Things as
They Are

Things as They Are

NEW DIRECTIONS IN
PHENOMENOLOGICAL
ANTHROPOLOGY

edited by
Michael Jackson

Indiana
University
Press

BLOOMINGTON AND INDIANAPOLIS

© 1996 by Indiana University Press

The paper used in this publication meets the minimum requirements of American National Standard for Information Sciences—Permanence of Paper for Printed Library Materials, ANSI Z39.48-1984.

MANUFACTURED IN THE UNITED STATES OF AMERICA

Library of Congress Cataloging-in-Publication Data

Things as they are : new directions in phenomenological anthropology / edited by Michael Jackson.
p.   cm.
Includes bibliographical references.
ISBN 0-253-33036-X (cl : alk. paper). — ISBN 0-253-21050-X (pa : alk. paper)
1. Phenomenological anthropology.   I. Jackson, Michael, date.
GN33.T55   1996
301'.01—dc20   95-45911

1   2   3   4   5   01   00   99   98   97   96

CONTENTS

PREFACE

In teaching and advising graduate students at Indiana University, I have been asked often to explain phenomenology, clarify its relationship to existentialism, radical empiricism, pragmatism, and critical theory, and justify its relevance for contemporary socio-cultural anthropology. This book is, in part, a response to these requests.

My previous work *Paths toward a Clearing* (1989) was steeped in existentialist-phenomenological thought. But I chose to foreground the radical empiricism of William James and the empirical naturalism of John Dewey because, though these philosophers evolved and applied ideas similar to those of continental thinkers such as Husserl, Heidegger, and Schutz, the Americans were, I believed, easier to understand and closer to home.

The trans-Atlantic links between philosophers like James and Husserl are well known (Edie 1987; Ihde 1986; Stevens 1974; Wilshire 1968), and there is always a certain arbitrariness in one's choice of intellectual forebears and reference points. But phenomenology and existentialism command our attention, not only because these schools of thought have influenced the development of anthropological ideas in both Europe and the United States, but because many contemporary ethnographers are drawing inspiration from these traditions and making such *leitmotifs* as practice, embodiment, experience, agency, biography, reflexivity, and narrative central to their work. It is perhaps time to explore the genealogy of these notions, to survey the ways in which they have been and are being used in anthropology, and to indicate how they imply a critique of doctrinaire forms of objectivism and subjectivism.

I also see this anthology as a way of bearing witness to the vitality of contemporary ethnography. I hope it will help illuminate some of the shared themes and preoccupations which inform the work of some of the most enterprising ethnographers writing today, and outline new directions for anthropology. These essays testify to the potential of anthropology to encourage and sustain cross-cultural dialogue in the vexed and uncertain climate of our times.

Finally, I wish to acknowledge the critical suggestions of colleagues who contributed essays to this volume. But in doing so, I should note that while phenomenology has provided a repertoire of developing ideas that has deepened our understanding of the manifold and ambiguous character of lived experience, our quite different genealogies and research experiences have determined different intellectual trajectories. No consensus is reached, or reached for. In this sense, one might well reiterate Roger Poole's observation that "there is no definitive account of phenomenology, no general agreement on terms, nor could there ever be. It is a subject in development, everyone making of it what he [she] will for his [her] own work. The insight has been fruitful, the doctrine remains a challenge" (Poole 1972:81).

REFERENCES

Edie, James M. 1987. *William James and Phenomenology*. Bloomington: Indiana University Press.

Ihde, Don. 1986. *Consequences of Phenomenology*. Albany: State University of New York Press.

Poole, Roger. 1972. *Towards Deep Subjectivity*. London: Allen Lane.

Stevens, Richard. 1974. *James and Husserl: The Foundations of Meaning*. The Hague: Martinus Nijhoff.

Wilshire, Bruce. 1968. *William James and Phenomenology: A Study of "The Principles of Psychology."* Bloomington: Indiana University Press.

ACKNOWLEDGMENTS

Some of the essays in this volume were previously published.

"Honor and Shame," by Lila Abu-Lughod, is reprinted from *Writing Women's Worlds: Bedouin Stories*, chapter 5, in a slightly amended version, with permission of the author and the Regents of the University of California and the University of California Press.

"Struggling Along," by Robert Desjarlais, is reproduced by permission of the American Anthropological Association from *American Anthropologist* 96:4, December 1994.

"The Cosmology of Life Transmission," by René Devisch, is excerpted from *Weaving the Threads of Life: The* Khita *Gyn-Eco-Logical Healing Cult among the Yaka*, with the permission of the author and the University of Chicago Press (© 1993 by The University of Chicago. All rights reserved).

"Reflections on a Cut Finger: Taboo in the Umeda Conception of the Self," by Alfred Gell, is reprinted from *Fantasy and Symbol: Studies in Anthropological Interpretation*, edited by R. H. Hook, 1979:133–148, with permission of the author and Academic Press London and Bailliere Tindall (© 1979 by Academic Press Inc. [London] Ltd.).

"Space and Sociality in a Dayak Longhouse," by Christine Helliwell, is a substantially revised version of "Good Walls Make Bad Neighbours: The Dayak Longhouse as a Community of Voices," first published in *Oceania* 1992, vol. 62 (3):179–193. It is reprinted here with the permission of Oceania Publications.

"In Defiance of Destiny: The Management of Time and Gender at a Cretan Funeral" by Michael Herzfeld is reprinted here from *American Ethnologist* 1993, vol. 20 (2):241–255, with permission of the author and the American Anthropological Association.

"Suffering and Its Professional Transformation: Toward an Ethnography of Interpersonal Experience," by Arthur Kleinman and Joan Kleinman is reprinted here from *Culture, Medicine and Psychiatry* 1991 vol. 15 (3):275–301, by permission of the authors and Kluwer Academic Publishers, Dordrecht, The Netherlands.

Back to things themselves.
—Edmund Husserl, *Logical Investigations*

And they said then, "But play, you must,
A tune beyond us, yet ourselves,

A tune upon the blue guitar
Of things exactly as they are."
—Wallace Stevens, *The Man with the Blue Guitar*

If every event which occurred could be given a name,
there would be no need for stories. As things are here,
life outstrips our vocabulary.
—John Berger, *Once in Europa*

Introduction

Phenomenology, Radical Empiricism, and Anthropological Critique

MICHAEL JACKSON

> How can we understand someone else without
> sacrificing him to our logic or it to him?
> —Maurice Merleau-Ponty (1964:115)

My intention in this introduction is to draw on several overlapping traditions of ideas, both European and non-European, in an eclectic and opportunistic endeavor to sketch some guidelines for a phenomenological anthropology. But though phenomenology provides a focus for our field, it is anthropology and not philosophy which is our central concern.

The unifying assumption of the phenomenology outlined here is that philosophies and theories, like political opinions, should be regarded as part and parcel of the world in which we live rather than transcendent views that somehow escape the impress of our social interests, cultural habits, and personal persuasions. The measure by which the worth or truth of any view is judged must be a worldly one. Whether one calls upon correspondence to the facts or force of personal conviction in claiming merit for one's point of view, such invocations indicate ways we construct, contest, and experience our worlds; they are not notions which can be arbitrated decisively, or regarded as arguments that can be won. It is not that phenomenology gives up on empirical rigor or critique, as we shall see. Rather, it refuses to invoke cultural privilege as a foundation for evaluating worldviews or examining the complex and enigmatic character of the human condition. It is a way of illuminating things by bringing them into the daylight of ordinary understanding.[1]

It is commonly but mistakenly thought that phenomenology is a kind of intuitive, solipsistic, or introspective philosophy that repudiates science (Schutz 1962:99–100). In fact, the domain of phenomenology is *being-in-the-world,* and this cannot be construed strictly in terms of "self-enclosed features of human subjectivity" (Casey 1991:xix). What phenomenology stands against is the fetishization of the products of intellectual reflection. Thus, objectivism

and subjectivism are equally untenable if by these terms we imply that one
domain of experience is to be privileged as the way to truth, while others are
disparaged and ignored. The phenomenological method is above all one of
direct understanding and in-depth description—a way of according equal
weight to all modalities of human experience, however they are named, and
deconstructing the ideological trappings they take on when they are theorized
(Goldstein 1961:225–226). Phenomenology is the scientific study of experience. It is an attempt to describe human consciousness in its lived immediacy,
before it is subject to theoretical elaboration or conceptual systematizing. In the
words of Paul Ricoeur, phenomenology is "an investigation into the structures
of experience which precede connected expression in language" (1979:127).

THE WORLD REGAINED

Many contemporary anthropologists have expressed dissatisfaction with the
arcane, abstract, and alienating character of much theoretical thought. Sometimes this is phrased as a criticism of the ways Western intellectual traditions
tend to be privileged over all others, as though no edifying account of human
social life could be rendered by using African, Islamic, Indian, Chinese, or
Polynesian traditions of thought. In addressing these issues, detailed descriptions of lived reality are seen as ways of resisting the estranging effects of
conceptual models and systematic explanation which, when pushed too far,
disqualify and efface the very life one wants to understand,[2] and isolate us from
the very life we have to live.

The knowledge whereby one lives is not necessarily identical with the knowledge whereby one explains life. Would one ever make a nest if one were
mindful that some day one would have to dig a grave? The ways in which
human beings reflect, analyze, and rationalize events in retrospect are seldom
isomorphic with the attitudes they adopt in the face of life.

In a moving essay entitled "Coping with Destiny," Meyer Fortes shows how
this paradoxical disjunction between doctrine and action, theory and practice,
episteme and experience, applies to notions of fate in societies (here, the
Tallensi of northern Ghana) which we all too often characterize as "fatalistic":

> Fate, which is in theory irresistible and irrevocable, is in practice taken to be
> controllable. . . . It is thus recognized that it is not in the nature of man to submit
> blindly to what purports to be mystically inevitable. Our Western science and
> medicine, our politics, cosmologies and moral or religious systems testify even more
> imperiously to this than do the attempts of Hindus, Buddhists or West Africans to
> control by ritual means what they designate as Destiny. (1987:145–146)

What is at issue here is the intellectualist fallacy of speaking as if life were
at the service of ideas (Dewey 1980:291; Merleau-Ponty 1962:39). By "intellec-

tualism" we do not intend to disparage intelligence and reason. Rather, we intend an indictment of the view that all experience is reducible to knowledge, and may be metamorphosed until it comes to resemble the objects of science. Observes Dewey: the "assumption of 'intellectualism' goes contrary to the facts of what is primarily experienced. For things are objects to be treated, used, acted upon and with, enjoyed and endured, even more than things to be known. They are things *had* before they are things cognized" (Dewey 1958:21).

Our argument is that the variety of human experience cannot be solidified in what Theodor Adorno calls "a body of enumerable theorems" (Adorno 1973:13). A changed philosophy, notes Adorno, would "cease persuading others and itself that it had the infinite at its disposal."

> Its substance would lie in the diversity of objects that impinge upon it and of the objects it seeks, a diversity not wrought by any schema; to these objects, philosophy would truly give itself rather than use them as a mirror in which to reread itself, mistaking its own image for concretion. It would be nothing but full, unreduced experience in the medium of conceptual reflection. . . . (ibid.:13)

A more homely way of phrasing this point of view would be to point out that exhorting a child or citizen to be "good," or urging a person to "be happy," "think positively," or "seek success," is as abstract and inefficacious as instructing a golfer who slices the ball (because of bad habits of body use) to "keep his or her eye on the ball." Concepts that might have some value in commenting upon life may have little practical efficacy in working out routines and techniques that will actually help a person accomplish his or her life goals.

The spirit of Adorno's critique of "identity-thinking" (in which a determinate relationship of "identity" is assumed to exist between words and the world) can be discerned in several essays in this volume. Attempting to cover or contain the flux of experience with finite, all-encompassing, and bounded terms is seen to be absurd. This argument, somewhat reminiscent of Heidegger's view that an experientially authentic language would make verbs its grammatical subject, informs Lila Abu-Lughod's use of a narrative account of the experience of a young Bedouin woman to call into question the status and authority of concepts of honor and shame in the ethnography of circum-Mediterranean societies. The force of this argument is also felt in Christine Helliwell's critique of anthropological attempts to isolate and define discrete social groupings, in the doubts Robert Desjarlais casts on the notion of "bounded individual lives," and in Jim Wafer's critique of the anthropological notion of the field as a "clearly delimited area of the anthropologist's experience, with neat geographical and temporal boundaries."

This argument also pervades what is loosely called postmodernism and post-colonialism: a breakdown of hard and fast distinctions between "highbrow" and popular culture, a dispersal of authorial authority, an undercutting of the privileges which European intellectual traditions have accorded them-

selves vis-à-vis non-European societies, and a shift in emphasis from explanatory causes to creative effects. At a time when the gap between the haves and the
have-nots is both widening and hardening, the theoretical question of how one
might understand the world yields to the practical question of how the world
might be changed. But in invoking Marx's second thesis on Feuerbach, we seek
only to underscore the point that what compels our interest in any idea is its
power to destabilize and unsettle received ways of seeing the world, replenish-
ing our sense of life's variety and possibility, and encouraging debate on the role
of the intellectual in the world of practical affairs.

Many ground-breaking ethnographies are providing us with timely and
ironic reminders that for the most part human beings live their lives independently of the intellectual schemes dreamed up in academe, and that the domain
of knowledge is inseparable from the world in which people actually live and
act. The essays in this volume may be read as a corrective to the "natural failing"
of intellectuals to exaggerate the significance of their theoretical knowledge.
They bring home to us that what people recognize as imperative and real in
most societies, most of the time, is not ratiocination, but commonsensical,
taken-for-granted knowledge, and that *this* constitutes, to all intents and
purposes, the effective and practical reality of life (Berger and Luckman
1966:26–27). In prioritizing the knowledge with which people live rather than
the knowledge with which Western intellectuals make sense of life, ethnography helps us place practical and social imperatives on a par with scholastic
rules and abstract understanding. It helps us recover a sense of those critical
contexts of existence where knowledge is not a matter of how to know but a
matter of life or death, when something is hazarded and risked in the process
of coming to know, when *"something is at stake"* (Kleinman A. & J. 1991:277).
Fieldwork brings home to us the ontological priority of social existence, and
fieldwork-based writing affirms that truth must not be seen as an unmasking
which eclipses the appearance of the thing unmasked, but a form of disclosure
which does it justice.[3]

This "anti-intellectualist" attitude, as William James called it, implies "a
looking away from first things, principles, 'categories,' supposed necessities;
and of looking towards things, fruits, consequences, facts" (James 1978:32). In
rejecting metaphysical abstraction, William James wanted to debunk all notions that it is possible to have the last word on the meaning of human
existence. The world is never something finished, something which thought
can bring to a close; the world is always in the making, and our thoughts, like
our actions, have meaning only in relation to the practical and social life in
which we are engaged. "The truth of an idea," says James, "is not a stagnant
property inherent in it. Truth *happens* to an idea. It *becomes* true, is *made* true
by events. Its verity *is* in fact an event, a process" (ibid.:97). The same pragmatic
spirit informs the work of the Frankfurt School, for whom the discovery of
immutable truths yields to a concern for the possibilities of changing the world.

In this endeavor, doctrinaire notions of ahistorical and anonymous truth are shown to serve the particular interests of power elites, and the mystique of objective knowledge to function as a means of obscuring the active, interpretive, and constitutive power of human subjectivity. More recently, Michael Herzfeld has argued along similar lines that the idea of transcendence legitimates not only Western myths of context-free, rational language, but ideologies of state power and bureaucratic authority (Herzfeld 1992:20–21).

To bring a pragmatist critique to bear on theoretical thought is to undercut its epistemological pretensions in order to disclose its *existential* meanings.

First, this means placing intellectual culture in its historical context, reiterating Horkheimer's and Adorno's argument (1972) that instrumental rationality, with its preoccupation with pattern and order, is linked historically to a concern for controlling nature and dominating other human beings. The bourgeois emphasis on intellectual rationality and order reflects the mentality of a class which feels that its power and privileges are always under siege from the class it excludes from its own as a world of chaos (Adorno 1973:21).

Second, a preoccupation with order and structure may be seen as a form of wishful thinking, a consoling illusion passing itself off as a privileged glimpse into the hidden workings of the world. According to this view, the systematic and objective order which the ethnographer "uncovers" in the course of fieldwork may not mirror any external reality but function as a magical defense against the unsystematic, disorienting reality he or she encounters (Jackson 1989:3–4). In Nietzsche's view, a preoccupation with systematic understanding may reveal little more than "the finickiness of scholars compensating themselves for political impotence by conceptually construing their, so to speak, administrative authority over things in being" (Adorno 1973:20).

Existentially, an unanalyzed world does not lend itself to control. If a person is to have any leverage or purchase on the world, he must "separate off from the environment and the group in which he, quite literally, lives, some things as being peculiarly himself" (Dewey 1958:13). Vanity, prestige and rights of possession are all involved in this splitting of the subject from a world of objects. Objective knowledge bestows a semblance of order on one's world, but at a price. The price is what Whitehead called "the fallacy of misplaced concreteness." For, in becoming tokens *of* the real, concepts easily become mistaken *for* the real, and manipulated magically as if they gave control over life. However, as Dewey pointed out, there is little difference between magic and science in the ways they serve to protect us from the perilous, aleatory character of life by making the unknown appear to be determined by the known. Thus, while magical spells work to superimpose the order of words on the disorder of the world, "Our magical safeguard against the uncertain character of the world is to deny the existence of chance, to mumble universal and necessary law, the ubiquity of cause and effect, the uniformity of nature, universal progress, and the inherent rationality of the universe" (1958:44). George Devereux makes a similar point. Both anthropomorphic thought and scientific thought, he argues, are ways in which we deal with our panic and "cosmic anxiety" over the unresponsiveness of matter by projecting human designs onto the non-human world, which we then imagine to conform to and respond to these designs (1967:32–34).

What is suggested here is that when we make cross-cultural comparisons between various "systems of thought," we would do well to construe these not as worldviews (*Weltanschauungen*) but as lifeworlds (*Lebenswelten*).

In an influential essay on African traditional thought and Western science (1967), Robin Horton sought to demonstrate that both scientific models and African models had explanatory value: they revealed order where there seemed to be chaos, identified the hidden causes of events, revealed unity beneath diversity, and showed that abstract rules underlay phenomenal reality. Our argument is that it is presumptuous and unedifying to try to give intellectual viability to African thought by assimilating it to the categories of Western scientific and philosophical discourse. Rather than examine the epistemological status of beliefs it is more important to explore their existential uses and consequences. Our emphasis is thus shifted from what beliefs "mean" *intrinsically* to what they are *made* to mean, and what they accomplish for those who invoke and use them. The sterile antinomies of rationality versus irrationality, or science versus magic, will be exorcised only when the criteria of truth encompass dialectically both antecedent causes *and* projective purposes. Moreover, it is only by abandoning the conceptual baggage anthropology inherits from colonial and imperial discourse that we are free to experience other worlds from the ground up, as it were, and recognize that many of the reified categories that still define our discourse—ritual, magic, totemism, witchcraft, lineage—are largely figments of our own intellectual imagination and have no counterparts in the vocabularies and views of those we study.

This prioritizing of lived experience over theoretical knowledge is already presaged by phenomenological studies of illness as it is lived through by the patient rather than conceptualized and defined by medical science (Kestenbaum 1982, Kleinman 1980, Leder 1992). Arthur Kleinman uses the term "local moral worlds" to draw attention to the "microcontexts of daily life"—the fields where macro-level socioeconomic and political forces are played out in particular life-settings, and the experience of illness is constituted *intersubjectively* as a particular moral reality (1992:171–173). There is now growing interest in applying phenomenological methods to the cross-cultural study of intersubjectivity—an imperative view, one might argue, given the ways in which the concept of culture often works, like the concept of race, as a tool for creating and perpetuating radical divisions between Western and non-Western societies in terms of distinctions between "us"—the rational and knowing subjects—and "them"—the undifferentiated objects of our inquiry (Abu-

Lughod 1991:143–147). It is equally urgent that we avoid ontologizing such terms as Westernization and Urbanization, implying that they invade, infiltrate, dominate and transform non-Western, non-urban societies *holus bolus*. New commodities and technologies are not in themselves determinative of irreversible change in Third World societies; rather, their meaning and use are shaped as much by the conventional wisdom and interests of particular consumers as by the product or technique itself (Appadurai 1986).

What phenomenology calls into question is the longstanding division in Western discourse between the knowledge of philosophers or scientists and the opinions of ordinary mortals.[4] Phenomenology seeks a corrective to forms of knowledge and description that, in attempting to isolate unifying and universal laws, lose all sense of the abundance and plenitude of life (Feyerabend 1987:118). The central tenet of William James' radical empiricism is that the field of empirical study include the plurality of *all* experienced facts, regardless of how they are conceived and classified—conjunctive and disjunctive, fixed and fluid, social and personal, theoretical and practical, subjective and objective, mental and physical, real and illusory (James 1976:22–23). In Richard Rorty's terms, "systematic philosophy," with its search for an ahistorical, universal framework for representing essential truths has to give ground to modes of "edifying philosophy" which react against epistemology by calling for open-ended conversation, shared experience, and accounts of the human condition which place all explanations on the same existential footing (1979:365–394). The justification of any knowledge claim thus becomes *social:* "a matter of understanding the social practices in which we justify beliefs" (McCarthy 1993:14).

Our intention is not to write programmatically, announcing a paradigm shift and assigning it a name. All modes of inquiry and systems of knowledge have their social and personal uses. The issue is not to decide which one accurately mirrors reality; rather, it is to refuse them all foundational status in order to critically evaluate the various realities they engender. As for the question of evaluating knowledge, the question of freeing our discourse from misjudgment and error becomes transmuted into a question of freeing our discourse from misjudgment and error *that has harmful human consequences.*

It is the worldly and life-affirming tenor of the essays in this volume that command our attention—the way they stress the importance of fieldwork-based writing and bearing witness to what Paul Riesman in 1977 called "life as lived." In this sense, they exemplify Lila Abu-Lughod's "tactical humanism"— a method for illuminating the lives people see themselves as living that does not reduce the meaning of those lives to some Eurocentric notion of humanism (1993:25–33). The focus is on what phenomenologists call the lifeworld—that domain of everyday, immediate social existence and practical activity, with all its habituality, its crises, its vernacular and idiomatic character, its biographical particularities, its decisive events and indecisive strategies, which theoretical knowledge addresses but does not determine, from which conceptual understanding arises but on which it does not primarily depend.

Sartre's notion of "situation" (1956:481–553), Wittgenstein's "environment of a way of acting" (1979), Bateson's "ecology of mind" (1973), Habermas's exploration of the lifeworld as a field of intersubjective communication (1987), Turner's use of Lewin's field theory in his analysis of Ndembu initiation ritual (1970), and Kleinman's work on "local moral worlds" (1992:172) are moments of reclamation when social theorists, alarmed at the alienating power of their professional discourse, have attempted to turn our attention back to what William James called "the world experienced."

After James, perhaps no American philosopher has made a better case for this reclamation than John Dewey, whose empirical naturalism refused to subject "things in their immediacy" to "cognitive certification" or reduce "primary experience" to intellectual meanings which were not self-evident (1958:126). Knowing, for Dewey, was "a factor in action and undergoing," an instrumentality rather than a goal, a way of accomplishing things in the world rather than a way of intellectually possessing it. For Dewey, empirical method begins and ends in the lifeworld—the world of our everyday goals, social existence, and practical activity. This is why an anthropology of the lifeworld is critical of "a spectator theory of knowledge" (Dewey 1980:23) in which intellectual goals are divorced from what Bruce Wilshire calls "the gritty and obscure drama of everyday life" (1990:190).

For anthropology, ethnography remains vital, not because ethnographic methods guarantee certain knowledge of others but because ethnographic fieldwork brings us into direct dialogue *with* others, affording us opportunities to explore knowledge not as something that grasps inherent and hidden truths but as an intersubjective process of sharing experience, comparing notes, exchanging ideas, and finding common ground. In this process our social gumption and social skills, as much as our scientific methodology, become measures of the limits and value of our understanding.

This calls upon the intellectual to resist the tendency to ontologize the results of his or her interpretative activity: the fallacy of thinking that what is conjecturally possible must be actually the case, or falling into the belief that what is conceived in the mind must perforce exist in the world. The fetishized products of intellectual activity all too often assume a life of their own, reinforcing the illusion that life can be possessed, controlled, captured, and pinned down. Our aim is to do justice to the lived complexity of experience by avoiding those selective redescriptions, reductions, and generalizations which claim to capture the essence of the lived in underlying rules or overarching schemata yet, in effect, downplay and deaden it.

The radical empiricism of William James, the empirical naturalism of Dewey, and the phenomenology of Merleau-Ponty insist that knowing must give up the illusion that it is possible to absent ourselves from the constraints of history and the contingencies of our situation. One may disengage from the world the better to grasp it, but this disengagement is not transcendence. ⟵ Rather, it should be construed as a way of seeing one part of the world from the vantage point of another—a form of lateral displacement rather than an overarching perspective (Merleau-Ponty 1964a:119). The implication is that no one cultural standpoint is central.

This shift from standing *outside or above* to situating oneself *elsewhere within* the field of inquiry implies a shift from an emphasis on explanatory models to lived metaphors. While models impose connections on experience, metaphors evoke and mediate connections within experience (Jackson 1989:142). Erwin Straus provides a good example of this in his famous study of upright posture. Upright stance, he points out, characterizes our humanity—biogenetically, ontologically, and cognitively. Uprightness has both physical and metaphysical connotations, as when we refer to a person's "standing," "substantiality," "estate," or "status" (1966:143). The "verticality schema" is, however, ambiguous: a sense of standing coexists with a fear of falling. Ludwig Binswanger's *Daseinsanalyse* provides an example of what this means in practice. When disoriented individuals speak of the ground giving way beneath them, of being thrown, of losing their footing, and of falling, these are not, Binswanger argues, physical metaphors of mental states. Body and mind are effectively one, and what these images give evidence of is the actual experience of disoriented Being.

> When, in bitter disappointment, "we fall from the clouds," then we fall—we *actually* fall. Such falling is neither purely of the body nor something metaphorically derived from physically falling. Our harmonious relationship with the world and the men about us suddenly suffers a staggering blow, stemming from the nature of bitter disappointment and the shock that goes with it. In such a moment our existence actually suffers, is torn from its position in the world and thrown upon its own resources. Until we can regain our equilibrium in the world, our whole existence moves within the meaning matrix of stumbling, sinking, and falling. If we call this general meaning matrix the "form," and the bitter disappointment the "content," we can see that in this case form and content are *one*. (Binswanger 1963:223)

I have argued elsewhere (Jackson 1989:142) that if body metaphors are interpreted non-dualistically, so that the idea or sensation and its bodily correlatives are not seen as an arbitrary or rhetorical synthesis of two terms— subject and object (tenor and vehicle—which can be defined more realistically apart from each other, then the meaning of metaphor lies in its disclosure of the interdependency of body and mind, self and world. Metaphors thus reveal or realize unities; they are not figurative means of denying dualities.

René Devisch's study of the *khita* healing cult among the Yaka of Zaire (1993) describes in depth how metaphors are the connective tissue of the lifeworld. For the Yaka, the life cycle of persons is metaphorically integrated with seasonal and lunar rhythms. This integration is likened to a fabric of firmly but delicately interwoven social, bodily, and cosmic threads. Infertility is a tear in this fabric of life, and regenerative rituals are ways of reweaving the damaged strands. However, this metaphorical warp and woof of person and world is not simply a semantic or conceptual artifice but a lived reality, a vital flow charged with bodily and sensory power, in which self, group, and world are one (Devisch 1993:257). "I contend," writes Devisch, "that ritual metaphors in Yaka culture are not the flickering touch of mind on mind but a blending and empowering of senses, bodies, and world" (ibid.:43). Elsewhere, observing that ritual symbols are not abstract images, but corporeal devices, processes, methods, or patterns that originate in the lifeworld (ibid.:280), Devisch points out that such a view implies "a reversal of most of the linguistic and semiotic perspectives on metaphor and its logical processes known today" (ibid.). And it implies a methodological shift as well, since understanding this lifeworld entails reaching beyond "dialogue and discursive reality" into participation and transference (ibid.:283).

THE PHENOMENOLOGICAL EPOCHE

Husserl's phenomenological method was one of suspending inquiry into "objective" reality in order to explore the reality of human consciousness (1931:107–111). For anthropology, this implies a practical relativism: the suspension of inquiry into the divine or objective truth of particular customs, beliefs, or worldviews in order to explore them as modalities or moments of experience, to trace out their implications and uses. Ideas are not so much discounted as deconstructed; they are seen as approximate expressions rather than exact explanations of experience. The phenomenological method involves "placing in brackets" or "setting aside" questions concerning the rational, ontological, or objective status of ideas and beliefs in order to fully describe and do justice to the ways in which people actually live, experience, and use them— the ways in which they appear to consciousness. Dewey calls this "the postulate of immediate empiricism," namely that "things are what they are experienced to be" (1905:228). This phenomenological *epoché* or "bracketing" implies a rigorously empirical attitude, without being empiricist. *Empirie, nicht Empirismus*, declared Dilthey, in order to emphasize that though phenomenology focuses on the facts of consciousness it does not strive to explain these facts away by reducing them to antecedent conditions, biogenetic determinations, unconscious principles, or invisible causes.

This is not to say that human experience is without preconditions; rather, it is to suggest that the *experience* of these preconditions is not entirely preconditioned. A human life is seldom a blind recapitulation of givenness, but an *active* relationship with what has gone before and what is imagined to lie ahead. In Sartre's words, "man is characterized above all by his going beyond a situation, and by what he succeeds in making of what he has been made— even if he never recognizes himself in his objectification" (1968:91). Adorno makes a similar point. Praxis, he writes, "is characterized above all by the fact that the qualitatively new appears in it . . . it is a movement which does not run its course in pure identity, the pure reproduction of such as already was there" (Buck-Morss 1977:54). Culture, therefore, cannot be set over or against the person. It is, rather, the field of a dialectic in which the sedimented and anonymous meanings of the past are taken up as means of making a future, and givenness transformed into design. In this sense, Merleau-Ponty notes, the human dialectic is ambiguous:

> It is first manifested by the social or cultural structures, the appearance of which it brings about and in which it imprisons itself. *But its use-objects and its cultural objects would not be what they are if the activity which brings about their appearance did not also have as its meaning to reject them and to surpass them.* (1963:176)

The implication is that life cannot be understood simply through the systematic study of its outward and given forms: symbolic images, conventional usages, habitual expressions, or the inherited past. In Adorno's view, Husserl tended to fetishize the given as a kind of "second nature," and failed to take into full account the social activity whereby "givenness" is produced and transformed. Adorno's notion of the dialectic emphasizes the relationship of non-identity between givenness and choice, the intended and the inadvertent, the particular and the general, subject and object. One's goal is to disclose the fugitive ways in which the seemingly fixed forms of custom are actually lived in both consciousness and activity. As Goethe observed, "Do not look behind phenomena; they themselves are the truth" (cited by Buck-Morss 1977:80).

The "phenomenological epoché" thus entails shifting one's emphasis from causes to consequences. The phenomenologist suspends inquiry into the hidden determinants of belief and action in order to describe the implications, intentions, and effects of what people say, do, and hold to be true. For Merleau-Ponty, it is a method of describing how human beings actively make the world over to themselves and remake it over to others (1964b:71–82). In this sense, a pragmatist notion of truth is implied. Truth is seen, not as an intrinsic or static property of a belief, as naïve symbolic analysis often assumes; rather, it is what happens to a belief when it is invoked, activated, put to work, and realized in the lifeworld. For example, in my essay on Kuranko witchcraft (1989), it is argued that witchcraft beliefs have no reality apart from the people who make use of them. The beliefs cannot be understood simply as products of tensions in the social system, or as explanatory stereotypes. In particular, one must consider in detail how the beliefs are actually used by the women who confess to witchcraft during terminal illness—as desperate stratagems for reclaiming autonomy in a hopeless situation. The self-confessed witch does more than passively submit to her misfortune. Nor does she blindly recapitulate the stereotypes which men promulgate. Rather, she actively uses the imagery of witchcraft to give voice to long-suppressed grievances, coping with suffering by declaring herself the author of it. She makes of her own body the site of the world's injustice. Thus, she determines how she will play out the role which circumstance has thrust upon her. She dies deciding her own destiny, sealing her own fate (Jackson 1989:101).

The phenomenological turn prepares the ground for detailed descriptions of how people immediately experience space, time, and the world in which they live. The "facts" of natural science, like the notion of objective reality itself, are treated as "phenomena" of human experience, to be placed on a par with "beliefs" and elements of so-called subjective reality. But to suspend disbelief in such notions as objectivity, cause, essence, and authority is not to banish them from our vocabulary. Denying such terms absolute explanatory power is simply a prelude to exploring their phenomenal power—the interests they serve and the transformations they effect. Consider for instance the terms "heredity" and "environment." Any attempt to decide empirically how "natural" and "cultural" elements interact in human behavior must be complemented by an analysis of the ways in which "nature" and "nurture" are invoked in social discourse to legitimate quite different worldviews (Tournier 1988:201). People who invoke biogenetic nature as determinative tend to be politically conservative; social inequalities, they argue, reflect the nature of things. By contrast, people who invoke nurture tend to be liberals for whom the world can be changed for the better through concerted political action.

Katsuyoshi Fukui's ethnographic research among the Bodi of Southwest Ethiopia provides an example of how "contradictory" models reflect, not logical confusion, but contrasted contexts of social use. The pastoral Bodi recognize numerous color patterns for cows, based on eight primary color terms. Mastery of this "color-pattern vernacular," and of cattle genealogies and clan classification, is crucial to decisions as to which cow it is symbolically appropriate to sacrifice on such critical occasions as sowing grain or summoning rain. What is striking for our purposes, however, is that the Bodi apply Mendelian genetic principles in selectively breeding cattle whose color patterns are useful for cosmological and ritual purposes, but do not apply this model to human life or human genealogies. The reason is that cows, not persons, occupy the crucial mediatory position between social microcosm and natural macrocosm, and ritually correct color combinations must be readily available if relations between humanity and cosmos are to be managed effectively (Fukui 1979; 1987).

Use, not logic, conditions belief. That the phenomenologist is loath to essentialize such terms as nature, femininity, or Aboriginality does not preclude an appreciation that a separatist, essentializing rhetoric is often an imperative strategy for besieged groups and ethnic minorities in laying claim to civil rights or cultural recognition. Similarly, the force of a Christian's commitment to a belief, say, in the divinity of Jesus, does not necessarily hang on the refinement or updating of evidence from archaeology and biblical scholarship concerning the objective life of the messiah. Somewhat the same principle holds true in medicine. The therapeutic efficacy of a drug or nostrum does not always mean that there are objective medical grounds for demonstrating its allopathic validity. It is estimated that between 25 and 50 percent of the non-Western pharmacopoeia is empirically effective even though it is based on magical and homeopathic criteria (Hughes 1978:154). Finally, it should be stressed that in practice, if not in theory, people tend to assent to notions of absolute authority and objective knowledge in situations of personal crisis. On occasion, therefore, such beliefs are instrumentally necessary and existentially true because they help people regain effective control over their lives. As I have argued in an essay on Kuranko divination, consulting diviners and accepting the truth of what they say helps a person clarify his or her situation and alleviate anxiety. Whatever the outcome of a prognosis, it is not subject to rational, retrospective evaluation. Its meaning lies in its immediate consequences (Jackson 1989:63). This point is also made by Florinda Donner in her account of working with Yanomamo healers. She describes how her attempts to extract a theory of knowledge from curing practices were frustrated by the "unsystematic, improvisitory, fluid" character of the events she observed. Indeed, one curer, doña Mercedes, refused to relate what she did to antecedent events, and objected to Donner's tape-recording everything she said. "Every time you ask me about curing I start talking without really knowing what I am saying. You always put words into my mouth. If you knew how to cure, you wouldn't bother writing or talking about it. You would just do it" (Donner 1984:7).

What makes the phenomenologist uneasy is the assumption that beliefs and ideas have to have some kind of ahistorical, supraempirical validity if they are to be workable. But ideas can be meaningful and have useful consequences even when they are epistemologically unwarranted.

In *The Crisis of European Sciences and Transcendental Phenomenology* (written in the last years of his life, between 1934 and 1937) Husserl gives ontological priority to what he calls the *Lebenswelt* (lifeworld) over the world of theoretical thought and explanatory ideas (*Weltanschauung*). This was, in part, a way of affirming questions of value and meaning in the face of Nazi ideology and propaganda (Natanson 1973:41). But for Husserl, the European crisis could be traced to a disenchantment with scientific rationality and a longing to make philosophy more open and responsive to the demands of human life. It was Husserl's hope that the alienating division between the explanatory models of empirical science and our everyday involvement in the world might be overcome.

One response to the crisis was to critically question the classical empiricist assumption that the observer could distance himself from the object of observation by using disinterested techniques and neutral methods, thereby gaining certain and consistent knowledge of the other. Another response was to question the very idea that the world of theoretical ideas could in fact be dissociated from the pretheoretical lifeworld (Husserl 1970:123–141).

In recent years, one of the most compelling anthropological explorations of the relation of abstract theoretical thought to the lifeworld has been Jadran Mimica's study of counting and mythopoeia among the Iqwaye of Papua New Guinea (1988). Mimica shows in great detail that the Iqwaye counting system answers practical needs in everyday life and depends upon specific techniques of the body. But though these practical, cosmological, and corporeal givens define the matrix in which the counting system operates, Iqwaye arithmetic is *logically* capable of extensions that carry us far beyond the immediate world of Iqwaye needs and usages. But, Mimica argues, these abstract mathematical possibilities—which in the West have been so comprehensively elaborated and formalized that we have lost sight of their original sources in the lifeworld—are not realized in Iqwaye practice because the Iqwaye have no use for them. Turning to the question of why Western philosophy has so systematically sought a transcendent conception of number in pure rationality, Mimica argues that it is a matter of reification and forgetting. An ethnographic description of Iqwaye numeration, cosmology, and practical life thus reminds us that historically and ontologically the very possibility of "our" systems of number is grounded in, albeit distantly, and points to, albeit obliquely, the concrete world of things.

Consider, too, the indeterminate and ambiguous character of experience. Merleau-Ponty used a Gestalt model to remind us of the ways in which consciousness continually shifts between figure and ground. Whatever is brought forth, embodied, and made visible bears with it a sense of other things which are co-present but backgrounded, peripheral, and ephemeral. Every modality or moment of experience entails its contrary. As John Dewey put it, a primary datum of *all* experience is a sense of contrast between that which is immediate and that which is non-immediate, between the visible and the invisible, the tangible and the intangible. Dewey suggests that "our" distinction between sensible experience and the ideas which make this experience intelligible is directly comparable to "primitive" distinctions between natural and supernatural domains (1958:43–44). We can put this another way. Experiences we tend to gloss as belonging to the unconscious—an abyssal region of the *mind*—are conventionally construed in many preliterate societies as belonging to the unknown—a penumbral, inscrutable *space*. Thus, in Polynesia, the world of light (*te ao*)—of ordinary, quotidian, workaday reality—is contrasted with the world of darkness (*te po*) which both precedes it historically and lies about it (Levy 1973:249). For the Kuranko of northeast Sierra Leone, the contrast between daytime and darkness is suggestive of a more far-reaching distinction between secular authority and "wild" power. The world of the village (*sue*) is thus contrasted with the world of the bush (*fira*) whose vital energies are both inimical to and necessary for human well-being (Jackson 1982a:9–10,71–72). In Central Australia, the contrast between waking and dreaming worlds also conjures up a distinction between the patent, visible world of quotidian existence and the latent world of the Dreaming from which all life comes and into which all life ultimately returns (Myers 1986:48–51; Jackson 1995:57–58).

However, none of these distinctions implies that the domains of darkness, wilderness, or Dreaming are other-worldly, super-natural, non-empirical. On the contrary, they are worlds that enter experience and of which direct experience is had. They are, so to speak, dimensions of the lifeworld not ordinarily brought into consciousness, *but they are integrally part of empirical reality.* Objective thought, by contrast, forcing its distinction between the world of ideas and the world of sensible experience, insists that explanatory ideas or interpretive models *transcend* the empirical world.

But in what does this going beyond really consist? Is thought as disassociated from life as it sometimes appears to be?

While acknowledging that "reason develops and transforms itself in the practical field" and that thought reflects our relations to the world and to others, Lévi-Strauss insists nevertheless that thought is pregiven "in the form of an objective structure of the psyche and brain without which there would be neither praxis nor thought" (1966:263–264). How can one account for this kind of insistence on locating the foundations of thought *outside* the lifeworld?

GENEALOGIES OF THE CONCEPTS OF LIFEWORLD AND CULTURE

Twenty years ago David Bidney observed that "the concept of the *lebenswelt* is the connecting link between modern anthropology and phenomenology" (1973:133). But the importance of phenomenology for anthropology goes further than any superficial similarity between the concept of lifeworld and the concept of culture. Indeed, phenomenology calls into question the ways in which we habitually deploy the "culture concept" in our discourse.

The notion of lifeworld is presaged in Wilhelm Dilthey's idea of the life-nexus. Dilthey regarded himself as a "philosopher of life," by which he meant that philosophers should strive to "get behind . . . scientific elaboration and grasp life in its raw state" (1976:178). The implication was that philosophy should arise from and find consummation in the world of experience. Its concern should not be for knowledge for its own sake but "knowledge of life" (ibid.:178–180). In his *Introduction to the Human Sciences* (1883), Dilthey observed that the natural sciences used abstraction and measurement to a degree which would be unacceptable in the human sciences. His program for the human sciences involved placing conscious experience at its core, acknowledging the *reciprocal* relation of self and world (the "life-nexus"), and emphasizing the significance of purpose, will and agency in human life.

There are clear echoes of Dilthey's notion of life-nexus in Husserl's notion of lifeworld (Gadamer 1975:214–225; Makkreel 1982), and Dilthey anticipates Husserl's insistence that we avoid reducing lived experiences (*Erlebnisse*) to causal principles of which the subject is not conscious. Gadamer speaks of the concept of lifeworld as "the antithesis of all objectivism" (1975:218). The concept represents a resistance to metaphysical and etherealizing notions of culture.

For Husserl, the *Lebenswelt* was the world of immediate experience, of sociality, common sense, and shared experience that exists for us independent of and prior to any reflection upon it. "The life-world is a realm of original self-evidences," he writes, "experienced as 'the thing itself'" (1970b:127–128).

In *Being and Time*, Martin Heidegger uses phenomenological methods to explore "Being-in-the-world" and "Being-with-others," and in his account of "Being-in" Heidegger tries to recapture the primordial sense of cultural life as a mode of indwelling.

> "In" is derived from "*innan*"—"to reside," "*habitare*," "to dwell" (sich auf halten). "*An*" signifies "I am accustomed," "I am familiar with," "I look after something." It has the signification of "*colo*" in the senses of "*habito*" and "*diligo*." The entity to which Being-in in this signification belongs is one which we have characterized as that entity which in each case I myself am (bin). The expression "*bin*" is connected with "*bei*," and so "*ich bin*" ("I am") means in its turn "I reside" or "dwell alongside" the world, as that which is familiar to me in such and such a way. "Being" (Sein), as the infinitive of "*ich bin*" (that is to say, when it is understood as an *existentiale*), signifies "to reside alongside . . . ," "to be familiar with. . . ." "*Being-in*" *is thus the formal existential expression for the Being of Dasein, which has Being-in-the-world as its essential state.* (1962:80, italics in text)

Heidegger reminds us that in its original usage, *culture* (from the Latin *colo*) did not imply any separation of conceptual or moral qualities from practical life and social activity. In this pragmatic view the gods were not looked upon to make people *morally* better but to control the natural forces upon which the material bases of prosperity and happiness directly depended. Practical and religious life merged (Ogilvie 1969:10–21). *Colo* meant to inhabit a town or district, to cultivate, tend, or till the land, to keep and breed animals, and generally to look after one's livelihood "especially in its material aspects"—clothing and adorning the body, caring for and attending to friends and family, minding the gods, upholding custom through the cultivation of correct moral and intellectual disciplines (*Oxford Latin Dictionary* 1969). This sense of culture as a field of dramatic, vital and corporeal reality, mediating past and present, person and person, visible and invisible, subject and object, defines the preliterate lifeworld (Devisch 1993:48–49).

However, throughout the late Middle Ages in Europe, "culture" began to denote moral perfection and intellectual or artistic accomplishment. From the mid-eighteenth century, when German writers began to apply the term to human societies and history, culture almost invariably designated the refined mental and spiritual faculties which members of the European bourgeoisie imagined set themselves apart from manual workers, peasants, and savages. In this "dissociation of sensibilities" one hears a distant echo of Aristotle's metaphysical doctrine that nature is an ordered series from lower to higher potentialities and actualizations. As Dewey notes, this doctrine served to legitimate crucial social distinctions.

> The old distinction between vegetative, animal and rational souls was, when applied to men, a formulation and justification of class divisions in Greek society. Slaves and mechanical artisans living on the nutritional, appetitive level were for practical purposes symbolized by the body—as obstructions to ideal ends and as solicitations to acts contrary to reason. The good citizen in peace and war was symbolized by the soul proper, amenable to reason, employing thought, but confining its operations after all to mundane matters, infected with matter. Scientific inquirers and philosophers alone exemplified pure reason, operating with ideal forms for the sake of the latter. The claim of this class for inherent superiority was symbolized by *nous*, pure immaterial mind. (Dewey 1958:251)

In eighteenth- and nineteenth-century Europe, such social distinctions implied an epistemological division whereby the spiritual was "lifted out of its social context, making culture a (false) collective noun" as in the idea of "Germanic culture" or "Greek classical culture" (Marcuse 1968:94–95). Accordingly, *culture* came to denote a realm of authentic spiritual values, realized through an "idealist cult of inwardness" (ibid.:129), radically opposed to the world of social utility and material means. Roy Wagner (1975) calls this an "opera-house" notion of culture. Individual soul was set off from and against the body, and sensuality was spiritualized in notions of romantic love and religious adoration. No longer pricked by conscience about the ways in which their enjoyment of so-called higher values depended upon the menial toil of the "lower orders," the bourgeoisie denied both the sensual body and the material conditions on which its class privileges rested. Exclusion of the body from discourse went along with the exclusion of the masses from political life.

In 1871 the English anthropologist Edward Tylor published his pioneering work *Primitive Culture,* borrowing the term *culture* from the German tradition but defining it, after Gustav Klemm, in an apparently neutral way as "that complex whole which includes knowledge, belief, art, law, morals, customs, and any other capabilities and habits acquired by man as a member of society" (cited in Kroeber and Kluckhohn 1963:81). Although culture was held to be a distinctive attribute of *all* humankind, varying only in degree, the pejorative and historical connotations of the word *culture* remained in place, and Tylor, like Klemm and Herder before him, applied himself to the task of tracing out progressive stages of social development in terms of the advance of scientific rationality and technological control over nature.

Taken up by American anthropologists as early as the 1880s, the term *culture* gradually lost its nineteenth-century glosses, and between 1920 and 1950 a new demarcation function was assigned to it: culture defined the emergent properties of mind and language which separated humans from animals. This view, already implied in Kroeber's seminal 1917 paper "The Superorganic," was reiterated in Kroeber and Kluckhohn's 1952 review of the concept, where they define *culture* as "a set of attributes and products of human societies, and therewith of mankind, which are extrasomatic and transmissible by mechanisms other than biological heredity, and are as essentially lacking in sub-human species as they are characteristic of the human species as it is aggregated in its societies" (Kroeber and Kluckhohn 1983:284).

Whether we consider the idealist traditions of the eighteenth and nineteenth centuries which "etherealized" the body or anthropological definitions of culture which play up conceptual and linguistic dimensions of human existence to the exclusion of somatic, sensory, and biological dimensions, one finds that science since the Enlightenment has been pervaded by a popular bourgeois conception of culture as something "superorganic" and *sui generis*— a self-contained world of unique qualities and manners divorced from the world of materiality and biology. As Norman O. Brown puts it, "Culture originates in the denial of life and the body" (1959:297). The term works to demarcate, separate, exclude, and deny. Although at different epochs the excluded "natural" category is variously focused on peasants, savages, women, children, animals, and material objects, a persistent theme is the occlusion of the somatic, a scotomacizing of the physical aspects of Being, a denial of the grounds of our natural humanity.

LIFEWORLD, HABITUS, AND LIFE STORY

How then might European thought address a non-European world? And how can phenomenology outstrip its European origins and contribute to cross-cultural understanding?

No doubt Adorno is right in criticizing the intuitional, essentializing tenor of much of the work of Husserl and Heidegger (Adorno 1982). There cannot be such a thing as pure intuition, or a transcendental, monadic ego, because all acts of so-called intuition are informed by social interests, cultural bias, and the claims of our particular lifeworld upon us. A universalizing, eternalizing theory of Being, grounded in the being of European bourgeois intellectuals, has little value for anthropology. Feyerabend puts the matter bluntly when he takes

Husserl to task for proposing that philosophers are "functionaries of humanity." It is a "phenomenal conceit," he writes, to imagine that any one individual can have sufficient knowledge of all societies to be able to speak of "the true being of humanity." What does Husserl know of the "true being" of the Nuer? (Feyerabend 1987:274).

Toward the end of his life Husserl read Lévy-Bruhl and came to see that one cannot assume a universal ontology or enter matter-of-factly into the experiences of people in other societies (Merleau-Ponty 1973:101–104), but this seems not to have been an issue for many phenomenologists who, like Heidegger, touching briefly on anthropology, suggested that "primitive" Dasein is a "less concealed and less complicated" form of the Dasein active in "highly developed and differentiated culture" (1962:76).

What ethnography demands of phenomenology is resistance to generalizations made on the strength of one's own self-understanding. This is not an argument against generalization *per se*; rather it is a refusal to accord generalizations objective or omniscient status. It is an invitation to appraise generalizing as a "tool for conviviality," as a way of mediating conversations and social relations (Illich 1973). This is the thrust of Edward Said's argument that generalizing makes it possible for intellectuals to distance themselves from the *status quo* in their own society and identify with and lend their voice to "all those people and issues that are routinely forgotten or swept under the rug" (1993:11–12; see also pp. 23 and 44). But generalizing here is a means of creating solidarity, not objective knowledge.

For anthropologists, it is the *social* reality of the lifeworld and forms of *social* consciousness which are of critical interest. In *The Crisis of European Sciences*, Husserl alludes to "human beings, with all their human action and concern, works and suffering, living in common in the world-horizon in their particular social interrelations and knowing themselves to be such" (1970:146). But this theoretical interest in lived sociality is not systematically developed by Husserl, and one must turn to the work of Alfred Schutz for an outline of a phenomenology of social life.

Schutz's work brings us from abstract questions concerning objective knowledge of the world to existential questions concerning *how* people actually live in the world of objects and others. While strongly influenced by Husserl, Schutz rejected Husserl's fascination with ahistorical essences and, like Heidegger, emphasized the horizons of mundane existence,[5] the immediacies of intersubjective life, and modes of human action. In *The Structures of the Life-World*, Schutz makes clear the importance he attaches to agency, intentionality, and praxis.

> The Life-world is the quintessence of a reality that is lived, experienced, and endured. It is, however, also a reality that is mastered by action and the reality in which—and on which—our action fails. Especially for the everyday life-world, it

holds good that we engage in it by acting and change it by our actions. Everyday
life is that province of reality in which we encounter directly, as the condition of
our life, natural and social givens as pregiven realities with which we must try to
cope. (Schutz 1989:1)

Schutz presages Bourdieu in seeing the lifeworld as a "province of human
practice (1989:1), but Bourdieu disparages Schutz's focus on lived experiences
(*Erlebnisse*) and encounters (*Erfahrungen*) as a kind of "flabby humanism"
(Bourdieu 1990a:4). While acknowledging his intellectual debts to Heidegger,
Husserl, and Schutz, Bourdieu repudiates phenomenology because it fails to
account for the historical and cultural conditions under which forms of self-
consciousness and sociality emerge (1990b:25–26). In other words, he repudiates the phenomenological epoché. Yet Bourdieu also repudiates objectivism,
on the grounds that it reduces agency to automatism and practices to theoretical rules (1990b:9). He rejects a spectator theory of knowledge in which the
observer stands apart from the action the better to grasp its objective significance (1977:96), but he also wants to avoid the observer becoming too closely
embroiled in the situation observed (1990a:60). The *habitus,* as he understands
it, is thus a domain of practical activity, improvisation, and invention that does
not as a rule depart from common codes, habitual dispositions, approved
procedures, and accepted ground-rules. In this sense Bourdieu's notion of the
habitus bears some resemblance to Chomsky's notion of linguistic competence—the deep structures which define the preconditions of intelligibility, the
parameters of performance, and the limits of creativity (Bourdieu 1990a:13).

Despite his caveats and cavils, Bourdieu's emphasis on mundane
strategizing, practical taxonomies, bodily habits, social usages, and agency
makes his notion of *habitus* directly comparable to the notion of lifeworld.
Indeed, he admits that his theoretical vision "started out from an intuition of
the irreducibility of social existence to the models that can be made of it or, to
put it naively, of 'life's profusion,' of the gap between real practices and
experiences and the abstractions of the mental world" (Bourdieu 1990a:21).
But in exploring this domain, Bourdieu wants at all costs to avoid slipping into
a form of existential irrationalism centered on the autonomous subject, or
falling into the objectivist trap of viewing practice as merely a "mechanical
reaction, directly determined by . . . antecedent conditions and entirely
reducible to the mechanical functioning of pre-established assemblies, 'models,' or 'rôles'" (1977:73).

Bourdieu often gives the impression that he is "locked within the alternative of subjectivism and objectivism" in exactly the same non-dialectic
manner which, he argues, flaws the work of Lévi-Strauss (Bourdieu
1990a:62). In his eagerness to avoid a subjectivist vocabulary, he often tends
to speak of the habitus in objectivist terms as "objective" or "embodied"
history (1990b:56–58), or as *topoi*—"a common set of previously assimilated

master patterns" by means of which individual practices are produced or generated (1971:192). Moreover, his definitions of the *habitus* are often muddled, or compromised by a series of oxymorons—"spontaneity without consciousness and will" (1990b:56), "structuring structures" (ibid.:53), "intentionless invention" (ibid.:57), and "intentionality without intentions" (1991:108). As Michel de Certeau observes, by assimilating the ethnographic "other" or native to the "invisible," "mystical," and "hypothetical" space of the *habitus,* Bourdieu follows in the structuralist tradition of locating generative forces outside the immediate, lived reality of the lifeworld. "*Habitus* thereby becomes a place of dogma, if by that term we understand the affirmation of a certain 'real' which discourse requires in order to make totalizing claims" (de Certeau 1980:20).

Yet the antinomy of "subjectivity" and "objectivity" ceases to be a problem if these terms are seen as indicative of the way human experience vacillates between a sense of ourselves as subjects *and* as objects; in effect, making us feel sometimes that we are world-makers, sometimes that we are merely made by the world. A phenomenological approach avoids fetishizing the words with which we name these different moments or modes of experience, refusing to make any one "cut" into the continuum of consciousness foundational to a theory of knowledge.

Accordingly, one does not have to prove the existence or non-existence of agency in order to acknowledge the force and the consequences of the idea. For example, among the Yoruba, *ase* suggests "the power to bring things into existence, to make things happen" (Drewal 1992:27). Human beings are thought to "possess this generative force, and through education, initiation, and experience learn to manipulate it to enhance their own lives and the lives of those around them" (ibid.). Margaret Drewal shows that this belief enables ritual praxis—a shared conviction that one can act with others to resolve crises, and transform one's experience of the world. My study of Kuranko storytelling came to a similar conclusion. Kuranko social life is full of dilemmas and tensions. It is often impossible to deal with these quandaries by changing external circumstances. But through stories these vexed issues are voiced, discussed, and reconfigured (Jackson 1982a). Though it is difficult to capture the kinds of transformed awareness that storytelling or ritual effects, it is important to stress that human intentionality, consciousness, and coping do not always find expression in the "practical functions" of language or the objectified forms of economic and matrimonial exchange.

SUBJECTIVITY

The central problem of structuralist and post-structuralist thought is without doubt the problem of the subject. Bourdieu's notion of *habitus,* like Foucault's notion of discursive formations and discursive practices (the domain of the *episteme*), excludes autonomous subjects from the anonymous labyrinths of culture.

Our argument is that no matter what constituting power we assign the impersonal forces of history, language, and upbringing, the subject always figures, at the very least, as the site where these forces find expression and are played out. Arguing for a dialectical understanding of subjectivity and objectivity, Adorno comments: "If the object lacked the moment of subjectivity, its own objectivity would become nonsensical" (1978:509). No matter what significance we attach to discourse or culture, the phenomenal world of human consciousness and activity is never reducible to that which allegedly determines the condition of its possibility. Even if one tried to expunge the subject from one's discourse, it is one's own subjectivity which accomplishes the expulsion. Every argument for the death of the subject is authored by a human subject. By dismissing the subject, Bourdieu and Foucault would deprive us of the very site where life is lived, meanings are made, will is exercised, reflection takes place, consciousness finds expression, determinations take effect, and habits are formed or broken. Any theory of culture, *habitus* or lifeworld must include some account of those moments in social life when the customary, given, habitual, and normal is disrupted, flouted, suspended, and negated. At such moments, crisis transforms the world from an apparently fixed and finished set of rules into a repertoire of possibilities. To borrow Marx's vivid image, the frozen circumstances are forced to dance by us singing to them their own melody (Jackson 1989:20).

Behind Bourdieu's and Foucault's refusal to admit the knowing subject to discourse is a refusal to give issues of existential power the same value as issues of political power. Questions of coping with life or finding meaning in the face of suffering are rated less imperative than questions of social domination and distinction. Yet, at times Foucault seemed to recognize the need to unveil the subject and author who had been so cunningly hidden in the oblique and allegorical world of his books. In 1962, freely admitting an interest in the self, he confessed that he had in his early work "insisted maybe too much on . . . techniques of domination"—surveillance, the clinical gaze, the confessional— and now felt the need to explore what he called "techniques of the self" (Foucault and Sennett 1962). It was the existential force rather than the sociopolitical power of these techniques that intrigued Foucault. In shifting his focus from power to the subject in his later work, Foucault wanted to explore the way in which techniques of the self such as meditation, sex, drug use, and aestheticism permitted individuals to experiment with and transform themselves (Miller 1993:322).

After structuralism and post-structuralism the subject will never again be foregrounded in the heroic manner of romanticism and modernism, but it is equally true that never again will the subject be banished from discourse— erased "like a face drawn in sand at the edge of the sea" (Foucault 1970:387).

Modernist and post-modern conceptions of the person define, not two competing ideologies of the subject, but two aspects of experience which are mutually
entailed and co-present in every period of history and every human society.

> To be born is both to be born of the world and to be born into the world. The
> world is already constituted, but also never completely constituted; in the first
> place we are acted upon, in the second we are open to an infinite number of
> possibilities. But this analysis is still abstract, for we exist in both ways *at once.*
> There is, therefore, never determinism and never absolute choice, I am never a
> thing and never bare consciousness. In fact, even our own pieces of initiative, even
> the situations which we have chosen, bear us on, once they have been entered
> upon by virtue of a state rather than an act. The generality of the "rôle" and of the
> situation comes to the aid of decision, and in this exchange between the situation
> and the person who takes it up, it is impossible to determine precisely the "share
> contributed by the situation" and the "share contributed by freedom." (Merleau-
> Ponty 1962:453)

Even in cultures where the idea of biography has little meaning, or in times—
like ours—when the idea of the individual subject is intellectually unfashion-
able, life stories can be told, and must be told, if only to remind us that meaning
takes shape in the transitory, multiplex, and phenomenal forms of particular
lives.

   It is this imperative that underlies Lila Abu-Lughod's approach to an
ethnography of the lifeworld through telling the stories of particular individuals. She sees this as a kind of "writing against culture."

> By insistently focusing on individuals and the particularities of their lives, we may
> be better able to perceive similarities in all our lives. Of course, to say that we all
> live in the particular is not to say that for any of us the particulars are the same.
> Indeed, even in looking at the everyday we might well discover fundamental
> differences, such as those between everyday experience in a world set up to
> produce the effect of structures, institutions, or other abstractions . . . versus
> worlds that have not. Yet the dailiness, by breaking coherence and introducing
> time, trains our gaze on flux and contradiction; and the particulars suggest that
> others live as we perceive ourselves living—not as automatons programmed
> according to "cultural" rules or acting out social roles, but as people going through
> life wondering what they should do, making mistakes, being opinionated,
> vacillating, trying to make themselves look good, enduring tragic personal losses,
> enjoying others, and finding moments of laughter. (1993:27)

INTERSUBJECTIVITY

It is often alleged that all forms of existentialism and phenomenology are
"privacy theories of meaning" (Geertz 1973:12), characterized by naïve subjectivism, introspection and irrationalism, and indifferent to the historical and

social determinants of experience (Bourdieu 1990b:26; Lévi-Strauss 1973:58; 1981:640). Structuralist and post-structuralist thought has tended to sustain these misunderstandings. Let us take, as a starting point, Lévi-Strauss's scathing remarks in *Tristes Tropiques:*

> Phenomenology I found objectionable in that it postulated a kind of continuity between experience and reality. I agreed that the latter encompasses and explains the former, but I had learned from my three sources of inspiration [Geology, Marxism, and Freudian Psychoanalysis] that the transition between one order and the other is discontinuous; that to reach reality one has first to reject experience, and then subsequently to reintegrate it into an objective synthesis devoid of any sentimentality. As for the intellectual movement which was to reach a peak in existentialism, it seemed to me to be anything but a legitimate form of reflection, because of its over-indulgent attitude to the illusions of subjectivity. The raising of personal preoccupations to the dignity of philosophical problems is far too likely to lead to a sort of shop-girl metaphysics, which may be pardonable as a didactic method but is extremely dangerous if it allows people to play fast-and-loose with the mission incumbent on philosophy until science becomes strong enough to replace it: that is, to understand being in relationship to itself and not in relationship to myself. Instead of doing away with metaphysics, phenomenology and existentialism introduced two methods of providing it with alibis. (1973:58)

Lévi-Strauss is speaking here of his student years, but he reiterates this scornful view of existentialism in the closing pages of *L'Homme Nu*—the last volume of *Mythologiques* (1971)—describing it as a "self-admiring activity which allows contemporary man, rather gullibly, to commune with himself in ecstatic contemplation of his own being," a philosophy which cuts itself off from scientific knowledge "which it despises" (1981:640). The notions of subjectivity and experience which Lévi-Strauss singles out for derision are manifestly those that belong to nineteenth-century introspective psychology and German romanticism, though, as Arjun Appadurai has recently observed, there is a longstanding tendency in Western discourse to assume a "normative break" between "inner states" and "outer forms" and so interiorize and essentialize affect (1990:92–93). In these traditions, experience is a matter of "deep interiority," of inward sensibilities based on soulfulness, love, passion, genius, inspiration, suffering, and authenticity. As Dewey observed, this concept of experience as something privileged, personal, and sealed off from the world—"as the equivalent of subjective private consciousness set over against nature, which consists wholly of physical objects, has wrought havoc in philosophy" (1958:11). But just as limiting is the conception of experience associated with traditional empiricism, which isolates, selects, and decontextualizes immediate, sensible experience, treating it as raw material or crude ore from which pure metal—essence, truth, order, totality, reality—may be extracted (ibid.:133). In this view, the subject, far from bringing knowledge into being through insight, intuition, or inspiration, is relegated to the passive and disinterested role of receiving impressions and discerning rules already written into the Being of the world.

Radical empiricism avoids both idealist and empiricist extremes. By expanding the notion of experience to include active and passive modes, facts as well as fictions, the precarious as well as the certain, the idiosyncratic as well as the shared, one goes from trying to establish foundations for knowledge to an exploration of the circumstances under which different modes of experience arise in the course of life. Contrary to the view of Lévi-Strauss, no underlying order or generative principle is assumed. Structures are not foundational to the lifeworld. Rather, they are to be regarded as simply one horizon of experience, one mode of human activity, tied to particular ends, serving particular purposes, and having particular consequences. Structuring is an ongoing, open-ended activity, not the completed product of activity which, in fetishized form, can be said to predetermine activity from without or within (Piaget 1971:4,9).

Consider, for example, the case of Kuranko clan totemism. Twenty years ago, enchanted by the apparent ease with which Lévi-Strauss discerned a structural logic underlying indigenous taxonomies and uncovered "invariants beyond the empirical diversity of human societies" (1966:247), I devoted many months of fieldwork to collecting data with which to test the possibility that a system underlay the complex totemic usages that identified as well as explained interconnections between Kuranko clans. The data suggested that social distinctions made by Kuranko informants themselves between non-Muslim and Muslim clans corresponded to totemic distinctions between forest-zone and savannah-zone animals, thus reinforcing the generally held idea that the core Kuranko area was a pagan forest-zone while "strangers," such as Muslims, hailed from riverine and grassland areas to the north. But it became apparent that totemic affiliations and inter-clan joking alliances (based on shared totemic bonds) tended to differ from place to place. No overarching system held true for every village. Sharing of totems often indicated an alliance between clans in the past, and everywhere suggested the perennial possibility of hospitality, assistance, and protection from those with whom one shared a common history and fictive kinship, signified by a common totem. Clearly, the meaning of totemic affiliations and myths was not determined by historical events or by the logical demands of any totalizing system, but by the exigencies of locality, co-residence, and hospitality. People who settled together in the same place tended to sink their differences and place the past in abeyance, foregrounding common, contemporary interests. These found objective expression in the sharing of totems, references to a unifying Godhead, intermarriage, exchange, and forms of economic cooperation and neighborliness. No impersonal system governed these tactical and strategic uses of totemic narratives and usages. Nor were these practical and local realities a product of a disinterested, humanistic impulse to break down the "closing in of the group into itself" or "promote an idea something like that of a humanity without frontiers . . . the rudiments of an international society" (Lévi-Strauss 1966:166,167). Rather, immediate imperatives of mutual support and amity informed the ongoing restructuring of totemic identifications. Kuranko totemism was a repertoire of instrumental possibilities whose operation could only be understood by reference to the Kuranko lifeworld at its most local level (Jackson 1974; 1982b).

It is important to stress that phenomenology and radical empiricism are not merely philosophies of the subject. Although, as James points out, *"the fons et origo of all reality . . . is . . . subjective, is ourselves"* (1950 vol. 2:296–297), he insists that experience encompasses the empirically singular "me" as well as all my "social selves" which emerge in various contexts of interaction, recognition, and relationship (1950 vol. 1:292–296). Subjectivity entails a reaching beyond the self. Insofar as experience includes substantive *and* transitive, disjunctive *and* conjunctive modalities, it covers a sense of ourselves as singular individuals as well as belonging to a collectivity. William James compared the way consciousness continually slips from one modality to another with the cease-less movement of a bird between flights and perchings. The flights stand for the transitive parts of experience; the perchings suggest the substantive parts (1950 vol. 1:243). Lévi-Strauss's structuralism stands as a critique of the atomistic tendencies of structural-functionalism and the subjectivist ontology of Sartre's early work. But it is important to remember that meaning lies in relationships as they are *lived* and not simply in the structural and systematic properties that analysis may reveal them to have.

For social phenomenology, praxis is seldom a matter of individuals acting alone. It is a mode of shared endeavor as well as conflict, of mutual adjustment as well as violence. Subjectivity is in effect a matter of intersubjectivity, and experience is inter-experience (Merleau-Ponty 1973:56). A person becomes a subject for herself by first becoming an object for others—by incorporating the view that others have of her. The self arises in social experience (Mead 1934), which is why one's sense of self is unstable and varies from context to context.

The task for anthropology is to recover the sense in which experience is situated *within* relationships and *between* persons if the lifeworld is to be explored as a field of intersubjectivity and not reduced to objective structures *or* subjective intentions. Recent studies of the anthropology of the emotions have made this point with great force, showing that affect is neither an intrinsic property of human nature nor of the individual subject, but culturally embed-ded in forms of interpersonal and intersubjective relationship (Lutz and Abu-Lughod 1990).

In this view, reality is not to be sought beneath the empirical—in uncon-scious forms, instinctual drives, or antecedent cause—but in the constructive and deconstructive dialectic of the lived interpersonal world. From the outset of our lives we are in intersubjectivity. As R. D. Laing notes, "The task of social phenomenology is to relate my experience of the other's behaviour to the other's experience of my behaviour. . . . Social phenomenology is the science of my own and of others' *experience*. It is concerned with the relation between my experience of you and your experience of me. That is, with *inter-experience*" (1967:15,16–17 italics in text; see also Esterson 1970:1–3, 221–230). Shared intentionality and intersubjective understanding are in evidence in children at seven to nine months of age, well before the acquisition of language, and constitute what Daniel Stern calls the "existential bedrock of interpersonal relations" (1985:125). Ego and alter-ego are mutually entailed. Identity is a byproduct of *inter*relationships. The lifeworld is primordially a social domain. Observes Merleau-Ponty:

> I may well turn away from it, but not cease to be situated relative to it. Our relationship to the social is, like our relationship to the world, deeper than any express perception or any judgement. . . . We must return to the social with which we are in contact by the mere fact of existing, and which we carry about inseparably with us before any objectivification. . . . *The social is already there when we come to know or judge it.* (1962:362, emphasis added)

For Mauss and Lévi-Strauss, reciprocity is born of social necessity—the necessity of exchange between groups. But sociality is not something based on rational calculation or necessity. Insofar as sociality *is* intersubjectivity, we might say that empathic identification—a reciprocity of viewpoints—is the ground of the very possibility of those modalities of reciprocity which Lévi-Strauss so brilliantly elucidates (Jackson 1982:69–70).

It is, however, not enough simply to assert that subjectivity and experience are socially constructed. For the lifeworld is never a seamless, unitary domain in which social relations remain constant and the experience of self remains stable. Nor is it ever arcadian; it is a scene of turmoil, ambiguity, resistance, dissimulation, and struggle. Although ideological and normative definitions of personhood give priority to certain modes of experience—foregrounding notions of individual autonomy or collective identity — these definitions do not determine the range of lived experience.

An empirically faithful concept of experience has first to recognize this multifaceted character of the person—the fact that experience of self, or of self in relation to other, is continually adjusted to and modulated by circumstance. Second, as Dilthey argued, the concept of experience must include not only what is habitual, typical, and customary (*Erfahrung*), but what is idiosyncratic, exceptional, and singular (*Erlebnis*). Third, our notion of experience must recognize not only our sense of things substantive and bounded but our sense of the transitive and unbounded if we are to avoid reducing experience to the conceptual orders we impose upon it. Finally, it is imperative to recognize what

James called the "double-barrelled" character of experience—the way the *objects* of experience tend to fuse with the ways those objects are experienced, i.e., the lived *processes* of experiencing. Only such a concept of experience, Dewey notes, does justice to the "inclusive integrity of 'experience'" by admitting no division "between act and material, subject and object" but, rather, containing them both in "an unanalyzed totality" (1958:9,8).[6]

Let us briefly consider this proposition that the field of intersubjectivity includes relations between people as well as relations between people and things. Marx's account of human labor in *The German Ideology* shows how these horizons come together in the metaphor of begetting or reproduction. The metaphor discloses the phenomenal unity of laboring to give birth and laboring to ensure the continuity of one's social group (Marx and Engels 1976:43). Marx argues that in expending time and energy on making an object, the object becomes "a prolongation" of the worker's body (1964:89). The body is, in effect, reproduced through the making of the object, in the same way that it is reproduced through begetting a child (ibid.:91).[7] Just as individuals speak of identifying with, giving themselves to, or losing themselves in others, so in building houses, making tools, tilling the soil, or writing a book, people will speak of putting their heart and soul into the work, investing their time and energy in it, giving it their all. It is thus understandable that people should anthropomorphize and talk to the things they work on, blaming their tools when things go wrong, feeling that a part of them has been violated if the object of their labor is stolen, and, as Mauss observed in his famous essay, feeling that something of their own vitality is passed on to others in the form of a material gift (Mauss 1954:8–10). In many cultures this intersubjective relationship between people and the earth, people and masks, the living and the dead, is accepted as a natural attitude. Thus, writing of Turkish traditional art, Henry Glassie notes: "In things they do not see things, but people" (Glassie 1993:103). "The artist's gift suffuses an object with spirit. . . . Art is the object that contains love" (Glassie 1994:5, 6). In the West such attitudes are often written off as supernatural belief, as "fetishism" or mere superstition, *even though these experiences are universal and commonplace.*

An emphasis on the transitive and intersubjective does not mean denying the substantive and subjective; rather it implies that these terms denote not contrasted entities, but moments of a dialectic.

Such a dialectical view of experience evokes the metaphor of journeying. But it is not only way-stations and termini that figure in our itinerary, but critical deviations, digressions, and delays. It is in this sense that we begin to recover something of the original meaning of experience as *empeiria* whose root *per* is the same as the Germanic *fahr* ("to travel"). Experience, like experimentation and empirical work, suggests a passage into the world, a going forth, a venture, a trial, a self-proving peregrination—a "thinking with one's feet," as

Ortega y Gasset puts it (Marías 197:40). This was the task Victor Turner set himself in his later work—moving beyond a structural-functional concern with the outward forms and manifest functions of ritual activity to "idiosyncratic clusterings," "individual symbolic objects and actions," and inward transformations of experience that "cannot be explained as epiphenomena of social structural processes" (1978:572). For Turner, an anthropology of experience brings one back from the domain of anthropological theory to the dramatic settings of the lifeworld (Turner 1985;1986).

To speak of experience as practical know-how, accumulated wisdom, or knowledge gained through the vicissitudes of life is to reclaim experience from classical empiricism for whom it is merely the starting-point for forms of rational inquiry, the goal of which is to move away from sensation, belief, opinion, and everyday reality in order to adduce necessary and universal truths (Dewey 1960:70–87). For radical empiricism, however, inquiry ceases to be simply a matter of controlled experimentation, cool observation, and disinterested data-gathering, because the anthropologist himself or herself is drawn into the lifeworld as a participant.

INTENTIONALITY AND SOCIALITY

We have already insisted on locating knowledge, experience, and the person in the lifeworld. This implies that consciousness cannot be understood in isolation, as pure cognition or disinterested observation. Consciousness is engaged with the lifeworld. It is "from the very beginning a social product" (Marx and Engels 1976:44). In this sense, consciousness is active and outgoing; it points beyond itself. Belief is always *about* something. Feelings and thoughts are always *of* something. For phenomenology, the ego works with or against others to constitute a world on the basis of that which is already given, that which is at hand. If, when all is said and done, the world so constituted through collective or individual praxis is objectively identical to the world which existed before, the significant fact for phenomenology is that the passage from one objective situation to another is always mediated by *subjective* life—by purposefulness, practical activity, and projective and strategic imagination (Sartre 1968:97–99).

The principle of intentionality is central to any phenomenological analysis. Once thought to be the discovery of Husserl (building on the work of Brentano), it is now known that Husserl's notion of intentionality was strongly influenced by William James for whom the *purposes or intentions* of thinking, believing, and feeling must be taken into account if one is to understand any thought, belief or sensation (Wilshire 1968; Edie 1987; Wild 1969).

In this view, society or culture cannot be conceptualized in terms of objective conditions that directly determine the possibility of thought or action from without. Society is equally a domain of instrumentality in which human beings make their lives and confer meanings whose existential import cannot, in the final analysis, be reduced to the meanings sedimented in preexisting cultural forms. As Merleau-Ponty notes, the very activity that brings about the appearance of social structures and cultural forms also has "as its meaning to reject them and to surpass them" (1963:176). Analytically, our understanding of human intentionality demands what Sartre called a progressive-regressive method—a disclosure of the dialectical tension between what is given and what we make of the given in the light of emergent projects, imperatives and contingencies. This is to say, what is possible for a person is always precondi- tioned by the world into which he or she is born and raised, but a person's life does more than conserve and perpetuate these pre-existing circumstances; it interprets them, negotiates and nuances them, re-imagines them, protests against them, and endures them in such complex and subtle ways that, in the end, human freedom appears as "the small movement which makes of a totally conditioned social being someone who does not render back completely what his conditioning has given him" (Sartre 1969:45; see also Jackson 1989:4; Kleinman 1992:173–174).

EMBODIMENT

In *The Crisis of European Sciences,* Husserl observed that physical bodies and living bodies are "essentially different." Unlike physical bodies, such as rocks and buildings, the human body "holds sway in consciousness" (1970:107).

The landmark work in developing this insight was Merleau-Ponty's *Phe- nomenology of Perception.* Like Husserl, Merleau-Ponty repudiated the idea that the "phenomena" of human consciousness, affectivity, and comportment could be equated with the "facts" on which mathematics and physics were based.

Descartes distinguished between an I or ego which is essentially a thinking entity, an active mind (*res cogitans*), and a body or *res extensa*—a supposedly different kind of entity whose defining characteristic was that it had extension in space. The world was thus divided into an unworldly, transcendent domain of mind and a worldly domain of body. As Drew Leder puts it, "In Cartesianism, the human mind is viewed as an island of awareness afloat in a vast sea of insensate matter" (1990:8). Since the Baroque logic of Descartes led people to see mind and matter as essentially different, it became of great scientific and philosophical interest to understand how mind could act upon matter. Some thinkers resolved this dilemma by saying that mind does not act upon matter. If I appear to move my hand it is not a physical action caused by a mental decision but a coincidence of two separate actions, each caused by the will of God. God alone is the primary cause of all movement and my will is an illusion. The early seventeenth century philosopher Geulinx used an analogy of two clocks, both keeping perfect time. The clock of mind points to the hour, the clock of matter strikes, and to the inattentive observer there seems to be a causal link between the two. But this is an illusion. It is God who set the two clocks running and synchronized them (Coe 1964:29). Samuel Beckett, amused by these extreme Cartesian scenarios, made many of his principal characters creatures of Cartesianism, like Murphy who, powerless to act, lies abed persuading himself to desire and need nothing, since nothing can be actually desired or needed unless God decides it. (Unhappily, in Murphy's universe God does not exist.) Or Molloy who contemplates his hands and feet with a disturbing detachment as though they did not strictly belong to him. Here is a description of how Beckett's character, Watt, walks:

> Watt's way of advancing due east, for example, was to turn his bust as far as possible towards the north, and at the same time to fling his right leg as far as possible towards the south, and then to turn his bust as far as possible towards the south and at the same time to fling his left leg as far as possible towards the north . . . and so on, over and over again, many times, until he reached his destination, and could sit down. (1958:32)

In this account of the hapless Watt there is no natural or habitual unity of body and mind. As Richard Coe notes, "What we observe is a series of actions, grotesquely analysed, which, by an imperfect coincidence, add up to the intention of 'walking' in Watt's mind" (1964:32).

The absurdity of Watt and of the philosophical positions into which post-Cartesian philosophy talked itself are not simply artifacts of our intellectual tradition. These descriptions of minds alienated from their bodies reflect a not unfamiliar mode of human experience. Indeed, Drew Leder argues, it is because such phenomena as absentmindedness, bodily disappearance, and out-of-body experiences are fairly common that we lend support to Cartesian views. Philosophical error begins when we reify such experiences, or make them foundational to our understanding of what the world is really like. Put another way, phenomenology does not claim that human beings never experience themselves as disembodied, or never experience their bodies as inert objects or physical encumbrances (see Gadow 1982); rather, it argues against reducing all human experience to them.

For Merleau-Ponty, the Cartesian division between subject and object implies an untenable view that the human mind is the sole locus of subjectivity, the human body being a physical object that the mind has to move, manipulate, or bestow meaning upon. For Merleau-Ponty, human "being-in-the-world" is bodily being. Behavior is not an outcome of conceiving or willing something in the mind which is then executed mechanically by the body under orders from the mind. Motility, Merleau-Ponty explains, "is not, as it were, a handmaid of consciousness, transporting the body to that point in space of which we have formed a representation beforehand" (1962:139). "Consciousness," he writes, "is in the first place not a matter of 'I think that' but of 'I can.'" Consciousness is "a being-towards-the-thing through the intermediary of the body" (ibid.:137).

For Merleau-Ponty, then, subjectivity is a bodily being-in-the-world; intersubjectivity, even when expressed through fantasy or empathy, is a modality of bodylife. Embodiment is thus as much a primordial aspect of human subjectivity as it is of sociality.

Merleau-Ponty's phenomenology of the body subject is equally critical of logocentric models which, having located the source of meaning in the mind or in "society," show how these meanings are inscribed as symbols or signs on the human body. Bodily activity is not a way of expressing or objectifying meanings first formed in the mind. The meaning of a bodily action is not *given to* the action by some external agent but is *in* the action itself. "In the action of the hand which is raised towards an object is contained a reference to the object, not as an object represented, but as that highly specific thing towards which we project ourselves, near which we are, in anticipation, and which we haunt" (Merleau-Ponty 1962:138).

This radical view of bodily subjectivity implies that meaning is not invariably given to activity by the conscious mind or in explicit verbal formulations. Meaning should not be reduced to that which can be thought or said, since meaning may exist simply in the doing and in what is manifestly accomplished by an action. As Merleau-Ponty notes, "My body has its world, or understands its world, without having to make use of my 'symbolic' or 'objectifying' function'" (1962:140–141). This mode of understanding Merleau-Ponty calls *praktognosia* (practical knowledge).

Aboriginal kinship provides a compelling example of this. In many parts of Aboriginal Australia, kin relations are designated by kin terms as well as by parts of the body (Kendon 1988). Representation is, therefore, not merely a matter of naming, but a matter of embodying. Indeed, the fortunes of a kinsperson may be divined in an ache or muscular twitch in the corresponding part of one's own body-self. Nor is the relation between signifier and signified entirely arbitrary. For the Warlpiri, touching the breast to signify mother or touching the abdomen to signify a woman's child suggest obvious links between these signs and embodied experience, and touching the shoulder to signify a junior sibling discloses the fact that junior siblings are in fact often carried on an older sibling's shoulder. This is not to say that signs are unmediated projections of bodily experience. Displacement is common—as when the chin is touched to sign "father" (possibly a displacement upward from the penis) or when the center of the chest is tapped with a fisted hand to sign "mother's brother" (probably a displacement from the mother's breast). But the point is that the body is never merely an inert object or surface on which the mind inscribes meaning.

This point may be underlined with another example. Anthropologists often analyze body tattooing in a representational manner, treating the patterns or designs as insignia of rank and status—objective signs of social meanings. It is thus implied that the body markings are secondary elaborations of meanings first held in the mind and embedded in "Society." In Samoa, for instance, various designs signify a person's genealogy (both on the mother's and father's sides), moral qualities such as caring, kinship amity, and a dutiful attitude toward one's sisters, and virtues such as confidence, courage, decisiveness, and firm standing (Paulo 1994:77–78). But a phenomenology of tattooing would seek to complement such a piecemeal deciphering of symbols with an analysis of how the key social virtues are actually inculcated through lived experience. In this view, the body is regarded not as a passive or inert site, but as a domain of intersubjectivity and agency where meanings are constructed through the person's bodily, sensible, and intellectual relations with those who carry out the operations. The end product—the body marking—is only one moment in an ongoing process in which the subject of the tattooing interacts with and is supported and advised by others. Tattooing is thus a process of initiation (Paulo: 77)—a coming to understanding through bodily ordeals endured with one's peers—and the pain of tattooing mediates a common bond between those who share it together. In Samoa, this initiatory process (*pe'a* connotes both initiation and tattoo) is thought of as a kind of robing or dressing, and is completed with a ceremony (*umusaga*) that lifts the tapu of the tattooing and marks the entrance of the initiate into manhood and the community. The meaning lies in the event, not before or after it.

Reference to pain reminds us, too, that social meaning is often generated in the interior space of libidinal and visceral being. Exploring the way country and person are coalesced *as body* in Warlpiri cosmology, I have noted that "what is distinctive about Warlpiri anthropomorphism is that the human body and the body of the earth are metaphorically fused in terms of internal, visceral physiology and not just in terms of external anatomy. Thus, a sacred site is a womb, the odor of a person's sweat may evoke the aromatic sap of a particular species of tree, and a deposit of white clay may be said to be the semen of a Dreaming ancestor. Relations between person and country are couched in terms of organic processes such as sleeping and eating, digestion and defecation, procreation and parturition that Western bourgeois poetics shuns in its attempt to separate humanity, animality, and physicality into discrete domains" (1995:162). Some of the most compelling work on the phenomenology of the body is now exploring the cultural significance of the senses (Howes 1987; Stoller 1989), and the relationship between cultural models and visceral processes centered on the mouth, anus, penis, breasts, vagina, as well as the *materia prima* of urine, shit, semen, sweat, vaginal fluids, blood, milk, odors and vapors (Drummond 1981; Mimica 1993). The essays by Desjarlais, Kleinman, and Devisch in this volume also explore the field of "sociosomatics," showing the manner in which visceral experiences of wellness, illness, and therapeutic change are intimately connected with the cultural construction of knowledge.

PRAXIS AND PRACTICE

If, as phenomenologists argue, knowledge of the mind is neither ontologically prior nor superior to knowledge of the body, then we have to accept that activity may be meaningful even when it is not couched in words, explicated in concepts, or subject to reflection. In other words, our gestures, acts and modes of comportment do not invariably depend on *a priori* cognitive understanding. Practical skills, know-how, a sense of what to do, are irreducible. The meaning of practical knowledge lies in what is accomplished through it, not in what conceptual order may be said to underlie or precede it.[8]

In most human societies, knowledge is a matter of practical competence and sensory grasp rather than declaration (Devisch 1993:50; Desjarlais 1992:26–27). Among the Cashinahua of eastern Peru, for example, the knowledge a person acquires through skillful work is said to be "in the hands," while emotional *savoir-faire* is "in the liver" and social knowledge is "in the ears" (an index of how sociality demands effective oral communication). The Cashinahua reject the idea that the brain is some sort of central controlling agency, separated from the body. "They insisted," writes Kenneth Kensinger, "that different kinds of knowledge are gained through and reside in different parts of the body. The whole body thinks and knows" (1991:44). Moreover, the validation of knowledge is how a person actually behaves. "It is in action, not in contemplation, that knowledge is both gained and given expression" (ibid.:45).

This may be taken as a critique of our intellectual tendency to observe practical and social activities which are highly effective and complex, only to reduce them to hidden principles, cognitive patternings and unspoken assumptions which we ourselves bring to the field. We thereby subtly prioritize theoretical knowledge, giving the impression that the meanings we make of an activity are somehow determinative of it, albeit in an underground way which the participants are ignorant of. The theoretician's emphasis on saying over doing, on intellectual grasp over practical accomplishment, can thus imply an invidious distinction between native intuition and anthropological reason.

Compelling examples of this can be drawn readily from cross-cultural studies of cognition where non-literate peoples are asked to respond to experimental protocols aimed at testing their abilities for abstract theoretical reasoning. Consider, for example, this excerpt from an interview between a Russian psychologist and an illiterate peasant called Rushtar, reported in A. R. Luria's essays on cognitive development (1976:109–110). It begins with the psychologist presenting the subject with a syllogism: "In the Far North, where there is snow, all bears are white. Novaya Zemlya is in the Far North and there is always snow there. What color are the bears there?"

"If there was someone who had a great deal of experience and had been everywhere, he would do well to answer the question."

"But can you answer the question on the basis of my words?"

"A person who had travelled a lot and been in cold countries and seen everything could answer; he would know what color the bears were."

"Now, in the North, in Siberia, there is always snow. I told you that where there is snow the bears are white. What kind of bears are there in the North in Siberia?"

"I never travelled through Siberia. Tadshibai-aka who died last year was there. He said that there were white bears there, but he didn't say what kind."

Luria notes that his subjects refused to discuss any topics that went beyond their personal experience, insisting that "one could speak only of what one had seen." For the Russian psychologist, the concrete, situated, practical character of such responses is seen as "failing to accepted the premises presented." It is evidence of a *lack* of abstract cognitive skills, such as conceptual generalization, syllogistic and taxonomic reasoning, rather than as a *positive* preference for other skills more compatible with immediate social concerns. One cannot help but take from these transcribed interviews the impression that the psychologists regarded the peasants as ignorant, if not stupid. Worse, their lack of logic, theory, and abstract reasoning capacity is alleged to indicate a kind of arrested historical and ontognetic development. But is it not the case that, given the absurd context of these exercises in deduction and inference, the psychologist is the one who seems alienated and obtuse?[9]

Michael Oakeshott helps us put theoretical knowledge in its place. He argues that what we like to think of as theoretical knowledge is more like a *post facto* rationalization of what is said and done than an explanation of it. What an ethnographer commits to writing and synthesizes as a series of theoretical propositions about social organization, symbolism, or belief, should not be thought of as rules which govern these various fields of social activity. In other words, what we make of a social world when we reflect upon it from afar is not essential to the world's workings. Speaking does not spring from a knowledge of grammar any more than good research is an outcome of methodological training, or good workmanship is guaranteed by reading how-to-do-it books. We fall too easily into the habit of elucidating general principles from observations made in the course of research, then hypostatizing these principles as "rules" which allegedly determine human activity from within culture itself or from within the unconscious mind. Oakeshott compares this misconception with the common error of thinking of a recipe book as a kind of "independently generated beginning from which cookery can spring." In fact cookbooks, like the rules and principles spelled out in anthropological theory, are "mere abridgements" of activity, abstracts of somebody's practical knowledge of how to cook. Because they "exist in advance of the activity, they cannot properly be said to govern it" or "provide the impetus of the activity." A rule, like a recipe, says Oakeshott, "is the stepchild, not the parent of the activity" (1962:90–91).

Ethnography offers a basis for a critique of Western metaphysics by showing that theoretical knowledge has its origins in practical, worldly activity, and by reminding us that in most human communities the measure of the worth of any knowledge is its social value. Knowledge is a *vita activa*, a form of *savoir-faire*, of knowing how to generate the wherewithal for life, and to comport oneself socially with gumption, propriety, and common sense. What is expected of the ethnographer is that he or she act in a socially adroit manner, evincing an understanding of how to greet people, sit with them, give and receive, work alongside, and express compassion in times of adversity. These social expectations tend to be couched in terms of the practical obligations of fictive kinship and hospitality, and all the abstract, theorized work of anthropology counts for little if these social imperatives are not met. Dialectic must, so to speak, be realized as dialogue (Strassner 1963:257). In this spirit, many contemporary ethnographers emphasize that ethnographic research is, in Karen McCarthy Brown's words, "a form of human relationship . . . a social art" (1991:12). But because our understanding comes from "talking to people" (Shostak 1981:7) we find ourselves caught between the "force field" of these vernacular dialogues and the "disciplinary field" of anthropology (Scheper-Hughes 1992:24–25). But the tension is also between cultural fields. Twenty years ago, Paul Riesman wrote that his "introspective ethnography" of the Fulani was a result of "the encounter of a man belonging to Western civilization, and haunted by questions which life there raises for him, with a radically different civilization which he investigates with those questions constantly in mind" (1977:1–2). How to reconcile these fields is a question which many of the essays in this anthology address.

SUBALTERNITY

Our task is clear: to revalidate the everyday life of ordinary people, to tell their stories in their own words, to recover their names. For anthropology, there can be no doubt as to the identity of this ordinary person, this common man.

> He is the murmur of societies. Always he precedes texts. He doesn't even wait for them. He pays no attention to them. But in written representations he gets along. Little by little he occupies the center of our scientific scenarios. The cameras have deserted the actors who dominated proper names and social emblems in order to fix themselves on the crowd of the public. The sociologization and anthropologization of research privilege the anonymous and the everyday where close-ups isolate metonymic details—parts taken for the whole. Slowly the representatives who previously symbolized families, groups, and orders are effaced from the scene where they reigned during the time of the *name*. Number has arrived, the time of democracy, of the big city, of bureaucracies, of cybernetics. It is a supple and continuous crowd, woven tightly like a fabric without tear or seam, a multitude of quantified heroes who lose their names and faces while becoming the mobile language of calculations and rationalities which belong to no one. Ciphered currents in the street. (de Certeau 1980:3)

To shift our focus from the privileged world of detached intellectual activity to the often underprivileged domains of the lifeworld is to reconstitute our notion of knowledge as something urgently of and for the world rather than something about the world. Nowhere are the political implications of such a shift more forcefully spelled out than in the ongoing work of the subaltern studies project, inaugurated by Ranajit Guha in the late 1970s. The import of this work for anthropology is only now being realized.

Our concern here is to explore the relationship between the subaltern studies critique of European historiography and the phenomenological epoché.

In his landmark study of peasant insurgency in colonial India, Guha launched a critique of political and historiographical discourse which constructs the history of peasant India as a history of "events without a subject" (1983:11). Guha takes issue with the assumption that the insurgent was never "the subject of his own history" (ibid.:4). He writes against the view that the rural masses were historically without consciousness, blindly and spontaneously reacting to domination, never organizing, exercising agency, or possessing political consciousness. Apart from providing us with sobering reminders of the ways in which Western thought still perpetuates stereotypes of non-Westerners as radical others, absorbed into a mass of undifferentiated humanity which holds life cheap, Guha's work indicates that rebellion and defiance grow out of forms of resistance and "intentional ambiguity" *in everyday life* (ibid.:12; see also Trawick 1990:41–42).

Veena Das observes that the published work of the subaltern studies group is a reminder to anthropologists that much of their "theoretical arsenal" is made up of concepts that "render other societies knowable in terms of 'laws,' 'rules,' and patterns of authority" (1989:310). But such a preoccupation with order echoes the managerial and administrative priorities of colonial elites, making it difficult for the anthropologist to come to terms with transgression, disorder, violence, and affective action (see Devisch 1995). Yet these terms define the modalities of action through which, in the course of colonial history, subalterns have defined themselves as the subjects of their own destiny. Far from inhabiting a natural world without consciousness of their own situation, an inert mass reacting blindly to forms of external domination, the subaltern possesses consciousness and will no less than the oppressor.

What is at issue here is the link between discursive suppression and political oppression. The disparaged world of subaltern consciousness is analogous to the disparaged world of bodily, social, and practical life which we have vowed to recover and place on a par with experiences we have hitherto esteemed as rational. If we are to dissolve once and for all the invidious epistemological divisions that mark off the world of the European intellectual from the world of the irrational "savage," that separate doxa from opinion and reason from affectivity, we must disclose the hidden agendas and instrumentalities behind the fictions of interpretive and explanatory totalization, and relate forms of knowledge to the existential contexts which foreshadow them.

Consider, for example, the question of history. Phenomenology is less concerned with establishing what actually happened in the past than in exploring the past as a mode of present experience. Michael Oakeshott sets the scene:

> A fixed and finished past, a past divorced from and uninfluenced by the present, is a past divorced from evidence (for evidence is always present) and is consequently nothing and unknowable. If the historical past be knowable, it must belong to the present world of experience; if it be unknowable, history is worse than futile, it is impossible. (1933:107)

This view urges us not to oppose oral tradition and written history, but rather disclose the different social realities they authorize. For a long time, a positivist view of history, emphasizing exact chronology, objective events, and linear chains of cause and effect, served to bolster the authority of Eurocentric criteria of truth. We are now seeing a shift of emphasis toward indigenous truths, in which oral history is seen as sustaining the life of the living rather than keeping a record of the past. In her work on Maori oral narratives, Judith Binney speaks of the importance of this shift in making colonizers aware of what is imperative for the colonized—a necessary step if the dominant culture is to change "its attitudes about its possession of 'truth'" (1987:17).

> Maori oral narrative histories convey what is seen to be the essence of human experience to the people who are living. As the Samoan historian Malama Maleisea has commented, if there *were* a truth, there would be no histories. Or equally, as the Nigerian writer Chinua Achebe put it, in his evocative novel about the colonization of his country, *Things Fall Apart*, "There is no story that is not true. . . . The World has no end, and what is good among one people is an abomination with others." (Binney 1987:28)

NARRATIVE

As Jürgen Habermas has shown, the everyday lifeworld is a world of discourse, language games, and communicative activity (1987:135–140). In Habermas's conception of the lifeworld, narrative plays a singularly important role, for narrative makes it possible for people to create coherent scenarios which articulate *shared* meanings (Habermas 1987:136). As Lyotard puts it, a collectivity "finds the raw material for its social bond not only in the meaning of the narratives it recounts, but also in the act of reciting them" (1984:22). Sociality is, therefore, both mediated by storytelling and objectified in stories told and passed on. If we are not to lapse into solitude or solipsism, we need scenarios and symbols—true or otherwise—with which we can identify, stories which speak to the things we have in common (Jackson 1982a). John Berger's stories of French Alpine peasant life illuminate this. Writing of gossip as a form of "close, oral, daily history," Berger observes that it allows the whole village to define itself:

> The life of a village, as distinct from its physical and geographical attributes, is perhaps the sum of all the social and personal relationships existing within it, plus the social and economic relationships—usually oppressive—which link the village to the rest of the world. But one could say something similar about the life of a large town. What distinguishes the life of a village is that it is also *a living portrait of itself:* a communal portrait, in that everybody is portrayed and everybody portrays. . . . Every village's portrait of itself is constructed, however, not out of stone, but out of words, spoken and remembered: out of opinions, stories, eyewitness reports, legends, comments and hearsay. And it is a continuous portrait; work on it never stops. (1979:9)

Unlike theoretical explanation, narrative redescription is a crucial and constitutive part of the ongoing activity of the lifeworld, which is why narrative plays such a central role in phenomenological description. Moreover, narrative activity reveals the link between discourse and practice, since the very structure of narrative is pregiven in the structures of everyday life. As Alisdair MacIntyre puts it, "stories are lived before they are told" (1984:212). Consider stories about journeys. It is not just that journeys provide the content of the tale; the very structure of the story replicates the structure of journeying. In a mundane and immediate sense, stories grow out of patterns of our everyday movements in the lifeworld: going forth to work or forage, returning at evening to a home, a hearth, a bar, to share food and drink and tell each other about our day's experiences. But there is also the more epic journey which encompasses a human lifetime: the movement from birth to death which passes through the critical moments of coming of age, marrying, bearing and raising children, growing old. Narrative, we might say, is a form of Being as much as a way of Saying. Our stories, myths, and histories all reflect the temporality of experience (Ricoeur 1980:165). It is a view echoed in Alasdair MacIntyre's notion that the unity of any person's life "resides in the unity of a narrative which links birth to life to death as narrative beginning to middle to end" (1981:205). As Hannah Arendt observes: "That every individual life between birth and death can eventually be told as a story with beginning and end is the prepolitical and prehistorical condition of history, the great story without beginning and end" (1958:184).

Narrative, then, is one mode of description or discourse which may satisfy our interests in commenting upon experience without a radical split from it (Desjarlais 1992:35). As Michel de Certeau puts it, "a theory of narration is indissociable from a theory of practices, as its condition as well as its production" (1988:78). Thus, pedestrian movements to and fro along village paths, or within a grid of city streets, already impose a precognitive disposition which will find expression in stories where moral or conceptual transformations take place from one mode of being to another. As de Certeau suggests, the mundane metaphors of walking, traveling, digressing, and to and froing, which pervade narrative, disclose the intimate connection between non-discursive and discursive fields of activity (ibid.:100–101). Theoretical knowledge pretends that this connection can be disrupted, that discourse can escape the preconceptual conditions of being-in-the-world. But theoretical discourse is profoundly shaped and haunted by mythical and narrative forms—something which is brought home in Misia Landau's study of narratives of human evolution, where she shows how paleoanthropological research reports are frequently couched in terms of classic folktale scenarios (1991). What is implied here is that the very comprehensibility of theory depends on pretheoretical narrative forms that are common knowledge. In other words, the argument that scientific theory and traditional storytelling gain legitimacy or assert authority in radically different ways is questionable. As Lyotard observes, the credibility of any discourse in the postmodern age is not decided by the facts speaking for themselves or by the data *per se*, but by the way facts and data are organized into a narrative. As readers we decide whether or not to accept an account rendered, not merely on the basis of evidence and arguments, but on the strength of how agreeable the story is to us. This bestowal of consensus implies, therefore, a *social* evaluation of the work, and reflects class interests, shared aesthetic values, and a political sense of community, rather than some neutral, dispassionate, objective method of verification. As such, every piece of scientific knowledge, every innovation in medical technology, every paradigm in anthropology wins acceptance and gains currency in part because it is informed by a metanarrative—a hidden story which is, in effect, the story which the group who bestows this acceptance wants to hear about itself.

A focus on the lifeworld is thus connected with a revived interest in narrative description in anthropology. This is not necessarily a reflection of the fashionable view that ethnography is a form of writing (Marcus and Cushman 1982), but the expression of a concern for writing about lived experience in ways which do it justice. There is a political edge to this. As Lila Abu-Lughod observes, storytelling works against the "culture concept" by subverting assumptions of homogeneity, coherence and timeless, and by revealing the struggle, negotiation, and strategizing that lie at the heart of social life (1993:13). John Berger makes a similar point. Insofar as stories preempt and forestall abstraction, they bear witness to realities which the well-heeled often prefer to ignore.

> In poor societies abstraction and tyranny go together; in rich societies it is indifference which usually goes with abstraction. Abstraction's capacity to ignore what is real (and the heart can abstract as well as the mind: unjustified jealousy, for example, is an abstraction) is undoubtedly where most evil begins. (1985: 266–267)

THE RED WHEELBARROW

William Carlos Williams's famous poem may serve to preface our exploration of the implications of radical empiricism and phenomenology for ethnographic writing.

so much depends
upon

a red wheel
barrow

glazed with rain
water

beside the white
chickens

That poetry should figure so prominently in phenomenology is attested in the work of Heidegger and Bachelard. The origins of the poetic image, Bachelard observed, cannot be determined. The resonances of the image carry us far beyond that which can be contained and encompassed by conceptual thought. "Forces are manifested in poems," he writes, "that do not pass through the circuits of knowledge" (1969:xvii).

The Red Wheelbarrow exemplifies William Carlos Williams's poetic dictum: "No ideas but in things." It bears a family resemblance to Husserl's dictum, "back to things themselves" (*zurück zu den Sachen selbst*), and implies the same phenomenological task which Heidegger defined as letting "that which shows itself be seen from itself in the very way in which it shows itself from itself" (1962:58). Williams's commitment was to the specific, the local, the vernacular, the embodied particular. He wanted to make writing faithful to immediate experience: direct, presuppositionless, open-ended. In his longest poem, *Paterson,* Williams gives presence to this bodily and sensory immediacy—of what he called the "jumps, swiftnesses, colors, movements of the day"—by sustaining an image of walking through a landscape. Elaborate reworking, conceptual redefinition, and rhetorical embellishment are eschewed in favor of describing one's sense of being-in-the-world (Tomlinson 1985:vii–xvii).

William Carlos Williams's poetry and ideas about poetry are deeply in "the American grain." One recalls Ralph Waldo Emerson's dictum: "Ask the fact for the form," and Thoreau's famous phrase, "The roots of letters are things." And one can readily discern in these homely adages the pragmatist spirit of James and Dewey—and the New World impulse to break with the metaphysical and narrowly empirical traditions of Europe by renewing a concern for practical doing, with "what works," with primary experience rather than rationally constructed, categorical systems of ideas.

The link between the radical empiricism of William James and Husserl's phenomenology is well established (Edie 1987; Ihde 1986; Gavin 1992).[10] Both philosophers insisted on the comprehensive description of experience as it is actually had prior to intellectual reflection.

At first sight this may seem naïve. But, as Alfred Gell observes in his phenomenological analysis of human time, logical perspicacity, methodological rigor, and rational inquiry must be included, not expunged, if such an analysis is to be complete (1992:328). What Husserl and James wanted to stress was that there are significant differences between the way the world appears to our consciousness when we are fully engaged in activity and the way it appears to us when we subject it to reflection and retrospective analysis. It is not that reflection, explanation, and analysis are to be extirpated from phenomenological accounts of human life; rather that these modes of experience are to be denied epistemological privileges and prevented from occluding or downplaying those non-reflective, atheoretical, and practical domains of experience which are not necessarily encompassed by fixed or definitive ideas.

When the World Trade Center in New York City was bombed on February 26, 1993, reporters were quickly on the scene, interviewing people fleeing the smoke-filled towers.

> "We crawled under pipes when we arrived and everything was on fire," said Edward Bergen, a 38-year-old firefighter who was one of the first to reach the scene of the blast. "Suddenly, a guy came walking out of the flames, like one of those zombies in the movie, 'The Night of the Living Dead.' His flesh was hanging off. He was a middle-aged man." (*New York Times* Feb. 27, 1993:10)

The manner in which lived experience incorporates and fuses immediate sensory experience with pregiven cultural knowledge (in this instance, a well-known horror movie) was, for me, reminiscent of Warlpiri accounts of Dreaming myths in which it is difficult to draw an unambiguous line between inherited cultural knowledge and personal experience (Jackson 1995). But in both these examples, the idiosyncratic and the cultural are co-present. Indeed, it is the shared symbol that enables everyone to find consensus and consolation in a story. The phenomenological method aims for verisimilitude, placing primary experience and secondary elaboration on the same footing. Both are seen as integral to how people manage the exigencies of life. This is brilliantly elucidated in Michael Young's study of lived myth in Kalauna (1983), where he shows how the horizons of myth and biography are effectively fused, so that an individual projects himself "as a synecdoche of his ancestors and lineage" (ibid.:19), blurring the line between fact and fiction, life story and exemplary narrative.

Phenomenology's skeptical attitude toward systematic understanding, bounded ideas, and totalizing explanations finds expression in styles of writing which resist the idea that knowledge may be won by a progressive interrogation of the object—the notion that the object can be captured, held, and possessed. It is not surprising, therefore, that so much inventiveness characterizes ethnographic writing in the phenomenological vein. Nor is it strange that women have been at the forefront of this phenomenological turn. Observes Adrienne Rich: "Men in general think badly: in disjuncture from their personal lives, claiming objectivity where the most irrational passions seethe, losing . . . their senses in the pursuit of professionalism."

Hélène Cixous also sees definition, categorizing, rationalizing, and enclosure as masculine traits. She celebrates instead a passive and open attitude toward life in which language is entered into rather than exploited.

> This mode of passivity is our way—really an active way—of getting to know things by letting ourselves be known by them. You don't seek to master. To demonstrate, explain, grasp. And then to lock away in a strongbox. To pocket part of the riches of the world. But rather to transmit: to make things loved by making them known. (1991:57)

One sees this naturalistic style exemplified in such recent ethnographies as Karen McCarthy Brown's *Mama Lola* (1991), Jim Wafer's *The Taste of Blood* (1991), Nancy Scheper-Hughes' *Death without Weeping* (1992), Lila Abu-Lughod's *Writing Women's Worlds* (1993), Brian Moeran's *Okubo Diary* (1985), Robert Desjarlais's *Body and Emotion* (1992), René Devisch's *Weaving the Threads of Life* (1993), and my own *At Home in the World* (1995). These works recall Goethe's notion of "exact sensuous fantasy," and Adorno's "exact fantasy" (1977–1978:131) and "paratactic style" (Rose 1978:13). They provide abundant evidence that it is never enough to say that ethnography is a form of writing, with various genre conventions coming and going like interpretive fashions, for in these instances writing is compelled by politics not poetics, by a vision of the world not a theory of culture. Realist in character, yes, but not because their authors embrace philosophical realism. Rather, they are motivated by an urgent sense to place on record and testify to human experiences that "speak to us, without flippancy, about things that matter" (Wolff 1983:xi).

NOTES

1. The word phenomenon comes from the Greek *phaenesthai* (to flare up, show itself, bring to light, appear).

2. George Devereux has explored this paradox in depth, noting that Niels Bohr's *Abtötungsprinzip* (life-killing principle) applies equally to the way that experimental probing can kill the organism an experimenter seeks to understanding as well as the way conceptual models can obliterate all trace of the phenomenon one seeks to grasp (1967:255, 287–288).

3. We are echoing here Walter Benjamin's cabalistic observation that truth "is not an unveiling which destroys the secret, but the revelation which does it justice" (Arendt 1968:41).

4. Paul Feyerabend traces this division back to Parmenides who distinguished between a way of inquiry "far from the footsteps of humans" that leads to what is "appropriate and necessary," and a way of inquiry based on "habit, born of experience" which contains the "opinions of mortals." Only the first procedure, he believed, could help us establish truths capable of superseding all traditions (1987:120).

5. Crucial to Schutz's phenomenology of the lifeworld are his distinctions between several horizons or existential modalities of social experience, based on whether relationships are directly or indirectly experienced. Thus, the world of a person's immediate consociates (*Umwelt*) is contrasted with the world of a person's contemporaries (*Mitwelt*), predecessors (*Vorwelt*) and successors (*Folgewelt*) which exist at one remove (Schutz 1989).

6. For anthropology, this means that there is no real distinction to be made between the culture we study and the process of studying it. Our understanding is neither of another, nor of oneself, but of the interplay and interaction between other and self.

7. In her illuminating account of how the Aboriginal people of Belyuen (Cox Peninsular, Northern Territory, Australia), conceptualize labor and work, Elizabeth Povinelli notes that all matter, including the human body, is "the congealed labor of mythic action" which penetrates the earth or human body as speech and as sweat (1993:137–160).

8. Consider, for example, small boat-building—where the "conception" of the craft is incorporated in the builder's experience and body memory, requiring no blueprint, plan or objective measurements.

9. It is worth noting that the air of scientific neutrality in this research masked political assumptions and cultural prejudices that were anything but neutral. Luria's researches were carried out in remote villages of Uzbekistan and Kirghizia in 1931–32 during the Soviet Union's drive to eliminate illiteracy, collectivize the economy, suppress Islam, and generally create a socialist "revolution in cognitive activity" (Luria 1976:vi).

10. Alfred Schutz was also a "careful and sympathetic reader of William James" (Natanson 1986:18), and in *The Origins of Pragmatism*, A. J. Ayer referred to James as "a strong phenomenologist" (Ayer 1968:224–242, 291–193).

REFERENCES

Abu-Lughod, Lila. 1991. "Writing against Culture." In *Recapturing Anthropology: Working in the Present,* ed. Richard G. Fox, 137–162. Sante Fe: School of American Research Press.
———. 1993. *Writing Women's Worlds: Bedouin Stories.* Berkeley: University of California Press.
Adorno, Theodor W. 1973. *Negative Dialectics,* trans. E. B. Ashton. New York: Continuum.
———. 1977–1978. "The Actuality of Philosophy." *Telos* 31–34:131.
———. 1978. "Subject and Object." In *The Essential Frankfurt School Reader,* ed. A. Arato and E. Gebhardt, 497–511. New York: Urizen Books.
———. 1982. *Against Epistemology: A Metacritique: Studies in Husserl and the Phenomenological Antinomies,* trans. W. Domingo. Oxford: Basil Blackwell.
Appadurai, Arjun, ed. 1986. *The Social Life of Things. Commodities in Cultural Perspective.* Cambridge: Cambridge University Press.
———. 1990. "Topographies of the Self: Praise and Emotion in Hindu India." In

Language and the Politics of the Emotion, ed. C. A. Lutz and L. Abu-Lughod. Cambridge: Cambridge University Press.

Arendt, Hannah. 1958. *The Human Condition.* Chicago: University of Chicago Press.

———. 1968. "Introduction: Walter Benjamin 1892–1940." In *Illuminations*, by Walter Benjamin, trans. H. Zohn. New York: Schocken Books.

Ayer, A. J. 1968. *The Origins of Pragmatism.* San Francisco: Freeman, Cooper and Co.

Bachelard, Gaston. 1964. *The Poetics of Space*, trans. Maria Jolas. Boston: Beacon Press.

Bateson, Gregory. 1973. *Steps to an Ecology of Mind.* Frogmore: Paladin.

Beckett, Samuel. 1958. *Watt.* Paris: Olympia Press.

Berger, John. 1979. *Pig Earth.* London: Writers and Readers Publishing Cooperative.

———. 1983. *Once in Europa.* New York: Pantheon.

———. 1985. *The Sense of Sight.* New York: Pantheon.

Berger, Peter L., and Luckmann, Thomas. 1966. *The Social Construction of Reality: A Treatise in the Sociology of Knowledge.* Harmondsworth: Penguin Books.

Bidney, David. 1973. "Phenomenological Method and the Anthropological Science of the Cultural Life-World." In *Phenomenology and the Social Sciences*, ed. Maurice Natanson, 109–140. Evanston: Northwestern University Press.

Binney, Judith. 1987. "Maori Oral Narratives, Pakeha Written Texts: Two Forms of Telling History." *The New Zealand Journal of History* 21(1):16–28.

Binswanger, Ludwig. 1963. *Being in the World: Selected Papers*, trans. Jacob Needleman. London: Souvenir Press.

Bourdieu, Pierre. 1971. "Intellectual Field and Creative Project." In *Knowledge and Control: New Directions for the Sociology of Education*, ed. Michael F. D. Young, 161–188. London: Collier-Macmillan.

———. 1977. *Outline of a Theory of Practice*, trans. R. Nice. Cambridge: Cambridge University Press.

———. 1990a. *In Other Words: Essays towards a Reflexive Sociology*, trans. M. Adamson. Stanford: Stanford University Press.

———. 1990b. *The Logic of Practice*, trans. R. Nice. Stanford: Stanford University Press.

Brown, Karen McCarthy. 1991. *Mama Lola: A Vodou Priestess in Brooklyn.* Berkeley: University of California Press.

Brown, Norman O. 1959. *Life Against Death: The Psychoanalytic Meaning of History.* London: Routledge & Kegan Paul.

Buck-Morss, S. 1977. *The Origin of Negative Dialectics: Theodor W. Adorno, Walter Benjamin, and the Franfurt Institute.* Hassocks, Sussex: Harvester Press.

Casey, Edward. 1991. *Spirit and Soul: Essays in Philosophical Psychology.* Dallas: Spring Publications.

Cixous, Hélène. 1991. *Coming to Writing and Other Essays*, trans. S. Cornell, D. Jenson, A. Liddle, S. Sellers; ed. Deborah Jenson. Cambridge: Harvard University Press.

Coe, Richard N. 1964. *Beckett.* Edinburgh: Oliver and Boyd.

Das, Veena. 1989. "Subaltern as Perspective." In *Subaltern Studies VI: Writings on South Asian History and Society.* Delhi: Oxford University Press.

de Certeau, Michel. 1980. "On the Oppositional Practices of Everyday Life." *Social Text* 3:3–43.

———. 1988. *The Practice of Everyday Life.* trans. S. Rendall. Berkeley: University of California Press.

Desjarlais, Robert R. 1992. *Body and Emotion: The Aesthetics of Illness and Healing in the Nepal Himalayas.* Philadelphia: University of Pennsylvania Press.

Devereux, George. 1967. *From Anxiety to Method in the Behavioral Sciences.* The Hague: Mouton.

Devisch, René. 1993. *Weaving the Threads of Life: The Khita Gyn-Eco-Logical Healing Cult among the Yaka.* Chicago: University of Chicago Press.
———. 1995. "Frenzy, Violence, and Ethical Renewal in Kinshasa." *Public Culture* 7(3):593–629.
Dewey, John. 1905. "Immediate Empiricism." *The Journal of Philosophy* 2:597–599.
———. 1958. *Experience and Nature.* New York: Dover.
———. 1960. "An Empirical Survey of Empiricisms." In *John Dewey on Experience, Nature, and Freedom: Representative Selection,* ed. R. J. Bernstein, 70–87. New York: The Liberal Arts Press.
———. 1980. *The Quest for Certainty.* New York: Putnam's.
Dilthey, Wilhelm. 1976. *Selected Writings,* ed. and trans. H. P. Rickman. Cambridge: Cambridge University Press.
———. 1989. *Introduction to the Human Sciences.* Selected Works, Vol. 1, ed. R. A. Makkreel and F. Rodi. Princeton: Princeton University Press.
Donner, Florinda. 1984. *Shabono.* London: Paladin.
Drewal, Margaret Thompson. 1992. *Yoruba Ritual: Performers, Plays, Agency.* Bloomington: Indiana University Press.
Drummond, Lee. 1981. "The Serpent's Children: Semiotics of Cultural Genesis in Arawak and Trobriand Myth." *American Ethnologist* 8(3):633–660.
Edie, James M. 1987. *William James and Phenomenology.* Bloomington: Indiana University Press.
Esterson, Aaron, 1970. *The Leaves of Spring: Schizophrenia, Family and Sacrifice.* London: Tavistock.
Feyerabend, Paul. 1987. *Farewell to Reason.* London: Verso.
Fortes, Meyer. 1987. *Religion, Morality and the Person: Essays on Tallensi Religion,* ed. Jack Goody. Cambridge: Cambridge University Press.
Foucault, Michel. 1970. *The Order of Things.* London: Tavistock.
Foucault, Michel, and Sennett, Richard. 1962. "Sexuality and Solitude." In *Humanities in Review,* general ed. D. Rieff, Vol. 1. Cambridge: Cambridge University Press.
Fukui, Katsuyoshi, 1979. "Cattle colour symbolism in inter-tribal homicide among the Bodi." In *Warfare among East African Herders,* Senri Ethnological Studies 3: 147–177, ed. K. Fukui and D. Turton.
———. 1987. "Diversified selection in symbolic ecosystem: what colour variations of domestic anaimals in an East African pastoral society suggest." Unpublished paper presented at *Symposium on African Folk Models and their Application,* Uppsala, August 23–30, 1987.
Gadamer, Hans-Georg. 1975. *Truth and Method.* New York: The Seabury Press.
Gadow, Sally. 1982. "Body and Self: A Dialectic." In *The Humanity of the Ill: Phenomenological Perspectives,* ed. V. Kestenbaum, 86–100. Knoxville: University of Tennessee Press.
Gavin, William Joseph. 1992. *William James and the Reinstatement of the Vague.* Philadelphia: Temple University Press.
Geertz, Clifford. 1973. *The Interpretation of Cultures. Selected Essays.* New York: Basic Books.
Glassie, Henry. 1993. *Turkish Traditional Art Today.* Bloomington: Indiana University Press.
———. 1994. "Turkish traditional art today," *Catalog,* published for the exhibition, "Turkish traditional art today," Indiana University Art Museum, Bloomington, Indiana, October 26–December 23, 1994.
Goldstein, Leon J. 1961. "The Phenomenological and Naturalistic Approaches to the Social." *Methodos* 13:225–238.

Guha, Ranajit. 1983. *Elementary Aspects of Peasant Insurgency in Colonial India.* Delhi: Oxford University Press.

Habermas, Jürgen. 1987. *The Theory of Communicative Action, Vol. 2: Lifeworld and System: a Critique of Functionalist Reason,* trans. T. McCarthy. Cambridge: Polity Press.

Heidegger, Martin. 1962. *Being and Time,* trans. J. Macquarrie and E. Robinson. San Francisco: Harper.

Herzfeld, Michael. 1992. *The Social Production of Indifference: Exploring the Symbolic Roots of Western Bureaucracy.* New York: Berg.

Horkheimer, Max, and Adorno, Theodor W. 1972. *Dialectic of Enlightenment,* trans. J. Cumming. New York: Herder & Herder.

Horton, Robin. 1967. "African Traditional Thought and Western Science." *Africa* 37:50–71, 155–187.

Howes, David. 1987. "Olfaction and Transition: An Essay on the Ritual Uses of Smell." *Canadian Review of Sociology and Anthropology* 24(3):398–416.

Hughes, C. C. 1978. "Medical Lore and Ethnomedicine." In *Health and the Human Condition,* ed. M. H. Logan and E. E. Hart, 150–158. North Scituate, MA: Duxbury Press.

Husserl, Edmund. 1931. *Ideas: General Introduction to Pure Phenomenology,* trans. W. R. Boyce Gibson. New York: Macmillan.

———. 1970a. *Logical Investigations,* trans. J. N. Findlay. London: Routledge & Kegan Paul.

———. 1970b. *The Crisis of European Sciences and Transcendental Phenomenology: An Introduction to Phenomenological Philosophy,* trans. D. Carr. Evanston: Northwestern University Press.

Ihde, Don. 1986. *Consequences of Phenomenology.* Albany: State University of New York Press.

Illich, Ivan. 1973. *Tools for Conviviality.* London: Calder & Boyars.

Jackson, Michael. 1974. "The Structure and Significance of Kuranko Clanship." *Africa* 44(4):397–415.

———. 1978. "An Approach to Kuranko Divination." *Human Relations* 31(2):117–138.

———. 1982a. *Allegories of the Wilderness: Ethics and Ambiguity in Kuranko Narratives.* Bloomington: Indiana University Press.

———. 1982b. "Meaning and Moral Imagery in Kuranko Myth." *Research in African Literatures* 13(2):153–180.

———. 1989. *Paths toward a Clearing: Radical Empiricism and Ethnographic Inquiry.* Bloomington: Indiana University Press.

———. 1995. *At Home in the World.* Durham: Duke University Press.

James, William. 1950. *The Principles of Psychology,* vols. 1 & 2. New York: Dover.

———. 1976. *Essays in Radical Empiricism.* Cambridge, Mass.: Harvard University Press.

———. 1978. *Pragmatism.* Cambridge: Harvard University Press.

Kendon, Adam. 1988. *Sign Languages of Aboriginal Australia: Cultural, Semiotic and Communicative Perspectives.* Cambridge: Cambridge University Press.

Kensinger, Kenneth M. 1991. "A Body of Knowledge, or, the Body Knows." *Expedition* 33(3):37–45.

Kestenbaum, Victor, ed. 1982. *The Humanity of the Ill: Phenomenological Perspectives.* Knoxville: The University of Tennessee Press.

Kleinman, Arthur. 1980. *Patients and Healers in the Context of Culture.* Berkeley: University of California Press.

————. 1992. "Pain and Resistance: The Delegitimation and Relegitimation of Local Worlds." In *Pain as Human Experience: An Anthropological Perspective,* ed. M-J. DelVecchio Good, P. E. Brodwin, B. J. Good, A. Kleinman, 169–197. Berkeley: University of California Press.

Kleinman, Arthur, and Kleinman, Joan. 1991. "Suffering and Its Professional Transformation: Toward an Ethnography of Interpersonal Experience." In *Culture, Medicine and Psychiatry* 15(3):275–301.

Kroeber, A. L., and Kluckhohn, C. 1963. *Culture: A Critical Review of Concepts and Definitions.* New York: Vintage Books.

Laing, R. D. 1967. *The Politics of Experience and the Bird of Paradise.* Harmondsworth: Penguin Books.

Landau, Misia. 1991. *Narratives of Human Evolution.* New Haven: Yale University Press.

Leder, Drew. 1990. *The Absent Body.* Chicago: University of Chicago Press.

————, ed. 1992. *The Body in Medical Thought and Practice.* Dordrecht: Kluwer Academic Publishers.

Lévi-Strauss, Claude. 1966. *The Savage Mind.* London: Weidenfeld and Nicolson.

————. 1973. *Tristes Tropiques,* trans. J. and D. Weightman. London: Jonathan Cape.

————. 1981. *The Naked Man,* trans. J. and D. Weightman. Chicago: University of Chicago Press.

Levy, Robert I. 1973. *Tahitians: Mind and Experience in the Society Islands.* Chicago: University of Chicago Press.

Lutz, Catherine A., and Abu-Lughod, L. 1990. *Language and the Politics of Emotion.* Cambridge: Cambridge University Press.

Lyotard, Jean-François. 1984. *The Postmodern Condition: a Report on Knowledge,* trans. G. Bennington and B. Massumi. Minneapolis: University of Minnesota Press.

Luria, A.R. 1976. *Cognitive Development: Its Cultural and Social Foundations,* trans. M. Lopez-Morillas and L. Solotaroff. Cambridge, Mass: Harvard University Press.

McCarthy, Thomas. 1993. *Ideals and Illusions: on Reconstruction and Deconstruction in Contemporary Social Theory.* Cambridge: MIT Press.

MacIntyre, Alasdair. 1984. *After Virtue: A Study in Moral Theory* (2nd ed.). Notre Dame: University of Notre Dame Press.

Makkreel, Rudolf A. 1982. "Husserl, Dilthey and the Relation of the Life-World to History." *Research in Phenomenology* 12:39–58.

Marcus, George, and Cushman, Dick. 1982. "Ethnographies as Texts." *Annual Review of Anthropology,* ed. B. Siegel, 25–69. Palo Alto: Annual Reviews Inc.

Marcuse, Herbert. 1968. *Negations: Essays in Critical Theory.* London: Allen Lane.

Marías, Julian. 1971. *Metaphysical Anthropology: The Empiricial Structure of Human Life,* trans. F. M. López-Morillas. University Park: Pennsylvania State University Press.

Marx, Karl. 1964. *Pre-Capitalist Economic Formations,* trans. J. Cohen. London: Lawrence & Wishart.

Marx, Karl, and Engels, Frederick. 1976. "The German Ideology," trans. C. Dutt. In *Karl Marx, Frederick Engels: Collected Works, Vol. 5,* 19–608. Moscow: Progress Publishers.

Mead, George Herbert. 1934. *Mind, Self, and Society.* Chicago: University of Chicago Press.

Merleau-Ponty, Maurice. 1962. *Phenomenology of Perception,* trans. C. Smith. London: Routledge.

————. 1963. *The Structure of Behavior,* trans. A. L. Fisher. Boston: Beacon Press.

————. 1964a. "From Mauss to Lévi-Strauss." In *Signs,* trans. R. C. McCleary, 114–125. Evanston: Northwestern University Press.

————. 1964b. *Sense and Non-Sense,* trans. Hubert L. Dreyfus and Patricia Allen Dreyfus. Evanston: Northwestern University Press.

————. 1973. "Phenomenology and the Sciences of Man." In *Phenomenology and the Social Sciences*, Vol. 1, ed. M. Natanson, 47–108. Evanston: Northwestern University Press.

Miller, James. 1993. *The Passion of Michel Foucault*. New York: Simon and Schuster.

Mimica, Jadran. 1988. *Intimations of Infinity: The Mythopoeia of the Iqwaye Counting System and Number*. Oxford: Berg.

————. 1993 "The Foi and Heidegger." Review of *The Empty Place: Poetry, Space, and Being among the Foi of Papua New Guinea*, by James F. Weiner. In *The Australian Journal of Anthropology* 4(2):79–95.

Moeran, Brian. 1985. *Okubo Diary: Portrait of a Japanese Valley*. Stanford: Stanford University Press.

Myers, Fred. 1986. *Pintupi Country, Pintupi Self*. Washington: Smithsonian Institution Press.

Natanson, Maurice. 1973. "Phenomenology and the Social Sciences." In *Phenomenology and the Social Sciences*, ed. M. Natanson, 3–44. Evanston: Northwestern University Press.

————. 1986. *Anonymity: A Study in the Philosophy of Alfred Schutz*. Bloomington: Indiana University Press.

Oakeshott, Michael. 1933. *Experience and Its Modes*. Cambridge: Cambridge University Press.

————. 1962. *Rationalism in Politics and Other Essays*. London: Methuen.

Ogilvie, R. M. 1969. *The Romans and Their Gods*. London: Chatto and Windus.

O'Neill, John. 1982. "Essaying Illness." In *The Humanity of the Ill: Phenomenological Perspectives*, ed. V. Kestenbaum, 125–141. Knoxville: University of Tennessee Press.

Paulo II, Sulu'ape. 1994. "Samoan Tattooing," in *Fomison: What Shall We Tell Them*, ed. Ian Wedde, 76–79; published on the occasion of the exhibition: Fomison: What Shall We Tell Them, City Gallery, Wellington, 1994. Wellington: City Gallery.

Piaget, J. 1971. *Structuralism*, trans. and ed. C. Maschler. London: Routledge & Kegan Paul.

Povinelli, Elizabeth A. 1993. *Labor's Lot: The Power, History, and Culture of Aboriginal Action*. Chicago: University of Chicago Press.

Ricoeur, Paul. 1979. *Main Trends in Philosophy*. New York: Holmes & Meier.

————. 1980. "Narrative Time." In *On Narrative*, ed. W. J. T. Mitchell, 165–186. Chicago: University of Chicago Press.

Riesman, Paul. 1977. *Freedom in Fulani Social Life: An Introspective Ethnography*, trans. Martha Fuller. (Originally published as *Société et Liberté Chez Les Peul Djelgôbé de Haute-Volta*, 1974). Chicago: University of Chicago Press.

Rorty, Richard. 1979. *Philosophy and the Mirror of Nature*. Princeton: Princeton University Press.

Rose, Gillian. 1978. *The Melancholy Science: An Introduction to the Thought of Theodor W. Adorno*. London: Macmillan.

Said, Edward. 1993 *Representations of the Intellectual. The 1993 Reith Lectures*. New York: Pantheon.

Sartre, Jean-Paul. 1956. *Being and Nothingness: An Essay on Phenomenological Ontology*, trans. H. Barnes. New York: Philosophical Library.

————. 1968. *Search for a Method*, trans. H. Barnes. New York: Vintage Books.

————. 1969. "Itinerary of a Thought." *New Left Review* 58:43–66.

Scheper-Hughes, Nancy. 1992. *Death without Weeping: The Violence of Everyday Life in Brazil*. Berkeley: University of California Press.

Schutz, Alfred. 1962 *Collected Papers. The Problem of Social Reality*, ed. M. Natanson. The Hague: Martinus Nijhoff.

―――. 1972. *The Phenomenology of the Social World,* trans. G. Walsh and F. Lehnert. London: Heinemann.

Schutz, Alfred, and Luckmann, Thomas. 1989. *The Structures of the Life-World,* Vol. 2, trans. R. M. Zaner and D. J. Parent. Evanston: Northwestern University Press.

Stern, Daniel. 1985. *The Interpersonal World of the Infant: A View from Psychoanalysis and Developmental Psychology.* New York: Basic Books.

Stoller, Paul. 1989. *The Taste of Ethnographic Things: The Senses in Anthropology.* Philadelphia: University of Pennsylvania Press.

Strassner, Stephan. 1963. *Phenomenology and the Human Sciences: A Contribution to a New Scientific Ideal.* Pittsburgh: Duquesne University Press.

Straus, Erwin. 1966. *Phenomenological Psychology,* trans. E. Eng. New York: Basic Books.

Tomlinson, Charles. 1985. "Introduction." *William Carlos Williams: Selected Poems,* ed. C. Tomlinson, vii–xviii. New York: New Directions.

Tournier, Michel. 1988. *The Wind Spirit: An Autobiography,* trans. Arthur Goldhammer. Boston: Beacon Press.

Trawick, Margaret. 1990. *Notes on Love in a Tamil Family.* Berkeley: University of California Press.

Turner, Victor. 1970. *The Forest of Symbols.* Ithaca: Cornell University Press.

―――. 1978. "Encounter with Freud: The Making of a Comparative Symbologist." In *The Making of Psychological Anthropology,* ed. G. D. Spindler, 558–583. Berkeley: University of California Press.

―――. 1985. *On the Edge of the Bush: Anthropology as Experience,* ed. E. L. B. Turner. Tucson: University of Arizona Press.

―――. 1986. "Dewey, Dilthey, and Drama: An Essay in the Anthropology of Experience." In *The Anthropology of Experience,* ed. V. W. Turner and E. M. Bruner, 33–44. Urbana: University of Illinois Press.

Wafer, Jim. 1991. *The Taste of Blood: Spirit Possession in Brazilian Candomblé.* Philadelphia: University of Pennsylvania Press.

Wagner, Roy. 1975. *The Invention of Culture.* Englewood Cliffs, NJ: Prentice-Hall.

Wild, John. 1969. *The Radical Empiricism of William James.* New York: Doubleday.

Wilshire, Bruce. 1968. *William James and Phenomenology: A Study of "The Principles of Psychology."* Bloomington: Indiana University Press.

―――. 1990. "Resistance to Tolerance and Pluralism in World-Community: Otherness as Contamination." *Public Affairs Quarterly* 4(2):189–201.

Wolff, Tobias. 1983. "Introduction." *Matters of Life and Death: New American Stories,* ed. T. Wolff, ix–xi. Green Harbor, MA: Wampeter Press.

Young, Michael. 1983. *Magicians of Manumanua: Living Myth in Kalauna.* Berkeley: University of California Press.

Bedouin
贝都因(人)

Honor and Shame

LILA ABU-LUGHOD

In the final chapter of *Writing Women's Worlds* I wrote about a young woman called Kamla, awaiting her marriage. I entitled the chapter "Honor and Shame." But honor and shame—the values widely thought to regulate interactions in circum-Mediterranean societies—have been seen as a mechanism for the sexual control of women. Associating honor with men and shame with women, discussions of this cultural complex have generally treated women's role as negative, or at best passive. Yet Kamla, a young woman who has been to school, proudly asserts the honor (through modesty) of girls like herself and struggles to maintain this modesty as part of her cultural identity. Moreover, although she talks in terms of these seemingly timeless values, she rejects some of their entailments, using arguments derived paradoxically from both her religious education and the romantic mass-media soap operas that enthrall her. Honor and shame in Egypt in the 1980s for a young Bedouin woman with some education, influenced by the ideas of urban Egyptians and sensitive to the moral pressures of increasingly persuasive Islamic groups, take on specific meanings. Indeed, the very possibility of an abstract moral code like "honor and shame" is thrown into question by the relentless specificity of Kamla's story.

In a letter sent to the U.S. from Egypt and dated July 30, 1989, Kamla wrote to tell me her good news:

> In the Name of God the All-Merciful and Compassionate. It gives me pleasure to send this letter to my dear sister, Dr. Lila, hoping from God on high, the All-Powerful, that it reaches you carrying love and greetings to you and your family while you are all in the best of health and in perfect happiness.

By name she mentioned my brother and sisters (none of whom she has met) and asked me to convey her greetings and those of her family to them and to my parents, as well as to the one American friend of mine they had met ten years ago—in short to everyone they knew about in my life in America. I had confided during my last visit that I would be getting married soon. She asked if I had; if so, she wrote, she sent a thousand congratulations and hoped, God willing, that he was a good man who would understand me. She hoped also that their new in-law was a noble man, the best in all of America, and that they would meet him soon. After wishing me many children (six boys and six girls) and more greetings, she squeezed her piece of news onto the bottom of the page:

> Your sister Kamla has become engaged to Engineer Ibrahim Selim, Aisha's brother.

I could hardly believe it. We had teased Kamla about him ever since his name had been floated four years ago as a prospect. This was the match she scarcely dared hope her father would arrange. Not that she had ever met the young man. What mattered was that he was educated, came from a family that believed in educating girls, and lived in a town. She would be able to escape the kind of life her family lived, a life that annoyed her—the only one in her family, male or female, to have made it through high school—more and more.

Because she complained so much, I had asked her in the summer after she graduated to write me an essay on how young Bedouin women's lives were changing and what of the past she hoped the Awlad ʿAli community to which she belonged would retain and what she wished they would abandon. She had proudly told me that her teacher had sent off for publication an essay on Awlad ʿAli weddings she had written in school. You can trace, in the stilted words of her essay and the candid comments (in parentheses) she made as she read it aloud to me, the outlines of the new world she hoped to gain by marrying the likes of Engineer Ibrahim Selim.

The Education of Girls
AN ESSAY ON THE YOUNG BEDOUIN WOMAN OF EGYPT
AND THE CHANGES IN HER LIFE OVER 40 YEARS

If we are to speak of the Bedouin girl in Egypt we find that her life differs from one era to another. The circumstances of the home and family relations change from one age to another. If we go back to discuss the way she was around forty years ago, we find that the Bedouin girl was living a life in which she was of no value. When she came of age, or maturity (*as the Egyptians say—I mean the years when she is ready for marriage*), she had to do housework at her family's home—for example, cooking, washing clothes, and preparing firewood. (*Her only value was in the housework she did—the sweeping and washing—and if she didn't do it they'd laugh at her and gossip about her laziness. She was forced to do it, even if she weren't capable. No matter what her health was like. I'm talking about those who were my age, from around the age of twelve on.*)

Also, she used to spin and weave even though it is very difficult, painful, and strenuous. (*When she was around fifteen, her mother or any woman in the household, an aunt for instance, would teach her. It's supposed to be the mother, though. Her goal was to teach her daughter to spin and to make something, anything. The important thing was for her to weave something, if only a border for the tent.*) She had to learn this skill. (*This is what is important for the Bedouins, housework, weaving and such things. Forty years ago this was what a girl had to put up with.*)

Kamla had been resenting housework. Now that she had finished school she rarely left the house. With two sisters, she was responsible for the cooking and cleaning one day out of three. On another of those days she was in charge of baking bread with them. She was on call much of the rest of the time, seeing to it that her little brothers and sisters were bathed, dressed, and out of mischief. Piles of laundry collected in the back room to be done when there was time.

Where before she had worn clean clothes for school, studied with her brothers in a quiet room of her own, and been given few household duties, now she had no privileges. Her clothes were as caked with dough and soot as her sisters'. Kamla's only escape was listening to the radio. She carried my transistor with her wherever in the house or courtyard she was working. She kept an eye on the time so as not to miss the soap operas. When she was free, she stared into space as she listened to Egyptian music, talk shows, and the news. So attached was she to the radio that I called it her sweetheart. Her mother, irritable from fatigue herself, scolded her and threatened to lock up the radio. When Gateefa complained, "My daughters are becoming lazy sluts," Kamla, like her sisters, ignored their mother.

Kamla had scored high enough on her final exams to secure a place in the agricultural college for which her high school had prepared her. She had no special interest in agriculture and had gone to this secondary school only because the regular high school was on the far side of town. Her uncles had given her a choice: quit school or go to the nearby agriculture school. School was still much on her mind. Her essay continued:

> Education for the Bedouin girl used not to exist. It was impossible for her to study. *(Forty years ago she lived a life, as I said earlier, that had no value at all.)* She was governed by the customs and traditions that the Bedouin families followed. These customs and traditions forbade a girl to leave the house under any circumstances. So going to school *(this is an example)* would be the greatest shame. She couldn't say that she wished to study, no matter what. Even if, as they say, she was the daughter of a tribal leader. *(So for example, a girl's father would be a tribal leader and she'd want to study but her relatives would say no you can't. She'd say, but I'm the daughter of the head of a lineage. I must learn. They'd forbid her.)*

This hypothetical example was, of course, from her own experience. She had been allowed to continue her schooling against the wishes of her uncles. They wanted to pull her out when she was no longer little. Because she was so determined, she and her parents had put up with the uncles' general suspicion and their occasional accusations. She was a fierce child who had early on decided she wanted to go to school. She was not allowed in the public school, though, because, as is often the case, her father had never registered her birth. She went each day anyway, as a visitor, borrowing her brothers' books. After three years of this her teacher finally required her to register officially. Her

father went and got her papers. From then on, she came in at the top of her class
while her brothers and male cousins flunked out. I had recorded in my notes
from 1979 her bashful reaction when her brother told their father she had been
appointed school monitor. Kamla's father had been hugging his youngest son,
then in his first year of school, proudly predicting that his son would come out
above the rest.

The school had been within sight of the camp and its students were mostly
relatives and neighbors. The secondary school, though, was about three
kilometers away. Kamla's class had only four Bedouin girls; the rest of the girls
were Egyptians from town. To get to this school she had to walk along the road
past houses of people who did not know her. She said she walked with her head
down, looking neither right nor left, but she still had to endure catcalls from
men driving by.

Her relatives' suspicions were harder to cope with. One aunt had come
twice to her mother to accuse Kamla of taking her son's schoolbook to give to
a boy from a neighboring tribe. Kamla's mother had defended her. True she had
given the boy a schoolbook, but it was in exchange for the book that he had
given her the previous year. And the book was one that her father had bought
her, not one she had taken from her cousin. Fortunately, when they questioned
the aunt's son, he backed her.

Kamla and her mother were angrier when Kamla's uncle told her father that
he'd seen his niece Kamla walking home with a boy. Her mother said she felt
she'd been hit in the stomach with a rock. She argued, to me, "If it were true,
why didn't he stop for her and put her in the car? Why didn't he get out and beat
her right there, if he really saw her? If he's so afraid for her, why doesn't he ever
offer to drive her to school?"

Kamla told the story as she knew it. She believed the problem began during
her second year of high school. Her uncle had not wanted her to continue but
her father had defended his daughter's right to stay in school. Furious, her
uncle did everything he could to prevent her from studying. If, for example,
guests came to the house he'd knock on her door to ask her to make the tea.
She'd try to escape, sneaking off to study outdoors under the trees. Two days
before her final exams (when, as we all know, she added, nerves are on edge),
she was walking home from school. Across the road a boy she had known since
she was small was going the same direction. Because she always walked with
her head down, she noticed her uncle drive by after he had passed. He went
straight to her father and told him, "Your daughter was walking hand in hand
with a boy." Her father had questioned him carefully, then called in Kamla's
mother. She in turn had come to Kamla ("And you know how upset she gets!"
she said to me) to ask her about it. Kamla refused to say "yes, no, or maybe"
unless her uncle came and accused her to her face.

Her father, she said lovingly, believed in her. He asked her why she didn't
always walk home from school with her cousin and she explained that she was

not about to go out of her way just to walk with him. If he wished to walk with her along her route before cutting off to his house, he was welcome to. Kamla's uncle had also told her father that this cousin had informed him that the boy waited for Kamla at the school gates to walk home with her every day. Fortunately for Kamla, her cousin happened to pass by the house that afternoon. Her father called him over to question him—right in front of her uncle. The boy swore that he had never said such a thing. That ended it.

ARRANGED MARRIAGE

The next paragraph of Kamla's essay took up the matter of marriage. Commenting on it, Kamla said, "This was a topic the Bedouin girl would hear nothing about and wasn't supposed to have anything to do with."

> She had no right to an opinion in any matter, however much the matter might concern her personally. She had no say even in the choice of a husband. She had absolutely no say in this matter. (*And to this day, no matter how educated she's become, very seldom can she express her opinion. The Bedouin girl has no say.*) In this matter what she had to do was carry out her family's orders even if she didn't want to. It was not right for her to refuse. (*Even if she didn't want him, she had to agree to it against her will. Even if he was older than she was, for example, or very different from her, she had to agree to what the family wanted. For example, if they said I had to marry someone and I didn't want him—I hated him—but if my kinsmen had agreed to the match and told me I had to marry him, what I would have to do, despite my wishes, was marry him.*)

I was surprised that Kamla depicted women as powerless in decisions about marriage. She had heard the same stories I had—stories like her grandmother Migdim's, of resistance to marriages arranged for them by their kinsmen. She knew plenty of young women like one who had been married briefly to Kamla's cousin. In love with someone else, she had gone home to her father's household at the slightest provocation, eventually forcing her husband to divorce her. The specter of forced marriage, especially to paternal cousins, may have loomed for Kamla because she, like her sister Sabra, was waiting. As her mother joked with a friend, "Kamla's got her diploma. Now we're going to give her the other diploma!"

Her religious training at school had given Kamla moral ammunition against arranged marriage. The Prophet, she would explain, says that it is wrong to marry someone you have never seen. Second, the girl must give her consent. The bride's relatives are supposed to ask her opinion. Kamla is not sure her opinion will be sought. Already she has made it known throughout the women's community that she does not want to marry her cousin Salih, the young man closest to her in age who has been lined up with her, at least according to the calculations made by his father and uncles about marriages between their children.

Kamla is fond of Salih but he is "like a brother." She and her sisters boldly ask him to get them things they want from town. They reach into his pockets to grab the latest cassettes he has brought for himself. Kamla sometimes teases him, threatening to make him wash the dishes and sweep the floor if he marries her. Kamla even jokes with his mother. I'd seen the woman grab Kamla and warn her to be good or else she'd exercise her prospective rights as a mother-in-law and make her quit school. Kamla broke free easily, laughing as she shouted defiantly, "Not until I come to live with you!"

Women in the camp mutter that Salih is not right for Kamla. Even her grandmother Migdim half-supports her. Although she tries to persuade her granddaughters of the virtues of marrying cousins, Migdim is angry with her sons for wanting "what nothing good will come of"—this set of matches within the family between children who have grown up together and say they feel like siblings. This was exactly the kind of match she had successfully resisted as a young bride. She fumed, "Her father wants Kamla for Salih and Kamla says she won't marry him. And Salih says he won't marry Kamla. She's older than he is!"

Her unmarried granddaughters enjoy provoking Migdim by maligning cousin marriage. They say they want out: marriage to men who live far away so they can have new lives.

"They're good for nothing!" insisted one of Kamla's cousins once about her male cousins.

Migdim scolded her, "You slut! What is this outrage? You gypsy!"

She and her sister laughed wildly, "Damn them, our cousins! What do you see in them?"

A cousin agreed, "They're all ugly. Not a handsome one among them. No, we'll marry outsiders, Grandma, ugly or handsome."

Kamla shook her head. "I'm marrying an Egyptian! Someone educated."

Her grandmother retorted, "Your father won't agree to it!"

Kamla hugged her grandmother. "We're just talking with you to see what you'll say. Is there anything in our hands, Grandma? Or in my father's? Only God knows what will happen."

GENERATIONS

In the past, according to Kamla, a girl had no say in the matter of marriage because, as her essay continued,

They thought that girls shouldn't be concerned with anything but clothing and food and drink. In her kinsmen's eyes a girl had no value. (*Even now it's true. You might think conditions had changed and advanced a bit, but it's still true.*) They did not know that a girl had something she valued more than food and such things—and that was feelings. (*Feelings were forbidden to the girl.*) But she had feelings and sensitivity and affections just like any other person on this earth. (*This is true. There is no person God has created without feelings or sensitivity.*) Her kinsmen had feelings and sensitivities and affections. (*Take my father, for example. My father loved in the days of his youth. But then he thinks a girl doesn't have any such feelings.*) But they did not care if the girl had feelings. Her feelings and desires were not important.

Kamla laughed conspiratorially as she read the next section.

So, for example, if she loved a person she could not show this love, however precious and strong her love was. She would be very afraid that her relatives would hear about it because they considered it a big scandal for a girl to love even though they had. They say that only men have the right—a young woman does not have the right to know or speak with any man except her brothers and their relatives. All of this has governed the Bedouin girl for as long as she has lived on this earth. (*This is true. For example, if a boy meets a girl and talks with her, they say it doesn't matter—"He's a man." But you, the girl, if you do this? They don't say anything to him. If my father heard that my brother was in love with someone and talked with her, he wouldn't say anything. But if it was me? That would be dealt with very differently.*)

This talk of love and vocabulary of feelings was new. Ever since I had known Kamla, from the age of twelve or so, she had been a tough little girl, the kind who would say to her uncle's new wife, "I don't even know what this 'love' is. I hear about it in songs and hear about this one giving her necklace and that one her ring, but I don't know what they are feeling." She used to amuse her great-aunts when they hugged her and teased her about which of her young cousins she would grow up to marry by defiantly shouting, "I'm never going to marry."

Just a year before she wrote this essay she had demanded of her mother, "Does a woman have to marry? Does she have to have someone to tell her what to do, to boss her around?"

"Yes a woman has to marry," her mother had answered. "If she doesn't, people will say, 'The poor thing!'"

But things had changed. Kamla now quoted from a book she had read at school: it was natural as one entered adolescence to begin thinking about members of the opposite sex. She admitted that such things had never even crossed her mind before. But then it had happened. It was at her cousin Selima's wedding that she had first revealed to me the new experiences she had begun to have at school. During a quiet period of the day before her cousin's wedding, we had gone for a stroll on the hillside. Scattered on the ridge were groups of women in two's and three's, sisters who rarely saw each other, aunts and their nieces, old friends, also talking privately.

Looking into the distance, and as it turned out, toward a certain house, Kamla had asked me, "What do you think, Lila? Is it wrong for two people to think about each other all the time?" I was puzzled. She told me about a young man at school—a well-behaved and good person, she added quickly—who had taken notice of her. He had asked her friends whether they could persuade her to agree to talk to him. She had refused at first. Finally she agreed to a brief meeting, with friends present. He wanted to know if she would be willing to marry him if he got his father to request her. She wondered if there was any hope that her father would accept. Knowing the family, I said I doubted it.

Usually she was more realistic. When I would ask who she wanted to marry she would give various answers. She was adamant about her cousins: "If they think I'm going to take any of these, my cousins, or anyone from the camp, they're wrong." Then she would deny that she cared whether or not it was the boy she knew from school. The brother of their family friend Aisha would be just fine. As long as the man was educated. Backtracking she would say, "It's not even important that he's well educated. But he must be knowledgeable." The boys in her camp didn't know anything; they would not know how to get on in the world. Dependent on their fathers to feed, dress, and marry them off, they were incapable of taking care of themselves. "They're men in name only," she scoffed.

She blamed her elder kinsmen, especially her father, for her cousins' failures. Despite the double standard in matters of the heart, she acknowledged that her cousins and her brothers were having almost as hard a time dealing with their old-fashioned elders as she was.

She thought the elders were mistaken to be so strict with the boys. They wanted the boys to be straight but all they would get from applying this pressure was stubbornness. The pressure, she warned, would produce the opposite of what they wanted. She gave examples. The men won't let the boys play soccer. "What's wrong with soccer? It's exercise." They won't let them have a television; they won't let them go to cafes. They aren't permitted to grow their hair long, or to go to the local cafeteria where videos are shown. The men wouldn't even let the boys get jobs, making them stay on the land and tend the new fig trees. Noting that her brothers and cousins had no money, Kamla added, "They treat them like girls. If only they would give them a bit of freedom."

THE DANGERS OF SCHOOLING

Kamla thinks her elders are wrong to fear an abuse of freedom. Her essay described what happened when her generation began to go to school:

> Life began to change for the Bedouins, a change of conditions and location. Those Bedouins who began living in town started sending their sons and also their daughters to school to learn right from wrong, prayer and writing. (*That was my father's single goal in educating us. He wanted us to know this. They don't put us in school to learn—who cared if I got educated? My only reason for being there was to learn right from wrong and the Qur'an. That's all.*) After that they would pull them out of school. (*Even if a girl was clever and came out first in her class, once she had learned right from wrong and had come to understand, they would say to her, "Come on, that's*

enough.") Some might let her stay through secondary school. *(Like me. After I finished secondary school, that was it.)* The Bedouin girl could even gain such a mastery of learning and knowledge *(it would be great if every girl could go to high school)* that she could enter university. *(In Alexandria you'll find Bedouin girls who've gone to university.)*

Kamla was grateful to have been allowed to continue so long in school. She had dreamed, when still in primary school, of going to college to study politics and economics. At the time, she says with amazement, she didn't understand the problem of being a girl. She had hope. Now they tease her younger sister for similar ambitions. Her father had proudly congratulated her for a good report card and said it was a pity her brothers had given her such a hard time when she announced that she wanted to be a doctor. Kamla was scornful. "They'll make her quit long before she becomes a doctor."

The problem with being a girl, as Kamla explained in her essay, was what other people would say and think about her family if they let her go to school.

What happened was that people began competing over the schooling of girls. *(For example, my father sees Aisha's father who has educated all his daughters. So my father looks at him and says, "Why should he educate his daughters and not me? I have to educate my daughters." One looked at the next until all of them started educating their daughters. . . . But around here, they see that others' daughters aren't in school. No one here has daughters in university. In Marsa Matruh [a city] they all sent their girls to school, each imitating the other. My father looks over at Aisha's father and his daughters. If one of them did anything wrong—May God protect us!—anything wrong, my father and all of them would decide not to follow. But when I look, I see that the Bedouin girl does not give up her Bedouin values. The girls went to school and nothing bad happened.)* They put them in school and the girls repaid their precious trust. The Bedouin girl made them see clearly that their daughter was as good as any girl from the biggest city. . . . She would get the highest grades in all fields of learning. *(This is true. If, for example, you compare someone from Marsa Matruh and someone from Cairo who've both graduated from the same school, you'll find them equally good. You'll even find that the Bedouin girl is better because she is also modest, pious, and respectful of her traditions and customs—better than the Egyptian girl who may have graduated from medical school but does not dress properly. Everything in her lifestyle is not right. Even if she gets educated, the Bedouin girl is better. You know, the Bedouins used to think that girls were a scandal. They used to think that if a Bedouin girl left the house she would have to do something wrong. They were sure of it. They'd say she can't go out—she's an idiot, she can't think. Like a beast of burden, she wouldn't know right from wrong. But when she got educated she showed them that what they had thought was wrong.)*

Kamla still struggled against community opinion. Her relatives opposed sending her to college. An aunt put it bluntly: "What? Let her study in Alexandria? She's a kid. What does she know? Someone might take advantage of her. If it were here in our territory, it would be fine. But it's in Alexandria. She's gotten enough schooling."

The positive model Kamla's father had for women's education was Aisha, the woman whose father had been an old friend, whose husband was a business partner, and whose brother he was eventually to accept as a son-in-law. Aisha was the only college-educated Bedouin woman they knew. Whenever she and her children accompanied her husband on a visit, Kamla assumed special charge. Although all the women were warm it was Kamla who saw to it that Aisha got water for ablutions, a prayer mat when she wanted, and who kept the conversation going.

Tall and slender, Aisha was elegant. She wore nicely styled full-length long-sleeved dresses. Instead of the usual black headcloth, she wore the fashionable modern headcovering that now marked Muslim modesty and piety. Unlike the Egyptian women who sometimes visited, she did not turn her nose up at the food that was offered her and she was relaxed with the women of the household. She'd just laugh when old Migdim teased her about her husband. "After He created your husband's tribe, God created the donkey." Insults were expected between people from Aisha's tribe and her husband's.

Aisha was and was not part of their world. A distant relative, she had people and interests in common with Migdim, Kamla's mother, and the others. But she was defensive about her family. Though they lived in the city she was quick to tell stories that showed her brothers to be Bedouins. Describing her own wedding, she recalled how her husband—whose family were real desert Bedouins—came to her house the evening before the wedding. He had brought a western-style suit with him, intending to have his photograph taken with her. Her brothers, she reported, had said, "If you're coming to have dinner with us, that's fine, you are very welcome. But if you're coming for anything else, don't bother."

Aisha switched easily between Bedouin and Egyptian dialects. When she and her husband entertained Bedouins in their home, she sat in a separate room from the men. She served them the customary lamb and rice. When they were with Egyptian friends, she served different foods and they all ate together. They even got different videos to entertain their guests. For Bedouins they rented the same film about the Libyans' struggle against the Italian colonists. Their guests, Aisha explained, love the early scenes showing a traditional Libyan Bedouin wedding and the scenes of men fighting on horseback. Egyptian films, she said, contained risque scenes so they never showed them to Bedouin guests. Aisha owns two photo albums. One she shows to their more traditional Bedouin friends and family. The other one she hides because it contains photographs, taken with a self-timer, of herself holding hands with her husband. Yet Aisha worries about trying to raise her two small children in an apartment on the outskirts of Alexandria. She does not want them to play with the neighbors. She fears they are picking up bad language. She apologizes that they have picked up the Egyptian dialect. Her five-year-old daughter has just begun school and has started denying that she's an Arab; she says she's Egyptian, her mother reports. "You know," Aisha says earnestly to Kamla, "Egyptians aren't like us."

EGYPTIANS

Could Bedouin identity be maintained after schooling? Kamla's essay took up this question.

> The Bedouin girl preserves the traditions and customs she was raised by. *(People stay with what they have grown up with because they came of age with it. Me, for example, I grew up knowing this was shameful and that was not right, there are customs, there's respect and modesty. Even when I'm old and my hair is gray I'll have to follow these.)* She has sense and preserves her family's reputation. *(Of course, she'd be afraid that if she did something wrong they'd pull her out of school.)* The Bedouin girl tries to overcome the special obstacles she must confront. *(For example, she doesn't let her customs and traditions, or people's talk—saying this is wrong and that is shameful—make her fall behind other girls. The Bedouin girl follows her customs but in a way that doesn't tie her up or block the path before her.)* She attempts to live a life enlightened by learning, happiness, and contributions to her country and family. *(She gives to her country. The Bedouin girl feels for her country and understands the meaning of Egypt as much as any girl from Cairo. The girl living in the Western Desert has feelings for Egypt that may be even stronger than the Egyptian girl's. The educated Bedouin girl knows the meaning of her country. . . . Boy, if my father heard this!)*

Kamla's comment about her father gives a clue about what obstacles she faces as she moves between home her state school run by Egyptian teachers. While her father bemoans the Awlad ʿAli's lack of foresight in failing to request an independent state from the British and chafes against every government restriction on his activities, Kamla patriotically defends Egypt and speaks proudly of President Mubarak. When her father confronted her for being a few hours late from a school trip she argued back. He then scolded her for raising her voice and waving her hands as she spoke. "This is the work of Egyptians!" he yelled. Anger fighting fear, she answered, "I *am* an Egyptian. And they are the best people and this is the best country!"

But Kamla will only go so far in her defense of Egyptians. She often criticized their poorer neighbors who had lived among Egyptians and had picked up different ways. As evidence of their immorality she disclosed that the men and women ate together. Another nearby household fared not much better. They knew no modesty, she said. As evidence she described how the son listened to cassettes in front of his father and the young daughter-in-law neither covered her hair with a black headcloth nor avoided her father-in-law. In her essay, and even more clearly in her commentary, she underlined this distinction between Bedouin morality and Egyptian immorality. Still writing about the young Bedouin woman who had become educated, she said:

> She doesn't forget her origins or her customs and traditions. She raises her children as well as the people of the city do. *(Now we're talking about what the Bedouin woman does after she gets educated. Does she forget her duties as a mother? The difference between the Bedouins and the Egyptians is that when the Egyptian woman has a baby, she gives it to her mother to raise for her and she takes it to daycare. She doesn't*

do her duty to the child nor give it the required care. For example, she nurses only up to the fortieth day or at most for two months. And then she leaves it with her mother, her sister, or daycare and goes out to work. But the Bedouin woman gives the child its due, even if she's educated and has an advanced degree. Not her mother, not anyone else—she herself does the work.

And she raises her child according to her customs. Let's say she's a Bedouin who marries an Egyptian or an educated Bedouin. She doesn't raise her child by the customs or traditions of the Egyptians. She raises her child with the customs and traditions of the Bedouin, except that she is slightly more informed. I mean, she tells her daughter "This is shameful," and "That is right." Take an educated Bedouin girl like me, for example. If I were to marry an educated man and live the city life, I wouldn't let my daughter follow the ways of the Egyptians where a girl wears short dresses or goes out to clubs. No, of course that is wrong. We must be modest. It is wrong for us Bedouins and we must respect our traditions. This is necessary. You wouldn't find an educated Bedouin woman allowing her daughter to do things that she could not do when she was with her family. Or maybe even if her parents permitted it, the girl herself would not do it. "No," she'd know, "that's wrong." Bedouin women are the ones who really know how to raise their daughters. They are better than Egyptians because the Egyptian woman won't hit her daughter. Very rarely do you find an Egyptian who can hit her daughter. But the Bedouin woman, if her daughter does something wrong, she must hit her. Even if she's not that young. She must hit her to teach her right and wrong. You don't learn right from wrong if you're not beaten. The Egyptians don't do it and their girls—well, you know. . . .)

Poets have long reflected on the differences between Bedouins and their peasant neighbors. Only fragments like the lines of a love story about a wealthy peasant and a beautiful Bedouin girl named Khawd are remembered. Drought had driven her family into his fields in search of pasture for their herds. He allowed them to graze their animals when he saw Khawd. When his beloved one day announced that her family had decided to return to the desert, she asked him to migrate with them. In despair the young man answered:

O Khawd, I have no camels that I might travel your distances
I have nothing but buffaloes and cows, who will find no pastures near you

Kamla's aunt Dhahab had once recited a short poem on a similar theme. It was her comment when I declined her polite suggestion that I marry her son so that I could come live with her. The song came, she said, from a story about a bull who fell in love with a camel and tried to follow her into the desert. She warned him that he would exhaust himself if he tried since he had to eat and drink every day and she drank only every five days. He said for her sake he'd drink only every other day but she knew he couldn't keep up with her. She told him:

You'll kill yourself bellowing
O bull, if you try to follow . . .

Kamla and Sabra had a younger sister who loved television. She thought her father was wrong not to let them have a TV set. Although she conceded that foreign films were immoral, she argued that Egyptian films were different. Her father had taken away the television set when he heard that the girls were watching films in which people hugged and kissed each other. "He didn't want us watching. He said it was shameful." But these films and stories, she persisted, always showed the correct path in the end, even though they had people doing such things earlier. Egyptian films show how the girl who went off with a man later realized that he had tricked and used her. The importance of proper moral behavior always became clear in the end.

Kamla's sister wondered anyway what her father could be thinking when he worried about his daughters' exposure to these things. Realistically, she asked, "Where do we ever go? Nowhere but this house or the rest of the camp where it's all family. Where does he think these things could happen?"

Kamla's father feared the influence of Egyptians on the Bedouin community. His opinion was that the most serious problem the Bedouins faced was what to do about intermarriage between Bedouins and Egyptians. In the past, he maintained, no Arab, even the simplest shepherd, would give his daughter in marriage to "a peasant," as they used to call all Egyptians, even if the man were a company president. Things were more difficult now. Where before the area had been almost completely Bedouin (except for a few Egyptians running things), now in regions like theirs that were close to large towns, Egyptians made up fifty percent of the population.

The trouble with the Egyptian presence, he went on, was that the Egyptian girls looked so pretty. They always dressed up, combed out their hair, and wore short dresses. A group of Bedouin elders had met recently to discuss what to do about these women who "walk around naked." Their concern was that the young men would find them attractive and want to marry them. Their fathers, of course, would want to make them happy and might agree. If the young men married Egyptian girls there would no longer be any difference between Bedouin and Egyptian in the next generation. Kamla's father had warned the elders of this danger at the meeting. He admitted, though, that the process would be hard to stop now that the boys see these girls in school. Although he was afraid that Bedouin girls might pick up things from Egyptians—like learning to have boyfriends, for example, which the Egyptian girls don't think twice about—his real fear was intermarriage. That would bring about the end of tribal bonds.

PIETY

Kamla reflected, in her essay, on what aspects of Bedouin life she would like to see preserved. Her father would have been proud of the list of positive features she drew up:

> We all know that everything in life has its good qualities and its bad. (*Weren't you asking what was good about the Bedouins and what wasn't?*) The virtues of the Bedouins are:

1. Their piety and their total adherence to the traditions of the Prophet, despite their lack of education. (*This is the thing I hope will continue until Judgment Day. This is the best thing—that they are religious. Even though ninety percent of them aren't educated, they are pious. Long clothing, respect, and modesty. The woman is as pious as the man. No woman can talk with a man she doesn't know or have him visit her at home. And she doesn't show her face or talk with any older man. This is what I hope Bedouin women and girls will never abandon.*)

2. Their total respectfulness. The old respect the young and the young respect the old, whether they are strangers or kin.

3. Their generosity. (*It's true. You won't find anything on this earth like the generosity of the Bedouins. Even someone they don't know—they must invite him to the house and bring him food. Maybe no one else has this quality. I hope the Bedouins will hold onto this.*)

4. Hospitality and respect for the guest.

5. The ties of kinship that link various parts of the family and the cooperation of relatives in all situations. (*The other thing I want them to hold onto is this mutual assistance—they help each other in all circumstances. For example, even someone from a family that is related distantly to another must help a person from that family. Even among the women. When a Bedouin woman sets up a loom, for instance, her neighbors come to help her. Others always come to help. I wish the whole world—never mind just families—the whole world would help each other and that Muslims would cooperate the way our religion tells us to. Ninety-nine percent of Bedouin women haven't been educated. But they are pious. They're ignorant and illiterate but they dress the right way, they fear God, and they pray. Sometimes they don't even know how to pray properly, but they pray anyhow. They are totally respectable and they follow the traditions of the Prophet. They say the Prophet used to do this, the Prophet used to do that. They learn it from their husbands or their educated sons.*)

Interestingly, Kamla did not have much to say about any of the traditional virtues except the first, piety. Although she was vehement about their importance, perhaps she could not afford to think through their implications. She was proud of her father's generosity and hospitality but it was also a source of tension since the burden of feeding his many guests fell on the overworked women of the household. And if she were to think about how the extensive bonds between kin are to be maintained, she would have to admit the virtues of marriages to paternal cousins, the kind of marriage she wanted desperately to avoid.

Piety was a different matter. Like many, Kamla was becoming defensive in the face of new pressure coming from those sympathetic to the Islamic activists in Egypt. She was correct to point out how tied up with their faith her kin were. They reckoned the months by the Islamic lunar calendar, the years by the annual religious feasts, age by the number of years a person has fasted the month of Ramadan, and the hours of the day by the five times for prayer. All the older women and many of the younger ones prayed regularly. Doing without the accoutrements of city people, women simply prayed where they were, facing southeast and laying down a small kerchief on the ground before them.

The men like Kamla's father tended to know more. They would have learned as children to recite the Qur'an and they continued to learn from the lectures at the mosque every Friday.

Their reactions to the sanctimonious Egyptians, and now some Bedouins from the cities, who were becoming, as they put it, "followers of the model," meaning the life of the Prophet, have been mixed. The older women are not cowed. They argue, as Kamla did, that they've always worn modest clothing and covered their hair with a headcloth. They resent being told that some of the ways they have been devout Muslims are wrong.

Kamla is more unsure. Sometimes she defended these Muslim Sisters and Brothers and sometimes she went along with the old Bedouin women as they made fun of them. One evening, having recited some poetry and told some traditional tales for my benefit, Kamla's aunt Dhahab turned to her niece and asked, "Hey Kamla, have you given Lila any songs?"

Kamla was coy. "I'm not a song person. I'm just a simple person minding my own business. I'm with God. I'm pious and know my Lord."

Her sister hooted, perhaps thinking of Kamla's love of the radio and scandalous movie magazines. But Kamla went on, only half-joking, "Auntie, I've become pious. I don't have anything to do with songs."

Her aunt mocked her, "What's this? You've become pious?" Everyone laughed as the old aunt continued, "God's blessings! God's Blessings! So, you're joining the Beard Family?"

There was a commotion, everyone talking at once about the topic that was so often in the air these days—the Islamists. Kamla spoke on their behalf. "They say 'We are religious people, . . . following God's path, the path to heaven.'"

Her aunt was hardly convinced. "I swear to God they've never seen heaven. God is the only judge. God is present."

Sabra thought they should be more respectful. But she admitted, "May God protect them, they do some things that aren't necessary. Do you know what our aunt who lives out west says? She says they say that the sugar dolls are wrong, even the food we make to celebrate the Prophet's birthday. Rotten life! The special food for the birthday that the whole world celebrates—they say it is forbidden!"

Her aunt concurred, "Have you ever heard of anything like that!"

Some women were even more irreverent. Once when an old friend from the nearby town was visiting, the evening conversation turned to the topic of these new religious types. She complained that they had forbidden celebrations of saints' birthdays including the candy and meat eaten at them. They had said it was wrong to call any holyman "Saint so-and-so." She said, "They have forbidden everything. Why, the next thing you know they'll forbid the clothes we wear and make us go around naked."

She then described to the group gathered around her how these people dressed. She told them about the wife of a Muslim Brother called Mr.

Muhammad who had moved to her town. She was offering lessons on religion every Tuesday afternoon for any woman who wished to learn. The woman wore a veil that covered her head and her face, "except for her eyes." She wore gloves, a dress down to the ground, and shoes. As the old woman put it, "She looks like a ghost."

Kamla showed off her knowledge of religion. "It is wrong for a woman to veil her face. What is required is that your head be covered; it is fine to expose your hands, your feet and your face."

The old woman then commented on the men. "They all run around with those beards. Why, Doctor Ahmed's sticks out like this! It looks like pubic hair."

Kamla had to raise her voice to be heard over the wild laughter. "But Auntie, the beard is a tradition of the Prophet."

Kamla had confided to me that she would have liked to replace her kerchief with the new Islamic headcovering but she was afraid her family would object. A photograph of her with her school friends revealed that she was the only one among them not wearing the new modest dress. Yet Kamla criticized some of her classmates who wore this type of clothing but added flowers and multicolored headbands to their veils. She said their religion teacher had given them a real talking to and had confiscated their flowers and headbands. He'd said, "If you want to take on the veil, do it seriously." Kamla said she would adopt this kind of veil "if God opens the way for me and I get to marry someone educated."

A NEW ORDER

The final part of Kamla's essay was to have been about what she hoped would change in her community. All she had written, though, was this:

> As for the bad things, I will talk about them.

She read this final sentence and looked at me. "What are the wrongs I wish the Bedouins would finish with? I've already discussed these. First, their ideas about girls. They are totally meaningless and wrong. I wish they would give her the opportunity to get educated. They see her as a worthless being. You know this, Lila. . . .

"Another thing I wish is that they wouldn't let their customs and traditions rule them to such an extent that they believe that the customs of the city people are wrong and theirs right. Whenever they see that a person is educated, they say he's wrong, we're right. I wish they would respect the educated. I wish they would preserve their customs and traditions but be a bit more advanced. A girl who goes to school doesn't forget her customs and traditions no matter how educated she becomes. Even if she goes to Europe or America, the Bedouin girl will preserve her customs and traditions. They should give her more freedom.

"Another thing I wish is that they would get more organized. I wish they

would put a little order in their lives. Among Bedouins, order is completely
lacking. In every area of their lives—in terms of food, in having too many
children, in the way they raise them—there's no order. And the house—
anything goes!" I was curious about what Kamla meant by "order." She gave
examples from close to home. "Say you've got two brothers living in one house.
If they organized their lives they'd put each one in his own house. And the
business of marrying more than one wife—I wish they'd change their views on
this. It is the biggest sin. The Prophet—it is not forbidden—but the Prophet
said only if you can treat them fairly. But a man can't, it can't be done. Even if
he has money he can't. As a person, in his thoughts and his actions, he can't be
fair. He'll like one more than another.

"The generation that's coming now, after my father's and mother's, they
wouldn't think of it or do it. Why? So they won't have a house with thirty or
forty people living in it. A household with two women in it will have thirty or
forty people in it. Their lives will be lousy. They won't have good food, good
clothes, or good child-rearing. They won't be clean. A woman alone in her own
house can handle her children. When there are two, one will say 'Why should
I hit my children when that one doesn't hit hers?' They watch each other. When
one does something, the other is looking. If one cleans and washes and the
other doesn't, she says, 'Why should I do this when she doesn't?' If she is alone,
a woman won't be able to say that. Who's going to do it for her? She'll do it
herself and she'll know what's what. When she's alone she doesn't have to
depend on anyone. And even her daughter will turn out well, like her mother.
The other way they're always getting into fights over any little thing. Even
without my saying this, you know it, Lila. This is what I wish would change.

"Bedouins think that as long as they have a house and can eat, drink, and
be clothed, that's enough. That's life. And they marry and have kids and marry
again. But a man should live a more ordered and relaxed life. Should a man
come home at the end of his day tired from working and find it filthy and the
kids and women fighting? He comes wanting to relax and finds this? This is
what makes someone say, 'No, there should be order.'"

For years I had heard Kamla's call for order. Living in a household of twenty
or more, half of whom are under ten years old, can be chaotic. Fed up, Kamla
would sometimes say, "This isn't a house, it's a breeding station!" She and her
sister often teased their mother, calling her Shalabiyya, the name of a character
they had seen in a family planning advertisement on television. Shalabiyya was
a woman with too many children. In her lap, on her shoulders, on her head—
when she tried to draw water or milk the cow, they climbed all over her and
trailed behind her. Gateefa would apologize, "We can't change the way we are."

When Kamla was young, she used to come home from school announcing
that she was going to marry an Egyptian doctor and only have one child. Other
times she'd say she was going to have only two children, both daughters. She
was going to live alone in a house with her husband, just the two of them.

Bedouin men make women work hard and don't pay attention to them. Even if they are ill, they won't lift a finger to help, not even to pick up a crying baby. Egyptian men help their wives, respect them and treat them well. When Kamla's younger sister, echoing their father, accused Egyptians of being stingy and not offering food to their guests, Kamla defended them to support her favorite theme. She argued that they just did things in an organized manner; they had special meal times, unlike the Bedouins who brought out food whenever anyone stopped by.

Kamla confessed that she belonged to two worlds. With her sisters and cousins she talked about the things they knew, not letting on that she was different. But there were so many things she could talk to her school friends about that she could not talk about with them—things like politics. Sometimes she seemed to accept her double life with equanimity. When I saw her spinning with her aunt one day, I asked, "Hey Kamla, so you know how to spin too?" She had laughed. "Yes, I can go either way. If it turns out I'm to be citified, I'll do that. And if it turns out I'll be a Bedouin, I'll know how."

When I suggested she might be lonely if she moved into a house of her own she was adamant. "No, I won't miss them at all." Yet this is someone who is fiercely proud of her father for being an important man who is generous and pious. Despite occasional confrontations, she spends, like her sisters, nearly every evening sitting close to her mother and talking. Even her brood of little siblings only sometimes drives her crazy. The youngest she can rarely resist grabbing to hug. Delighted by this two-year-old's every new accomplishment, she whispers new words in her ear and kisses her when she repeats them.

Most of the time, though, she says she wants to get out. I worry about Kamla's blithe confidence that life in the city will be so much better. I disagree with her assessment of Bedouin women's lives. I argue with Kamla that she deliberately ignores the richness of their relationships and the ways they have always struggled back (and were expected to). Her own life is evidence. There was not a single woman in the camp who had not admired her for being a wilful little girl. Even her father had been amused by her opinions and determination. As she had grown up, her strength of purpose had enabled her to withstand the social pressure against her schooling. The kind of independence she displayed reminded me of her grandmother Migdim, with her stories of resistance to marriage and her struggles to have her way with her sons. It even reminded me of her mother Gateefa, who had earned the respect of her husband.

Yet, when her letter arrived I was happy for her—happy that it was her fate not to have to marry her cousin after all and glad that her father had been willing to take her wishes into consideration. Armed with romantic visions inspired by Egyptian radio melodramas, cloying love songs, and her tattered collection of hokey postcards showing blonde brides and grooms looking deeply into each other's eyes, she will go off to live with her Egyptianized, educated husband in a small and ordered household. She will never work outside the home. She will rarely even leave her apartment. She expects to clean house, cook meals, and serve her husband. If God brings children, she'll take care of them.

Because she has none of his sister Aisha's feminine refinement, I was worried. What would her husband think when he first saw this sturdy young woman with her wide feet and calloused hands? Because she is the daughter of a wealthy tribal leader, the fabric of her dresses would be expensive and she would bring many with her; but they would have been tailored by local seamstresses whose renditions of city clothes are always awkward. And would she know how to dress for the wedding night, this girl who has had to fight her mother's horrified accusations of immodesty when she wore a home-made bra? Would Engineer Ibrahim Selim find charming her outspoken ways?

I wrote back to wish her all happiness and to apologize for not being able to attend the wedding. An older sister would sing at the henna party on the eve of her sister's wedding so I looked through my collection of Bedouin wedding songs to see if any seemed right. I ended my letter with three that I hoped would mean something to her. The first let her know how much I thought of her family:

> Her father has a good name
> and those who've come to marry will find happiness . . .

The second reminded her that I knew how much she wanted this:

> Her morning is blessed
> she got what she desired and was honored . . .

And the third expressed my best wishes for this young woman, vulnerable and beautiful as are all young brides heading off into the unknown:

> Neighbors, come say farewell
> a gazelle from our land is about to journey . . .

Struggling Along

ROBERT DESJARLAIS

This essay began as an experiment in ethnographic writing, based on my fieldwork in a shelter in downtown Boston for the homeless and mentally ill. I wanted to answer the Nietzschean call of the French philosopher Gilles Deleuze, to attend to the "pulsional intensities" of life rather than to any given cultural codes or symbolic orders (such as that of "the person"). And so I organized my fieldnotes in terms of the intensities common to the shelter—intensities of pain, of taking pharmaceuticals, of bodily sensations, of hearing voices, of using language, and of relating to others.[1] This method led me to develop an intensity-centered phenomenology over a person-centered ethnography, which lent priority to the gamut of forces and sensations that course through the lives of the shelter residents. This shift from a focus on bounded individual lives to a focus on the forces common to—and often constitutive of—those lives also helped me to bracket more effectively the category of experience and to see that the elements of everyday life in the shelter are distinct from the elements of "experience" as the process is typically understood. In brief, the residents of the shelter tend not to experience—defined here as an inwardly reflexive process that proceeds, coheres, and transforms through temporally integrative forms—but rather "struggle along" by way of an acutely tactile mode of perception that attends to episodic, temporally finite encounters. Building on this observation, I argue that the category of experience, which many take to be universal, natural, and supremely authentic, is not an existential given but rather a historically and culturally constituted process predicated on a range of cultural, social, and political forces.

AN APPROACH TO EXPERIENCE

Alice is a fortyish native of New England who lives in a shelter of cots and partitions set up on a basketball court in the basement of a large government center in downtown Boston. If she is not staying in the shelter, she is sleeping in a psychiatric hospital or on the city's streets. She considers herself "estranged from society" since the state took her child away ten years ago; she now spends much of her time bumming cigarettes and reading the Bible. She bums cigarettes because she lacks money and does not want to start buying packs of her own lest she pick up an expensive habit. The Bible helps to lessen the noise, worries, and distractions that are part of shelter life. "If I can just read the Bible for fifteen, sixteen hours a day," she says, "and just block out all the rest, then I'm okay." Given the lack of calm in the shelter, and Alice's own troubles, the task is not an easy one. When we cross paths in the building, and I ask how she is doing, she often says she is "struggling along." Her response aptly describes what life is like for her and many of the fifty other "homeless mentally ill" who sleep on the basketball court. The nature of the struggle, where people live a routine existence marked by stress, fear, and distractions, has led me to question one of the basic goals of my ethnographic work there. I set out to understand what Alice and her companions experience of the everyday. But the apparent absence of some of the distinguishing features of experience—reflexive interiority, hermeneutical depth, narrative flow—leads me to question the universal relevance of the term.

The concept of experience is one of the most problematic in contemporary anthropology, with the problems relating, at least in part, to the rhetorical and analytic needs that it serves. Some use the word because it appears relatively free of the baggage that concepts like "self" or "mind" or "affect" carry (Kleinman and Kleinman 1991). Some rely on it to provide the "missing term," as E. P. Thompson (1978:170) found, through which "structure is transmuted into process, and the subject re-enters into history." And some build theories on its turf because they find it gets at something more real and more immediate than the stuff of meaning or discourse (Jackson 1989, Desjarlais 1992). The word is of such value that even scholars critical of experiential approaches fear that without it or something like it "cultural analyses seem to float several feet above their human ground" (Geertz 1986:374; Scott 1991). Experience, it seems, is a crucial element of contemporary academic thought; to try to write about humans without reference to experience is like trying to think the unthinkable. Yet despite its apparent necessity, as something that can and must be thought, its universality remains in question. We must ask if experience is as essential or as commonplace as many take it to be.

In anthropology, the ontology of experience has taken a back seat to its epistemology. Perspectives on the study of experience generally divide anthropologists into two camps. There are those who advocate an anthropology of experience to investigate, chiefly through phenomenological means, domains of life—pain, bodies, emotions—that one can only poorly apprehend through cultural analysis; and there are others who find that such an anthropology is epistemologically unfounded, since one can never really know the felt immediacies of another person or society, and irrelevant to more important social and political concerns. In listening to the debates sparked by these different orientations, one gets the sense that everyone knows what is meant by experience. Yet it is rarely defined, and when it is defined, it involves a generic "we." Indeed, the very fact that the category of experience goes undefined, or is couched in universalist terms, suggests that it is taken as a fundamental, authentic, and unchanging constant in human life.

The current focus on experience stems from Romantic sensibilities toward the incongruous and nearly unfathomable aspects of everyday life. It follows from Boas' distinction between physical and historical methods, whereby "physicists" sought to "bring the confusion of forms and species into a system" and "cosmographers" considered the phenomenon itself "without regard to its place in a system" and sought to "penetrate into its secrets until every feature is plain and clear" (1887:644–45; Stocking 1989). Boas, Sapir, and Geertz have advocated the latter, idiographic approach, as has much of American anthropology. Yet experientialist approaches also echo a "widespread aspiration" in post-romantic thought "to retrieve experience from the deadening, routinized, conventional forms of instrumental civilization" (Taylor 1989:469; Gadamer 1975:63). Here, experience is held to be a truer aspect of life rich enough to defy conceptual models. The sentiment has passed from Schiller to Dilthey to contemporary anthropologists, who claim that theoretical and medical formulations fail to account for the intensely felt and personal dimensions of human life and suffering.[2] The emphasis is on felt realities rather than cultural categories, the near rather than the distant, and the sensate over the semantic. The sensate begets immediacy which, in turn, begets authenticity. In the end, however, the logic is haunted by a unique but problematic collapse of ontology and epistemology, in which the primary ontic nature of experience translates into a supreme facticity.

The problem with taking experience as an uniquely authentic domain of life is that one risks losing an opportunity to question either the social production of that domain or the practices that define its use. Connotations of primacy and authenticity lend legitimacy to the anthropologist's craft, but they can simultaneously limit inquiries to descriptions of the terrain of experience when what we need are critical reflections on how the terrain comes about (Williams 1979:164–170, Scott 1991). Asking about experience can tell you about some things, such as how the everyday comes together, just as asking about labor relations or clan lineages can tell you about other things.

In asking a few questions here, I want to suggest that experience is not an existential given but rather a historically and culturally constituted process predicated on a certain way of being in the world. Since this way of being is only one possibility among many, some people live in terms different from experience. This appears to be the case with Alice and many of her companions. Their worlds, to be sure, are marked by interiority and a sensate reflexivity, but the subjective and temporal contours of their lives are distinct from the act of experiencing as it is commonly defined. If we take experience to be simply a sensate awareness of life, or "to be alive when something happens" (which is the traditional meaning of *erleben*, a German word for experience), then the people in the shelter certainly do experience. But today experience (or "Experience," if you will) entails something more, and I want to understand what conditions are necessary if people are to experience or, alternatively, to struggle along.

The etymology of experience suggests how European cultures have gradually produced a distinctly interior, introspective process. "Experience," like "experiment" and "expert," comes from the Latin *experiri*, a compound verb, formed from the prefix *ex-* 'out' and a prehistoric base **per-* denoting 'attempt, trial', that meant 'to try, test' (Ayto 1990). *Per-* also relates to the Latin *periculum*, "peril, trial, danger," through the suffixed extended form **peri-tlo* (Turner 1982:17). The modern English word "experiment" best preserves the original meaning of "experience," though the latter also meant at first "putting to the test." From this came the idea of "actually observed phenomena in order to gain knowledge of them," which in turn led to the more subjective "condition of having undergone or been affected by a particular event" (Ayto 1990). The subjectivist connotations of experience are only a recent innovation; the idea that to experience is to feel, suffer, or undergo is first recorded in 1588 (Barnhart 1988:357). Similar to the trajectory of the Western self, which initially marked an exterior relationship to one's environment but later came to entail a moral, reflexive agent (Taylor 1989), experience evolved from a verb denoting an external engagement with or testing of one's surroundings to a template marking a person's subjective awareness of that engagement. As Lévy-Bruhl, Hallowell, Lienhardt, and others have pointed out, however, human functioning need not depend on such reflective assessments but can assume a wealth of non-introspective forms.[3] Experience involves only one rather inward-looking arrangement of human agency among many.

The stress on interiority ties into the affirmation of ordinary life that has earmarked humanist thought and literature and relates to the Romantic sensibility that the most authentic truths lie in our selves (Taylor 1989). A focus on the truths of personal revelations relates closely to modern religious concerns, particularly the Pietist emphasis on religious devotion, with personal experience—as a state of mind or feeling—forming an integral part of the inner religious life. The inner states cultivated through such devotion reveal truths worth talking about. Raymond Williams notes, for instance, that in nineteenth-century Methodism there were *experience-meetings*: classes "held for the recital of religious experiences" (1983:128). Today as well, experience is largely rooted in individual agency. A person "has," "learns from," or "discloses" an experience. Privacy, individuality, and reflexive interiority are intrinsic to experience; no one else can experience my toothache, though they might empathize with my suffering. Experience thus readily equates with a person's "inner life" or "consciousness" and is often synonymous with subjectivity.[4]

The notion of interiority encourages some to try to understand the "very marrow" or "essence" of experience (Desjarlais 1992) and leads others to suggest that "experience is sensual and affective to the core and exceeds objectification in symbolic forms" (Good 1993:139). The excessiveness of experience points to a second distinguishing feature: experience possesses hermeneutical depth. The sense of depth, like that of interiority, ties into the Western genealogy of the self. While the writings of Augustine, Descartes, and Montaigne brought successively stronger declarations of human "inwardness," only with the expressivist yearnings of Wordsworth, Hölderlin, and others to discover and articulate our inner nature does this interiority come to possess significant depth—"a domain," that is, "which reaches farther than we can ever articulate, which still stretches our furthest point of clear expression" (Taylor 1989:289). In modernist times, the grounds of experience, rather than those of the self, have possessed the richest depths because experience is often seen as the foundation of human agency (Taylor 1989:465). As Gadamer describes the philosophy of Dilthey and Husserl, "essential to an experience [*erlebnis*] is that it cannot be exhausted in what can be said of it or grasped as its meaning. . . . What we call an *erlebnis* in this emphatic sense thus means something unforget- table and irreplaceable, something whose meaning cannot be exhausted by conceptual determination" (1975:67). The import of experience is inexhaust- ible because experience, like a text or a work of art, carries forth a wealth of meanings that can never be conclusively interpreted (see Ricoeur 1970).

The hermeneutical depths of experience distinguish it from the subject matter of traditional cultural analysis. Human experience eludes social science analysis and resists symbolization. The idea of an excessive, hermeneutically rich plane of being entails the view that the only way to safely study experience is to attend to the perimeter of expressions, stories, and social formations in which it is cloaked.[5] To say that thick description is the best method of analysis here is not to denigrate the available methods but simply to point out the kind of phenomena in question: experience is too complex, too subtle, and too private to be understood through anything but phenomenological assessments. Even then, "it's all a matter of scratching surfaces," as Clifford Geertz puts it (1986:373). Talk of surfaces, cores, and bone marrow suggests a shadow play of interiors and exteriors: we cannot penetrate the containers of experience. The body is often held to be one such container, with the skin serving as an "envelope" within which, Faulkner writes, "the sum of experience" resides (1986:54).

The sum coheres. Despite the immediacy, richness, and contingency that characterizes lived experience, experience works on a principal of unity. John Dewey (1926) talks about the "inclusive integrity" of experience, while Michael Oakshott (1933) ponders its "concrete totality." James, Dilthey, Husserl, Merleau-Ponty, and others agree that the sum of experience is greater than its parts. Joyce's Leopold Bloom, Freud's Wolfman, and Proust's remembrances exemplify the integrity of experience; memories, dreams, and sensations snowball into a unified, epiphanic whole. The appeal to wholeness apparently relates, for many, to a modernist desire to develop a concept that might safely absorb the many select features of human agency, such as "thought," "feeling," and "sensation."[6]

Experience builds to something more than a transient, episodic succession of events. The intransience of experience ties into the fact that it affects a lasting and memorable impression on the person who undergoes it. "To undergo an experience with something," Heidegger writes, "—be it a thing, a person, or a god—means that this something befalls us, strikes us, comes over us, overwhelms and transforms us" (1971:57). By undergoing an experience, a person picks up something new; "experience means *eundo assequi, to obtain* something along the way, to attain something by going on a way" (1971:66). Experience is fundamentally transformative; an experience "does not leave him who has it unchanged," or so says Gadamer (1975:100) in his specification of a "genuine experience" (*Erfahrung*). To have an experience or to learn by experience suggests an education that can accrue in certain skills, knowledge, or wisdom, though the education hinges on a flux of subjective reflections that other kinds of learning (such as operant conditioning) do not. Thus the *Oxford English Dictionary* reports that, since the sixteenth century, experience has involved "knowledge resulting from actual observation or from what one has undergone" (*OED*, 7).

"To experience," Heidegger writes, "is to go along a way. The way leads through a landscape" (1971:67).[7] The landscape is organized through temporal, as well as spatial, lines. Experience, by definition, collects itself through the rhythmic pacings of time. As Carr, who draws from Husserl, puts it, "Our experience is directed towards, and itself assumes, temporally extended forms in which future, present, and past mutually determine one another as parts of a whole" (1986:30–31). Narrative typically helps to form the sense of temporal integration. The idea that experience accumulates in time through stories builds chiefly upon musings on the relation between forms of life and narrative orderings of time. From Aristotle to Heidegger to Ricoeur, the interpenetration of narrative and experience has grown stronger in correlation with the predominance of literature in the lives of the educated. The present state of the art is that we can only grasp our lives through narrative, though few question to what degree this "inescapable" fact applies outside the modern West.[8]

Experience as a whole is subject to similar queries. In much the same way that the truth of sexuality grew out of an economy of discourses that took hold in seventeenth-century Europe (Foucault 1978), so a set of phrasings of depth, interiority, and authenticity, sensibilities of holism and transcendence, and practices of reading and writing have, in the modern era, crafted a mode of being that many in the West call experience. In taking experience to have a specific meaning and to possess a limited reality, the task is to identify where and when people experience and the conditions that make the process possible. Thinkers such as Taylor and Foucault, who emphasize the priority of language in shaping our lives, tend to speak of incarnations of self or power as generic to an age. Yet these kinds of theories seldom consider the plurality of social, sensorial, and technological forces that occasion diverse ways of being within a society. I find cultural discourses as well as day to day contingencies to be evident in the shelter where Alice stays. Experience there is a possibility, not a given, with certain conditions necessary if people are to experience.[9]

THE SHELTER

The shelter was set up in the early 1980s by the Massachusetts Department of Mental Health (DMH) to provide temporary housing for persons troubled by mental illness. To gain a bed one must be both homeless and mentally ill, which means owning a diagnosis of "schizophrenia," "bipolar disorder," or the like. A "guest" arrives from a local hospital, another shelter, or the streets (often through contact with "homeless outreach" teams) to sleep on one of fifty-two cots set up in the gym of a mental health center that occupies one third of a vast government center (with the top floor housing a locked, "in-patient" psychiatric ward). A staff desk guards the entrance to the shelter, which abuts a lobby where many residents spend much of their time talking, sitting, and pacing. Within the shelter, standing partitions separate the men's and women's sleeping areas. Each person sleeps in an open space filled by a bed and a locker. In the morning and in the evening, residents can sit in a day room or watch television in a smaller room. Some stay in the shelter for a few weeks, while a handful have been there over five years. They typically leave when they return to the hospital, find a more permanent place to live, hit the street, look for a better life outside Boston, or get kicked out due to infractions of the shelter's rules concerning drugs or theft.

I frequented the shelter at a time when there was great interest—among psychiatrists, policy-oriented academics, and the general population—in the improvement of services for the chronic and persistent mentally ill, despite severe cuts in health services for the poor and a general push for privatization.[10] Program cuts affected the shelter in two ways: residents lost out on case-managers and treatment programs, and staff worried about losing their jobs.

The staff maintain that the shelter is perceived as the Rolls Royce of shelters. While their guests do not hold the same level of enthusiasm, many do find it to be one of the better shelters in the Boston area. Part of its appeal lies in the safety it provides. "People feel safe in the shelter," Bill, a staff member, told me. "A lot of people feel that things are not going to get out of control here. Once they're here, they don't want to move out, because it's threatening. The strategy then becomes, 'How can I stay here?'"

The strategy of the staff, in turn, is to maintain the impermanence of the shelter and make it clear, at meetings and in conversations, that it is "not a home."[11] For the most part, they are successful in getting their point across by balancing safety with a modicum of comfort and a set of rules. Discipline includes throwing a person outside the shelter for an hour (typically for acting up or swearing or talking too loud for too long) or sending them out for the night for more egregious acts. While the latter punishment is the "final form of discipline" because staff cannot bar people from the shelter unless they steal or take drugs, there is also the threat, if one "decompensates" too radically, of being restrained and escorted by police to a psychiatric hospital for evaluation.

The staff's proclivity to displace people contributes to a distinct political system. In contrast to Foucault's model of "disciplinary" power in the industrial age, which centered on acts of confinement and panoptic visibility, power in the shelter typically involves acts of displacement and obscurity.[12] And whereas the staff, who maintain a proper and durable place, rely on "strategies" that enable them to keep to themselves in a position of withdrawal, foresight, and self-collection, the residents lack such a place, and so have few grounds— spatial, political, economic—on which to stand.[13] To get something done, or to effect something in their own interests, they resort to tactical actions that depend less on an appropriation of space and a concerted technology of knowledge than on diverse opportunities in time, rhetorical phrasings, and other isolated actions.

The therapeutic orientation of the staff includes a range of rules and protocols that set the tempo of everyday life. A resident must shower every other day, leave the shelter from 9:30 in the morning to 3:30 in the afternoon, perform a rotating set of chores, dine at 5:00, take medications in the evening, and return to the shelter by 9:00 at night. The staff holds that "the rules are there to provide structure to your lives," as a nurse told several residents one evening. Residents find that the multiplicity of restrictions, as well as the way in which they are asserted, are unpleasant and infantilizing. Freddy, for instance, says that the shelter is "not a home. There are too many rules and regulations." The management's philosophy is that "it's a question of choices," as one staff member put it to a group of residents gathered for a meeting one evening. "Take Freddy, for instance. He has choices. If he wants to stay here instead of in-patient [the locked psychiatric ward on the fifth floor], then when he's feeling nervous and anxious, he can either come up to us and ask for more medication, or he can try to throw a door through a window." Freddy nodded his head and smiled in accommodating agreement.

To understand why people stay in the shelter for months or for years, one needs to know something about "the street," which is where many come from and where many go to if they leave without locating an apartment. The shelter residents talk about the street as if it was a single location with a singularly forced sensorium of cold weather, fear, anonymity, transience, and a constant, unsettling tendency to get on one's nerves. Roy, like others, says the street is a "pretty tough place." He used to panhandle in front of Dunkin' Donuts and kept mostly to himself for "safety reasons." If you're on the street, he says, you get beat up, cheated, robbed, disrespected. You end up sleeping in subways, with people stealing money from your pockets, and eating at McDonald's, Burger King, "or even out of trash cans if you're desperate." Julie, who lived on the streets for several weeks before I met her, says the isolation snuffs out a person's will to talk and be with others. "People in the street don't talk to anyone." She wore a Red Sox T-shirt, twisted a piece of paper, and paused after each sentence. "A part of you dies on the street. Your spirit dies. You lose the wanting to live inside, the wanting to talk with someone. That part dies too. Once you're outside, you can't come back inside. The street is tough. Homeless people are dying out on the streets. You lose everything but a sense of survival."

The street tends to reduce people to a few material possessions, a couple of friends, and the redundancy of walking, hiding, eating, bumming cigarettes or change, and sleeping on benches, in the subways, in the woods, or in different shelters. The lack of shelter or privacy leads to a condition of supreme exteriority that derives from transience, a distanced sociality, and a restless engagement with one's surroundings. For many, the fears and discontinuities of the streets are amplified, in both the mathematical and sensory scales of the word, by concerns commonly associated with mental illness, such as hearing voices, anxiety, or fear of harm. Bruce hears voices, "Young women telling me they're easy to sleep with. That scares me, it scares me." Julie fears that people are planning to kill her on the street. One day she and her daughter escaped from two men in the subway. She fears the voices would get worse if she lived on the streets. "Right at this moment," Martin said one day, "I have this impending sense of doom—that something terrible is going to happen in a few minutes, like this ceiling could fall in on us."

"When you're homeless," Richie says, "you end up with just your body, cause you don't own anything else." With the loss of many possessions, and the public slant to physical movements and functions, the body becomes, at times, the most prominent instrument of engagement, awareness, and retrospection. "Look what I did to my arm," Freddy says of a track of scars up his forearm. Some scars are fresher than others. "I did it to prove that I'm sick, the government's sick, the state is sick, and you're sick." Nadia, an aging Polish woman who speaks of concentration camps, says she is losing her voice because of a thyroid problem. One day she lies on the grass with a necklace, an ankle bracelet, and a wrist bracelet made out of interlocking safety pins. "I thought I would adorn my tortured body," she tells me.

Distinct as the residents' concerns are, they suggest that everyday life is marked by a frail sensitivity toward the noises, activities, and potential violence of Boston's streets. The states of feeling common to those who are homeless result less from inherent dispositions than from the constant and tiresome afflictions of the street. A basic orientation—the product of cold nights and fearful sounds—pivots on the sensory range between "nervousness" and "staying calm," with many bedding down in the shelter in hopes of finding more of the latter. People talk of being "emotionally tired" when they arrive in the building and refer to an inability to deal with "distractions." "We're sensitive," Joan says at a group meeting one day. "We can't deal with things. Every little thing bothers us, and we can't take shit. That's why we're here [in a DMH shelter]. We're not like the people outside." She says she needs to be "familiar" with an area before she is comfortable. She does not want to be in a place where she always has to be on the lookout. "It's the adjustment that's the problem. It's okay when you're well. But when you're sick, it's hard to start off fresh each day." She came to the shelter after sleeping in basements and doorsteps. Molly would like to get a job, but she would need "a smooth day" at first, just ringing up the numbers on a cash register, before she could do it for real. She says she cannot "react" to people when she has a job. "I can't hold that in my mind. I can't sit still."

Given these concerns, many people come to stay in the shelter because there are simply "less worries" there, as one man put it. "I feel safe as long as I'm in the building," Joey once said when I asked how he was doing. Tommy finds that the place as a whole is good for "detuning": "there's not much pressure here." Louise, who is "desperate to find an answer to the rambling" of her mind, is looking for a place "to recover from the shock of the elements outside." She says she will stay in the shelter until she feels it is safe for her to move out. Some stay for years for quite similar reasons.

Within the shelter, much of everyday life orbits around efforts to keep shocks to a minimum and so "hold oneself together." "Hypersensory residualness wants to be within equatorial lines" goes the last line of one of Charles's poems. For many, there is a common and practical need to keep the senses within equatorial lines—to seek comfort and safety in the routines of shelter life, and so spend one's days in a way that skirts the fears, worries, and afflictions that impinge. Some try to stay calm by holding onto a thought, a word, a gesture, or a cigarette. Jimmy says he "used to pick up a newspaper, you know, and hold onto a word, and that would calm me down." Chuck works on puzzles for the same reason.

By three in the afternoon, five to ten tired people are usually waiting for the shelter doors to open. When they do, many lie in their cots for an hour or so. One of the chief complaints of shelter life is that it is hard to find time and space to oneself. "I suppose you can't ask for much," says Julie. "It's a place for people with problems. And it's a place where everybody's together. You have to be together." But being together has its problems: each resident must sleep with twenty other same-sex fellows on the same half of the basketball court; no partitions separate the beds from one another. During the day, they share six tables, four armchairs, one couch, the TV room, the lobby, and the far reaches of the building. Most confrontations within the shelter involve disputes over these limited resources. One day Matthew sat down at a table where Barbara was seated. "I want to be alone," she said. "Alone?" he asked. "How can you be alone here? Everybody's together. You could be off somewhere by yourself." A minute later, Matthew walked off.

On the basketball court, much of the tension builds on distracting sights and sounds—the hypersensory residuals of which Charles spoke. "There are fifty tensions here," Sally tells me, one for each person living in the shelter. "It's hard to get a decent sleep here," she added. "Someone is always singing a song." Matthew, a middle-aged man from Mississippi, likes to sit in the plaza on the third floor. "There's too much going on downstairs," he says. "There's two televisions on, radios. I can't see how you can watch TV with all that going on." A similar distraction nags Jimmy. "The building," he says, "keeps you out of your own little world. It's kind of distracting."

"What do you do when the building distracts you?"

"Play dead."

People pace, play dead, or hold onto a word or Bible to get through the day. The staff thinks the "routine" is "self-defeating," but for many who live in the building, it is a question of survival. "It's all right, it's better than nothing," Joey said of a new coat bought at a discount market. "I'm trying to hang in there, you know. Hanging in is good. I'm all right as long as I'm busy. My father says an idle mind is an ill mind."

For most, hanging in there is good enough. People stay busy by talking, smoking cigarettes, and pacing. The goal of many of these activities is to be doing something. Time consists of a grab bag of concrete activities marked by expanses of silence and waiting. "I smoke cigarettes, drink coffee, listen to music, talk with people, you know," Roy says of his daily routine, with the phrase "you know" referring to activities taken for granted. I ask Patty what she did today. "Oh, you know, the usual boring stuff, smoking and eating and talking. In and out, in and out, and I paced a bit today."

Pacing helps people to keep busy and calm their nerves. Warren finds that "there's too much pressure sometimes" from staying in the building and so spends much of his time walking around the city. One of Joseph's poems, jotted in a notebook, consists of four lines:

Pacing the floor
pacing my mind
walking the floor
walking my thoughts

For Joseph "pacing up and down" is the way to change his luck. His advice for a newcomer is, "Live one day at a time, don't get ahead of yourself, and don't get too worried." Worries for him are the main problem in the shelter; they throw off the equilibrium, the balance. "If you have to get copies for something, or records at the hospital, it can get compressed in here, because of the close quarters and tight spaces." He gets to feeling "tight" inside, "constricted." Pacing helps because it uses up energy, "so much energy from the medication."

Psychotropic drugs are a clear presence in the sensory range of everyday life. Almost everyone who sleeps in the shelter takes medications prescribed by a psychiatrist and given by a nurse; those who refuse risk a trip to a hospital. The medications help with the voices and lower anxiety, but they can also cause a body to stiffen or to shake. People get "hopped up," feel "anxious" or "hyper," or get "the Haldol shakes." There is no "gray area" with Ralph's medications. Not enough and he gets to hearing voices. Too much and he walks around stiffly in a stupor. "They make you walk around real stiff." "I got coffee coming, I got coffee coming. I just took my medication—to smooth out the joints," Joey tells me. Leona takes her meds to make the chemicals connect with one another "like fingers tied together." Richard's head was "a mess" until the medication helped him to get his "equilibrium" back. For many, medication is one way to get desensitized or "detuned," as Tommy put it. They make Jimmy go into his "own little world."

Shelter life, despite its many distractions, can be too mundane; it is difficult, at times, to keep from playing dead. Martin says he walks around too much because he has nothing to do with his time. One day he shows me a poem he wrote called "Sheol," which is the word for the Hebrew netherworld. The poem tells of the LA street scene, where "people are hanging out, with no thoughts, no feelings." Others refer to similar affinities between mood and setting. "Sometimes I go to my bed area," Leona says, "and it seems so kinda gloomy, dark. It looks moldy, though it isn't really moldy, you know?" Vicki finds that the shelter is like death row, and says you sometimes see the same faces in different shelters. How does that make her feel? "I don't feel anything," she says. "I lost my mind," Lisa said in introducing herself one day. What does that feel like? "I don't feel, I don't feel. I feel numb." Richie says he "acts crazy" to stop from being bored. He gets the "shelter blues" when he feels depressed and worthless and tries to make himself and others feel "more alive" by touching and talking to them. "I don't know what I was thinking about then," said Henry of a razor put to his wrist some years back. "I guess I did it because I was really depressed. When I cut myself, I felt alive, more alive than I felt before. Anyway, I wasn't depressed any more after that."

The mundane distractions of shelter life, and the occasional deadening of feeling, thus turn on the feel of razors, caffeine, footsteps, touches, and the constant exchanges between bodies and voices. With these exchanges, abrupt interactions soon grow tiresome. Matthew was talking one day, partly to me, partly to himself: "Moses was a wise man." Nancy walked up and interrupted: "Matthew, can I have a cigarette?" "I don't want to hear that, Nancy," Matthew said. "We're doing the same old song and dance."

Much of everyday life repeats the same old song and dance: the bumming, selling, and sharing of food, cigarettes, and Walkman radios. The staff gives out paper tokens to a "guest" if she takes a shower, makes her bed, or waters the plants. People use the tokens at night to pay for snacks, soda, or soap in the evening; they also use them to buy cigarettes from each other. People walk over to a convenience store to buy coffee, cigarettes, or food for others; their cut is fifty-five cents or so or a share of the bounty. The going interest on a loan is a hundred percent; if Sally loans Chuck five dollars today, he should pay her ten by next week. Cigarettes can be exchanged for conversation, radios for friendship, and sex, at times, for money. "If you have the money," Martin said, "you can get anything you want on the street." Last spring, he bought Valiums on the street for a dollar a pill and was trying to get a constant supply set up in the building. Drugs, cash, food, and bodies flow in and out of the building in a vast common market.

Language is an integral part of this political economy. A few kind words can set someone up for a free cigarette or a cigarette can be offered in exchange for conversation. The street value of words was brought home to me one October evening when I was talking, in Harvard Square, with someone who tends to frequent the Government Center. He was selling flowers, which he found in a trash bin behind a florist's shop, for 25 cents each. He said he could offer people bits of his poetry or translations of Chinese characters he wrote on a piece of cardboard, but they might steal his words. "How do I know," he asked, "that if I put my words on this cardboard, or put them into the air, you or someone else won't take my words and sell them somewhere else? No, you gotta be more careful than that these days."

Words are therefore some of the key commodities in Boston; they can be bought, sold, shared, or stolen by peddlers, psychiatrists, or ethnographers alike. Words spoken often relate to the exchange of money, and "talking" to someone can entail an ongoing social and financial contract.

Bruce walks up to Larry one afternoon and says, "Larry, can you talk to me today?"

"Yeah, can I give you twelve [dollars]?"

"That's great, that will make the week easier."

Later, Bruce tells Larry not to be too stern in lending out money. You have to "work in international waters," give "some room in between," and tend to "the give and take." The advice captures well the ethics of a place where money can be tight but where debts are not soon forgotten.

One reason for the brevity of conversations is that residents find it difficult to follow through on them. As Julie asked me, "Would you want to have a conversation with someone who is talking to themselves, who is caught up with their own conversation?" While some hear and respond to voices, others "talk ragtime," which, Peter explains, is talk "about the sky falling down or cows on the roof." He spoke softly. "It doesn't make any sense. How can you listen to that? . . . People are fickle here, they're unpredictable, they don't make sense." "It's awkward," Joseph said. "People seem rational when they first sit down with you, but then, the next thing you know, they're bouncing off the walls." As it is, conversations frequently involve two planes of discourse, with the distinction leading either to arguments, miscomprehensions, or a complex ambiguity of meaning.

Helen, who sometimes uses a cane, walks slowly through the lobby.

"Where's your cane?" Phillipe asks.

"You shut your mouth!" she says to him, and then to me: "He's talking dirty."

Edward was telling Sally and me about the nonfiction novel he intends to write "about making it in the city, today, not yesterday, you know what I mean?" Leona walked by, held a cross at him for several seconds, and flicked her head. "I thought you was a demon," she said, "I thought you was a *demon*! We don't understand one another. We don't *understand* one another!" And then more to me than to Edward: "We live in the same place, but we don't *know* one another. And that's how most arguments get started around here!"

The risk of conflict caused by "loose tongue fits" (as one woman put it), and the struggle for many to hang in there leads to the general consensus that the shelter is "not a place to make friends," as Julie puts it. "Everyone here has problems," she adds. "Each goes their own individual way. So I have no real friends here." "You cannot have real friends here," says Sally.

While many lament the lack of friends in the shelter, many also find comfort in the detached but constant companionship that characterizes shelter life. "I like it here," said Sally. "It's good here because I don't feel lonely. There's always people to talk to here. In an apartment by myself, I was going crazy, losing my mind." Sally likes being around people, but tries not to get too involved in their lives because they can cause her to have a "nervous break-down."[14] The building provides an arrangement where she can keep to herself in the company of others. Others also tend to share a word here and there but largely go their own ways. Except for a few close ties and love interests, lives are kept separate. Anonymity is more the rule than the exception.

Since social ties are so difficult to maintain, the acquaintances that Barbara spoke of are often made out of constant economic exchanges—loans, payments, negotiations. With these exchanges, companionship, like words, can be for sale. Gary walks over and sits down with Janie. "Janie, do you have an extra cigarette?"

"Only if you sit with me."

"Okay."

Janie slides out a cigarette and hands it to Gary.

"You better remember me when I need a cigarette."

"I will."

They smoke in silence.

The economic bases of friendship are evident in the exchanges between Bruce and Larry. The main interactions between these two involve a constant exchange of money, cigarettes, and lottery tickets, and negotiations on those exchanges. In August, Larry moved into a halfway house while Bruce stayed on in the shelter. Two days after Larry left, Bruce sat down with me and a staff member named Lisa, who asked what he thought about Larry's departure.

"I think a lot about him leaving," Bruce said. "He bummed a lot of cigarettes from me, you know."

"Oh yeah, you also seemed to get a lot in return."

"Yeah, we treated each other right. I don't know, he kind of let it go the last week. I lent him some money the last week, ten dollars one day and some cigarettes the next, but I guess he thought I was setting him up."

"Maybe, you know, he was trying to get some distance from this place."

"Yeah. Maybe so."

As with Bruce and Larry, many ties between shelter residents rest on an ethos of exchange. The most significant consequence of this economics has to do with typical activities in and around the building, which often center on acts of collecting. People bum cigarettes, panhandle for money, and scavenge back alleys for clothes, food, and empty soda cans. "I'm sorry. I'm collecting bottles. That's what I do," one man says after brushing the sore arm of a woman sitting next to a trash can. The identity of this man, who stays in the psychiatric ward and scours the building for empty cans, is that of many. An old man always seems to have with him a bag stuffed with, among other things, *Popular Mechanics* magazines and a package of envelopes. Patty is known to wear up to five hats, even in the summer. Emily walks by a table, spies the *Boston Globe*, looks at an ad for Jordan Marsh, reads it, tears it off the page, and carries the clipping to her locker.

The tendencies to collect or to hoard relate, as do many aspects of shelter life, to the economics of homelessness. Joan, for instance, lost her apartment, her library, and her record collection when she fell ill. "It's all gone now." Without a home to keep things ("Home is the place where you keep all your stuff," George Carlin once quipped), possessions soon fill bags and lockers. "It's not right to take all the things we have," Leona said on hearing that the staff was going to limit the articles "guests" could keep in their bed areas. "We don't have enough money for a place. That's why we have all our things here, and we can't even keep our own things or our own children." Collecting also arises from marginal shares of Boston's makeshift economies (see Hopper et al. 1986). Spending money can be gained by collecting bottles or selling the few quality items found in the trash. A lack of money leads a few to pick through dumpsters in search of food, blankets, or clothing. And food or drink that cannot be immediately consumed tends to be given away or hidden until it can be eaten in privacy.

The principles of accumulation do not end with economics. At a basic level, shelter lives tend to consist of the repetitive collection of the elements of those lives. Memories, for instance, often involve such a collection. Gathered like so much spare change, they are characteristically dreamy and drifting. "One night I was scared of something," Peter says of his nights on the street. "I pulled an alarm because I was scared, and the fire engines came. I told them I was scared and alone and I thought that if I pulled this alarm, they would be able to make me feel good. They threw me in jail for that." Patty recalls, with a similar opacity, an apartment she fixed up in the North End before she got "sick." "Oh, it was beautiful," she says. "There were chairs there, and a table, and a tablecloth. I had all my things there. But people were trying to break in, they were trying to kill me." With Patty and Peter, each image shines like a new coin—*this* alarm, *that* tablecloth—but the memory as a whole lacks a dominating narrative fabric. Many other memories have a similarly strong eidetic quality; people remember dates, names, and specific acts and dialogues as if reciting a court docket: "On December 5, 1987, I broke into a real estate office," Phil says one day. But experiential or motivational underpinnings often do not play a role: "I don't know why I did this," he adds. "Maybe 'cause I wanted money, I can't remember." And then, as if an afterthought: "See, that's why I wonder about these drugs."

The inability to clearly remember an incident or why it occurred relates to several factors: the wear and tear of pharmaceuticals, the affective and cognitive disturbances of mental illness, the tactical focus on single encounters, and, most importantly, a training distinct from the more mainstream arts of memory. I once asked Phil where he slept the night before he returned to the shelter after a hospital stay. "I forgot." How could he forget? "I can't use my memory all the time," he said. "You see, I never learned how to use my memory like most people do. I have to think about something at least three times before I can remember it."

Like Phil, many residents learn to use their memories in ways distinct from most non-homeless people. Much of the education relates to the pragmatics of time that comes with living in shelters. The episodic quality of shelter life, where you need to live one day at a time and not get ahead of yourself and where nobody does nothing and you only know people from the same old monotony, fixes time as a diffuse and sporadic order. There are eddies when the mundane occurs, and whirlpools when someone is restrained or hospitalized, but much of the day, week, and month consists of a vast ocean of the same old song and dance. There is more routine than in the street,[15] and Chuck says he drinks coffee to keep up with it, but for the most part, it is only a routine: out by 9:00, lunch at 12:00, back by 3:00, dinner at 5:00, snacks at 7:00, checks in on the first of the month. Because of this event-dependent organization of time, people recall specific dates and events, and everyone talks about the time Walter punched a nurse, but there is little reason to notice the potential links between events and the motivations for actions. The poetics of time are more like those found in Beckett than in Proust; recollections depend on momentary occupations more than any deftly woven remembrances of times past. When the occupations change, the memories take new forms. "You have a child?!" Joan asked a woman she was talking to. "Yeah? Excuse me, I forgot. I've been moving back and forth between hospitals, moving back and forth between the hospital and this place, and I forgot."

As with Julie, who found that the lack of "structure" in the shelter led her to forget how boring it actually was, a constant migration leads Joan to forget something she once knew, as if a person needs a solid footing to remember. The structure of memory relates to the structure of time. In the shelter, the routines of the clock, the realities of power, the influence of pharmaceuticals, the constant exchanges, and the relative lack of privacy and "structure" create a sensitivity toward singular moments and exchanges and desires. We cannot speak of a strong narrative line here, for while people tell stories and events tumble along the episodes rarely add to a narrative whole dependent on a poetics of coherence, continuity, and climax—as narrative is usually defined.[16]

Barbara and Walter are sitting on the benches in the lobby outside the shelter. She asks him to go to the store to buy her some cigarettes and a soda. He returns to the lobby, hands Barbara a can of Pepsi, a pack of cigarettes, and some coins, and sits down on the far bench with a soda of his own.

"Where's the rest of my change?" Barbara asks.

"What's a few pennies?"

"A few pennies are a few pennies, that's what they are, especially when they're mine."

The two sit and drink their sodas. There is no catharsis to the dispute. They both appear to be angry, but everything seems to diffuse abruptly. The conversation entails a transfer of words that involves less a narrative frame (as I would have anticipated) than a poetics of exchange, confrontation, finite acts, and momentary occupations.

CONCLUSION

All told, the themes common to many shelter lives are a political agency built out of tactical movements, an acutely tactile engagement with the world, a constant focus on daily concerns, a distanced style of communication, a poetics of pacing and talking that centers on generally unconnected episodes, a makeshift economy of cigarettes, loans, and conversations, and a ragtag collection of words, memories, images, and possessions. These basic orientations, in tandem with other cultural, linguistic, and political forces, pattern the conditions of, and the grounds for what is possible in, people's lives. They set up a form of life that we might tentatively gloss as struggling along.

The aesthetics of this form of life center on the pragmatics of stasis, expediency, staying calm, and holding oneself together. Given the basic conditions of life on the streets, finding a "smooth day" where nothing much happens has its value. Since one way to stop thinking about the cold or other distractions is to step out of the flow of time, the acme of this predilection is the pursuit of timelessness. For many, there is a need for days where hanging in there is good enough. To get away from the constant tensions and the fleeting distractions, some suspend the minutes of a day.

Too much calm can get to a person after a while, however. An idle mind, after all, is an ill mind, and pacing and other activities help to lessen the worries that come with living in the shelter. The trick is to keep the senses within the equatorial lines, to find the "gray area" between sensory vitality (which can include hearing voices) and walking around in a stupor. A desire for balance is evident in other aspects of shelter life, including the benefits of working in "international waters" when bargaining with one's colleagues and the perceived need to keep a certain distance from others. In the realm of economics, relations, and the senses alike, the residents of the shelter tend to work toward points of "equilibrium," which often come down to a sense of stasis. The stasis, which makes a good deal of sense given how much is impermanent and transient in their lives, tends to grow more fundamental the longer people stay in the shelter.

How does all this compare to the act of experiencing? Although experience and struggling along are not mutually exclusive categories, in which the elements of one would imply the absence or negation of corresponding elements in the other, the two processes do involve distinct aesthetic, temporal, and phenomenal features. Experience entails an aesthetics of integration, coherence, renewal, and transcendent meaning—of tying things together through time. A good day for someone who experiences might be one in which there is a novel integration of personal undertakings, a tale to be told bordering on the adventuresome. The features of such a day build on the stuff of novelty, *employment* transformation, emplotment, and movement. A good day for someone who struggles along, in contrast, might be a smooth one, where nothing much happens, where a few bucks are earned, where the voices are not too bad, where pressure is relieved through pacing, and where there are enough cigarettes to last the day. The ingredients of such a day draw from the forces of expediency, equilibrium, and stasis.

Sitting in the same place for several hours each day has its consequences. The temporal order of experience, involving as it does a cumulative layering of events that builds to a whole greater than its parts, proceeds along narrative lines of an Aristotelian bent. The gist of experience is that it goes beyond the situation at hand. The temporal order of struggling along, in contrast, involves a succession of engagements, which can include a constant but purely episodic unfolding of events. In the shelter, economic concerns, the press of everyday distractions, and a tactical mode of agency directs the struggles toward temporally finite forms in which future, present, and past need not have much to do with one another.

The phenomenal plane of experience is a thoroughly reflexive one; to experience is to engage in a process of perception, agency, and reflection that is couched in mindful introspection. Struggling along also entails a firm sense of interiority and reflexivity, but the reflections are not as intense as they are with experience. The distracting sights and sounds of the building, which draw or drag a person in different directions, prompt an acutely tactile mode of perception with little room or need to introspect or to contemplate. Day in, day out, things happen much more with the retina, on the skin of the eardrums, and in the tips of the fingers than in any detached haven of mind or body. Experience implies a contained, integrative, and occasionally transcendent adaptation of sensations, images, and lessons; struggling along entails a diffuse and external rain of distractions that prompts more a retreat from the world than an incorporation or an assimilation of its parts.

What occasions the differences? While the disabling troubles of mental illness surely play a role here, it is a set of specific political, social, cultural, and environmental forces, rather than any inherent will or disposition, that leads people to either experience or struggle along.[17] Both processes are patterned by longstanding cultural orientations, strengthened through a lifetime's interactions, such as a sense of personhood as something unique, interior, and well-contained. Yet different formations of time, space, and agency are also at work. Whereas experience derives from environments that offer a lasting sense of privacy, in which a person can dwell within his or her own world for some length of time, acts of struggling along are borne of extensively public spaces, with agency taking shape through constant concerns with one's surroundings. Those concerns can contribute to an episodic orientation toward time, with each incidence taking precedence over any larger temporal context, as well as to the need, at times, to stop the rush of events and find some point of equilibrium or stasis. Much of the difference thus rests on the kind of environment in which a person lives: a condition of permanence, detachment, and security gives rise to a process which entails, among other things, a sense of transcendence, of going out into the world and so be transformed through those movements; a state of unsettledness, unrest, and constant engagement, in turn, necessitates the act of holding onto a word or a Bible to get through the day.

Each of these ways of being are context-dependent, with the contexts themselves framed by a mix of political and economic forces. In the shelter, struggling along relates directly to a politics of displacement, to a world of acutely public spaces, and to an economics of exchanges and ragtag collectibles. Living in the shelter for any length of time prompts a way of being that enables most people to attend to these concerns.

When the context changes, so do the features of one's life. Henry, for instance, spends a lot of time away from the building. Son of a New Orleans doctor, he prefers smart clothing and "proper" people and long walks through Boston. "Tension builds if you stay in one place all day," he says, "whether you're mentally ill or not." He typically walks about five miles each day, drifting from the park to Newbury Street to the Fenway, and returns around five o'clock to speak of his adventures. "I kissed a woman on the lips today," he said one evening. "She was sitting on a bench, and she was crying, and so I kissed her. Now she wants to know where I live." As Heidegger might put it, the kiss befalls Henry, strikes him, overwhelms and transforms him. He goes along a way. The way leads through a landscape. The journey through this landscape, with its landmarks, education, and suspenses, is what we call experience. Like Henry, a few other residents, principally those who are new to the streets and spend a lot of time away from the building, also carry on in continued reference to a constellation of inwardness, hermeneutical depth, renewal, and narrative pacings of time. A quite different constellation of speaking, moving, sensing, and remembering takes form, however, among the majority of those who spend most of their time in the building, making do with day-to-day contingencies.

The presence of two distinct ways of being, with their own defining features, conditions, and constraints, suggests that anthropologists need to rethink their approaches toward the everyday. The ordinary-language notion of experience as the phenomenal, palpable charge of life will probably thrive in anthropology as long as the metaphysic motivating it has its uses—as long, that is, as practice opposes theory and the sensate parries meaning. But for those who get their hands dirty figuring out what the process of experience might imply, a revaluation of methods and motives is called for. Rather than take experience as an authentic, intensely human, existential given, we need to bracket the category. We need to consider how the word serves rhetorical needs that help carve out a way of looking at the world. And we need to consider how the process itself relates to specific social, cultural, political, and material forces.

For the residents of the shelter, a politics of displacement, an episodic sequence of events, and a world of constant, acutely public transactions contribute to a certain tack in life. Indeed, some of the most fundamental constellations of time, space, and agency behind this and other struggles appear to be changing in the late twentieth century. In the modern industrial era, experience might have seemed an essential part of human nature for some people because its defining features—reflexive depth, temporal integration, and a cumulative transcendence—blended so well with the reigning aesthetics of that age. But the poverty, transience, and contingency that is increasingly coming to characterize life on the fringes of post-industrial societies suggests that experience might become, at least in some circles, a relic of the past.

NOTES

Fieldwork at the shelter, conducted while I was an NIMH post-doctoral research fellow in the Department of Social Medicine, Harvard Medical School (Grant #MH1-8006) was linked to the McKinney Research Demonstration Project at Boston, directed by Stephen Goldfinger, M.D. (see Ware et al. 1992). This essay, which appeared in a slightly different version in *American Anthropologist*, benefited from comments from the project's ethnographic team—Norma Ware, Byron Good, Tara AvRuskin, and Joshua Breslau—as well as from Arthur Kleinman, Terri O'Nell, Lindsay French, Jamie Saris, Tracy McGarry, Toni Tugenberg, and other members and affiliates of the Department of Social Medicine, Harvard Medical School. Editorial advice from Barbara and Dennis Tedlock, comments from members of the Department of Anthropology, University of California, Santa Cruz, who heard a version of this paper in February, 1994, and critical reviews from Vincent Crapanzano, Kim Hopper, Don Pollock, and an anonymous reviewer were exceptionally helpful. Thanks as well to the shelter's residents and staff, and to Michael Jackson for including this essay in the present volume.

1. As set forth in Deleuze's essay "Nomad Thought" in *The New Nietzsche*, edited by David Allison (New York: Delta, 1977), and in *A Thousand Plateaus*, coauthored by Felix Guattari (Minneapolis: University of Minnesota Press, 1987).

2. See, for example, Bruner 1986, Jackson 1989, Wikan 1991, Kleinman and Kleinman 1991, and DelVecchio Good et al. 1992:199.

3. See Lévy-Bruhl 1938; Hallowell 1955; Lienhardt 1961; Leenhardt 1979; Crapanzano 1977; and Kleinman and Kleinman 1991.

4. See Geertz (1986:373), for instance. The private aspects of experience make some wary of experiential approaches in anthropology. Those critical of such approaches tend to question the legitimacy of the research more than the universality and relevance of the concept. Finding that experience denotes a subjective realm that can only be poorly comprehended, they uphold the view that experience is interior, private, and ubiquitous.

5. See DelVecchio Good et al. 1992:200; Jackson 1989; Bruner 1986.

6. See Williams (1983:127–28), who notes that the concept of "culture" holds a similar attraction.

7. Heidegger is drawing on the fact that *Erfahrung* comes from the Old High German *infaran*, to travel, traverse, pass through, to reach or arrive at (see Needham 1972:171).

8. Taylor holds that a narrative orientation to life is "inescapable" (1989:47). Becker (1979), Rosaldo (1986), and Good (1993) offer three studies that systematically inquire into the forms of, and conditions for, narrativity in, respectively, Javanese, Ilongot, and Turkish societies.

9. All this raises a question. How can one conduct a phenomenology of a group, particularly one that has quite diverse backgrounds, concerns, and futures? My response, which is a somewhat unsatisfactory one, is to attend to the dominant concerns of the group, while bearing in mind its diversity and heterogeneity. As it is, the ubiquity of regulations, the constancy of routines, and the commonality of afflictions (fear, hearing voices) lead shelter residents to lead quite similar lives.

10. Much of my research, conducted from March 1991 to August 1992, involved participant-observation in the daily life of the shelter and its surroundings several afternoons and evenings each week. Because I could not and did not want to use a tape recorder, and structured interviews made both residents and staff uncomfortable, I spent much of my time hanging about, listening to and entering into conversations, and then immediately finding a place to write down the content of these exchanges. See Aviram 1990, Goldfinger 1990, Dennis et al. 1991, and the special issue on homelessness in the *New England Journal of Public Policy* (1992, Vol. 8, no.1) for recent assessments of homelessness among persons considered to be mentally ill.

11. Consequently, my research interested the shelter manager in part because he wanted to learn if there was any way he could make shelter life less accommodating to his guests.

12. Foucault 1977; Desjarlais n.d.1.

13. The words in quotes, and the idea of "strategies" and "tactics," come from de Certeau 1984; see Desjarlais n.d.2.

14. The common desire to be alone in the company of others compares to Corin's (1990) finding that many people with schizophrenia seek out a stance of "positive withdrawal" toward their worlds. Estroff (1981) and Strauss and Carpenter (1981) come to similar conclusions in their studies of mental illness.

15. Anne Lovell writes of the "permanent temporal dislocation" common to New York city's homeless street people. "I feel dead," one man tells her, "'cause that's what dead people do. They never change. . . . it's all been like one god damn long humble day." "It's a one-day-at-a-time-Sweet-Jesus kind of thing," says another (Lovell 1992:98,94). Gounis (1992), in turn, writes insightfully about the institutional routines of several "homeless" shelters in New York City.

16. See Ricoeur 1984, Carr 1986.

17. I find that acts of struggling along have more to do with environmental and political forces than with the vagaries of mental illness because I know of other people who must contend with similar afflictions (including the "deinstitutionalized" residents of a halfway house where I worked in the mid-1980s) yet whose lives are organized much more along the lines of "experience." To hear voices, feel paranoid, and think and act differently than others can have a tremendous and often disabling effect on a person's life, but the environment in which one lives determines so much more.

REFERENCES

Aviram, Uri. 1990. "Community Care of the Seriously Mentally Ill: Continuing Problems and Current Issues." *Community Mental Health Journal* 26:69–88.
Ayto, John. 1990. *Bloomsbury Dictionary of Word Origins.* London: Bloomsbury.
Barnhart, Robert. 1988. *The Barnhart Dictionary of Etymology.* New York: H. W. Wilson.
Becker, A. L. 1979. "Text-Building, Epistemology, and Aesthetics in Javanese Shadow Theatre." In *The Imagination of Reality,* ed. A. L. Becker and A. A. Yengoyan, 211–243. Norword, NJ: Ablex.
Boas, Franz. 1940 [1887]. "The Study of Geography." In *Race, Language, and Culture,* 639–647. New York: Macmillan.
Bruner, Edward. 1986. "Experience and Its Expressions." In *The Anthropology of Experience,* ed. V. Turner and E. Bruner, 3–32. Urbana: University of Illinois Press.
Carr, David. 1986. *Time, Narrative, and History.* Bloomington: Indiana University Press.
Corin, Ellen. 1990. "Facts and Meaning in Psychiatry: An Anthropological Approach to the Lifeworld of Schizophrenics." *Culture, Medicine and Psychiatry* 14:153–188.
Crapanzano, Vincent. 1977. "Introduction." In *Case Studies in Spirit Possession,* ed. V. Crapanzano and V. Garrison, 1–40. New York: John Wiley.
de Certeau, Michel. 1984. *The Practice of Everyday Life.* Berkeley: University of California Press.
DelVecchio Good, Mary-Jo, Brodwin, Paul, Good, Byron, and Kleinman, Arthur. 1992. "Epilogue." In *Pain as Human Experience: An Anthropological Perspective,* ed. M-J. DelVecchio Good, P. Brodwin, B. Good, and A. Kleinman, 198–207. Berkeley: University of California Press.
Dennis, Deborah, Buckner, John, Lipton, Frank, and Levine, Irene. 1991. "A Decade of Research and Services for the Homeless Mentally Ill Persons: Where Do We Stand?" *American Psychologist* 46:1129–1138.

Desjarlais, Robert. 1992. *Body and Emotion: The Aesthetics of Illness and Healing in the Nepal Himalayas*. Philadelphia: University of Pennsylvania Press.

———. n.d.1. "Power and Obscurity." Paper presented at the 93rd Annual Meetings of the American Anthropological Association, Washington DC, November 1993.

———. n.d.2. "The Office of Reason." Paper presented at the 94th Annual Meetings of the American Anthropological Association, Atlanta, GA, November 1994.

Dewey, John. 1926. *Experience and Nature*. Chicago: Open Court Publishing Company.

Estroff, Sue. 1981. *Making It Crazy*. Berkeley: University of California Press.

Faulkner, William. 1986 [1936]. *Absalom, Absalom!* New York: Vintage.

Foucault, Michel. 1977. *Discipline and Punish*. New York: Pantheon.

———. 1978. *The History of Sexuality, Volume 1: An Introduction*. New York: Vintage.

Gadamer, Hans-Georg. 1975. *Truth and Method*. New York: Crossroad Publishing Corporation.

Geertz, Clifford. 1986. "Making Experience, Authoring Selves." In *The Anthropology of Experience*, ed. V. Turner and E. Bruner, 373–380. Urbana: University of Illinois Press.

Goldfinger, Stephen. 1990. "Introduction: Perspectives on the Homeless Mentally Ill." *Community Mental Health Journal* 26:387–390.

Good, Byron. 1993. *Medicine, Rationality, and Experience*. Cambridge: Cambridge University Press.

Gounis, Kostas. 1992. "Temporality and the Domestication of Homelessness." In *The Politics of Time*, ed. H. Rutz, 127–149. Washington, DC: American Ethnological Society Monograph Series, Number 4.

Hallowell, A. Irving. 1955. "The Self and Its Behavioral Environment." In *Culture and Experience*, 172–183. Philadelphia: University of Pennsylvania Press.

Heidegger, Martin. 1971. On the Way to Language. New York: Harper and Row.

Hopper, K., Susser, E., and Conover, S. 1986. "Economies of Makeshift: Deindustialization and Homelessness in New York City." *Urban Anthropology* 14:183–236.

Jackson, Michael. 1989. *Paths toward a Clearing: Radical Empiricism and Ethnographic Inquiry*. Bloomington: Indiana University Press.

Kleinman, Arthur, and Kleinman, Joan. 1991. "Suffering and Its Professional Transformation: Toward an Ethnography of Interpersonal Experience." *Culture, Medicine and Psychiatry* 15:275–301.

Leenhardt, Maurice. 1979. *Do Kamo: Person and Myth in the Melanesian World*. Chicago: University of Chicago Press.

Lévy-Bruhl, Lucien. 1938. *L'Expérience Mystique et les Symboles Chez les Primitifs*. Paris: Alcan.

Lienhardt, Godfrey. 1961. *Divinity and Experience: The Religion of the Dinka*. Oxford: Clarendon.

Lovell, Anne. 1992. "Seizing the Moment: Power, Contingency, and Temporality in Street Life." In *The Politics of Time*, ed. H. Rutz, 86–107. Washington, DC: American Ethnological Society Monograph Series, Number 4.

Needham, Rodney. 1972. *Belief, Language, and Experience*. Chicago: University of Chicago Press.

New England Journal of Public Policy. 1992. Special issue on homelessness, Vol. 8, no. 1.

Oakshott, Michael. 1985 [1933]. *Experience and Its Modes*. Cambridge: Cambridge University Press.

Ricoeur, Paul. 1970. *Freud and Philosophy*. New Haven: Yale University Press.

———. 1984. *Time and Narrative*, Volume 1. Chicago: University of Chicago Press.

Rosaldo, Renato. 1986. "Ilongot Hunting as Story and Experience." In *The Anthropology of Experience*, ed. V. Turner and E. Bruner, 97–138. University of Illinois Press.

Scott, Joan. 1991. "The Evidence of Experience." *Critical Inquiry* 17:773–795.

Stocking, George, ed. 1989. *Romantic Motives: Essays on Anthropological Sensibility.* Madison: University of Wisconsin Press.

Strauss, J. S., and Carpenter, W. T. 1981. *Schizophrenia.* New York: Plenum Press.

Taylor, Charles. 1989. *Sources of the Self: The Making of the Modern Identity.* Cambridge: Harvard University Press.

Thompson, E. P. 1978. "The Poverty of Theory or an Orrery of Errors." In *The Poverty of Theory and Other Essays.* New York: Monthly Review Press.

Turner, Victor. 1982. *From Ritual to Theatre.* New York: Performing Arts Journal Press.

Ware, Norma, Desjarlais, Robert, AvRuskin, Tara, Breslau, Joshua, Good, Byron, and Goldfinger, Stephen. 1992. "Empowerment and the Transition to Housing for the Homeless Mentally Ill: An Anthropological Perspective." *New England Journal of Health Policy* 8:297–314.

Wikan, Unni. 1991. Toward an Experience-Near Anthropology. *Cultural Anthropology* 6:285–305.

Williams, Raymond. 1979. *Politics and Letters.* London: New Left Books.

———. 1983. *Keywords: A Vocabulary of Culture and Society.* Oxford: Oxford University Press.

The Cosmology of Life Transmission

RENÉ DEVISCH

COMPREHENSION FROM WITHIN

My experience with Yaka people in Southwestern Zaire (1971–74, 1991–) and Kinshasa (1986–) has led me away from current postmodern trends that aim at a self-conscious, narrative account of a dialogical or bargained reality. Fundamentally, my perspective does not involve a rendition of a dialogical encounter as such with Yaka people, nor of their experience—I am not speaking for them—but aims more radically at disclosing the "bodily" ways in which people create and engage in a culture from within its own genuine sources. Yet surely, since I write at some physical and cultural remove from them, I portray processed visions of their world. Indeed, while my assumptions and questions in the field may sometimes be at odds with those of my hosts, we both firmly believe in the reality and probity of our affective and intellectual ventures (cf. Boddy 1989:356ff.). I do consider my ethnographic endeavor very much as an esthetic and moral experience, grounded in participant observation or rather observational participation, and reciprocal sympathy, friendship. To overcome the traps of prejudiced interactions of a colonial and missionary type I opted for an intensive participation in the daily life scene and activities of the Yaka. In the village setting, my attempt was to adopt a status of full member-ship, not that of a visitor or a guest, becoming "part of the goings on in the village, immersed in its sights and smells and sounds" (Jackson 1989: 7). Most of my contacts and information dealt with the worlds of oral lore, kinship, hunting, the councils of elders, divinatory seances, initiatory and healing dramas, and the cosmology. These have increasingly become the scenes of our joint ventures, of both a passionate, affective, and intellectual nature.

I see respect, genuine sympathy, participation, and associative dialogue as the golden means to acquaintance from inside the culture, that is, to "knowl-edge through transcendence of the self in the other," as Janice Boddy (1989:358) has put it. Indeed, this kind of gnosis or search and inquiry through acquaintance with someone (cf. Mudimbe 1988:ix) includes also a very Yaka perspective on knowledge gained and shared through sociality. As a man, I had no unbiased entry to the female life-world, but I might have a sense of it through the experience that my wife Maria conveyed to me, as we shared the last four months of field work, as well as through my acquaintance with the healing cults. Yet I venture to say that I am making major dimensions of Yaka culture accessible within the framework of its own arrangements, within the terms of its own epistemological locus (cf. Mudimbe 1988:x).

Elders, diviners, and healers have forcefully initiated me in their world of intensive, esthetic, and moral exploration into the opaque layers of the imaginary register and into the multilayered fabric of symbols and acknowledged intersubjective structures (De Boeck and Devisch 1994, Devisch 1988, 1990, 1991, 1993a, b). They have conveyed to me an eagerness to capture its often elusive signs and forces in the daily encounter and the life-world, offering ever new and renewed virtualities of meaning and empowering. Symbolic (re)production and the concomitant recycling of forces constitute the crux of senior men's almost daily endeavor. For example, on opening a council of elders, a pair of senior men solemnly proclaim, dancing all the while to the rhythm of their clapping hands: *Thuna ha muyidika maambu*, "We are here to generate things." Their rhetorics are mostly of a metaphoric kind, and may culminate in a melodious song. Ritual drama is even more creative and body-centered. Healing ritual develops a bodily, sensuous, motoric, affective, and musical approach to the life-world. It is not a deciphering of a message, nor a recollection or commemoration. Healing ritual aims at emancipating the initiate's destiny, that is, at clearing and enhancing lines of force in the wider weave of family and life-world of his or her genuine history. Such experiences led me away from regarding culture as a mere text or program. I became acquainted with the Yaka view of culture as a fabric, a patterning of continual (re)generation: culture is present in its creation rather than in its statics—a very postmodern position with which I am in agreement. It inspires or molds the healing drama as a womb-like regeneration of meaning and forces in the patient, therapy management, and the life-world. The healing drama is the texture that engenders new meaning, new relationships, renewed contact with the life source to reinforce the patient, while reasserting the basic rule of exchange (matrimonial, avuncular, and so on) that transmits life and sustains ritual rebirth.

I contend that my allegiance to the Yaka people makes my swirling field experience into a centered practice and effort committed to acquaintance and comprehension from within, in which no particular creation of social science or western medical understanding is taken as prior or determining, or as the principle to which all else must be reduced. Inasmuch as the interpretive method has grown out of the field experience and of the very nature of ritual practices, I consider it an internal, phenomenological approach with an emphasis on production of meaning and regeneration of forces. My internal approach and emphasis on metaphoric, hence metamorphic production is meant to render the subject's genuine presence at, and presencing of, the heart and womb of Yaka culture. Rituals do not consist so much of a body of knowledge and practices, but of an ongoing, basically self-generative practice.

My account is meant to decipher the texture of practices and ritual at a level that is self-generative and that reaches beyond its mere reproduction in the authoritative speech and institutions in the center of diurnal village life. Rituals divine a most original, wonderful, and practical insight into human reality and the world. While opening himself up to this source of culture, and "transcribing" the metaphoric and imaginary fabric of ritual transformation and healing, and transposing that deep level of Yaka culture, the anthropologist cannot avoid putting his assumptions at risk.

TRANSVALUATION OF FIELDS

Yaka oral lore, cults, and ritual activities depict the seasonal, lunar, and life-cyclical changes in the cosmos and in the plant and animal worlds as fundamentally processes of life transmission. To the Yaka it is self-evident that the processes of conception, flowering, fruit-bearing or birth, ripening or maturation, decay, death, and rebirth are never ending and bring together both the sexes and the successive generations. Because the cosmic world order is less tangible than the social patterns of gender, descent, marriage, and labor division, there is, in major rituals, a pervasive transvaluation (see Flax 1990) of the social and corporeal onto the cosmic. It is not so much "representation" that orders the life-world and gender relations, but an intertwining of forces and meaning pertaining to the realms of gender, kin, and life transmission, with the cosmological fields of regenerative forces. This indirect cosmological portrayal of gender and life transmission, since it is so encompassing and very much acted out in an unspoken way in daily practice, gains the quasi-autonomous status of a self-evident world order. Space is not so much shaped by a visual journey or by a will to power that would gradually turn the life-world into a man-made layout of located forces to subjugate, of pathways and divisions to impose, or of predefined goals to achieve. Space is differentiated through awareness of and participation in various centers and vectors of forces, events, and movements. In discussing these spatial layouts, I mainly render the perspective of men in both their discourse and daily activities. However, the homestead and the home, as well as the cults, display a more maternal sensing, and reembodying of space (see Devisch 1993a: ch. 5).

In this essay I argue the following points: First, concerning public daily life, the social categories of maleness, patrilineal descent, and seniority are correlated with lineal order, uprightness, and verticality, while femaleness, uterine filiation, and mediatory roles are correlated with a cyclical and concentric space-time order. The asymmetric attributions of gender reflect and also act as a paradigm for the cosmological field: they undergird the interplay between the agnatic life force (*ngolu*) and the uterine vital flow (*mooyi*), and also between the life-bearing processes of bloodshed in the hunt and of cooking in the home. Gender arrangements and categories are associated with one or another of the various processes of plant growth—rising of sap, flowering, bearing and ripening of fruit. There are, moreover, appropriate foods and medications for men as distinct from the ones for women. Second, particular space-time aspects that are related to the various habitats of fauna or flora, to the lunar and female cycles, or to colors are imbued with motifs of death, (re)generation, (re)birth, and sexual maturation. The same motifs are the core of the transition rituals of boyhood, political enthronement, and funeral. Third, dance is a practical and gendered means of world-making through rhythm, melody and song giving the body over to the senses and the life-world. In dance women celebrate the love of life: it is a quest to transmit, enhance, and optimize life. It makes one fundamental statement: that this world is prolific, all-encompassing, composite, interrelated, and thus accessible. The weaving of body, group, and world makes tangible, tasteable, visible—concretely approachable—the fact that life is this world, and is lived as an interactive alignment of lingering, actual or lasting power and affect. It is the weaving, by means of the body-senses, of bodies with each other and of bodies with the world.

HORIZONTAL AND VERTICAL SPACE

Movements through horizontal and vertical space offer a weave, rather than a map, for gender differences and their mediation. Culturally encoded meanings and values related to such pairs as upstream/downstream, present/past, dry/wet, cold/hot, bitter/sweet, open/closed, accessible/concealed, raw/cooked, propitious/ominous, right/left, light/darkness, day/night, visible/invisible, and life/death are all components or conceptual underpinnings of this spatial ordering and of the gender-appropriate activities that are associated with the various spatial domains.

1. *The cardinal points of cosmological space originate in a specific and practical interaction with the surrounding life-world.* They are not fixed in reference to some objective, "universally" valid, criteria. For example, when standing, Yaka men indicate the direction of the rising sun with the right arm and the setting sun with the left. In such a position the individual will have a horizon (*ndilu,* "border, limit") both in front and behind. The courses of the great rivers in Kwaango land—the Waamba, Twaana, and Kwaango—offer the Yaka specific points of orientation. Needless to say, these orientations do not necessarily correspond to a set of objective geographical directions established mechanically in relation to abstract points—as with the aid of a compass, for example. North, south, east, and west are a terminology alien to Yaka culture. In practice the Yaka define the directions of the rivers with reference to the heavenly course of the sun from dawn to dusk. Folktales and ritual texts, like the elders, explain that the sun rises upstream of the great rivers and sets downstream. The sun emerges from the earth in the morning after having traversed its breadth by following a subterranean watercourse. It exits the earth at the source of the large

rivers. Upstream and rising sun—situated toward the east—all acquire in this manner a significative value relative to diurnal origin as well as to masculine rule. During the accession to power of a political chief at the local or regional levels, the handing over of white clay or kaolin coming from this Luunda cradle to the chief, followed by his anointment with it, contributes to his ritual "birth" into power. The anointment confers on him the status of sovereign ruler and supreme mediator of animal and human fertility (see Devisch 1988). Just as upstream and river source connote, in the male view, the masculine origin of life, conversely the water flowing downstream connotes the law of exogamy and the succession of generations, as expressed in the proverb: "As water does not flow upwards to its source, so the man does not marry his mother." In other words, the descendant does not spill his life-giving capacity into the ascendant. The sorcerer who takes the lives of his descendants by withdrawing the life which he himself had previously transmitted to them is furthermore likened to an incestuous person. A proverb applied to both the sorcerer and the committer of incest declares that for such persons "the source and mouth of the stream are situated at the same point on the Yingubu plains."

In folktales, the notions downstream (*kubaanda,* "below") and setting sun—as does also west—signify a decline or end, but one pregnant with a new beginning; the male perspective associates this world with the onset of motherhood. In the evening the sun appears to submerge into the tributary of the great rivers. Some oral lore associates this tributary with the Zaire river, more than six days walk from the northern border of Yaka land, or with the "river of salt" (the Atlantic Ocean). Folktales report that, with the exception of paramount chiefs and powerful ritual specialists, commoners may be stricken with blindness when reaching the place where the sun sets. Here also, it is thought, life is extinguished, and from this site come death and its agent, evil sorcery. According to popular narratives, the forests of the river valleys are, by extension, populated by nonancestral spirits (*m-fu*) and monstrous dwarfs (*yitsuutsu*) roaming around to molest (*-tsuutsa*) the wayward individual or drag him down to the underworld where he will visit with the ancestral shades.

Every act that has no further bearing on the present situation is carried downstream, as is every stain from which the newly circumcised, the initiate, the patient, or the bereaved ritually rids him or herself by bathing in the stream or wading upstream toward its source. The corpse is likewise buried with its gaze fixed in the direction of the water's descent. Tradition recommends that one lie in the same direction when retiring at night; ideally, one faces the north when getting up in the morning, so that the rising sun is on the right hand.

Front and back, left and right offer the cardinal points. The south is opposed to the north, as is behind to front, the shadow to that which is clearly perceived, and as strange or dreaded phenomena are contrasted to that which is known and controllable. The oral lore describing the great migrations relates that the Kwaango river was crossed from the left bank. It is striking, furthermore, that the Yaka groups tend to consider people living to the left bank of the great river of reference to be backward; its inhabitants are dubbed "the people who eat dogs"—in other words, those who do not practice exogamy, held to be the distinctive human trait.

These lineal directions and flows in the cosmological order, as they are depicted in the folktales, display a concentric and cyclical pattern in the female realms of the conjugal home and of the house of seclusion in the healing cults. Source and mouth, high and low, upstream and downstream, left and right meet in the initiand couched in fetal position on its bed: the positions of ascendant and descendant, male and female intertwine in the androgynous identity of the initiand in a process of self-gestation. In Yaka symbolism, the same positions fuse in the couple in conjugal union.

2. *Village, forest, and savanna, day and night, as well as origin and end are key polar concepts that differentiate between the realms of inhabited and noninhabited space.* The distinction between "village" (*hata*) and "forest" (*n-situ*) is primarily of an ontological rather than a geographical or sociological order. Village corresponds to the realm of life, day, the known, organized, and licit, in opposition to forest, the realm of the dead, night, the obscure, unknown, uncommon, where the ancestral shades, spirits, and forces that deflate or empower mix, where toxic and edible plants grow side by side, and both illness and healing find their sources. In other words village designates the space of the *societas,* the organization of life for the good of all, the relations of subordination, familiarity, and mutual aid within a particular group, that is, their recognized activities and social bonds. Those persons forming a community or hamlet in a village aid each other in working the fields, gather at the well to steep manioc, launder clothes or draw water at the stream, and may well travel together or attempt to resettle in the same neighborhood when migrating to the capital city of Kinshasa. Domestic animals belong to that same village realm: chickens, pigeons, goats (approximately three to every household), and pigs (a third again the number of goats). They serve especially as means of exchange and symbolization.

The category "forest," in contrast, is applied either to the fantasy or imaginary realm including people and spirits one has no relation with—the foreigner and all monstrous spirits—or to the domain of the wild, including the predatory animals, the evil sorcerers and the revengeful deceased who are kept out of the ancestral world. In the eyes of the Yaka, any individual who does not figure among one's acquaintances and who lives in a distant region—that is, far enough away such that one does not go there to contract a marriage or exchange goods or services—is considered *n-ndzeendza,* literally, "the separate." It is, however, especially the deviant plotting in secret who is counted as a forest dweller: such include the sorcerer, thief, or individual who violates the rights of another, in particular matrimonial rights. When an illness or a disorder in the village life is held to stem from some illicit act, it is understood that the forest has taken hold of or encroached upon the dominion of the village. Popular fantasies hold that shades, sorcerers, and monstrous figures live in the twilight of the forest. Night and forest are opposed to the social visibility of the *societas* and infringe on the inhabitable space: one presses close to companions on the dark moonless evenings. A solitary stroller at night draws suspicion. For this reason the Christian missionary, for example, in the habit of taking the air at twilight, became suspect of seeking to draw the deceased into his service.

Only men may enter the forested areas and marshlands. The forest galleries are situated in the humid valleys of the great rivers and shelter the majority of the larger game animals (greater herbivores); hunting them is a highly valued activity restricted to the men. Similarly, only men may penetrate the marshlands bordering the streams. Braving snakes, they there cultivate bananas and tap palm wine. Secondary forests are to be found on the plateau bordering the forest galleries. It is on this plateau and on the hillsides flanking the valleys that each family unit engages in subsistence agriculture. The cultivation of crops (*sodi*) on burnt-off land makes it constantly necessary to relocate the fields and consequently renders impossible any demarcation (*ndilu*) of the field being worked (*yilanga*), other than the name of the valley or forest where it is found.

The sandy savanna plateau (*tseki*) covered with herbaceous vegetation is recognized as a feminine milieu. The women engage in various sorts of gathering on these steppes and savannas. The men do not venture onto the plains except for the collective hunts carried out during the dry season when the grasslands are burned. As the savanna gives way to denser vegetation, it is usual to distinguish between the wooded steppes or secondary forest (*mabwaati*) and the more lightly wooded savanna (*bikwaati*), where grasses are more abundant. Vegetation thus readily serves as an indicator of seasonal differences.

3. Certain zones and activities assure the transition or mediation between the realms of village and forest. Inasmuch as they allow transition, they are propitious. Thus the outskirts of the village serve as a meeting place in the evening for youth where recreational sex and in particular joking relations (*-mokasana*) have free reign. Again, it is at the periphery of the village, or at the stream where the villagers bathe, that the numerous healing and purification rites, as well as the phases of seclusion and reintegration belonging to the rites of passage, are held, frequently at twilight or at dawn. In these transitional realms men and women mix freely, in contrast with gender and age arrangements observed at diurnal assemblies held in the center of the village.

Menstruation is associated with the transitional zone at the edge of the village, where in former times women had their little houses for menstruation; it is there that garbage is disposed. Unprocessed goods from the bush— firewood or plants—are brought in, although not on the regular paths, and left at the edge. Once disassembled, they may be brought into the homestead.

Beyond the village itself, arrangements of space become more and more unmarked. The zone in which the inhabitants live and carry out their activities is called n-totu, "land that yields food." The category is distinct from that of the "chiefdom or territory" (tsi), which groups a particular population under the same traditional political authority. Referring to the tributary relations (-laambula) of that population to the ruling chief to whom they should pay a tribute (n-laambu), the territory is also called n-laambu. Yikoolu designates the familiar region that extends in concentric waves around one's village and within whose limits the adult might move about, or at least not hesitate to do so, in order to engage in matrimonial relations, or to exchange goods or services. Any distance within this familiar region appears to its inhabitants to be significantly shorter than an equivalent distance beyond its bounds. The point of reference here is not one's own domestic space but may depend on any of several possible orientations: the positions of the sun corresponding to the traveler's points of departure and arrival, the number of nights one must spend on the journey, and precise spatial landmarks including related households, chiefly residences, or the homes of diviners or ritual specialists. The rites of puberty, by which pubescent boys prefigure their marital condition, allow them access to the yikoolu. The newly circumcised are permitted to organize dances with masks involving several dozens of the villages in the region during which they strike up ludic relations with girls of similar age.

In the yikoolu, plains and forests are divided into named sections with imprecise and partially overlapping boundaries; the region's rivers and the watercourse serve as the main reference points for locating them. Their partitioning reflects the activities that take place there—hunting, collecting, agriculture—activities which themselves are especially determined by the ecology and types of vegetation to be found in the region. Lineage groups may relate to one another in terms of geographical landscape: rivers, hills, forests, savannas, graves mark the routes of migration and give a stability to the past. The land bears the signs of the sequentiality of the journey and helps to fix the order of successive migrations: the most prestigious group, by referring its deeds to the source of a river or to hills "up high," earns primacy in time. The landscape becomes a cultural one. Lineage names may recall such located deeds. The land tells a story of lineage hierarchy and sustains relations of cooperation, for example, in the seasonal collective battues.

Any area beyond the yikoolu is foreign land: it is usually out of reach for childrearing women and their children. Young marriageable and married men may venture into this area in search of school education or paid labor. Sometimes senior men and women will enter this unknown region to meet with a renowned diviner. On a journey into the foreign land, men walk ahead and women follow. Indeed, the world is open far wider for men than women. The young men who travel to Kinshasa outnumber by far their female peers.

The noninhabited land within one's region, in particular the savanna area, figures as a benevolent transitional zone between related locales as well as

between the genders. An in-married woman is referred to as one who has
followed the path through the savanna. Recreational sex or any seductive
demonstration on the part of a married woman evoke this in-between zone.
Popular imagery situates extramarital relations on the edges of the fields
(n-teetwa sodi); in folktales or palavers, a woman's lover is indicated with the
expression: "he from the top end of her field." Popular judgment thereby
practically excuses the woman for her behavior; however, the offended party
tends to situate the extramarital affair in the conjugal home.

The crossing of paths (phaambwandzila) forms the junction point for all the
partitions and directions of the horizontal space, especially when it is found in
proximity to a village: it links upstream and downstream, the village with
forest, savanna, stream, and fields, hunting tracts and the inhabited space,
different locales with each other, the homestead and the lineage quarter.
Intersections located at some distance from the village, near a spring or stream,
are sites where the solitary wanderer is likely to be whisked underground by
ghosts, or where he may reach or reemerge from the underworld. The ground
of such crossings is trod by all inhabitants of the village without distinction; it
is here that the footprints are superposed (-dyaatasana) and that misfortune
may settle itself upon the individual, or may be chased away. The numerous
rites of purification and incorporation intentionally make use of these points in
order to exclude the participants from the inhabited space as it was before and
to reintegrate them into it after cleansing. It will also be seen that a crossing of
footpaths constitutes a junction in the vertical spatial ordering between high
and low, surface and underground, and between the living and the dead. It is
at a crossroads, at the outskirts of the village space, that foreign merchants set
up their business: it is here that cassava and peanuts are compiled and packed
for trading, when very rarely a truck comes along.

COSMOLOGICAL PORTRAYAL OF GENDER

Certain mythic statements or ritual activities depict reproductive union between sun, moon, and earth, or between fire and water. Transposed onto the
human domain, this macrocosmical union sets the scene for depicting both
gender differences and their surpassing in the transmission of life. The rainbow
palm, parasol, and banana trees, the he-goat, the earthen jar set in the fork of
a three-pronged stick, the cock crowing at dawn, the laying hen, and the
termite mound all serve as cosmological icons of life-bearing sexuality.

1. *Palm tree and earthen jar are metaphors of the world.* The oil (mbati or
tsaamba) and the raffia (yiimba) palms, which grow both in the village and the
forest, are rich in cosmological and sexual symbolism. When the tree has
reached an age of approximately fourteen years, its trunk may attain a height of
eight meters or more: it becomes smooth, except at the base and immediately
under its sphere-shaped crown of abundant leaves. The buds of the crown

successively engender female and then male inflorescences; by bearing these simultaneously, the palm tree fecundates itself. The clusters of palm nuts require six months to mature. As soon as the whitish sap of the raffia palm seeps from the trunk and is collected in a calabash, it begins to ferment and produces palm wine, a drink highly prized by the men. This sap is gathered either by making an incision in the stem of a male cluster or by cutting the trunk at the base of a leaf. In certain narratives the cluster of red nuts nested in the center of the leafy crown symbolizes the sun placed in the center of the firmament, as well as the paramount Luunda ruler, regional dynasts, and vassals. The trunk of the palm tree denotes the junction between the earth, where one stands, and the firmament. The azimuth, the vertical link between the sun at its zenith (which bears male connotations) and the earth's surface (which bears female connotations), is signified by the long, smooth trunk of the parasol tree that grows on fallow land. It is also represented by the trunk of the palm tree as well as of the banana plant which produces a lengthy inflorescence curved down toward the ground and strikingly colored with violet and reddish-brown shades.

The palm tree is first an icon of the diurnal life-bearing journey of the sun. The sap rising up within the trunk and oozing from the male inflorescence is associated with the rising sun. The sun itself is considered as a body of water emerging from the spring which is the source of the great rivers of Yaka land. Both the sun's trajectory and the rainbow's arch are said to outline or demarcate the heavens. At the height of its heavenly course, the sun may sometimes "boil over" and flood the earth with a downpour, especially when it appears in its rainbow form, *khongolu*, as the rainbow-serpent *n-kongolu*. At the moment of flowering the palm tree fertilizes the inflorescence with its white sap. The Yaka believe that through fermentation (*fula*), the whitish inflorescence is transformed. This is their way of saying that the male flower-cluster is changed into the female inflorescence, thus producing the growth of a bunch of red palm nuts. The rising of sap is seen as a kind of fermentation which results in the bearing of the red fruits at the top of the trunk. Once ripened, the reddish palm oil may be extracted from the nuts through a laborious process of cooking done by men. Thus the sun, which at its height seems to boil over onto the earth, is metaphorically associated with the maturation of the palm tree, its flowering, and the effusion of sap.

The palm tree, moreover, metaphorically depicts how much the genitor and genitrix—like the initiate—tap from a maternal source of all life. The emergence of the palm nuts and the movement of the sap downward in the palm tree and back into the earth for cooking or gestation serve as metaphors of pregnancy. In the rites enthroning the political titleholder and in the healing cults, the macrocosmic significance of the palm tree is transferred to the seclusion house and to the initiate's body. The *khita* or *ngoombu* initiate, for example, is returned to "the egg-like womb of the world" by being confined in the ritual house (De Boeck and Devisch 1994). Through seclusion, the initiate relives the fetal condition, experiencing both gestation and self-generation, *ngoongu,* by sponsoring in his or her body the cross-fertilization of the white (palm) sap and the red life-giving fluid (extracted from palm nut). *Ngoongu* includes the cosmogonic images of "arche," the "arch-mother" or "arch-womb," the primal and ever-renewed generation of life from the egg- or palm tree-like "macrocosmic womb" suspended between the heavenly and subterranean trajectories of sun and moon. In the Yaka worldview, this womb is bounded by the trajectory of the sun, which is thought to be parallel to the great Kwaango river that drains the whole Kwaango basin, a major part of Yaka land. The palm tree thus evokes the unceasing emergence of life when male fecundation "ferments" into maternal potency.

The double-edged sword of the ruler is an icon of the palm tree whose form is depicted in the shape of sword and scabbard. Itself a macrocosmic metaphor for life regenerating itself, the palm tree may well display a "ternary" logic, that is one of mediation overcoming the separation between the realms of heaven and earth, upstream and downstream, white (of the blossom) and red (of the palm nuts, the sun), male and female, polity and autochthony (see Devisch 1988). This symbolism receives an iconic embodiment in the chief's sword of rulership, called "the sword of life and death." As commonly interpreted, the sword, wrapped in a leopard pelt or brandished in the Luunda war dance, recalls the bloody Luunda invasion. It is a long, double-edged sword, with two parallel lines engraved in the middle and over its whole length and with a pointed, spherical metal hilt. The blade and hilt thus evoke the mythical and virile *kyandzangoombi* python inhabiting the trunk of the palm; the parallel lines represent the palm sap that first rises within and then, after fermentation, oozes down the trunk. The sword's scabbard is indeed shaped like a palm tree; it depicts a vagina-cum-uterus. Male and female connotations are thus joined in sword and scabbard. As such, the sword stands for the chief's mediating (ternary) function: he combines male and female attributes and metaphorically represents both himself and his offspring; that is, he is his own life source. His sword is a political weapon and a symbol of his chiefly power over continuity and rebirth, life and death. The act of enthronement, like the chief's sword, transfers the basic metaphor of the palm tree to the Yaka nation. The region under the direct control of the paramount ruler in Yaka land, *Kyaambvu,* can be figuratively depicted as that cluster of palm nuts that is the most central and the closest to the trunk and its original blossom. Other clusters gravitate around this central cluster, and this serves as a metaphor for the various regions and subregions in Yaka land. Like palm nuts, the clusters of villages are axially situated on the stalks that stand for the autochthonous landowners.

The earthen jar (*loondu*) is an icon of the cosmos. Pottery is made exclusively by women who are widowed or whose husbands have left home for a time as migrant workers. In molding a jar from clay, the widowed or celibate potter anticipates a new pregnancy. She forms it in the image of the macrocosm, the universe formed like an egg; she also fashions a neck that depicts the male principle of life transmission. She then allows the jar to dry in the sun and fires it, preferably on an evening when the (male) sun tints the (female) moon with a blood-red hue as it rises above the horizon at the beginning of the lunar cycle.

2. *The hen about to lay and the cock crowing at dawn are core symbols in the cosmology and healing cults.* They introduce the particular ability to surpass the conventional arrangements of vertical and horizontal space. The hen and the cock ensure not only the transition between the forest and the village or between the various familial and domestic spaces—these fowl peck about in all the dwellings without distinction—but also between earth and sky, low and high, and day and night. As a two-legged creature of the domestic realm that cuts across core spatial and temporal divisions, the hen is the optimal symbolic substitute of the human being in mutation. The hen about to lay as well as the crowing cock inspire core metaphors underlying the eclosion of clairvoyance in a mediumistic diviner-to-be (Devisch 1991).

The crowing cock *(khokwa khookula),* and in particular the white-feathered cock with a blood-red comb *(buluundu),* which announces sunrise while standing on one leg, is an icon of the rising sun. By substitution the cock also depicts the seminal hearts of the palm tree, the parasol tree, and the banana plant. Alike diviners, renowned healers are buried with the inflorescence of the palm or parasol tree placed on their head. In ritual context, the crest of the cock and the one claw on which it postures itself metonymically trace the vertical line stretching from the point on which one stands to the firmament above. The pose struck by the cock is named *kataku* and depicts the virile and fecundating erection. At sunrise and sunset while in seclusion, the young newly circumcised initiates, naked and chanting songs of their role in life transmission, are required to hold themselves erect on one leg; the other leg is bent with the sole of the foot resting on the inside of the other knee. Just as the *kataku* position implies virility, a fractured leg instead expresses impotence. Family elders adopt this virile stance when they address the agnatic cult spirits. The guardian and healer of masculine fertility (the *yisidika*) who presides over the numerous rites of puberty proper to the *yikubu* cult, also called *n-khanda,* and who is meant to foster the boys' potency during the circumcision ceremonies, is the same person who practices the ritual art of healing bone fractures. There is another position considered equivalent to the *kataku* posture which consists of pressing the legs against each other and crossing the toes. This gesture, called *-lama,* refers rather to sexual union, to the "union or intertwining of the legs" *(-biindasana maalu),* and to taking possession of the conjugal space.

3. *The trope of color displays gender and moral properties.* By virtue of their capacity to reflect the successive phases of day and night, of heat and coldness, from one sunrise to another and in the various stages of the lunar cycle, the colors red, white, and black serve to symbolize the complementary arrange-

ments of the genders; they also frame the definition and handling of illness, healing, and health. Combined with spatial polarizations, they denote the boundary-trespassing value of fecundation, gestation, and delivery, and the links between generations crossing over death.

Blue (*buundi*) signifies the sun at rest. The sun as it is about to rise is associated with the subterranean world and with what is not erect, with whatever is considered low on the vertical axis, with the river source from whence the sun emerges, or with cold. In this phase it is thought to have a bluish hue, that of water in the shade or of "blackened wood, pulled from the hearth" (*bundyambaawu*). When used in fertility rituals, the *bundyambaawu* connotes the virile member at rest. For curing masculine impotence, it is a piece of a trunk of the banana tree blackened by the fire which serves as a *bundyambaawu*. For circumcision, it is a log extracted from the fire lit near the house of *yifiika*, "mother" of the circumcised, around which the initiates and the whole community have danced through the preceding night. At dawn, the *bundyambaawu* is placed on a path which leads away from the village to the circumcision camp located on the periphery. The most senior of the circumcision candidates is seated straddling the log before undergoing the operation. Shortly before the ceremony and dressed in a red loin-cloth, he would have executed a chiefly dance on the roof of the house while displaying the chiefly sword.

Just as red may evolve from being pure color (*tona*) to fire red (*mbaawu*), it is said that pubescent boys and girls have the inner capacity to grow to full ardor and fertility. The rising sun is associated with the vertical "high up" and with the sky. It is emphasized that the rising sun "feeds or strengthens itself" (*taangwa buditsaatsa*), in that it constitutes its own vital source. That vigor (*khoondzu*) incarnated by the rising sun is what men wish each other when, in the morning, they exchange the red cola nut (*kaasu*), a stimulant. Circumcision or rites of reintegration that conclude an initiation, healing, or mourning period also take place at sunrise. A final step in the reintegration may be arranged for on the roof of the conjugal home, or if necessary on an elevated platform erected in the middle of the village for the occasion. There, initiate and partner are invited to exchange pepper and to "entwine the legs" (*-biindasana maalu*) in a gesture signifying the lifting of the conjugal prohibition. In line with this, ritual vocabulary designates defloration and the first experiences of orgasm with the term *-yoka tona*, that is, "to make the color incandescent," with reference to the sun. According to ritual symbolism, the sun at zenith maintains itself in a constant state of ebullition (*taangwa budifusukidi*): to it are attributed the characteristics of fire (*mbaawu*, a term designating anything that gives off heat or light), and, consequently, it is associated with blood (*meenga*). Fire red is equally identified with upstream—the "above" of the horizontal axis and the east, and further may evolve into an icon of the androgynous principle of autogeneration, after the manner of the crowing cock and the hen about to lay.

In line with this, the sun is assimilated to an origin and a source of heat and force (*ngolu*). Oral lore, in evoking the sun which rises and approaches its zenith (*nyaangu*), describes the ardor (*ndzuundza*) of the conquerors, the great hunters, or those who legitimately seek revenge. One also turns to this metaphor in order to depict high fever, inebriety, or liminal experiences such as parturition, mortal agony, or trance. In situations such as these in which certain limits are exceeded, the color red, considered as self-sustaining, connotes existential completeness. The red of the morning sun, depicted as *tona*, pure color, is the harmonious blending of colors and of spaces. This red similarly indicates a fulfilled and mature human condition. Once news of her pregnancy has been made public, the young wife is adorned with a belt of red pearls, after she has been spat upon with water on her womb. Paramount chiefs monopolize red garments.

Dark reddish brown, *khula*, also labelled *ngula* or *luundu*, evokes longing and readiness for fertility, pregnancy, and the setting sun. The setting sun is also associated with ravines and the downstream direction of rivers, where it enters the earth for its nocturnal subterranean journey. Red takes on an ambivalent value when it is mingled with the white of the moon at the onset of the lunar cycle. During initiatory seclusion the small brownish termitary (*mbaambakhuku*) is suspended from a branch or fastened in a treetop with a liana; the object thus carries, to put it in metaphoric terms, the fetal signification of the setting sun and first moon. The moment the darkening sun disappears over the horizon is in ordinary language expressed with the terms *budisika khula*, "when the sun prepares *khula*." This phrase also applies to the novice preparing a paste by rubbing a section of the red wood of the *n-kula* tree against a wet stone. Mixing it with palm oil he oints his body with this paste. Identified with the fetus bathing in its mother's blood, the novice is therefore required to avoid the sunshine of broad daylight and never leaves the ritual dwelling except at evening. Other prohibitions see to it that values of the setting and rising suns should not contaminate the novice. He must avoid any allusion to spotted animals, for their skins may combine different shades of red or mix red with white. It is also forbidden to have anything which might resemble lightning in the initiate's presence, hence the prohibitions against bringing fire into the cult house, throwing water or allowing a piece of firewood to fall nearby, offering the novice some manioc which during preparation has spilled over into the fire (*luku lwatyaamuki*), or any reference to birds of prey who dive out of the sky, or birds whose plumage or legs are red in color. The setting sun, as well as the night and red clay that are associated with it, connote concealment, subjacency, latency, rest, or gestation. Ritual practices and some folktales allow a glimpse of the following cosmological scheme through their layers of metaphorical transpositions. At twilight the sun descends into the waters downstream and disappears into the earth by way of the ravines (*mbeengi*) to which the sun has conferred its reddish color (*kabeenga*), or by way of the caves (*yitadi*) situated along the water's edge. During the night the sun returns to the upstream side by way of a subterranean river. The reddish clay (*luundu*) collected in the ravines and that which one might find in discarded snail shells or in hollows inside the caves (*muundu*) thus come to depict the earth as a place of gestation.

White is basically associated with kaolin clay. Since kaolin is collected at marshy spots that evoke the cradle from whence the full moon emerges, it carries life source in emergence. It is believed that the moon retires in or rises up from one or another marshy spot near the main river Kwaango. Kaolin is primarily the privilege of the maternal uncle to link up his sister's child with the uterine source of life. In the agnatic line of political titleholders and sodalities, the agnatic role is passed down through the male line, but it needs to be vitalized by the uterine life-flow to gain a capacity to regenerate itself. When a patriarch, a political chief, or the initiate of an agnatic sodality (as, for example, the blacksmith) is close to death, the ancestral kaolin (*pheemba yibati* or *pheemba ya yitsi khulu*) must be applied for at least one night to the erectile muscle behind the scrotum of the dying man. Popular exegesis has it that the hereditary kaolin put near the scrotum of the patriarch in mortal agony absorbs the vital flow or life source which is in the process of escaping the person near death. The kaolin of rulership is transmitted to the successor when he is ritually "born" into his function. It is brought into the home of the new owner at dusk, and, like other ancestral objects (*bisiimba*), it must be protected from the light of day. These ritual items and the kaolin may, however, be found outdoors at the full moon in the case of their owner's illness or of repeated failures in the hunt. White clay is then painted on the cult objects and around the eyes of the ritual figurines, thus repeating one of the gestures that the initiate himself was exposed to during initiation. It is said to "wash" or "distemper" the cult objects: *-kusa pheemba,* or *-yebala pheemba.* As the different names used for it imply, kaolin represents that which revivifies health (*pheemba yakolala baatu*) and sustains longevity (*pheemba yiziingu; pheemba yiziingisa baatu*). The ancestral kaolin further insures an abundance of game (*pheemba yabambisi*). It unifies members of the same homestead or lineage quarter and demarcates them from outsiders. After a family reconciliation or rite of passage in the community, certain patriarchs will spray the kaolin in all directions before kindling the fire and distributing it to all the members. The uncle, or the healer who has confirmed avuncular links with his client, whitewashes the left arm of his "uterine descendants" or the left-hand side of the cult objects with his kaolin in order to enhance the transmission of life from its uterine source. This practice takes place on the occasion of an initiation or its commemoration. Kaolin may also be utilized along with the red *muundu* clay in similar transitional contexts. These two types of earth are different yet complementary, as are the full moon and the setting sun with regard to one another.

Pitch black, *kaphiinda,* is associated with the moonless night: it is a quality associated with charcoal (holu), black ashes, or the darkish-red pearl referred to as *ndiimba*, literally, "stain" (Devisch 1979:132–35). The latter refers to blood-shed or the violent and bloody work of an abusive sorcerer. Red shades off into the value of black when high and low intersect in one of its symbols, as, for example, in the case of lightning, birds of prey, or bloodshed. Charcoal and *ndiimba*, like dark night, and in particular the black of midnight (*katan-kolu*) during which the villagers are in deep sleep and incapable of self-defense, are the marks of the violent and bloody work of abusive sorcery. Ensorcellment that belongs to the black of night is one of illicit violence, inasmuch as the selfish sorcerer appropriates the life of another, bringing the victim to an immutable death of never-ending darkness. Black may be associated with low, cold, the inanimate, and with the darkness of night during the new moon. Articles of kitchen refuse (such as corncobs, banana peels, pressed palm nuts, and so on) that have been blackened over the fire denote "that which can no longer reproduce." These blackened waste elements can be placed alongside the corpse of someone who has succumbed to his own mischievous deeds or to a mysterious disease, or also alongside the corpse of a deformed or sterile individual, in order to prevent the unfortunate being or its defect from ever reappearing among the descendants. The black of night as a trope of degrada-tion, impurity, negative death is a basic constituent of the "ritual arms of war" (*mateenda*). These arms contain charcoal, gun powder (*thuya*, black in color), dark-colored feces whose appearance connotes the decomposition of lost blood, and the blackish and poisonous *loombi* ashes that are obtained by charring a mixture of toxic ingredients in a casserole over the fire. For the popular imagination a sorcerer may appear at the receiving end of his own wrongdoings and thereby kill himself with these *mateenda*: in death-agony his body swells up, discharges black blood, and vomits a substance similar to charcoal. Such a "black death" [my expression] with no after-life (the latter being associated with a white condition) strikes culprits undergoing the poison ordeal. The black of night contrasts with the positive values of white and red. A blood sacrifice in rituals of family reunification and of healing aims at compensating for [or: restoring the] blood shed illegitimately. Then black becomes red, thus recovering its positive qualities of height and heat. The subsequent application of kaolin clay has the capacity to "whitewash, whiten" (*-seemasa*) the stain or defilement (*mbviindu*), to make it "blank." On the ontological level the black/white antinomy, associated with the perversion of red and with the rising sun, serves to designate certain vices. By manipulating this antinomy the group may succeed, for example, in expressing its rejection of the sterile individual when at the death of this person the community seeks to definitively disassociate him or her from society: a banana peel, a corncob, and a piece of sugar cane—all whitish in color—are blackened in the fire, wrapped up, and placed on the buried corpse. This practice expresses the wish that the individual disappear forever.

White and red are in a kind of balance. White, *kaseema,* may positively be associated with lowness, coolness, with fluid or animate life, and with cold and the full moon. It may denote *mooyi,* the uterine life flow that connects each individual through the blood ties with his mother, mother's mother and maternal great-grandmother, with the uterine source of life. As *kaseema* is the polar complement of positive red proper to *buundi* and *mbaawu, mooyi* is the uterine complement of agnatic life force, *ngolu,* when the heat has hardened the bone. Medicines obtained through boiling but administered cool are powerful (*ngolu*). When in denoting the full moon white mixes with the red of the sun— which also means that it is associated with vertical height—it acquires an ambivalent or transitory value. The kaolin clay (*pheemba*) which serves to mediate between high/low, hot/cold, day/night, daylight/darkness, and red/ black neutralizes this ambivalence. Kaolin is used at ritualized moments of transition in the life of an individual, a family, or a community. Finally, white is charged with a negative value, and is defiled or degraded to black, when it connotes the last quarter of the moon, that is, when vanishing moonlight and rising sun, day and night, high and low, are conflated. The smithery manipu- lates the colors black, red, and white: it is an instance of both violation and foundation of cosmic order. The forge (*luufu*) is situated on the outskirts of the village. The smith dispenses both life and death, for he fashions agricultural and artisanal tools, on the one hand, and weapons, on the other. The smith is regarded as capable of reanimating the bodies of the dead or of treating anemia. In times past the forge had been transformed on occasion into a sort of tribunal where conflicts of interests between competing brothers, that is, of conflict between the realm of diurnal village and nocturnal forest, were adjudicated through the ordeals of poison or fire: "Is not my brother at the source of my lasting failure in the hunt? Is he not the one who causes my wife's repeated abortions by intruding upon her in nightmares?" The smith has earned the name of *ngaangula:* literally, "the artisan who is able to undo someone's secret arts."

DANCE AND THE WEAVE OF LIFE

Dance, in particular moon-dancing, intertwines rhythm with intimate fellow- feeling, olfactory exchange, erotic transport, sexual communion, and repro- duction. Underlying the rhythm, tempo, and pace in dance is a sense of presencing-oneself-in-the-world, a sense of lustful collective celebration of body and solidarity so as to enhance the flow and force of life.

Lunar and female cycles parallel one another. The lunar cycle at full moon enlivens the night as "a threshold to a new beginning" (*-kyeela*), and it may also chill it into the fallow state of the new moon. Night, inasmuch as it is a time category, is portrayed in the oral lore as that which separates one day from another and which leads to the dawning of the new day. The duration of a journey or of some exceptional activity is normally measured in terms of the number of nights involved. Some narratives deal with the mediative role exercised by the moon on behalf of the sun, in order that the latter may reappear. The idea of gradual progress toward the dawn of a new day is otherwise expressed by the term -kyeela; it designates the collective celebration by means of which the community, in dancing the whole night through, celebrates the social rebirth and newly acquired status of one of its members.

The new moon, in particular its total obscurity, connotes coldness: it evokes negative feelings and keeps the villagers indoors and self-absorbed, making them more anxious and feeling more vulnerable to sorcery. Oral lore marks it as an intrusion of the forest realm into the order of the village. The passage from the new moon or moonless nights to the crescent moon connotes the end of menstruation. The crescent moon is associated with the state of fallow land ready to be cleared for a new cycle of agricultural production. It evokes menarche and the bride after joining the groom. Partners may then resume conjugal communion. It is moreover associated with the sap that starts rising in the palm tree.

In folktales and healing cults, the crescent moon is figured by a gourd—an object that in certain contexts signifies the uterus—which is hung next to a cluster of ripe red nuts in order to collect the whitish sap oozing from the incision in the inflorescence of the palm. One thinks here of the folktale that adults tell to children in which the tortoise wagers with man as to who is best capable of reaching the sun. Each time the tortoise attempts to climb up into the sky the lightning takes the gourd from the animal and throws the tortoise back to earth. The tortoise then hides itself in the gourd and is thus successful in reaching the heavens. The archaic formula implicitly points to the appearance of the crescent moon as the moment when the palm sap rises and is about to spill over, a sign of life which attempts to regenerate itself. According to popular accounts, the young bride should wait for the crescent moon before moving into the conjugal home. It is always at the crescent moon that cult initiates behave as if they have come back to life. Once the period of seclusion has been completed, they prepare themselves to once again face the light of day by eating of the tonifying cola nut, usually in the morning. At crescent moon, the household of a chief may temporarily suspend the means of union within the familial and domestic unit by dampening the hearth, abstaining from cooked food and sexual intercourse, and avoiding contact with knives. In order to do this each person will "administer himself an aphrodisiac" (-diseengula) while "pronouncing his motto" (-ditaandumuna) evoking the origin and role of the institution or cult that each represents. The following day familial union may be restored: the hearth is rekindled, the family shares a cooked meal, and conjugal communion may be resumed. The confusion between day and night brought on by the crescent moon is thus resolved.

At the time of the full moon, joyful dancing and singing, in celebration of rhythm and desire, revivify and interweave the flow of life in and between people and their life-world. Mostly only women join in the dance at full moon to celebrate the never-ending fluctuation between life and death. These dances are most vivid at the onset of the seasons of seedtime and harvest, or to anticipate and celebrate collective hunting during the long dry season. According to the Yaka, the succession of lunar cycles and of the seasons, like the passing on of life and the succession of generations, are all an outflow of rhythm. Transmission of life, growth, and healing are rhythm. In singing and dancing, in particular at full moon, women, children, boys, and a few married men usually celebrate a collective arousal and sharing of the life source and libidinal forces. Songs may voice libidinal desire, themes of love and loss, but indirectly in the imagery of forest spirits, of popular animals, or of cooking. Women's dancing possesses mediating and ordering functions. In rural Yaka areas, women always dance in groups. Women's dancing seems to arouse the effervescent vital flow in themselves, the community, and their life-world, while superimposing a weaving movement onto the group and their world. An oblong wooden cylindrical drum (ngoma) with a single leather membrane is usually accompanied by one or two shorter but larger drums (yimbandu), each of which has a different tonality, along with shakers (sakila, bisaangwa). Keeping time with the rhythm of the drum and chants, each woman swings her hips and belly in a kind of wheeling involving a skillful circular rotation, while slightly undulating her upper body. The women interrupt each rotation by extending their left hips in a powerful rolling wave. While dancing they remain fixed to one spot. Within the bonds of conjugal intimacy, the wife may dance in a similar way as a prelude to conjugal intercourse, during which she is expected to make similar movements with her belly; -niingasana n-ti myathaangi, "rhythmically shaking the sticks of the bed" is an expression for conjugal communion. Dance reinforces the Yaka ideal of the female form: a round belly, generous hips and breasts that suggest nurturing, fullness and ripeness—maasi kuthulu, kuvumu kaanda dyabaatu, "breasts filled with grease, and the womb with offspring." The dancer's movements evoke the mysterious transmission of life through the act of insemination and childbirth. Maintaining a tense (ngaandzi), erectile (khoondzu) posture, the male drummer grasps the phallic-shaped cylindrical dance drum between his legs; some songs, particularly those employed in the context of circumcision rituals, make the association between the drum's appealing rhythm and the erect penis's movement.

By dancing at transitions in the group and seasonal calendar, the community engages in a rather lustful celebration of the vital flow. The success of the transition in the life of an individual, the group, or the life-world is anticipated by a night of celebration (-kyeela) at full moon, involving an all-night vigil of nonstop dancing by women, children, and young men. The themes and style of the mourning song dance in which both men and women participate are not very different from the women's normal dancing at full moon. It is as if the libidinal affects in women's undulating movements and in their singing intensely mediate between life and death, sorrow and vital flow, chaos and order. The women seem to share and express their affects through their bodies. Moreover, in the chants that accompany the dances the women are offered a unique opportunity to voice their feelings, especially toward the men's group.

Dancing is a form of weaving and a reenactment of the universe's birth. Weaving, like dancing, seeks to symbolically regenerate, re-empower, and reorder the life-world. Weaving raffia palm fibers requires the coordinated manipulation of the weaving-hook (n-noongu) and the fibers. The hook's movements are determined by the progression of the weaving itself: from top to bottom (high to low), left to right, back to front. The raffia cloth connotes the effervescent, sexual, and cosmological symbolism of the raffia palm, and the ascending and descending flow of its sap. The weaving-hook bears a virile sexual connotation and is shaped in the form of the palm tree's inflorescence that later develops into a cluster of palm nuts—itself a metaphor for both the sun and offspring. Women's dancing—in particular in the undulating movement of the hips, as the dancing movement in sexual union—links weaving to the celebration or act of life transmission. Dance acts as a fabric, namely as a genuine method of articulating the vital flow with the collective, and the world. The weaving of the loincloth is both an expression of this articulation and an unspoken pattern of dance. In other words, the vital flow manifests itself as rhythm and cosmogenetic formation. As a metaphoric form of weaving, the women's dancing from sunset to sunrise reactualizes the cosmogenetic significance of ngoongu, the earthly womb, that is, the pristine cosmic emergence of (re)generative forces in the universe which ceaselessly renew themselves at their point of origin. By mimicking the flow of life in the palm tree, both dancing and weaving reenact the birth of the universe and the individual by celebrating the constitutive imbrication of the polar principles that characterize beings and things: east and west, up and down, front and back, heaven and earth, decomposition and rebirth, sowing and flowering, ascendance and descendance, genitors and offspring, masculine and feminine. Dance produces a reorganization of synergies, channeling the vital flow from body to world and vice versa.

REFERENCES

Boddy, J. 1989. *Wombs and Alien Spirits: Women, Men, and the Zar Cult in Northern Sudan.* Madison: University of Wisconsin Press.

De Boeck, F. and Devisch, R. 1994. "Ndembu, Luunda and Yaka Divination Compared: From Representation and Social Engineering to Embodiment and World-making." *Journal of Religion in Africa,* 24:98–133.

Devisch, R. 1979. *Mort, deuil et compensations mortuaires chez les Komo et les Yaka du Nord du Zaïre,* ed. R. Devisch and W. de Mahieu, 1–18, 69–112. Tervuren: Annales du Musée royal de l'Afrique centrale.

———. 1988. "From Equal to Better: Investing the Chief among the Northern Yaka of Zaire." *Africa, Journal of the International African Institute,* 58(3):261–90.

———. 1990. "The Therapist and the Source of Healing among the Yaka of Zaire." *Culture, Medicine and Psychiatry,* 14(2):213–36.

———. 1991a. "Mediumistic Divination among the Northern Yaka of Zaïre." In *African Divination Systems,* ed. M. Peek, 104–123. Bloomington: Indiana University Press.

———. 1993a. *Weaving the Threads of Life: The Khita Gyn-eco-logical Healing Cult among the Yaka.* Chicago: University of Chicago Press.

———. 1993b. "Soigner l'affect en remodelant le corps en milieu Yaka." *Anthropologie et sociétés* (Québec), 17:215–37.

Flax, J. 1990. "Postmodernism and Gender Relations in Feminist Theory." In *Feminism and Postmodernism,* ed. L. J. Nicholson, 39–62. New York: Routledge.

Jackson, M. 1989. *Paths toward a Clearing: Radical Empiricism and Ethnographic Inquiry.* Bloomington: Indiana University Press.

Mudimbe, V. 1988. *The Invention of Africa: Gnosis, Philosophy, and the Order of Knowledge.* Bloomington: Indiana University Press.

Reflections on a Cut Finger

Taboo in the Umeda Conception of the Self

ALFRED GELL

My theme is the nature of taboo and its role in the definition of the self, and in the articulation of the self into a social world. Partly, I have attempted here a revision of the too-featureless "ego" whose presence in symbolic anthropology has hitherto mainly been that of a detached bystander "classifying out" an already constituted world. Instead of a "transcendental" ego, occupant of a zero point at the center of a cognized world while always remaining somehow external to it, I have sought to delineate the ego as immanent in a network of relations, defending an at best vicarious transcendence, not always successfully. I am concerned with grasping the oscillatory movement whereby the ego both recoils from the world in constituting itself and is simultaneously drawn back into the world in accomplishing its projects. I argue that the notion of "taboo" stands for the negative, denying aspect of egohood, while the corresponding notion of "lapse" stands for the reabsorption of the ego into the world.[1]

The investigation is set among the people of Umeda village in the West Sepik District of Papua New Guinea, where I carried out field research.[2] The topic with which I am concerned is sufficiently narrowly defined as to render any detailed discussion of the Umeda setting unnecessary, except perhaps to forestall a possible misconception that the ensuing text will be devoted to accounts of pig-festivals, big-men, or ceremonial exchange. Suffice to say that all three are remarkably absent in the vicinity of Umeda, isolated as it is either from the sea or river trade routes and situated in a most unproductive terrain from which the inhabitants derive a slender subsistence based on sago. The village and its neighbors form a collection of exogamous hamlets, permanently occupied by one or more patrilineal clans, whose relations with one another take the form of matrimonial exchange and matrilateral alliance. Viewed from afar, the individual hamlets resemble becalmed ships amid an ocean of trees, each one perched on a ridge too low to make it more than barely discernible above the forest plain. The huts are clustered in little groups beneath the shade-giving coconut palms, and may be abandoned, for much of the time, by occupants who prefer to live among their hidden and somewhat desultory gardens, or in hunting lodges deep in the bush.

Such, very briefly, is the social and physical context of the present investigation: an equable, low-keyed existence, dominated by the monotony of sago production and the hardly less monotonous quest for game, and punctuated by too-infrequent hunting successes and annual performances of ritual of surprising splendor.

But with these I am not concerned here.

It is apposite that an investigation which focuses on the twin notions of "taboo" and "lapse" should commence with the analysis of an incident, involving myself, which well exemplifies both.

I happened once, during my fieldwork, to be peeling a stick of sugar-cane together with some companions from Umeda village. Clumsily, I allowed my knife to slip and it embedded itself in my finger. Unhurriedly, but still unthinkingly, I deposited the offending kitchen knife and the still unpeeled stick of sugar-cane and raised my bleeding finger to my lips. The external world ceased momentarily to exist for me, conscious only of the familiar saltwater taste on my tongue and a just perceptible pulsation where the sting would be. My world contracted to a simple circuit, a chain of actions and sensations completed by finger, lips, and tongue tentatively exploring the extent of the wound, which was only slight, in fact. Slight enough to be in itself entirely unremarkable, and the momentary lapse into unreflectiveness prompted by it equally so, were it not that, reflected in the distorting mirror of an alien, or at least partially alien, set of cultural categories, my lapse of consciousness was a lapse indeed, as the shocked countenances and expressions of disgust evinced by my Umeda companions told me soon enough, just as soon as I recovered my wits and looked about me.

Naturally my curiosity was aroused and my observations somewhat sharpened by this incident. It was evident that I had, in Umeda eyes, *broken a food taboo*, though one so fundamental as not to figure in the recitations of such taboos which my highly taboo-bound informants would readily provide—and of which the prime one, as had been impressed on me from the very first days of my stay in Umeda, was the *taboo on consuming self-killed game*. It did not need much to perceive the kinship of my own unwitting "breach of taboo" with what was, for them, the taboo *par excellance*. It occurred to me, as it had not done previously, that Umeda ideas of taboo had little or nothing to do with real or supposed anomalies within their system of animal or plant classification, and everything to do with avoiding eating one's own self.

Nothing, I subsequently learned, prevented Umedas from ingesting blood, *per se*, but ingestion of one's own blood was in the highest degree revolting. Pig's blood—derived from a pig killed by somebody else, of course—was a most acceptable delicacy. It was the auto-cannibalistic aspect of my behavior which they so remarked, the more so in that Umedas disdain to practice cannibalism in any guise, while continually harping on its terrors in their myths and stories. With opened eyes, I was enabled to see the significance of the entire absence of auto-cannibalistic habits among the adult population, the absence of such things as nail-biting, moustache-chewing, the swallowing of dried nasal mucus, etc.—practices which among ourselves vary in degree of niceness without ever attaining the status of major sins.

It was, then, but a short step from the realization that to lick blood from a cut finger was to breach a taboo which protects the body in all its aspects from auto-cannibalistic violence and confusion, to the further realization that the whole spectrum of Umeda food taboos might repay examination from precisely this point of view. For it is not only the debris of the body which is protected in this way, but everything in the environment which stands as an emblem or appurtenance of the self. And it is tabooedness, specifically, which singles out these entities, emblems, for this particular role. In Umeda, taboo clarifies the phenomenology of the self, in placing under its interdictions those parts of it whose separateness, far from disqualifying them for this function, permits them to express its individuation and separateness from its congeners.

It may be helpful to cite an example at this point.

An important food taboo prevents children and ritual novices from eating the river fish *pannatamwa*, whose red markings are said to recall the red body-paint sometimes worn by this category of persons. The "category of persons who taboo the *pannatamwa*" are distinct from the rest of society precisely, and perhaps only, in that they *do* observe the taboo: of broadly comparable social status, their shared category membership is by no means founded on over-whelming resemblance between observers of the taboo as individuals. They differ in age, in clan and hamlet affiliation, in physiognomy, in accomplish-ments, and in the esteem in which they are held. In everything, in fact, by the tabooed status that *pannatamwa* has for them, they are situated differently vis-à-vis the total society, yet, in the light of the taboo in which they all share, they do form a category, and do have a common status. Because the taboo, in this instance, applies to the whole species, all of whom appear to resemble one another in every minutest particular, it serves to codify the less palpable resemblances which unite the category of those who must observe the taboo. Should we say, then, that the *pannatamwa* is tabooed "because it stands for the self"— because it situates the self in an intelligible order? But just as the class of "persons who taboo the *pannatamwa* fish" has no basis outside the actual observance of the taboo, so, it seems to me, outside the specific acts, obser-vances—and taboos—which specify a self as *my* self, there is nothing for an emblem of the self to be an emblem of.

To observe a taboo is to establish an identifiable self by establishing a relationship (negative in this case—*not* eating) with an external reality such that the "self" only comes into existence in and through this relationship. In phenomenological language, the self only comes about in "intentional acts" and the observance of a taboo is such an "intentional act." It is nowhere except in what it accomplishes.

Umeda food taboos establish and specify the individual at a number of levels: (1) through taboos incumbent on humankind in general such as the incest taboos, the taboo on eating self-killed game, on cannibalism or the eating of dogs; (2) through other taboos which are incumbent on certain social categories such as the *pannatamwa* taboo, or a taboo which prevents little girls from eating pandanus sauce; (3) through taboos which apply only to individuals whose careers have been marked by certain specific incidents, such as a taboo which prevents men who have undergone a certain curing ritual at which white cockatoo feathers are worn from eating these birds; and finally, (4) through taboos which are entirely personal and idiosyncratic, though always socially recognized, as when a man taboos a variety of sago in memory of a deceased wife, or a fruit tree from whose branches he once suffered an unlucky fall. The Umeda individual, at any given point, is always observing a specific constellation of taboos, some collective, some personal, and many perhaps unacknowledged. In this constellation of taboos one may discover the outlines of a *soul* or *personality*, no longer a shadowy even if believed-in counterpart of the physical body, though the body is included, but immanently present in a privileged segment of intersubjective reality. The "I" does not stand apart from the world in placing a portion of it under a variety of interdictions: it is present only in the network of intentionalities which bind it to the world, its contours outlined in the very substance of that world. Taboos on eating, on killing, on sexual intercourse, on looking at, touching etc., together circumscribe a "hole" in the texture of shareable intersubjective reality which, privileged with respect to a specific individual, constitutes his soul, or ego, or personality. Taboo does more than express the self: it constitutes the self.

Such a philosophical account of taboo, whatever advantages it might possess in terms of generality, does not, at first glance, seem to offer very much by way of cultural insight. Culturally, it implies no more than that a system of food taboos, or taboos of any other kind, functions as a set of diacritics situating the observers of taboos within an intelligible social order. I want, in what follows, to focus attention more narrowly on "eating" and "not eating" in Umeda, not so much as indices of status as aspects of a culturally specific personality system. Let us suppose that I have established my view of the anthropological "ego" as a network of relations, having its origin in intentional acts: it is now desirable that I should reconstruct, in more detail, the actual form that this network of relations takes in Umeda. In order to do this I have narrowed the field down to just one aspect of this general system, namely the relations subsumed under the Umeda verb *tadv* meaning "eat."[3]

Or, to be more precise, I am concerned with "*tadv* relations" as constitutive of the ego both positively, eating (and also drinking, biting, striking, shooting, killing, and copulating with, since *tadv* means all these things), and negatively (not eating, not striking or killing, not copulating with, etc.). In Umeda such *tadv* relationships, fanning out from each individual, punctuate intersubjective reality and set up a series of fields of identity at various levels. *Tadv* has no "basic" meaning, since the context determines which of a wide variety of *tadv* or *tadv-maivem* (not eating) relations is the operative one. But in all contexts in which *tadv* relationships are found identical principles apply. We may approach the elucidation of the *tadv* relation system by bearing in mind the following criteria:

1. I distinguish three basic *modalities* of *tadv* relations. These correspond to the separate "meanings" of *tadv* in various contexts in which it is used, that is "biting," "striking," "shooting with an arrow," "copulating with," "eating," and so forth (or for any of these preceded by "not"). These may conveniently be reduced to just three modes, viz., the *sexual, gustatory,* and *aggressive* modalities of *tadv* relations.

2. Next, we may distinguish two possible *senses* or "directions" of *tadv* relations; the *active* sense (*tadv* is transitive) or the *passive* sense, in which ego is defined as undergoing the *tadv* activities of others.

3. Finally, we may distinguish a number of *planes* of *tadv* relations, that is, the plane of the individual's own sexual—gustatory—aggressive experience, the planes of his vicarious experience, his dreams, myths, sociological constructs, etc.

Utilizing these three criteria as the dimensions of a coordinate system it is possible to define *tadv* relations and *tadv-maivem* relations in terms of a "semantic space" having three dimensions: modality, agency-passivity, and immediacy-transcendence. And if, as I would suggest, the *tadv* relation system in Umeda subsumes the fundamental ego-world relationships (the structures of relevances which define the Umeda ego) a model of the *tadv* relation system is also a model of the ego itself.

More interesting, though, than the mere static outlines of such a system are the consequences of the interactions of events in different senses, modalities, and planes of *tadv* relations within the ongoing life process. A *tadv* relation, that is to say, is not simply a "point" in the coordinate system, but is generally found to correspond to a spectrum of other *tadv* relations on other planes, in different modalities, etc., which are "activated" simultaneously. A *tadv* relation is not single-stranded by nature, but comes as part of a bundle of such relations. These co-activated relations are discussed below as the "paradigmatic equivalents" of a particular *tadv* relation. An example is needed for clarification here: let us take the sexual mode of *tadv* relations as a case in point.

Anthropologists are familiar with languages, such as Umeda, which use the same word for both "eat" and "copulate." The sense of this transaction, as expressed in speech, is overtly man/eater/active *versus* woman/eaten/passive. But even a purely physiological interpretation of the situation, as it would be conceived by the Umedas, would not make the transaction appear entirely one way. If their language is understood by Umedas as making the man the eater, the situation is reversed when one takes into account the masculine role in reproduction, also as understood by the Umedas. In the one act the man both "eats" the woman and also contributes semen which is the food of the embryo, that is, he is himself "eaten." Hence the practice, widely encountered in New Guinea and elsewhere, of continuing sexual intercourse during the earlier months of pregnancy, supposedly to further the development of the unborn infant: the Umeda father is simultaneously a consumer (active sense of *tadv* relations, sexual mode) and a nourisher (passive sense of *tadv* relations, gustatory mode). This reciprocity of senses in the eating/sexuality nexus is nicely brought out by the Umeda words for the female sexual organs: a trio of closely related words mean, respectively:

1. daughter, young girl, vagina (*mol*)
2. fruit, daughter (metaphorically) (*movwi*)
3. gullet, vagina (euphemistically) (*mov*)

The vagina has a double significance both as what is "eaten" (that is, fruit and girls) and as the organ which consummates eating, the gullet down which the eatables disappear.[4]

The same point can be made in a more general way. The reciprocal of the verb *tadv* is the verb *yahaitav*. This verb expresses the notions of (1) "dying, being killed" (the reciprocal of the aggressive modes of *tadv*); (2) "fainting" including experiencing orgasm (reciprocal of the sexual mode of *tadv*); and (3) "being satiated," "falling asleep" (reciprocal of the gustatory mode of *tadv*). It is derived from the adjective *yahoi* which means basically "soft" and in addition "ready to eat" of cooked food, sago, fruit, etc., and "ready to faint, sleep, die, etc." Umeda men discuss their sexual experience explicitly in terms of "fainting" and "dying" thereby revealing the reciprocal character of sexual—aggressive "eating" of the other (women also "die" in the sexual act). The same is true even if one is merely talking of food; eating food—which is seen incidentally as an incitement to love, as well as sleep—warms and excites the body, as a prelude to softening and relaxation followed by fainting and death. Food is an active as well as a passive substance; while it submits to being eaten, the eater must also submit himself to the power inherent in it, as is seen in the usage which demands that a young man must eat his sago as hot as possible, and is forbidden to blow on it so as to cool it. He has to submit to the "heat" of the sago in order to conserve and augment his own "heat."

The situation becomes still more complex and nuanced when we bring into consideration parallel sequences of events, not only in different modes or senses but also on different "planes" of *tadv* relations. A *tadv* relation, let us say the sexual one we have been considering, has correspondences with other *tadv* relations on other planes. The plane of the dream is a case in point. In terms of the standard repertoire of Umeda dream interpretations a sexual *tadv* relation corresponds to the following dream: "your sister comes to you bringing a gift of food"—this being the dream which is supposed to foretell imminent sexual gratification. It will be apparent, and this is not fortuitous, that the dream which prefigures a *tadv* relation (sexual) is itself a dreamed-out *tadv* relation, but not a sexual one. The "crossing over" from the physiological to the symbolic—prefigurative plane of events (whose mechanics I will consider in more detail below) is accompanied by a shift, not in the sense of the relation, for ego is active in the dream (as eater), but in the modality of the *tadv* relation. The dream representation of having sexual access to a woman is receiving food from the hands of a sexually inaccessible one. Sexuality becomes eating. But there is also, in the patterning of the dream, a reference, which is less obvious, to yet a third plane of *tadv* relations, the sociological plane. For why should ego be in receipt of a gift of food brought by his sister? Such a gift is not simply a token of affection, but represents a structural feature of Umeda society. It is not biological individuals alone who become bound together in the nexus of *tadv* relations: social groups, sibling sets, patrilines, hamlets and whole villages are definable in terms of such relationships. In Umeda, ego is by definition a member of a group whose relationship to other groups is mediated in the form of the transfer of women, the passage of gifts of food, and on occasion by mutual violence. Relations between social groups are *tadv* relations; the structure of ego's *tadv* relation system is integral with the structures of *tadv* relationships which define his group membership. Returning to the dream, then, the "sister's gift of food" is an aspect of *tadv* relations on the sociological plane. Ego's married sister returns periodically with gifts of food whereby affines recipro-cate the sexual rights they have in ego's sister—with whom ego himself identifies and whom he definitely does not eat. It need hardly be said that the incest taboo can be most readily incorporated into the approach to taboo I have adopted here.

Accordingly, a twofold shift from the original plane of physiological events can here be seen: (1) a shift from the "real" meaning of the dream to the dream events themselves wherein "sexuality" is replaced by "eating," and (2) a further shift from these dream events (posited as "real") to their sociological interpre-tation. Here a second transformation occurs in the mode of *tadv* relations, which results in their assuming the sexual mode once more, in that ego is being reciprocated with food for being sexually "eaten" (in the person of his sister) by his affinal group. But the sense of the transaction is inverted, passivity replacing the active sense of the transactions figuring on the planes of physiological and dream events: *qua* wife's brother, ego submits to the sexuality of the other.

A *tadv* transaction, in whatever mode or plane, can therefore be seen as forming part of a set of *paradigmatically equivalent* transactions in other senses, on other planes, or in other modes. The example just given of the correspon-dences between bodily experience and dream events, and between dream events and a certain sociological reality, comprises such a set of paradigmatic equivalents, though an incomplete one no doubt. But rather than explore the merely paradigmatic aspects of the system of *tadv* relations further—since of such substitutions there is perhaps no foreseeable end—I should like to look in more detail at the enchainment of events within the reality of everyday life. How is it that certain among the constellation of *tadv* relations encompassing ego become salient from moment to moment, how are they articulated to his vital interests, and how are they translated into specific patterns of action?

In other words, having sketched in the *tadv* relation system as it is paradigmatically, I turn now to the problem of *syntagmatic* ordering in the enchainment of *tadv* relations in the flow of social life. And by contrast with the paradigmatic axis, along which *tadv* relations are seen as equivalent to one another, when viewed syntagmatically *tadv* relations are characterized by being mutually exclusive, even mutually inimical within one plane of events. This discussion will also lead me back to the themes of taboo and lapse with which I began.

A *tadv* transaction is by no means an isolated event; it is integral with the texture of interconnected events which make up the social process. A *tadv* transaction has its origins in events which are themselves *tadv* transactions, and it has consequences, and these consequences are further *tadv* transactions, and so on. For detailed examination I have chosen the hunting/sexuality nexus. Not only are these the pivotal elements in Umeda masculinity, but an analysis of the relationship between hunting and sexuality enables one to see, in a particularly striking fashion, the orderly—that is to say, repetitive or oscillatory—character of the enchainment of *tadv* transactions within the social process.

Our initial situation is as follows: a young Umeda man, having waited patiently and sleeplessly in his deserted garden by the light of the moon, succeeds, at length, in shooting and killing a marauding wild pig. What are the *tadv* relations involved here? Up to the moment of the pig's demise the man was in a *tadv* relation with the pig, and it with him, indirectly, in that it was from his garden that the pig came to steal. Subsequently, though, the situation is transformed: having consummated his relation with the wild pig in the modality of hunting, the killer is precluded, by the very strict taboo on eating self-killed game, from consummating the relation subsequently in the modality of eating.

Or, where we find paradigmatically:

$$killing = eating$$

syntagmatically, we find:

$$killing—not\ eating$$

Identifiable here is a basic principle having implications for the whole spectrum of Umeda behavior, which asserts that if, on the plane of real life events, say, a relationship, **A** *tadv* **B**, is paradigmatically, equivalent to **A'** *tadv* **B'** on another plane (for example, dream) then the latter relation, **A'** *tadv* **B'**, is inimical to or contraindicative of the original relation **A** *tadv* **B**, should it occur on the same plane. This has profound consequences, for if the relation of **A** *tadv* **B** corresponds to ego's vital interests, then it must be that the relation **A'** *tadv* **B'** will be shunned, or, in other words, **A'** *tadv-maivem* **B'**. Hence, if "ego shoots pig" is paradigmatically equivalent to "ego eats pig," as indeed it is on the basis of the general schema, *tadv* = hunt = eat = make love, etc., it follows that ego cannot eat the pig he has killed. The "principle of syntagmatic exclusion" motivates both the taboo and its sanction, for the consequence of eating self-killed game is not being able to hunt successfully subsequently.

To return to the situation of the hunter: the death of the pig has the consequence of creating a *tadv-maivem* relation which prevents him from eating its carcass. At the same time this constitutes a redefinition of his "field of identity," since, as I argued above, the observance of taboo creates a privileged segment of intersubjective reality, so far as ego is concerned, not so much *his* as *him*. Having witnessed the demeanor of Umeda men at the butchering of wild pigs they have killed, the diffident, sidelong, almost embarrassed glances they direct toward the dismembered animal, I am convinced that I am not being fantastic in suggesting that they are personally strongly identified with their hunting prey.

In the working out of the logic of *tadv* transactions, it is the hunter himself who now becomes the passive object.[5] The pig, edible, but inedible by him, now enters the sphere of matrilateral—affinal food exchanges briefly alluded to above. His closest relatives, his father, his mother if he is an eldest son, his elder brothers and certain individuals with whom he is ritually associated, may no more eat the pig than may he, since they are too closely identified with him and his kill. It is another matter with the members of his opposite hamlet moiety, his mother's brothers and their families, or, if he is married, his wife, brothers-in-law, and wife's parents. These "others" now eat ego's pig. In this guise ego is now, in a sense, dismembered and eaten, most significantly by those with whom he has, or may have, *tadv* relations of a sexual kind. These are: wives, marriageable girls, and female cross-cousins who, though actually too close for marriage, are the likeliest partners in unsanctioned liaisons.

Ego is not passive in all respects even during this phase of "dismemberment." Ego, as food, is active inasmuch as food is a potent substance in its own right. Even in being the object of *tadv* relations in the gustatory mode, entering the bodies of ego's potential sexual partners, food becomes the instrument of ego's active *tadv* relations in the sexual mode. Food softens the hearts of wives and girlfriends in a remarkable way, and it is the accepted consequence of hunting success that ego will now become the target of amorous advances, to which he will succumb.

A paradoxical situation ensues, for lovemaking is a paradigmatically equivalent *tadv* transaction to hunting success and is, both according to our hypothesis and in Umeda eyes, highly inimical to it. The dream betokening a sexual conquest was, it will be remembered, a gift of food: the dream betokening a hunting success is dreaming of making love. The hunter's integrity, the virtue he derives from the strict rein he places upon his appetites in order to succeed in the chase, is dissipated at the very moment of coming to fruition. Triumphant, he falls into the arms of his amorous cross-cousins, who play the role of so many Delilahs to his Samson.

We may now begin to grasp the pattern in its totality. Ego is embroiled in a sequence of active and passive movements: first active (pig-killer) then passive (food provider) then active again (sexual conqueror) then passive again, since ego is "softened" by his sexual partners, just as he softened them originally with his gifts of meat. At this point, these active and passive oscillations of *tadv* relations are interrupted, since ego, physically and morally threatened by his love-making, must now eschew *tadv* relations altogether and resume the ascetic mode of life of the hunter awaiting his kill, patiently watching by night in the lonely forest.

Two types of rhythmic alternation can be sensed here. First "short cycles" of active/passive (*tadv/yahaitav*) alternations: "eating" followed by "softening" and dissipation. *Tadv* relations, modalities of ego—world interactions which constitute the ego as an open, energy absorbing system, contain also, because of their intrinsically reciprocal character, the promise of the ego's dissolution and incorporation into the other as a thing "softened," eaten, and destroyed. But these short cycles of *tadv/yahaitav* alternation, tending toward dissolution and death, are only episodes within a longer cycle of indulgence, activity, followed by asceticism and withdrawal from activity. The hunter has consummated his vital interests in the realms of venery—in both senses of that convenient homophone—but only at the cost of placing himself in jeopardy from which the only escape is via asceticism, that is to say, via taboo. If the short cycle is definable as a *tadv/yahaitav* alternation, then this, the longer cycle, is definable as *tadv* (consummation) followed by *tadv-maivem* (taboo). *Tadv-maivem* (taboo) is the condition of rejecting both "eating" and "softening," since the latter only follows on the former. Taboo restores the ego by reconstituting it as a closed system, protected by the *tadv-maivem* relations which demarcate an inviolable region. Having first of all described taboo as the means whereby the ego comes into existence as a privileged segment of intersubjective reality, we are now able, by tracing the vicissitudes of the ego in the flow of social process, to grasp taboo as a "moment" in the dialectics of the ego—world interaction.

But there is more to it than this. The phase of ascetic withdrawal at which the hunter has arrived is not a *terminus* but is only a stage on the way to the renewal of the overall cycle of events. We need to understand the mechanism whereby this alternation (eating/tabooing) becomes prolonged. The mechanism involved is the dream.

Umedas explicitly associate dreaming with the ascetic mode of existence. The fully fed man, the sexually satisfied man, will sleep a sound and untroubled sleep, while the man who is neither tosses and turns beside his fire and dreams. The impoverishment of his waking hours is compensated for by the enrichment of his vicarious experience, the nobler for not being real. Our ascetic hunter, benighted, hungry, and solitary, also dreams. He dreams of the women from whom he has voluntarily absented himself in order to restore his integrity, and of gifts of food brought to him by his sister. In either case, the dream is a negation of actuality, while being also, according to the logic of the system of dream omens, a prognostication of what is to come. Detached from the entanglements of worldly *tadv* relationships, the ascetic has access to the sublime, to symbolic truths unavailable except in dreams or in the world-ordering magical formulae of his hunter's incantations over his dog.[6] A spirit will guide his steps to the pig's lair in the forest, and a wonderful dream about women, of which he must say nothing subsequently on pain of its losing its efficacy, will set the seal of ultimate success on his endeavors. Awakening from his ascetic trance, he encounters a world subtly transformed by the action of the dream into one demarcated as the scene of his future projects, its inner constitution now laid bare, inviting him, drawing him in. He picks up his bow, whistles for his dog, and sets off in search of his predestined pig. And not in vain: crouching by a gap in the perimeter fence of a garden he first hears a rustling, a snuffling in the under-brush, which can mean but one thing. A dark form looms and in the same instant his arrow flies from his bow. . .

The cycle is complete: we have arrived at our point of departure.

Vita activa, vita contemplativa—between these contraries we are forever vacillating, and in Umeda as elsewhere. Gorging, lovemaking, as well as the noble pursuit of killing pigs, constitute vital interests in the eyes of the Umeda male, but their consummation comes in the moment of *lapse,* which in turn carries with it the suffering, dissipation and extinction. Contemplation, transcendence, asceticism, reestablish the integrity which is threatened by lapse, but also, by giving access to apodictic symbolic knowledge, reopen the mundane sphere for renewed activity. In this way an oscillation is established which corresponds to the life-process, between immanence, involvement, entropy (*tadv/yahaitav,* agency/passivity, tending toward death and absorption) alternating with transcendence, ascetism, negentropy which only succeeds in directing the ego back toward its immanent role in the world (fig. 1):

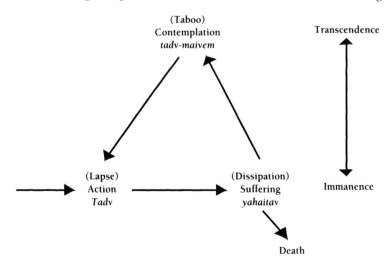

1. The "phenomenological" stance I adopt in this essay is derived from Maurice Merleau-Ponty, whose *Phenomenology of Perception* (1962) I was constantly reading in the field. A great deal also derives from Alfred Schutz (1962) and Peter Berger (1973). Robert Murphy's *The Dialectics of Social Life* (1972) was another immediate stimulus. The basic idea of the "cycle" of hunting, sexuality, and asceticism was worked out some time before, however, as a result of being asked to lecture on Umeda at the University of Sussex, an exercise from which I greatly profited.

2. I have described the Umedas in a monograph (Gell 1975).

3. I am not saying that no food taboos reflect taxonomic anomalies, "interstitial" categories, etc. (Leach 1964; Douglas 1966). I am saying that Umeda food taboos are not of this kind. I am well aware that paradoxical consequences can be drawn from my assertion here that Umeda food taboos reflect an "identification" between the thing tabooed and the observer of the taboo. For instance many male-dominated societies in New Guinea impose taboos on young men forbidding them to consume foods which can be plausibly said to be identified with women, feminine sexuality, menstruation, etc. (Meigs 1976). Such taboos would appear to be definitive of the ego by negation, rather than by association, as here. We are by no means required to make a choice between these alternatives.

Umeda men or women would not eat menstrual blood, or feces or earthworms or any of a large class of entities thought to be "disgusting" (*ehe*). These are at one level certainly in a different class from entities which are "emblems of the self" such as *pannatamwa*, trees bearing the same name as ego, self-killed game, etc., that is, things known to be desirable to eat apart from their tabooedness. My point is not that tabooed entities have to fall into one or other category, but that whichever category they do fall into the effect of taboo is to create a relationship in the *public* sphere between "ego" and an external reality communicated by *acts*. Taboo creates and specifies an ego. Umedas, in fact, predominantly taboo things which are independently known to be good to eat. But the total structure of the food system is too complex to analyze completely here. We have to distinguish among: things which are good to eat and are eaten, things which are good to eat and are not eaten, things which are not good to eat and are not eaten, and an apparently paradoxical class of entities which are known not to be good to eat but which are nonetheless eaten—such as the dogs' penises that Baktaman novices are forced to consume, or, less spectacularly, the ultra-hot sago Umeda bachelors have to swallow (Barth 1975, p. 65). No matter how taboo and "prescriptive eating" are distributed among these categories, which would vary from culture to culture, I think my essential point would stand.

My emphasis on the public character of the self descends at some removes from Wittgenstein (1953) and Ryle (1949). Barth's monograph on the Baktaman (1975) contains a chapter on "Taboo," whose argument is in some respects parallel to the one advanced here.

4. Cf. Gell (1975, chapter 3), on Umeda lexical symbolism.

5. What motivates this "principal of exclusion" cognitively? Why should a sequence of events on a "higher" plane, such as dream, mean something *else* when transferred back to mundane reality? Essentially, I think, this arises from a separation, which has to be maintained, between "metaphors of experience" and what is *meant*. The principle of exclusion keeps the metaphors which generalize experience "meta-." The switch-over in modality which accompanies a crossing over from one plane to a higher one is a frame-marking device: metaphorical reality, dream reality, give access to vicarious transcendence, but only while they can be kept separate logically from the "paramount

reality of everyday life" (Schutz 1962:341) from which they all start. On psychological "framing" cf. Bateson (1973:157). The metaphor of *tadv* relations, which generalizes the ego—world interaction (eating, aggression and sexuality) at the same time motivates an Umeda preoccupation with keeping separate in reality what metaphor unites in terms of a cognitive paradigm.

6. In a paper related to the present one but concerned with Umeda magical perfumes (Gell 1977) I have discussed Umeda hunting magic and its mechanisms in more detail.

REFERENCES

Barth, Frederik. 1975. *Ritual and Knowledge among the Baktaman of New Guinea.* Oslo: Universitetsforlaget. New Haven: Yale University Press.

Bateson, Gregory. 1973. *Steps to an Ecology of Mind.* London: Paladin.

Berger, Peter. 1973. *The Social Reality of Religion.* London: Penguin.

Berger, Peter, and Luckmann, Thomas. 1971. *The Social Construction of Reality: A Treatise on the Sociology of Knowledge.* London: Penguin.

Douglas, Mary. 1966. *Purity and Danger: An Analysis of Concepts of Pollution and Taboo.* London: Routledge & Kegan Paul.

Gell, Alfred. 1975. *Metamorphosis of the Cassowaries: Umeda Society, Language and Ritual* (LSE Monographs in Social Anthropology, no. 51). London: Athlone Press.

———. 1977. "Magic, Perfume, Dream . . ." In *Symbols and Sentiments: Cross-Cultural Studies in Symbolism,* ed. Ioan Lewis, 25–38. London: Academic Press.

Leach, Edmund. 1964. "Anthropological Aspects of Language: Animal Categories and Verbal Abuse." In *New Directions in the Study of Language,* ed. Eric H. Lenneberg, 23–63. Cambridge: MIT Press.

Meigs, Anna S. 1976. "Male Pregnancy and the Reduction of Sexual Opposition in a New Guinea Highlands Society." *Ethnology* 15, no. 4, 393–407.

Merleau-Ponty, Maurice. 1962. *The Phenomenology of Perception,* trans. Colin Smith. London: Routledge & Kegan Paul.

Murphy, Robert. 1972. *The Dialectics of Social Life.* London: George Allen & Unwin.

Ryle, Gilbert. 1949. *The Concept of Mind.* London: Hutchinson.

Schutz, Alfred. 1962. *Collected Papers I. The Problem of Social Reality.* The Hague: Martinus Nijhof.

Wittgenstein, Ludwig. 1953. *Philosophical Investigations,* trans. G. E. M. Anscombe. Oxford: Blackwell.

Space and Sociality in a Dayak Longhouse

CHRISTINE HELLIWELL

Anthropology, like sociology, has long approached the study of social relations as if its primary concern were the discovery of order, or "structure," in social life. This structure is, in turn, most usually thought to rest upon the existence of discrete social groups: moieties, clans and lineages, societies, corporations, and households. Or, as one of the most widely used contemporary anthropology textbooks puts it:

> When anthropologists speak of the "social structure" or "social organization" of a tribal or peasant community . . . they are looking at a social system as comprised of *groups*, looking at social relations in terms of interlocking positions and roles. (Keesing 1981:212, emphasis in original)

This perception of the essence of social life as found in "society," that is, in the orderly workings of a system of discrete groups, is curious, since there is much evidence to suggest that the presence of such a system represents but one mode of social relationship among many. Strathern, for instance, has demonstrated that Papua New Guinea Highlands sociality cannot be assimilated to conventional anthropological models of group dynamics (Strathern 1988), while Sartre has argued convincingly that many forms of collective action are better understood as the outcome of shared intentionality with respect to a singular, specific goal than as that of the workings of an accreted, identifiable social entity (Sartre 1976).

Both this anthropological view of social life as vested in discrete groups and Sartre's alternative to it are obviously closely linked to the dominant perception in the West of the human "individual": as a highly autonomous, self-directing subject of its own meanings and experiences. Western social theory has commonly regarded such individuals as prone to anti-social behavior in the absence of internalized constraints. It is for this reason that "society" is viewed as acting to structure, or to "socialize," the actions of these atomistic individuals vis-à-vis one another. It does this through organizing them into discrete groups, which define and order the interactions between them. These groups constitute social structure for anthropologists because they are understood to "structure" individual thoughts and activities so as to make individuals capable of mutually beneficial interaction with others. In searching for such groups, then, anthropologists believe themselves to be searching for the foundations of society itself.

But the stress on groups as lying at the heart of orderly social relations is also almost certainly linked, *inter alia*, to a rather deeper characteristic of Western cognition. This is what Fabian has termed "visualism": "a cultural, ideological bias toward vision as the 'noblest sense' and toward geometry qua graphic-spatial conceptualization as the most 'exact' way of communicating knowledge" (Fabian 1983:106). There are two rather different elements here: where the first suggests an abstraction from the realm of sensory experience in favor of its visual components, the second points to a further abstraction from the visual itself in favor of its geometrical properties. This second abstraction is responsible for the pervasive visualist critique of "mere" appearances, on the grounds that these obscure what are thought to be more fundamental underlying structures. Thus, Tyler points out that one of the effects of visualism is a hierarchy of "thingness," such that "substances" or "objects" are experienced as more "real" than "attributes," "qualities," "actions," "events," or "relations" (Tyler 1984:23). Furthermore, he argues, visualism "promotes the notions that structure and process are fundamentally different, and that the latter, which is only sequentiality, can always be reduced to the former, which is simultaneity" (ibid.).

With respect to the study of social relations, the implications of the above are obvious: Western anthropologists (and others) will tend to accord bounded social entities a higher facticity—to see them as more "real"—than more fluid, relational forms of sociality. In addition, where social life is more fluid or disordered (in Western terms), they will tend to carve it up into discrete "pieces" of sociality that can easily be represented in visual-spatial terms, and hence accorded a high degree of "thinghood." In other words, the stress by anthropologists on "structure" as opposed to "process," and on discrete social groups as the bearers of such structure, can be linked to Western cognitive processes.[1] The stress is made more pronounced, of course, by certain methodological features of the discipline. Primary among these is the emphasis on observation (linked, no doubt, to a concern among anthropologists to validate their claims to be *scientists*), and the production of diagrams, charts, maps, and so on which this entails. In this respect, the time-honored method of beginning ethnographic research through the taking of a census—the identifying and mapping of groups with high visibility—predisposes the fieldworker to conceptualize social relations in terms of such easily identifiable social "pieces." The result is a tendency both to overlook altogether more fluid and unstructured forms of sociality, and to reduce such forms to the order of well-defined groups. Since the existence of such groups is taken as a given of society itself, the ethnographer's professional reputation may depend on their identification, as may the putative viability and integrity of the society under study.

This is not to suggest that anthropologists should reject out of hand all visually based information: clearly this has its place, as is indicated in what follows by my use of diagrams and my stress on the importance of the gaze as a regulatory technique (cf. Fabian 1983:123).[2] Rather, we should resist what Tyler refers to as the "hegemony of the visual": the *privileging* of vision over other forms of experience in the quest for ethnographic knowledge. In this way, we might begin to relinquish our reliance on visualist categories—"individual," "society," "group," and so on—in the study of social relations, and on the static models of sociality which these models engender. Thus, the purpose of my argument is not to deny that discrete groups may in fact occur in many of the communities which we study. It is, however, necessary to question the presuppositions, taken for granted in many anthropological accounts, that such groups play *the* central role in social life. Too often, the anthropologist's quest for order means a loss of anything resembling disorder: the insertion of boundaries into what may, in fact, be a more seamless form of sociality. Where this is the case, the disparity between anthropological analysis and indigenous reality may be so great as to render the former essentially fictive.

The remainder of the essay takes up this point with respect to the ethnography of Borneo Dayak peoples. This literature is unusual among those of "tribal" societies in that, whereas in most such societies the "primary" social groups are seen to be based in kinship,[3] in the Borneo literature it is the household that is understood as the constituent unit of social structure (see King 1978:13). It was the early ethnographer of the Iban, Derek Freeman, who first identified households as the bearers of social structure in a Dayak society. In the absence of identifiable "kin groups" among the Iban, he characterized the primary social grouping as constituted with respect to a dwelling, and as highly discrete in the context of broader social relations: a "sovereign country" as he coined it (Freeman 1958:22, see also Freeman 1960, 1961, 1970. Cf. Appell 1976:4–6). A heavy emphasis on the household has been "the hallmark of studies on Bornean peoples" (King 1978:13) ever since.

In a critique of Evans-Pritchard's concept of social structure, Rosaldo (1986:94) notes that his use of the concept recalls "a house with many rooms that people pass through over the course of their lifetimes." Significantly, in the literature of Borneo Dayak peoples, the "houses" that people pass through—the overarching, unambiguous entities that "structure" their activities vis-à-vis one another—are tangible dwellings on the ground. Here, the building blocks of society are described not simply as if they resemble dwellings, but as if they were *constituted* by the dwellings which apparently divide members of the community up into tidy social units. This means that while African ethnographers draw kinship diagrams and so reify the "lineage" (Jackson 1989:10), their Borneo cousins draw diagrams of dwellings, and so reify the "household": the group whose existence is said to be bounded by that dwelling. Given the visualist context in which these representations are read, the Dayak household thus takes on an extraordinary facticity; since the diagrams themselves are understood as representations of "real" houses, households themselves are understood to be visible, seen in the walls of the houses which provide their boundaries. In addition, and connected with this visual apprehension, they take on the quality of extraordinary discreteness: the boundaries of the group are clearly marked in the walls of the apartment, and hence in the lines that represent those walls on paper. There is no space for fluidity or even ambiguity here, and hence little scope for a more relational or processual understanding of social relations in these communities.

One of the features of Dayak peoples is their widespread propensity to live in longhouses (although these are now disappearing in many areas). Significantly, within the ethnography of the island, these longhouses have typically been depicted as each consisting of little more than a line of independent household apartments.[4] It has consistently been argued, within this literature, that the appearance of community suggested by the fact that apartments are not freestanding, but rather are joined into a single longhouse structure, is an illusion: that, appearances notwithstanding, each apartment is, in fact, a structurally discrete entity. In this view, the independent character of the apartment reflects the autonomy of the household and the insignificance of more fluid, interhousehold modes of sociality. Several ethnographers have taken this so far as to draw a parallel between the structure of a Dayak longhouse—with its "public" veranda and "private" walled-off household areas—and that of an English-style street of terraced houses.[5]

This essay sets out to demonstrate that while such a depiction might work well on paper and successfully locate the holy grail of "social structure" in these communities, it might, simultaneously, reveal very little about modes of sociality and forms of relationship pertaining there. The essay starts from the premise that any conclusions concerning the character of social life to be drawn from the structure of either longhouse or apartment must be based not only on the abstract arrangements of those spaces, but also on the ways in which people live and use them. As we will see, when applied to longhouse life in the Dayak community of Gerai,[6] this approach provides a radically different conception of Dayak sociality from that which results from a simple "mapping" of apartments, and therefore households, vis-à-vis one another (cf. Bourdieu 1977:1–2). Social relations in Gerai can be seen to have a more fluid and seamless character, once they are released from the artificial confines imposed by the insistent search for social structure.

THE GERAI LONGHOUSE: *SAWAH* AND *LAWANG*

The Gerai longhouse is a massive structure, with its floor set some two-and-a-half to three-and-a-half meters above the ground on heavy ironwood piles, and its thatched roof rising to a peak of almost eight meters. It consists of a number of apartments built side by side; the final structure is the result of the addition, over the years, of new apartments at the sides of already existing ones. Of the two longhouses still found in the village,[7] one contains nine apartments and the other fourteen; the resultant structures are respectively thirty-three meters and fifty-four meters in length.

GERAI LONGHOUSE - Apartment

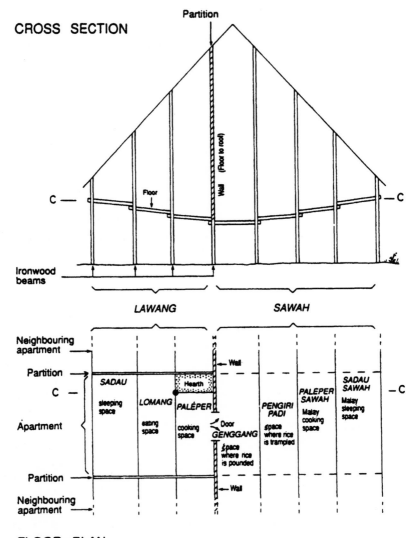

CROSS SECTION

FLOOR PLAN
(Scale approximate)

As can be seen from the accompanying diagram, the longhouse is divided into seven named spaces. These run its entire length, cross-cutting each individual apartment and unifying it with those on either side. Each of these named spaces occurs on a slightly different level from those adjoining it, such that the overall arrangement resembles a system of wide steps dipping down to its lowest point in the middle. The difference in levels serves to differentiate each space from those on either side, as does the fact that each is identified with a distinct "true function" (*guno nar*), also given on the diagram. Although each of the spaces may be used for a variety of purposes, it is its "true function" that Gerai informants will emphasize when describing a longhouse apartment.

Between the *paléper* and the *genggang* spaces, a wall, rising from floor to roof, stretches the entire length of the longhouse. This divides each apartment into an "outer" gallery area, which is not partitioned, and an "inner" cooking, eating, and sleeping area, which is partitioned off from the equivalent areas of those apartments on either side. Into this wall of sawn planks a door is set, providing access between the "outer" open gallery and the "inner" section of the apartment. The outer section is usually referred to simply as *sawah* ("outside"), but it can also be called *ruang* ("space"). The inner section is most commonly termed *lawang* ("door"), although it is almost as frequently referred to as *lem rumah* ("inside of the dwelling").

This division between an "outer" open area and an enclosed "inner" one occurs in Dayak longhouses throughout Borneo. In line with Western understandings of social relations, it has usually been portrayed by ethnographers of the region as representing a separation between a "public" community area and a "private" household one. At first sight, a description of the Gerai *sawah* and *lawang* as "public" and "private" spaces respectively would seem to be borne out by Gerai Dayaks' own account of the differences between the two. If pressed, Gerai people will describe *sawah* (outer area) as *ramo*, and *lawang* (inner area) as *yeng diret*. *Ramo* means literally "available to anyone," and refers to the fact that *sawah* is an area where anybody from within the longhouse or the wider community may stroll, sit, weave, carve, or whatever, without requiring permission from the household inhabiting that apartment. *Yeng diret,* on the other hand, may be translated as "pertaining to the self," and so suggests that *lawang* is an area which cannot be used freely by anyone at any time. In fact, use of this area is governed by strict rules of etiquette. If, for instance, the *lawang* section of any apartment is empty, or if its inhabitants are sleeping, it should not be entered by anyone other than household members. The *sawah/lawang* division, then, does appear to be very similar to the distinction commonly made in the West between the open "public" street and the closed "private" houses which it links together.

Yet, with respect to the Gerai case, such a reading of this "outer"/"inner" division would seriously misrepresent both the character of relations between any individual household and the wider longhouse community, and the role of *lawang* space in the creation and reaffirmation of those relations. There is no doubt that the Gerai *sawah* corresponds to the "public" area found in other Borneo longhouses: like Dayaks elsewhere, those of Gerai come to this covered, open space in the late afternoon and evening to share gossip, tobacco, and betelnut, or simply to stroll in the breeze. However, the accompanying conception of *lawang* as a series of "private" areas, reserved for the more exclusive use of individual households, is much more difficult to sustain. As we shall see, forms of cross-household sociability take a different, less immediately visible, form in the inner, partitioned area. This fact, combined with Western presumptions concerning the character of domestic life as everywhere according with the common Western pattern (cf. Harris 1981), has led to the "public" character of this inner area being ignored in the literature in favor of the more obvious conviviality of relations on the outer gallery.

In fact, description of *lawang* space as *yeng diret* suggests a rather different conception of the area than can be accounted for in terms of "private" households. This is because while *yeng diret* might superficially translate as "pertaining to the self," the notion of *diret* ("self") does not, in fact, easily accord with Western conceptions of a distinct, bounded ego or subject. Thus, while the term's use often appears to parallel that of the English "self," it extends far beyond this to denote also what English would translate as "we" or "us": any group of people which includes the speaker and which is engaged in some shared enterprise is referred to as *diret*. Like "we" or "us" in English, *diret* has no specific, delimited referent; exactly *who* is denoted by it varies from context to context. Describing *lawang* as an area "pertaining to *diret*," then, designates it as pertaining to the English "us" as much as it does to the English "self" and, furthermore, does not limit the "us" in question to the household. This reflects the fact that, in Gerai, subjectivity and agency are not linked to autonomous individuals (and groups), as they are in the West; rather they are conceived in terms of the *mutuality* of human sociality (cf. Strathern 1988). There is, in other words, no individual/society or household/community opposition involved here, since these oppositions are foreign to Gerai sociality. It is the lack of any such oppositions which has made it so difficult for ethnographers of Borneo to grasp the character of longhouse sociality,[8] and which has rendered description of it in terms of opposed "public" and "private" areas deeply inappropriate.

The "private," as opposed to "communal," ownership of the materials which go to make up any one longhouse apartment is a feature of Borneo longhouses which has been stressed relentlessly in the literature. In this respect, the longhouses at Gerai are no exception. Each individual household provides the nails, planks, strips of bamboo, lengths of rattan, units of thatch, and so on, which together comprise its longhouse apartment. Such a pattern has often been taken to indicate the existence of a set of property relations similar to those operating in the West, and to attest to the independence of any Dayak household from those others surrounding it. However, there is no necessary link between responsibility for the materials that together go to make up an apartment and exclusive rights over the finished structure and over the space which it circumscribes. In the Gerai longhouse, while apartment space "belongs" to a particular household, it is also identified as belonging to the community at large (as we will see). No Gerai Dayak would ever claim that an apartment is radically isolated from those on either side of it, in the way that the proverbial Englishman wishes to claim that his home is his castle. This holds as true with respect to the inner, partitioned *lawang* as it does with respect to the outer, open *sawah*.

For Gerai people, then, *sawah* and *lawang* do not represent a division between a "public" and a "private" realm. Yet, there is a distinction made between these two sections of the longhouse and between the two corresponding sections of each individual apartment. This distinction is so salient that it is marked by a solid plank wall, the most solid wall found anywhere in the longhouse. If we relinquish our presumption of the individual/society, private/public opposition as lying at the heart of Gerai sociality, and begin to take account of its relational and mutual character, then the aptness of Gerai people's own descriptions of these areas becomes apparent. Here, we have a distinction between "outside" and "inside," as the expressions *sawah* ("outside") and *lem rumah* ("inside of the dwelling") make clear. Implicit in this outside/inside division is one between not "they, the community" (*sawah*) and "us, the household" (*lawang*), but rather, one between "they, the world out there" (of which we may also at times be a part) (*sawah*) and "us, the longhouse community" (*lawang*). In other words, the spatial separation parallels a division not *within* the longhouse community, but between that community and those without it: between "us" and "other."[9]

This portrayal of the nature of the *sawah/lawang* divide is supported by the fact that while *rumah* may be taken to mean "apartment," it may equally be taken as referring to the longhouse as a whole. Thus, the "inside" space designated in the description of *lawang* as *lem rumah* ("inside of the dwelling") may refer as much to the entire *lawang* area of the longhouse as it does to the *lawang* section of any individual apartment. The equation of the *sawah/lawang* divide with one between "us" and "other" is also evidenced by the identification, among Gerai Dayaks, of the *sawah* with strangers and outsiders. Thus, although this area most often functions as one of easy community sociability, the "true functions" of two of its four spaces are to do with Malay guests to the longhouse: the *sadau sawah* and the *paléper sawah* ("outside" equivalents of the *sadau* and of the *paléper* respectively, the latter both being found in the *lawang*) function most essentially as a sleeping place and a cooking place for Malay visitors to the longhouse. Since Gerai Dayaks, like many other Dayak peoples, tend to define themselves ethnically in opposition to Malays (to the degree that they will often use the term *reng Melayu* ["Malay"] to mean simply non-Dayak), the association of the outer *sawah* with Malays identifies it as an area for "others," as opposed to the inner *lawang* which is "our" space (see Helliwell 1991).[10]

Before the arrival of the Dutch, Gerai was under the putative control of the Malay *raja* based in Sukadana, some eighty kilometers away on the coast. Although Gerai's location far from a river deep enough to be used for transport meant that it remained relatively free of direct Malay interference over its affairs, in 1986 Gerai myth and oral history remained full of references to the *raja* and his emissaries. Unlike Dayaks from other longhouses or villages who, during the days of Malay control, arrived at the longhouse as either friends or enemies (and so could be treated accordingly), Malays had come as neither. Their fealty to the *raja* demanded that they be treated with care and respect in order to avoid his wrath, but they were nevertheless perceived—then as now—as a different order of being, one which refused pork and rice wine (both prized by Gerai people) and engaged in an incomprehensible set of practices with respect to its deities. It is partly because of these taboos, Gerai Dayaks claim, that they still deem it most sensible to banish Malay guests to the outer *sawah* area, where they are least likely to be offended by Dayak customs.

But the practice reflects a more deeply held conception of the *lawang* as "our" area and the *sawah* as the area of Malays, that is, of "others," than can be accounted for simply through reference to Gerai wishes not to offend. Thus, informants told me that in the past a Malay was not permitted, on pain of death, to enter the *lawang*, although Dayak strangers were generally invited to do so. Further, a suggestion made early in my fieldwork, that I might build myself living quarters on the *sawah* area of one of the apartments, elicited the following disapproving response: "Only people who don't eat pork should eat and sleep out on the *sawah*. You are one of us—it wouldn't feel right to have you living out there." This not only points up the conception of the *sawah* as a Malay area, but also demonstrates the degree to which Gerai Dayaks conceive of the world as divided essentially between "us" and "those who don't eat pork" (that is, Malays). Another response made to the same suggestion emphasizes the gleeful Gerai joke which underlies the banishment of their erstwhile masters to the outer veranda space. In order to dissuade me once and for all from building on the longhouse *sawah*, it was pointed out that each household's pigs are kept immediately beneath this section: as living quarters such an area would therefore be noisy and foul-smelling. How much more so for Malays, to whom pigs are so unclean that contact with them of any kind is strenuously avoided!

It is not my intention to discuss in detail here the nature of *sawah*, and the ways in which it is distinguished from *lawang*. It is sufficient for my purposes to have demonstrated that the Gerai *sawah/lawang* division constitutes a conceptual distinction between outsiders and community, rather than one between "public" and "private" areas *within* that community. For the remainder of this essay I shall focus on *lawang* space. Because of its conventional identification as the "private," domestic realm, the character of this "inner" space, and the forms of wider sociability that take place within it, have been seriously neglected in the anthropological literature on Dayak societies.

LAWANG CONSTRUCTION AND *LAWANG* SPACE

Among Borneo ethnographers there has long existed, as already noted, a largely unquestioned belief in the walled-off, "private" character of the inner section of the apartment, and hence of the household which cooks, eats, and sleeps there. Because of this belief, ethnographers have conventionally approached the study of the Dayak longhouse via the study of a single apartment within it. The assumption has been that apprehension of the character of one apartment simultaneously induces apprehension of the character of the longhouse as a whole, since this latter consists of nothing more than an aggregation of several apartments.[11] The problem with this approach is that it leaves no space for an awareness of relationships that might operate *between* apartments, especially for those occurring in the "private," inner area.

While the Gerai longhouse consists of a number of individual units arranged next to each other, it also consists of a single spatial entity, which one can traverse from end to end. To isolate a single apartment and describe nothing more than the relationships which unify its seven levels across the width of the longhouse would be to neglect those relationships which unify individual apartments along its length. In spatial terms, these latter relationships are clearly marked: neither the seven spaces, nor the wall between *sawah* and *lawang,* stop at the edges of any one apartment. Rather, they continue, in identical form, into those on either side, and so on down the entire length of the longhouse. This is as true of the three *lawang* spaces as it is of the four *sawah* ones. Indeed, while cross-household ties may at first sight appear to be sustained primarily through easy interaction in the open *sawah* area, they achieve much greater frequency and intensity within the closed-off *lawang.*

It has long been recognized by anthropologists and sociologists that the arrangement of domestic space is closely linked to the nature of the relationships occurring within that space. Therefore, the analysis of such arrangements is able to provide important clues to the character of social relations, and to indigenous conceptions of those relations.[12] For all their value, however, most such analyses have suffered from the bias of visualism in focusing on the visible, "spatial" divisions of the dwelling. In examining the Gerai *lawang,* on the other hand, I am concerned to "bracket out" this apparently obvious significance of geometry, and to concentrate instead on the way the space is lived and used in everyday life.

In this respect, the character of the partition separating the *lawang* section of an apartment from that next to it is highly revealing, for in the formal diagrams of longhouse layout, it is this partition which marks the edge of each apartment and so represents its independent, "private" character. Yet, in reality, the partition is constructed of flimsy pieces of bark and other materials propped against each other in such a way as to leave gaps of varying sizes; through these dogs, cats, and small children climb, people hand things back and forth, and neighbors stand while they chat together. This is, in other words, a highly permeable boundary: a variety of resources moves through it in both directions. Like everything else in the longhouse, this partition is "owned" by only one of the two households whose apartments it delimits (by the household which built its apartment first). But in *practical* terms it is shared by both, and its very character not merely expresses, but generates, that sharing. The partition constitutes an opening into—and a promise of—the neighboring apartment as much as it constitutes the boundary of the apartment to which it formally belongs. In this respect, the way these partitions may appear in the context of some formal anthropological representation of longhouse space, and the way they are experienced in the daily lives of those who build and use them, are two quite different things.

The character of the partitions marking *lawang* off from one another—their very ricketiness and permeability—lies at the heart of longhouse sociability. For they promote not simply the movement of resources from household to household, but also the flow of sound and light from one end of the longhouse to the other. It is this dual flow which constitutes and locates each "independent" household as coterminous with all others, and with the longhouse community as a whole.

While living in the Gerai longhouse, I wrote many letters back to Australia in which I described myself as part of a "community of voices." Although this perception was not, at the time, finding its way into my notebooks it was, nevertheless, the most apt way that I could find to describe the central quality of longhouse residence. Voices flow in a longhouse in a most extraordinary fashion; moving up and down its length in seeming monologue, they are, in fact, in continual dialogue with others. Speakers and listeners may be (and usually are) invisible to one another, but they are profoundly present in each other's lives. Through the sounds of their voices, neighbors two, three, four, or five apartments apart are tied into each other's worlds and each other's company as intimately as if they were in the same room. Within the longhouse, voices create a powerful sense of community.

During my first two months in Gerai, while living with a household in its longhouse apartment, I was unable to understand why my hostess was constantly engaged in talk with no one. She would give long descriptions of things that had happened to her during the day, of work that she had to do, of the state of her feelings and so on, all the while standing or sitting alone in her apartment. To a Westerner, used to the idea that one's home stops at its walls, and that interaction beyond these involves a projection of the voice or of the self which makes impossible the continuation of normal domestic chores, her behavior seemed eccentric, to say the least. It was only much later, on my second field trip, that I came to realize that the woman's apparent monologues had always had an audience, and that they were a way of affirming and recreating the ties across apartments that made her a part of the longhouse community. In addition, I recognized with time that she had been responding to questions floating across apartment partitions that I, still bewildered and overwhelmed by the cacophony of sound that characterizes longhouse life, had been unable to distinguish.

Eventually I, too, was able to appreciate and make sense of this tapestry of sound, and to recognize individual voices as they wove together with others in the air and flowed through the spaces of different apartments. These voices were never raised as the dialogue moved across four or even five partitions, but their very mutedness reinforced the sense of membership in an intimate, privileged world. Conversations were taken up at will and relinquished according to the demands of work or body; they were never forced, never demanding of participation, but always both gentle and generous in their reminder of a companionship constantly at hand. Even now, the memory of such conversations fills me with emotion; it is they which most clearly define longhouse life for me, and which distinguish that life from the Australian one to which I have since returned.

Light also flows the length of the longhouse, particularly at night, when the structure is demarcated from the surrounding blackness by the tiny lights glowing up and down its length. In explaining why they sow the seeds of a plant bearing red flowers with their rice seed, Gerai people told me that once in bloom, the flowers serve as "lights" for the growing rice: "Just as human beings in the longhouse at night like to see many lights around them and so know that they have many companions, in the same way the rice sees the flowers at night and does not feel lonely."[13] In the longhouse at night, one is aware of the presence of neighbors by the glow of their lights and their hearths. If a light is not showing in any apartment, its absence is a source of concern and investigation. On at least three occasions, when I had developed a fever in the late afternoon and by evening was too ill to get off my mat and light my lamp, it was the darkness in my apartment that brought people anxiously to my aid. "Why is your apartment in darkness, Tin?" was always the first query, taken up immediately in the conversation flowing to further parts of the longhouse, and bringing neighbors on either side to the apartment partitions. If there was no reply, within moments someone would be pushing open the door.

While *lawang* partitions may demarcate the space of each household, then, they simultaneously incorporate that household into a larger community space defined by the movement of sound and light. This movement continually reaffirms—to any individual household, as well as to those on either side of it— its status as part of the longhouse, and thereby of the community of neighbors that is encapsulated within that longhouse. It is the character of these partitions as they are lived and used—their flimsiness and permeability—which allows for the creation of community in this way, a point of which Gerai people themselves are perfectly well aware. Thus, my attempts, in the early days of residence in my own apartment, to create more privacy for myself by filling in some of the gaps in my two partitions with strategically placed pieces of cardboard and bark, were viewed with extreme disapproval by my neighbors. They saw such behavior as constituting a denial not only of my own "need" for community, but also of their needs in this respect, since by blocking up my partitions I was effectively stopping, or reducing, the flows of sound and light which linked *them* into the larger longhouse neighborhood. In response, they so frequently "accidentally" knocked askew my assorted pieces of filler that I eventually resigned myself to living with the holes. There is, then, a profound difference between the way in which these partitions and the *lawang* spaces which they enclose might appear in any abstract representation and analysis of the spatial structure of the longhouse, and the way in which both are experienced in the day-to-day activities of longhouse life.

The status of *lawang* space, as coterminous with the community as much as it is with the household, is, in fact, asserted explicitly within Gerai customary law. I shall elaborate on this with respect to two of the obligations which apartment owners have to the wider longhouse community.

Firstly, a household must ensure that a fire is lit in its apartment hearth (located within the *lawang*) every five or six days. Gerai people are quite clear that this is an obligation owed to one's neighbors rather than to the spirit world. For this reason, they say, any neglect of this obligation is punishable not by the supernatural, but via litigation against the head of the household. Such litigation would normally be carried out by those neighbors whose apartments adjoined that of the delinquent, and the largest share of any ensuing fine would be paid to them. Although Gerai people told me that nowadays neighbors are reluctant to sue one another on these grounds, I noted that the obligation is still strictly adhered to by longhouse members.

The requirement to light a fire in the hearth every few days is clearly linked to the flow of light already described. A dark, unlit apartment creates an uncomfortable fission in the smooth flow of sociability from one end of the longhouse to the other, and detracts from the sense that neighbors have of being tied into a larger community, of being a part of the "we in here" as opposed to the "that out there." For the same reason, those households which stay at their farm huts for extended periods during the rice cultivation cycle are spoken of with passion as *jat* ("bad"): "They don't care about their neighbors, they just want to live alone at their rice fields." Significantly, when a household decides to move as a whole to live at its farm hut for a time, it asks one of its two neighboring households, rather than one related by kinship, to take on the task of lighting a fire in its hearth every six days. Longhouse neighbors themselves, then, assume responsibility for one another's *de facto* presence in the community during any absence.

Secondly, the members of a household must demonstrate their love and respect for their apartment by taking care of it. In the recent past, if they failed in this undertaking, it was, again, the households living on either side which sought compensation for the neglect. Still, today, any signs that an apartment is not being cared for (such as holes in the roof or floor) are cause for community gossip, and for shame on the part of its inhabitants. Gerai people say that an apartment that is *buro'* (literally, "rotten") is essentially an apartment without people. Its presence, therefore, constitutes a denial of the rights of neighbors to live next to an apartment that is inhabited, and thereby to be incorporated into the wider longhouse community.

In summary, the space marked off by internal *lawang* partitions is not a "private" one, radically separated from the equivalent ones on either side in the way that the space within an English terraced house might be. Any temptation to understand *lawang* space in such terms results from the tendency among anthropologists, outlined earlier, to construe social relations in terms of "pieces" of sociality. The resulting account of Dayak "society" as resting on the existence of private, independent households resonates strongly with Western experiences of our own sociality, and so reinforces the apparent "correctness" of that account. As a result, ethnographers have been led to overlook the crucial evidence of how *lawang* space and the partitions which divide it are lived and used in the lives of those who inhabit it. This evidence points not to the autonomy of the household, but to the *mutuality* of interhousehold relations: not to the opposition of household and community, but to a complex merging of the two. As Gerai people put it when describing the longhouse: *Biarpun banyak lawang, pokok-e sebetang ja* ("Although there are many doors, at essence there is only one trunk").

THE GERAI HOUSEHOLD:
"SOVEREIGN COUNTRY"?

The flow of light and sound through the permeable *lawang* partitions provides the means whereby the human gaze and its auditory equivalent may also pass those boundaries. It is significant that so much Western social theory has focused on the repressive effects of the gaze (see Jay 1994), for it is clear that other senses may also be used in régimes of regulation and control (cf. Fabian 1983:19–20). While there is no doubt that vision has certain unique properties as a means of access to, and therefore interaction with, the world, what is crucial with respect to its use as a regulatory technique is the context in which it occurs. Thus, as in H. G. Wells's "country of the blind," where social regulation is dependent on the use of senses poorly developed in the sighted (and hence disadvantaged) interloper, we would expect to find other senses being used to this end in non-visualist settings. This is the case in Gerai, where what we might call the "audit" is as important as the gaze to the monitoring of behavior across household boundaries. Movement of both gaze and audit are ensured by the permeability of apartment partitions, and the former is also facilitated by the requirement that apartments be lit.

Examination of the audit and the gaze demonstrates further the problems inherent in the conventional view of the Dayak household as strictly bounded by the four walls of its apartment: as a "sovereign country." The wide use, in the ethnographic literature, of terms such as "individualistic," "anarchistic," and so on to describe Dayak people conveys an impression of individual and household activity as largely unconstrained by social rules and norms (see Helliwell in press). This parallels, of course, the conception of households as discrete, autonomous entities, and reflects the difficulty of accounting adequately for social regulation within such atomistic models of human relations. If we start from a conception of Dayak household and community as merging into one another rather than opposed, then the operation of social regulation and control in these communities can easily be understood.

The openness of the *lawang* section of an apartment to the gaze and audit of neighbors places those inhabiting it under much greater pressure to conform to recognized community standards of behavior than would be the case if *lawang* were walled off into "private" areas, exclusive to the use of the household. Gerai values, for example, place enormous emphasis on sharing between households, such that when any household obtains a relative abundance of a foodstuff, it is expected to share it out among neighbors and close kin. Only rice (which, as already noted, has a special status) and certain store-bought foods are exempt from this requirement. Thus, a longhouse resident who hears her immediate neighbor return from a hunting trip, from checking his fish traps, or from gathering fruit and vegetables listens carefully to what he has to say to other members of his household about the success of his trip, and may even move to their shared partition in order to examine what he has brought home. Concomitantly, at any time that she herself arrives back at the longhouse with (or without) game, fish, vegetables and so on, she knows that her neighbor's gaze and audit will be upon her.

This knowledge is generally sufficient to overcome any temptation to miserliness that might otherwise be present, and to lead any household which has more goods than are necessary for its immediate needs to share them out with neighbors. By not sharing, such a household would risk the networks through which it receives as well as gives, for neighbors will quickly tell others of any lack of generosity. Not to share is also to risk general opprobrium and the *jat nar* ("very bad") label: an unpleasant prospect in such a small community.

In addition to monitoring relations between any household and those around it, neighbors are also able to regulate those which take place *within* a household. Just as goods, light, and sound flow back and forth between apartments so, too, do advice, opinions, and soothing words. I was once in a friend's apartment several doors down the longhouse from my own when a heated argument between husband and wife broke out in the apartment next door. My friend moved immediately to the partition, arriving in time (as she told me later) to see the husband, squatting on the floor in the eating section, kick out and strike his wife on the leg. "What's going on?" my friend inquired, while the wife burst noisily into tears. The husband launched angrily into speech, telling us that in the heat of argument his wife had snatched the plate that he was eating from, and emptied its contents through the bamboo-slatted floor. He had kicked her in response. By the end of this tirade his passion was diminishing, and his wife's sobs had quietened. My friend's presence had calmed the situation and prevented any escalation of events. Even without such a direct reminder of the presence of neighbors, a household's awareness of its own visibility and audibility to those around it ensures that, most of the time, its members behave toward one another in ways that are generally considered acceptable.

The construction of longhouse apartments, far from mirroring household independence, actively promotes community interference in the activities of individual households. Longhouse members themselves are well aware of this fact. The wish to escape such interference was the main reason given to me by a number of younger couples for their intended moves to free-standing dwellings. In particular, with the growing importance of the cash economy in Gerai, more and more households are reluctant to share resources with others. Yet, the very structure of an apartment, with its highly permeable boundaries on either side, means that longhouse living is almost incompatible with such a reluctance, leaving these households with little option but to move. It is significant, in this respect, that the two households at the very ends of the longhouse in which I lived in Gerai, each of which had only one neighboring household, were both much less amenable to community interference in their affairs than were other households in the longhouse.

A recognition of the extensive character of cross-household regulation in Gerai should not be taken to imply a kind of Lévy-Bruhlian conception of the community as lacking diversity and differentiation. The reduction of sociality to "society" is as absurd as the reduction of it to independent "individuals" or "groups." While, in Gerai, *lawang* space is coterminous with larger community space, it is simultaneously identified with a particular household. Although anyone may, theoretically, enter the *lawang* section of an apartment if household members are present, only very close and trusted friends or kin may do so if they are not, and then only for some clear purpose (such as to borrow a utensil or to deliver a basket of rice). Visits made during the absence of household members which are more prolonged, or which are made by those who are more distant from the household in question, may result in accusations of intention to steal or, worse, to introduce malevolent spirits into the hearth and so induce illness or misfortune in the household. Any loss of household items or illness among household members, following such a visit, may well lead to litigation.

In addition, household residents who spend a great deal of time monitoring the goings-on in neighboring apartments are said themselves to be *jat* ("bad"), and a variety of motives—ranging from theft to sorcery—may be attributed to them. Ironically, it is the constant possibility of monitoring that keeps in check excessive use of the technique: neighbors become quickly aware of over-monitoring by others. There is, in fact, a code of etiquette in operation with respect to gazing into and auditing neighboring apartments. This specifies one's intention in looking or listening at any particular moment, and one's willingness to notify one's neighbor that he or she can be seen and/or heard, as the two most important factors in distinguishing a "good" from a "bad" neighbor in this respect. One may peer or glance casually into a neighboring apartment, or listen briefly to a conversation taking place there, but gazing or auditing for any length of time should occur in accordance with this code. One should never stand and stare into an apartment whose inhabitants are sleeping or are absent, for instance, since the gaze lacks the element of notification. For the same reason, one should never try to listen in on a conversation taking place there that one is not prepared to join. Similarly, one should never watch or listen to a neighbor's misfortune, such as a household fight or a person's grief, unless one has good intentions in doing so (such as attempting to calm the situation). The apartment, then, is identified as the space of a particular household at the same time as it is identified as community space.

This results in what is, for the Westerner, a curious paradox in Gerai social relations: because of its openness to the ears and eyes of others, the *lawang* area of an apartment is almost the only place in the village where one may comfortably and easily be alone. Gerai people view being alone as an undesirable state, and regard with suspicion anyone who appears to seek this state out. People normally seek company for any tasks that they need to perform away from the village, and even in the village a lone person sitting working in the *sawah* section of the longhouse, or on the steps outside a freestanding dwelling, will soon attract cries of "'you poor thing—sitting there all alone!,'" followed, almost always, by a companion or two. The only place where this does not happen is in the *lawang* section of one's own apartment. Here, aloneness does not engender suspicion or concern in others, because it is recognized that unless the entire longhouse is empty, or its inhabitants all on the *sawah* (both highly unlikely events), one is necessarily surrounded and touched by the flow of sociality that characterizes *lawang* existence.

Again, this should not be read—as the Western tendency to oppose "private" and "public," "individual" and "society" might lead us to—as meaning that there is no room for more intimate, household needs even in the *lawang* section of the apartment, and that the household is constantly subject to the intrusive and repressive interference of neighbors. On the contrary, the relaxed openness of the apartment's *lawang* to a neighbor's eyes and ears means that only extraordinary behavior within makes a deep impression on those without. Otherwise, the presence of its inhabitants is largely taken for granted; they are part of the background audience which always surrounds one while in a longhouse. A neighbor's glance into the adjoining *lawang* space, or her momentary pause to listen for the sounds of its inhabitants, generally involves nothing more than a casual orienting of herself vis-à-vis the members of its household. While neighbors are always aware of one another's presence and activities, this does not imply either constant monitoring or relentless interference. For my own part, I found that my longhouse neighbors quickly became highly sensitive to my own need for "privacy," and that as long as they were able to locate my presence in my apartment from time to time they were perfectly content to leave me "alone"—since here, I could never be alone.[14] More than anything else, this apparent paradox encapsulates the incomensurability of Western and Gerai experiences of sociality.

CONCLUSION

The conventional anthropological depiction of Dayak "societies" as constituted in discrete pieces of sociality, in this case households, is far removed from the Gerai experience of social relations as constituted in the mutuality of person, household, and community. This becomes clear when the longhouse is approached not as an abstract "structure" to be mapped, but rather as a *place* to be lived and used. The stress on discrete groups arising out of the opposition of individual and society and the visualist focus on structure at the expense of process—both characteristic of Western thought—leads to a tendency among anthropologists to overlook the fluidity and ambiguity which characterizes much social life. In the case of the Borneo Dayak ethnography, this tendency is exacerbated by the similarity of the resulting representation of social relations to those found in the West; the Borneo ethnographer is quickly in the familiar terrain of "private" household and "public" community. As a result, permeable or ambiguous boundaries between apartments are read and represented as dense and rigid, the groups which they enclose as discrete and isolated.

The deeper concern for anthropologists, in this respect, is the tendency that we have to deny our own experiences of sociality in the communities that we study, in order to produce the kinds of "ordered" ethnographic accounts deemed professionally acceptable. It must be presumed that most ethnographers of Borneo Dayak peoples have spent considerable time in longhouses. It is astonishing, then, that so little of what makes these distinctive as places to work, play, eat, and sleep—their sounds and smells, the endless sense of movement and the unique mode of relationship associated with them—has ever found its way into the public ethnographic record of the region. This points to the discipline's conventional reliance on a very narrow range of data, most specifically on that of the visual-spatial type. The result of this self-censorship is the endless production and reproduction of Western social categories in accounts of non-Western peoples, and an accompanying inability to capture in any meaningful sense what constitutes sociality in communities very different from our own.

NOTES

This essay started life in October 1987 as a seminar presentation in the Department of Prehistory and Anthropology at the Australian National University. It was originally published in *Oceania* 62(3):179–92 (March 1992). I am grateful to the editors of *Oceania* for permission to print a revised version here. For helpful discussion and comments I wish to thank the editors and anonymous referees of *Oceania*, James J. Fox, Michael Jackson, Douglas Miles, Nicholas Thomas, Michael Young, and, most particularly, Barry Hindess.

1. See Tyler (1984) and Jay (1994:9–11), who both make it clear that this "hegemony of the visual" is not a cross-cultural universal.

2. This essay is also pervaded by visual metaphors ("perceiving, "seeing," "viewing," and so on), which I have made little attempt to avoid. As Tyler (1984) points out, Western cognition is so linked to the visual that we find it very difficult to think or represent in other than visualist terms.

3. This is clearly one of anthropology's "othering" techniques: "modern" peoples are seen to have left kinship "behind" (cf Fabian 1983:75–76).

4. "Apartment" is the term conventionally used in the Borneo literature to refer to each household's section of a longhouse. We shall see, however, that there is no precise equivalent of this term in the language of the Dayak community of Gerai. While the Gerai term *rumah* may be taken to mean "apartment," it may equally be taken to refer to the longhouse as a whole.

5. See, for example, Geddes (1957:29) and Freeman (1970:7, 1958:20). Some accounts of Dayak societies have emphasized the embeddedness of the household in wider social groupings, but they are unusual. See especially Sather (1976, 1978) on the "household cluster" among the Bajau Laut; Harrison (1976) on the "hamlet" among the Dusun of Ranau; and Appell (1978) on, particularly, the longhouse among the Rungus Dusun.

6. Gerai is a Dayak community of some 700 people, located in the *kabupaten* (subprovince) Ketapang in the Indonesian province of Kalimantan Barat (West Borneo). Almost 20 months' fieldwork in Gerai was carried out between March 1985 and January 1987. It was funded by a Ph.D. scholarship from the Australian National University.

7. In 1987, the Gerai community contained 121 permanently inhabited dwellings, 106 of which were found in the village and 15 outside. Only 23 of the 106 village dwellings were found in either of the two longhouses.

8. Freeman, for instance, is quite explicit that these spheres of life are mutually exclusive: "a longhouse must be conceived of, not as a unified group, but rather as a territorial aggregation of discrete units; not as a communal pavilion, but as a street of privately owned, semi-detached houses" (1970:129).

9. It needs to be made clear that this division between "us" (the community) and "they" (outsiders) is also one that should not be read in oppositional terms. Just as household merges into longhouse community, so does longhouse community merge into wider village community and the world at large.

10. Among anthropologists the problem of distinguishing between the ethnic identities of Dayaks and Malays has usually been seen as a very complex one, since Dayak groups which adopt Islam and form separate communities after their conversion generally are known as Malays, even though they may live as part of Dayak communities with pagan Dayaks and share many of their traditions and practices (see Avé 1972:185; King 1979:28–34).

11. Appell is a notable exception. He stresses the linkages existing along a longhouse, and states that the longhouse is not "merely an aggregate of member families" (1978:160).

12. Mauss was perhaps the first to engage in such an analysis with his pioneering study of Eskimo dwellings (Mauss 1979). More recently, Bourdieu's scintillating analyses of Kabyle domestic arrangements has demonstrated the power of this type of approach (Bourdieu 1973, 1977).

13. Gerai Dayaks believe that rice shares a descent line with human beings and so must be treated as if it were human. As a result, in a number of respects the layout of a rice field parallel human life within a longhouse.

14. Cf. Geddes (1957:32): "(t)he Land Dayaks have solved a great human problem—how to be independent and yet never be isolated. . . . In the longhouse it is possible to be an individualist and yet lead a cozy life of company."

REFERENCES

Appell, G. N. 1976. "Introduction." In *The Societies of Borneo: Explorations in the Theory of Cognatic Social Structure*, ed. G. N. Appell. Washington: American Anthropological Association.

———. 1978. "The Rungus Dusun." In *Essays on Borneo Societies*, ed. Victor T. King. Oxford: Oxford University Press.

Avé, J. B. 1972. "Kalimantan Dayaks—Introductory Statement." In *Ethnic Groups of Insular Southeast Asia, Vol. 1*, ed. Frank Lebar. New Haven: Human Relations Area Files Press.

Bourdieu, Pierre. 1977. *Outline of a Theory of Practice*. Cambridge: Cambridge University Press.

———. 1973. "The Berber House." In *Rules and Meanings: The Anthropology of Everyday Knowledge*, ed. Mary Douglas. Harmondsworth: Penguin.

Fabian, Johannes. 1983. *Time and the Other: How Anthropology Makes Its Object*. New York: Columbia University Press.

Freeman, J. D. 1958. "The Family System of the Iban of Borneo." In *The Developmental Cycle in Domestic Groups*, ed. Jack Goody. Cambridge: Cambridge University Press.

———. 1960. "The Iban of West Borneo." In *Social Structure in Southeast Asia*, ed. G. P. Murdock. Chicago: Quadrangle Books.

———. 1961. "On the Concept of Kindred." *Journal of the Royal Anthropological Institute of Great Britain and Ireland* 91:192–220.

———. 1970. *Report on the Iban*. London: Athlone Press.

Geddes, W. R. 1957. *Nine Dayak Nights*. Melbourne: Oxford University Press.

Harris, Olivia. 1981. "Households as Natural Units." In *Of Marriage and the Market: Women's Subordination in International Perspective*, ed. Kate Young, Carol Wolkowitz, and Roslyn McCullagh. London: CSE Books.

Harrison, Robert. 1976. "Hamlet Organization and Its Relationship to Productivity in the Swidden-Rice Communities of Ranau, Sabah, Malaysia." In *The Societies of Borneo: Explorations in the Theory of Cognatic Social Structure*, ed. G. N. Appell. Washington: American Anthropological Association.

Helliwell, Christine. 1991. "Evolution and Ethnicity: A Note on Rice Cultivation Practices in Borneo." *Indo-Pacific Prehistory Association Bulletin* 10:209–17.

———. In press. "Autonomy as Natural Equality: Inequality in 'Egalitarian' Societies." *Journal of the Royal Anthropological Institute* 1(2), June 1995.

Jackson, Michael. 1989. *Paths toward a Clearing. Radical Empiricism and Ethnographic Inquiry*. Bloomington and Indianapolis: Indiana University Press.

Jay, Martin. 1994. *Downcast Eyes: The Denigration of Vision in Twentieth-Century French Thought*. Berkeley: University of California Press.

Keesing, Roger. 1981. *Cultural Anthropology: A Contemporary Perspective.* New York: Holt, Rinehart & Winston.

King, Victor T. 1978. "Introduction." In *Essays on Borneo Societies,* ed. Victor T. King. Oxford: Oxford University Press.

King, Victor T., ed. 1979. *Ethnic Classification and Ethnic Relations: A Borneo Case Study.* Hull: Centre for South-East Asian Studies, University of Hull (Occasional Papers no. 2).

Mauss, Marcel. 1979 (1950). *Seasonal Variations of the Eskimo: A Study in Social Morphology.* London: Routledge & Kegan Paul.

Rosaldo, Renato. 1986. "From the Door of His Tent: The Fieldworker and the Inquisitor." In *Writing Culture: The Poetics and Politics of Ethnography,* ed. James Clifford and George E. Marcus. Berkeley: University of California Press.

Sartre, John-Paul. 1976. *Critique of Dialectical Reason.* London: New Left Books.

Sather, Clifford. 1976. "Kinship and Contiguity: Variation in Social Alignments among the Semporna Bajau Laut." In *The Societies of Borneo: Explorations in the Theory of Cognatic Social Structure,* ed. G. N. Appell. Washington: American Anthropological Association.

———. 1978. "The Bajau Laut." In *Essays on Borneo Societies,* ed. Victor T. King. Oxford: Oxford University Press.

Strathern, Marilyn. 1988. *The Gender of the Gift: Problems with Women and Problems with Society in Melanesia.* Berkeley: University of California Press.

Tyler, Stephen A. 1984. "The Vision Quest in the West or What the Mind's Eye Sees." In *Journal of Anthropological Research* 40(1):23–40.

In Defiance of Destiny

The Management of Time and Gender at a Cretan Funeral

MICHAEL HERZFELD

LAMENTS AS MODELS FOR ACTION

The lament tradition in modern Greece has been an object of fascination for scholars, from the earliest folklorists contesting questions of national identity (Menardos 1921; Zambelios 1859), to modern philologists who have sought a less ideological basis for recognizing cultural persistence (Alexiou 1974; Tuffin 1972–73), to folklorists working on performance (Caraveli 1986; Caraveli-Chaves 1980), and to social anthropologists (Danforth 1982; Herzfeld 1981a; Seremetakis 1990,1991). The more recent works have raised some important theoretical issues. Danforth's (1982:27–31) exploration of the phenomenology of emotion, for example, addresses current worries about the parochiality of formal analysis (see Geertz 1988:12–13; cf. Rosaldo 1989:1–21), while the contextualized analysis of lament texts has offered fruitful insights into the gender-specific basis of social protest (see Caraveli 1986) and resistance (Seremetakis 1990, 1991).

The very diversity of approaches to this durable topic should alert us to the dangers of any single-stranded interpretation. The nationalist folklorist who sought to prove that the modern laments continued an ancient tradition documented their argument exhaustively and—within the limits they set for themselves—far from unconvincingly; yet, in their single-minded pursuit of cultural continuity, they largely ignored the social significance of the phenomenon. By expropriating lament texts, they not only silenced any hint of gendered or class protest but reproduced patterns of domination at the national level. For such is the paradox of resistance against a truly powerful social régime: when resistance has no observable impact on the long-term trajectory of the larger society, when its vehicles are all indirect and allusive, its victories can at best only be highly "contingent" (Loizos and Papataxiarchis 1991:13).

Relief from social grievance may, it is true, be provided by such victories: hilarious inversions of the social order by riotously antiauthoritarian Iranian theatricals (Beeman 1981) and Greek shadow puppets (Danforth 1976); tales of illicit sexuality that recognize the wonder of faithful love amid the strict morality of Bedouin life (Abu-Lughod 1986:250); Cretan women's mockery of the alleged immorality of nonlocal women, a mockery couched in the rhetoric of male-authorized values (Herzfeld 1991); employees' pleasurable encroachments on "company time" (de Certeau 1984:25). Greek women's lamenting offers some similar glimpses in a more somber mode.[1] As Seremetakis (1990:507) remarks, women's performance of ritual lament "publicly resists those male-dominated institutions and discourses that fragment female practice and devalue the social status of women's labor." There may be some question as to whether it does so through the direct voicing of discontent with women's burdens, the articulation of a distinctively female solidarity, or the expression of women's embodied understandings of the communal past, but these are not mutually exclusive possibilities.

An important question nevertheless remains: do these lament performances actually change anything? Too definite an answer risks trivializing the lamenters' predicaments. What from a male perspective may appear as inchoateness makes it difficult for an observer to "read" lamenting or to elicit interpretations that are more than an intellectualist exercise (see Cowan 1991:181–182; Herzfeld 1991:94–96). A search for "the" meaning of these texts, moreover, hardly improves on survivalist and nationalist dreams of finding "the" origins, or on teleological analyses of "the" functions, of such phenomena. Only recently have ambiguity, uncertainty, and indeterminacy been recognized as central aspects of culture (see Bourdieu 1977; Fernandez 1986). How do we record the inchoate? How do we capture that sense of possible but as yet uncertain outcome that pervades the local understanding of events?

In this essay I am concerned with just such indeterminacy. By examining a single set of laments performed by the adolescent daughter of an elderly male villager, I focus deliberately on the ambiguities of text production—on some possible understandings whose very lack of clear definition raises intriguing questions about how and why things happen in social life and about why some events seem significant in hindsight even when at the time they may not have seemed significant at all. The article will necessarily be inconclusive—suggestive, I hope, but resistant to closure. This is a recognition of local perceptions, which are themselves highly tentative even though they do incorporate the "mastery" that the observer loses upon leaving the community (Bourdieu 1977:123). The key text bewails loss and destruction, as we shall see, but may also have initiated a process that allowed a young woman to redress her low social status. Issues of uncertainty and ambiguity are especially germane in the face of death, where "a final resolution . . . can never be achieved" (Danforth 1982:30).

The mourner in question faced several social drawbacks. She was a woman, an orphan, the child of a second marriage, and very poor. Her actions during the funeral suggested, however, that she found strength in these very disadvantages. She did not resign herself to what others regarded as her fate. On the contrary, a possible view of her actions is that she directly affected it.

The idea of even partially managing fate may seem logically perverse. This sense of paradox springs from a misreading of the Greek view of fate as irrevocable. In the words of a commonly heard proverb, "What fate writes, it does not unwrite."[2] To interpret this proverb as fatalistic, however, would be to overlook the social uses to which actors put the idea of an irrevocable destiny. These uses invariably work retroactively as strategies for the legitimation of failure and are often the only defense against rivals who seek to reify one's temporary setbacks as conclusive evidence of a fundamental moral flaw. The logic of fate and personality is clear: my failures and your successes are just a matter of luck, whereas my successes and your failures are proof of radical differences in "character" (*fisiko*). Such is the enabling logic of strategies of denigration and self-defense.

While the term usually given to funerary laments, *miroloya*, can be glossed etymologically as "words of fate,"[3] laments do not necessarily signal passive resignation to the inevitable. Caraveli (1986; Caraveli-Chaves 1980) has already discussed Greek laments as expressions of social protest, in which the pain (*ponos*) of bereavement metonymically expresses the pain of women's suffering in general. Such messages, however, work to alleviate the burdens of female identity, not only as a categorical and collective plaint but as a specific means of reordering the lamenter's own circumstances. This is instrumentality, not resignation. It is a powerful—because recognizable and socially accepted— weapon against the social corrosion of pity and contempt. While Caraveli and others rightly see in lamenting a source of female solidarity, however, competition over status and internecine hostility may also, among women, take the form of reciprocal assessments of lament techniques and styles (cf. Johnson [1988:147] on Hakka Chinese women). Moreover, lamenting can express individual protest while, by restating the premise of male control, it also confirms women's reasons for discontent (see Johnson 1988:138–139). It is much harder for women to transcend an androcentric morality when the terms of their struggle remain those of androcentrism.

I shall focus on a single funeral that took place in "Glendi," a highland village in west-central Crete, in 1974.[4] I shall discuss not only the lament proper but also the talking that accompanied it. Much of that conversation pointed to the lamenter's personal and social predicament. The lament itself, albeit ambiguously and sometimes indistinctly, also played on the theme of the lamenter's personal dilemmas. Its very ambiguity left open the possibility of future action.

About a year after the funeral, the young mourner requested (and later received) a copy of the tape I had made at the time. It was thus she who reopened the discussion, which has continued since then—a rare chance to probe the performer's own retrospective attitude toward the events in question in addition to the reactions of others. The advantages of such a longitudinal perspective far outweigh the restriction of textual variety that we encounter in this case.

TEXTUAL CONVENTIONS:
TIME PAST AND TIME USED

Since one of my goals in this essay is to indicate some of the mutual relevance of traditional textual concerns and social context, I shall briefly defer discussion of the funeral in order to discuss some of the imagery that has been central to folklorists' analyses of funeral laments in Greece. It is crucial here to keep in mind the semantic lability of texts that orthodox folklore studies represent as fixed and referential. In this regard, Caraveli's excellent 1986 study has proved particularly effective in showing how laments may permit the subversion of authoritative orders, not through direct, frontal rhetoric but through challenges to normative articulacy. Indecipherability may be subversive in itself (see, for example, Messick 1987); personal protest may also be expressed through the strategic and systematic manipulation of pronouns (see Trawick 1988).[5]

The linguistic evidence of a shared symbolic universe, too often dismissed by anthropologists as merely the product of old-fashioned folklorists' search for original, uncontaminated texts, may be evidence of a shared symbolic code whose internal coherence gives meaning to apparently aberrant or oblique performances. Thus, Greek laments frequently represent death as marriage to the black earth or to Death (*Kharos*) personified. The relevant literature is extensive (Alexiou 1974; Bloch and Parry 1982:4–6; Danforth 1982; Herzfeld 1981a; cf. Johnson 1988:157–158; Kligman 1988; Trawick 1988:21) and explains the metaphor in terms of a generic structural similarity among personal rites of passage. Here I shall be more concerned to show how, in social practice, the metaphor links actual funerals to actual marriages.

In an earlier study, I noted that whole phrases of a lament from Rhodes shared numerous lexical and semantic formulae with a wedding song from nearby Khalki (Herzfeld 1981a:54–55; Baud-Bovy 1935:1, 266).[6] The similarities transcended the different ritual contexts, different places, different metrical schemata. The woman who composed the lament for her mother did not necessarily "know" the wedding text; as far as I know, it may not have existed in her village at all. In normal anthropological practice, such resemblances would be treated as fortuitous, so as not to invoke suspect abstractions such as "folk memory" and the "collective unconscious." Individual borrowing of motifs and formulae might explain the diffusion of these elements but could not tell us why a performer should consider them immediately appropriate— could not tell us how, in other words, the *longue durée* of textual evolution translated into lived time. Linking of different time frames in this way is central to Greek lamenting (see also Seremetakis 1991:226).

Well-known songs about such historic events as the sack of Christian citadels by the Turks provide a stable repertoire of formulae suitable for the bricolage of personal lamentation. Without necessarily thinking of direct parallels between her personal bereavement and the grand catastrophes memorialized in these laments,[7] a mourner relies on the common stock of formulae to link personal experience with collective representations of grief. The analogies that her lamenting may suggest are not those of direct comparison between specific kinds of event, but are *indexed* [8] by recognizable, common phraseology. Through this phraseology, the mourner's unutterable pain becomes utterable as collective pain, her personal grief a refraction of collective loss. More formally, we can say that performance creates meaning by playing on the complex links among three kinds of time. The longest is the *longue durée* of *textual evolution*, in which the grand events commemorated in the song texts are scarcely more than generic markers for repetitive experience. This kind of time undergoes transmutation into *biographical time*: the imagery of the fall of cities or of death personified informs the public view of personal disaster. The effectiveness of such imagery, finally, depends on *interactional* or *performative time*, which corresponds closely to Bourdieu's (1977:7) *tempo*. It is the management of this interactional time that allows actors to recast biographical time metonymically as the *longue durée*—for example, the death of a loved son as the Passion of Christ.[9] Such linkage contributes to a lamenter's effectiveness: if she can evoke a sufficiently rich image of collective suffering, she will move others to tears because she has recast individual as common experience, her personal pain as a shared past and present.

Each lamenter performs in the face of ever-ready gossip by neighbors and distant kin. If she succeeds in moving them to sympathetic understanding and above all to identification with her personal pain, she may also eventually succeed in raising her social status. The full impact may not be at all apparent in the immediate aftermath of the funeral. Her subsequent life course, however, may prove suggestive. Indeed, Greek laments often have a prospective thrust. It is common for a lamenter to accuse her recently deceased parent or brother, for example, of having left her unprotected; the theme is one of well-documented antiquity (Alexiou 1974:193). This pattern of confusion turned to anger, so evocatively described by Rosaldo (1989:1–21), gives lamenting women a medium in which to anticipate what might be said of them—or even done to them—once their source of moral support in an androcentric world has been stripped away. The great benefit of working from a vantage of hindsight, as here, is that one can seek possible links between a mourner's subsequent life course and her condition at the time of bereavement.

Pain (*ponos*) is, as Caraveli (1986) and Seremetakis (1990, 1991) have both noted, a key element in the strongly gendered solidarity of women who lament. Deceased husbands have left them to widowhood, a status made socially vulnerable by the assumption that widows are sexually frustrated and so susceptible to temptation (see de Boulay 1974:123), and this may be as much a source of grief as the actual bereavement. In daily life, men often exercise authority over their wives by telling them "not to speak," and men also regard male self-control in speech as the analog of male sexual continence.[10] At a funeral, however, all this goes by the board. It is the women who articulate the family's grief in words of acknowledged power and beauty, while the men who are closest to the deceased display an overwhelming inability to speak coherently at all, and stagger about as though incapable of walking without support, weep, and throw themselves at the open grave. Women's grief is at once more explicit and more complex in its implications, and its reversal of women's ordinarily quiet and verbally inarticulate bearing highlights the solidarity that women seek in the face of death. It is not only the internalized pain of bereavement. It is also an externalized complaint, the public expression of protest against a husband who leaves a woman widowed and potentially dishonored, a father who has failed to provide for his children's future, even a charismatic politician like Archbishop Makarios III—the first president of Cyprus—at whose funeral "[w]omen knelt and sobbed 'Why have you abandoned us? What shall we do without you?' all along the [funeral procession] route" (Anonymous 1977).

But to leave the matter there is to assume that women only protest, that they cannot improve their lot. Such a view ignores the transformative capacity of laments and attributes "fatalism" to the women. No doubt the charge of fatalism would suit the men's interests. In the illustration that follows, however, we shall see a woman attempting to "usurp" a male role and, what is more, succeeding. Superficially, perhaps, it may be possible to interpret her words as a bitter cry of complaint at the irreversibility of her destiny. Subsequent events, however, show that she was no fatalist at all. Viewed in the light of her own history, her words suggest the emergence, inchoate and confused as it may have been, of an effective strategy to escape the trammels of a lowly birth and a penurious home. If, in the end, she measured her success in terms of the androcentric ideology whose constraints she tried to overcome, this should not overshadow her achievement—and the achievement of the "words of fate" she performed. But the fact that we cannot in the final analysis be certain whether she had consciously intended her lamenting to achieve these goals also illustrates the contingency that limits its impact on the course of events.

MATERIAL FROM WESTERN CRETE:
PRELIMINARY OBSERVATIONS

Western Crete is not as well known for its lament traditions as some other areas. One lengthy study of west Cretan laments is mainly concerned to establish continuity with Homeric tradition (Tsouderos 1976), while another study includes some laments from a single village (Kalokiris 1970). Both these studies suggest more thematic cohesion than is usual in actual performance. Caraveli's 1980 study (Caraveli-Chaves 1980), which addresses issues of more current concern, was based on materials from an east Cretan village. There may be a number of reasons for the comparative neglect of western Crete. The laments of Mani and Epirus seem to have attracted special interest from the earliest folklore collectors on, and some long texts have been recorded. Many laments (though not the majority of those of Mani or western Crete) are couched in the 15-syllable scheme common to much Greek verse. When confined to a single pair of lines, they often achieve explosive force: stylistic parody, pithy juxtapositions, analogies between the human and the divine, contrasts between life on earth and the oblivion beyond. The laments of the west-central Cretan highlands are less clearly designed to carry these contrastive devices but do draw on some of the same sets of imagery and convention.

Their supposed deficiencies occasion some local scholarly embarrassment. While most Greek comments on the lament tradition are fulsome and tend to emphasize possible connections with ancient styles and motifs,[11] a study of one village near Glendi sounds almost apologetic:

> Whether the deceased is young or old, woman or man, child or elderly, the kinsfolk will speak their laments to him. Perhaps these laments lack technique and profundity; as improvisations, however, they are important creations of folk poetry and when one hears them one feels genuine emotion. [Kalokiris 1970:84]

Note the emphasis on "speaking" the laments, the term usually employed in the villages. Early folklorists made an issue of whether these could be considered "songs" (*traghoudhia*), a term usually associated with (and sometimes a metaphor for) joy (*khara*), a term that also, significantly, often serves (though usually in the plural) as a poetic term for marriage. We shall see that villagers are concerned with this connection too but recognize artistry in both lamenting and more unambiguous song performances. More suggestive, perhaps, is the ethnographic parallel provided by Abu-Lughod's (1986:251) study of Egyptian Bedouin poetics, in which "song" is categorically opposed to the dominant norms and structures of the social order.

West Cretan "weeping" (*klama*) begins with more or less unverbalized lamenting (*moungres*; Kalokiris [1970:81] rather unhelpfully describes it as "hysterical cries") as the first announcement of death. It rapidly becomes verbal. Each brief verse line normally ends with a formulaic address to the dead—most commonly a vocative noun followed by the enclitic pronoun *mou* (my, mine, belonging to me) or the verb *leo* (I say, I speak)—assertions of possession, endearment, and the desperate will to communicate with those who are now forever beyond reach. The examples that Kalokiris gives seem far more coherent than what I shall report from my own field materials, and they have the virtue of suggesting the underlying structure more clearly (see also Trawick 1988:204). The laments follow the pattern of ordinary spoken discourse, except that the first syllable of each line may be high-pitched and protracted, as may the penultimate syllable of the terminal apostrophe.

In one woman's lament for her brother, a villager turned urban banker (Kalokiris 1970:86), the verses seem at first to express only grief. Closer examination, however, reveals an almost grim satisfaction that this successful local son's career did not bring him back to the "fresh [literally, 'pure'] air" in time. City life is morally corrupt; the expatriate villager finds redemption upon his return to his roots and to the soil: "You should be proud . . . that you died on Mount Ida . . . on the high peak . . . in the fresh air" (see also Herzfeld 1985:155).

During my fieldwork in Glendi, which is close to the village described by Kalokiris and has virtually the same lament tradition (Herzfeld 1985), I attended several funerals and memorial services and heard a good deal of lamenting. Lamenting is not confined to the actual funeral. Immediately after a death, kin gather around the bed on which the body is laid out, usually for an overnight wake. Close kin and neighbors keep watch over the body; others come to visit and offer their condolences (men with a solemn handclasp) to the close kin (siblings, parents, children) of the deceased. Kalokiris schematically insists that women lament while men (presumably those who are not directly affected and so can maintain a degree of equanimity) tell tales of the deceased's life, thus emphasizing and idealizing the gendered distinction between these two performative modes. In my own experience, however, women were no less inclined to join in the storytelling than men.[12] Only close kinswomen would sob and from time to time break into fits of lamenting, but even they interrupted these dramatic outbursts quite suddenly to remark, in more "normal" voices altered only by increasing hoarseness, on some incident in the dead person's life. This sudden switching between raucous lament and relatively calm recollection, so much at odds with the pure sense of archaic tragedy sought by the earlier folklorists, is especially common at the funerals of old people and suggests that the villagers recognize a need for conventional outpourings of grief even when inner feelings may not fully correspond to those outpourings. The performance of a lament is not necessarily a marker for deeply felt grief, and in fact one local scholar reported that west-central Cretan women sometimes sang laments to pass their time in a pleasurable, even "joyful," way (Tsouderos 1976:13).[13]

An old person's funeral is considered less "serious" than that of a young one—especially than that of an unmarried man or woman, whose wedding the funeral symbolically reproduces, with red wine and meat replacing the funeral hospitality of the colorless but fiery tsikoudhia (grappa) and white cheese. Very different was the funeral of a married woman in her mid-twenties who had died in Germany (where she and her husband were living as labor migrants), allegedly after taking inexpertly prescribed medicine. Her husband, prostrate with grief, staggered about at the funeral in the arms of his scarcely more composed brothers, while his wife's female relatives lamented with loud cries and sobs—the characteristic funerary reversal of male articulacy and female silence. The bereaved husband, with several children to care for, remarried within a year. A widower is usually too old to conform to the ideal of the virginal young warrior, or *pallikari* (see Campbell 1964:280; Machin 1983). This widower's dramatic pursuit of an attractive young woman whose family was of a status roughly equivalent to his, however, as well as his adamant refusal to accept any diminution of status and the speed with which he then created a new family with his second wife, protected him from such social erosion. The new bride's father, initially dismayed that his young daughter would have to raise another woman's offspring but swayed by her obvious determination to marry the man, could use the clear evidence of the groom's intense sense of family sentiment to counter the objections of his own agnates to the marriage. For, while the first wife's death had seemed to leave the young man quite inconsolable, it had also allowed him to enact the encompassing role of loyal family man and strong supporter of village values despite his long absence abroad. One would not have to be cynical in order to notice that public grief provided a morally fine background to his second marriage.

The funeral to which we now turn, while lacking such tragic power in the villagers' own eyes, similarly suggests the possible anticipation of future developments in the protagonists' lives. The deceased was nearly 90 and had not been a person of great consequence in village affairs. (Perhaps this was why I was encouraged to record the lamenting.) A poor member of the prestigious third-largest patrigroup of the village, he had been widowed and had remarried. His second wife was from the least prestigious patrigroup. She herself, manifestly beset by mental health problems, had been in no position to make a "good" marriage. As one of the neighbor women remarked at the time of the funeral, this woman had been "mad" (*palavi*) to marry so much older a man (she was now about 40, a half century younger than he), but she had been poor and so had hardly had much choice. At least it was more respectable to be a widow than an elderly spinster. Her lack of sons was another social demerit, but less serious than childlessness. Her two daughters, then aged about 15 and 12, were virtually the only lamenters besides herself.

This was not considered a "serious" funeral. People would still "weep," I was told, but if all the village came it would be because bad weather had interfered with work rather than because there was much interest in paying last respects. People also noted that even the older daughter did not know "serious things" (that is, how to perform good laments), while the younger daughter's attempts to imitate her sister elicited only condescending pity.

At this funeral, the great age of the deceased allowed most bystanders to take a philosophical stand. Not so the family, however: theirs was a social as well as a personal loss, and one that endangered their future. None doubted the genuineness of their grief; few admitted to sharing it. The mother, never a clear speaker at the best of times, was so hoarse from the vigil of the night before that one could barely make out the words in her lamenting. Because the younger daughter had no real knowledge of how to perform, the older girl carried major burden of expressing the family's concerns. But what she enunciated, very clearly, was her own concern at being left an orphan in a world hostile to women without fathers or brothers to defend their reputations and their chastity. Her mother did not appear to count as an active parent, and indeed subsequently became more of a dependent than a protector. The girl did the only thing that was left to her: she so vehemently stated her predicament that even a woman of a "good" patrigroup was moved to observe that it was "very sad" (*poli lipiro*), adding that the family did not have many kin to "support" (*na vastaksoune*) them. Note the contrast here with the physically enacted "support" of males who have just suffered bereavement. Familial support is crucial: the older girl's assumption of a supporting role toward her sister earned her some respect, permitting a kinder view of her status to emerge.

The public ideology of this community is androcentric. Men seek any available means of demonstrating that they have strong agnatic backing (brothers, patrilateral cousins, and so on), in order to intimidate potential enemies. Agnatic kin "support" a male mourner, as we have seen. Children suddenly bereaved of their father are "now on their own" (*monakha tora*); their mother is at best an ambiguous agnate (see Mandel 1983). The death—and, socially, the funeral—of their father weakens their claim on agnatic "support." A woman observed that if the two sisters were to marry, their kin would have to "find meat" for the wedding, implying the need for strong agnatic support: agnates, especially those who are active animal thieves, bear special baskets of meat (*kaniščia*) at weddings, thus demonstrating the solidarity of the patrigroup to potential foes. A mother, debarred from raiding and therefore unable to perform the role of shepherd, cannot protect her offspring alone. On the other hand, she also may not remarry, since both she and her children now "belong" to the patriline (*soi, fara, yenia*) of her late husband. A daughter in Glendi who loses her father is thus far more disadvantaged than is her counterpart in less strongly agnatic communities (see, for example, du Boulay 1974).

Thus, the daughters' only hope for social redemption now lay in appealing to the villagers' sympathy. At the same time, as unprotected young women, they would always, and automatically, be suspected of sexual abandon. Women can, it is true, anticipate such suspicion. The widow of a young man who was killed in a tractor accident made a great display of her lamenting as she walked from her house to the cemetery and back, never pausing on the way. She also let it be known that she had been pregnant at the time of the accident. She and her brothers-in-law, whose reputation would be the most affected by any fall in her moral status, thus forestalled interpretations of her pregnancy as evidence of post-mortem infidelity. Whereas a widow in a less strongly agnatic Greek community might have to put up with innuendo and derision (de Boulay 1974:183), in Glendi a widow's husband's agnates take rapid, preemptive action to protect their collective good name. Similarly, these two young girls had to start staking claims to chastity from the moment of their father's death. But with no brothers-in-law already in place to support those claims, who would believe them? And who would accept them as brides?

After presenting the funeral material, I shall briefly discuss the two girls' subsequent fortunes. It should become clear that the words of the lament look forward to a resolution of this dilemma. While the elder sister's "solution" might have been unsatisfactory for a woman of higher status, it was far better than might have been predicted at the time of the funeral. It is important to remember that a person's social worth (*timi*) is always relative to the expectations fellow villagers entertain of him or her (Herzfeld 1980:342–343). A woman of low status, no wealth, and dubious sexual reputation who still manages to get married may thereby earn at least grudging respect.

TEXTS

The laments from this funeral seem very disjointed. Some fragmentary elements come through the crunching of feet on gravel on the way to the graveside and the exhaustion of the mother's voice, the elder daughter's inexperienced gropings for the right style, and the younger daughter's largely wordless wailing. What follows is a representative sample of texts which repeat certain key phrases over and over (especially those imploring the deceased to speak).

M: *e do spitarkhagha [sic]*.	eh, the head of the house.

Then a conversational moment:

D: Siko mana mou . . . pam'pio omorfa.	Get up, mother . . . let's go in a more dignified way.

But the mother laments:

Oghrighora pou m'ekapses,	Quickly have you burned me,
pedhi mou, oghrighora	my child, quickly—[see] what I
inda'patha, pedhi mou.	have suffered, my child!

Here the widow addresses, not one of the daughters, but the dead man himself. *Pedhi mou* (my child) is an endearment and implies nothing about age or generation. We shall see that the elder daughter addresses her *father* as "my *mother*": the mother, fount of the deepest love, becomes the key metaphor for all close kin regardless of generation or gender. This semantic conflation alone should warn us against excessively literal interpretations (see also Trawick 1988:211).

Another source of confusion is the constant commentary from the women accompanying the principal mourners and helping them on their stumbling way. At one point, a woman comments, "Say [the laments] properly [*leye omorfa*]." A man observes, perhaps not unsympathetically, "She weeps, she weeps [*klei, klei*]." Then, at one outburst from the elder daughter asking her father to speak to her, a woman mutters to her, "Quietly [*sigha*]!" And then, in a louder and more matter-of-fact tone: "Quietly! Since, you might say, [he was] an old man, look, [it was] his time. But quietly!"

These admonitions, and especially the comment that "it was his time," suggest in a fairly explicit way that the young woman should resign herself to her immediate fate, since her father has not escaped his ultimate one. It does not do any good to protest too loudly. Women should band together in silent acceptance of their social and emotional pain. Significantly, however, these pieties have little effect. That the deceased father will never return is undeniable. In asking him to speak to her again, however, the elder daughter is denying just that. In rejecting the soothing bromides of her companions, she is also expressing a more realistic rejection of fate—social as well as physical. If, as Greeks say, "fate" for a woman can simply mean "marriage" (that is, to a specific partner),[14] this is a destiny that she can do something about. Events were soon to reveal as much.

Her appeal to her father to "get up and speak to me" is a cry for the solace of human companionship. It also, however, underscores the reversal of roles that takes place at a funeral. For now *she* is verbally articulate, a woman calling on a man to speak when she and all around her know that he will not do so. Again and again she cries out, in raucous, often incoherent pain, such lines as the following:

Ke ya to khatiraki sou to leo,	And for your sake I tell you, get
siko ma, mou milisis, pali leo.	up to speak to me, I say again.

Note that the most central formula of all is the rejection of silence in a phrase apparently unique, in Glendiot poetic diction, to the laments: "I say again." It is a claim to articulacy and a demand to be heard. Words provide the best weapon against the determination of one's social lot.

Siko na dhis ts' anthropous 'dho,	Get up and see the people here, my
mana mou,	mother,
pou irthane sto ghamo sou, khara	who have come to your wedding, my
mou,	joy,
yati se aghapoune, pali leo,	because they love you, I say again,
ke tha sou poune pali.	and they'll tell you again.
Siko na mou milisis, pali leo,	Get up and speak to me, I say again,
na yano sti kardhia, egho 'pa.	so I may get well in my heart, I said.
Siko, o patera mou,	Get up, O my father,
ke a'plisiaz'i ora kale, leo,	and if the time comes nigh, I say, fine
	man,

<table>
<tr><td>

ke tha se valo mesa se allo spiti pale,
gale leo.
Ma egho tha-n erkhome ke kathe
mera, leo,
če omorfa troparia na sou leo, gale leo.

Emis ton ekhasamene, leo, mana mou,
emis i-to patera mas, dhoulia mou.
Siko na mou milisis, yoka, leo,
na yano sti kardhia, egho dhe leo.

yati allios tha dhiaolo, mana mou,

an dhen mou milis, sou leo, khara
mou.
ke ya 'a pa' 'gho, ga-le'on'a mou.
Konda tou na tou po dhio-tria
troparia, lemonia mou!
Siko na mou milisis dha, patera mou,
ya na, na yano sti kardhia egho.
Ya plisiaz' i ora, gale leo,
ke tha se valo, lei, sto mnima, kale leo,

ma egho than erkhome kathe mera,
leo,
če na se thesi, 'nia mou. Ke omorfa
troparia, pali leo, če na tou pite,
leo, tou kalou mou yati egho
dhe katekho yati 'ne,

'dha tin kria aghapi, leo,
edha ine kria, egho 'pa.

</td><td>

I'll put you in another house, I say
again, fine man.
I'll be coming and every day I'll say,

I'll say fine hymns to you, I say again,
fine man.
We have lost him, I say, mother mine,
we our father, [O] my labor.
Get up and speak to me, son, I say,
that I may be cured in my heart, I
don't say [otherwise],
because otherwise I'll go crazy[?], my
mother,
if you don't speak to me, I tell you,
my joy,
and I'll go, my [?] lemon tree.
Beside him I'll sing two or three
hymns, my lemon tree!
Get up and speak to me, my father,
so that I may be cured in my heart.
The hour draws nigh, I say again,
and I'll place you [she says] in the
tomb, fine man, I say,
but I'll be coming every day, I say,

and to [?] put you to sleep, my [?]
lemon tree. And fine hymns I
say again, tell my love, say I,
because I don't understand why
[it] is,
[why] love is cold now, I say,
now it's cold, I said.

</td></tr>
</table>

This lament, metrically far more uneven and semantically more opaque than one would expect on the basis of Kalokiris' transcriptions or indeed than the majority of funerary performances I heard, displays several points of interest. First, there is an indisputable wedding theme, in which the wedding is a metaphor for the death of the mourner's father; but the incoherent remarks about love also suggest an allusion to the lamenter's own marriage prospects, now imperiled by the loss of her protector. When she speaks of love, the ambiguity seems almost deliberate, so that death identifies her beloved father with her eventual groom. This apparent confusion has emotional roots: a little later in the funeral, a man would remark, "Tomorrow we'll be dancing," which suggests a similar sense of the close relationship between joy and grief, as well as of the emotionally transformative passage of time. The *troparia*, "hymns," are the dirges themselves. When, a year later, the young woman asked me for a copy of the recording, she used this term, which represents a claim to respectability and articulacy. Listen to these hymns, says the mourner, for they are real hymns, respectable and religious in inspiration, rather than just "weeping." But they are expressions of a tradition that the church has often, and assiduously, tried to stamp out.

The text is full of formulaic elements that occur more coherently in the laments recorded by folklorists. The very disjunctiveness of the lamenter's utterances, in a public performance which none found masterly but none described as nonsensical, suggests that ulterior or at least ambiguous meanings are present. Death is incomprehensible at many levels, and lamenters predicate many signs upon this "inchoate subject" (Fernandez 1986:31). Death is and is not a marriage; the father is and is not a nurturant mother; the lamenter's "love" is and is not erotic affect. All this ambiguity permits a diffuse linkage among events past and present and opens up as yet unclear possibilities in the future as well.

A sympathetic woman who evaluated the lamenter's skill gave a very literal explanation of what the mourner meant. She complained that the latter did not have "fine things" (*spoudhea pramata*) to say: she did not lament with "enthusiasm," "gusto," and "tasty food" (*thousiasi, ghousto,* and *to fai to nostimo*). Note the link, so unlike English usage, between types of intense emotion. Joy and grief require effective performance, marked by gusto or by the rather more technical kind of enthusiasm called *meraki* (see Herzfeld 1981a:49, on the very similar *kaimos*). Aesthetic appreciation is as appropriate to funerals as it is to marriages. These rites of passage are also joined by casually aggressive verbal play—good wishes with sinister undertones—predicated on the analogy between them (Herzfeld 1985:126).

The observer's comments show that for her the effectiveness of lamenting would lie in the ability to convey the sensuality of grief—to turn grief into commensality. What she found instead of "tasty food" was a self-absorbed expression of misery:

Baba, fevghis ke pou mas finis, emas ke monakha mas? Afou ine ke i mama mas arrosti, ke pios tha mas prostatefsi emas ta monakha? . . . Ksipna, Baba, na mase dhis pou klemene yiro sou, ke mes emilis, mono eklises ta matia sou ya panda.

Papa, you are leaving, and how are you leaving us behind? Since our mother is ill too, who will protect us orphans? . . . Wake up, Papa, and see how we weep around you, and speak to us, but you've closed your eyes forever.

This observer's paraphrase eliminates the marriage metaphor, as well as any hint of a constructive future orientation. Only in the next stage of her life did the mourner herself actualize the latent possibilities of her situation.

AFTER THE FUNERAL:
FROM DEATH TO MARRIAGE

For some months after the funeral, the elder daughter did not appear much in public. Then, after failing to attract the interest of a fellow villager of relatively high status, she decided to adopt a conventionally male role—specifically, that of a father or an elder brother—by initiating negotiations to marry off her sister before allowing herself the luxury of marriage.[15] The man she found for her sister was a middle-aged deaf-mute from another village, a man who was himself to die only a few short years later.

In boasting that she had "married off her sister," she was claiming for herself the principal role that her father, in dying, had shirked. As a woman, she would ordinarily have had to get married herself before the younger girl could do so. In fact, she waited until she had married off her sister, then fell in love with a dashing but poor young man from yet another village and married him. Her triumph in marrying off the sister was not marred by the early death of the latter's husband, since widowhood is considered at least marginally better than spinsterhood and since the sister apparently offered no objections at any point.[16]

In the manner of her lamenting, we can discern some anticipation of the older girl's firm determination to make her own way. Although she did not fit the female role well, she made an unanticipatedly dramatic effort. Since nobody took her very seriously and everyone had low expectations of her, moreover, she emerged with much more dignity than the same actions would have conferred on a woman of even slightly higher status.[17] Today, she lives in a dank and poorly furnished basement apartment in one of the coastal towns. Her husband is a taxi driver who must struggle to make enough money to support her, her (now very ill) mother, and four small children. But she also has the solace of knowing that she achieved rather more than expected.

First through her lamenting and then through some decisive moves, she acted upon the conventional structure of social relations and values. She was not only categorically protesting her lot as a woman, she was also protesting, and rejecting, the categorical definition of herself as a woman limited by her gender. She was indeed biologically and, for most of the time, socially a woman; but when she had to adopt the social role of a man, she was ready to do so and later took explicit pride in this aspect of her actions. I certainly do not intend to suggest that she managed to prophesy this sequence of events through her lamentations. Her unusual and superficially faulty management of the formulaic structure, however, may conceivably suggest some impatience with convention. More substantively, the license accorded her as a very young and inexperienced lamenter allowed her to create dignity out of potential humiliation. Nobody could deny that she had tried to grieve like a mature woman. Her very solecisms highlighted her determination to act appropriately and so helped to deflect the fatalistic self-image that lies in wait for any young woman in circumstances comparable to hers.

Bemoaning her fate thus ultimately had the effect, if not the immediate and conscious purpose, of changing that fate. Superficially a passive expression of despair, it—or, rather, she—acted upon a critical situation with the poetic tools available. I use "poetic" here in its technical sense, as pertaining to performative expressions that, through deformation of social and aesthetic convention, may create new insight and understanding.[18] The lamenter's attempt to stake a claim on bystanders' admittedly grudging and qualified approval through her determination to keep lamenting may have suggested a reversal ("unwriting") of time-as-fate: in improving a humiliating social status, she (perhaps unwittingly) created for herself a kinder destiny in the long term—hardly the work of a fatalist.

Her imagery incorporated the reversible death-as-marriage theme. The fated descent into despair can be recast as an ascent to "joy" (khara, a synonym for "marriage"). The occasional use of the future tense in the lament suggests an orientation that is not exclusively to the past. Her statement "I'll put you in another house," ostensibly an allusion to the act of transferring the body to the grave, also reflects the conventional language, in a neovirilocal community, of a parent transferring a daughter to another home and another agnatic allegiance at marriage. The death of a father, marked by these lamentations, led by short stages to the marriages of both daughters. This was not prophecy but the creation of a field of meaning in which there existed more possibilities for future action than the literal surface conveyed. What is written cannot be unwritten; but what is sung or keened can most certainly be reinterpreted. The paradox of fate is that it can only be understood provisionally, because new events and new performances may change what people claim its mandate to have been all along. Thus, the daughter's lament was doubly performative: a projection of self, and plausibly if by no means certainly, an attempt to alter circumstances.

I have tried here to establish certain connections between a biography and a performance and to suggest that these converge in a symbolic vocabulary that is rich with past communal experience. The links I have advanced, while suggestive, would certainly be very difficult to "prove." Language resists reduction to literal, singular meanings, a fact that both makes resistance possible and constrains its practical effects. That my analysis is provisional respects the uncertainty the mourners themselves experience in interpreting events.

The lack of final closure, moreover, preserves a key feature of the young woman's continuing situation. Her life remains difficult, lonely, threatened by poverty. Did she "succeed"? At what did she succeed? Like the reading of fate at the time of a death, the answers to such questions are always, at best, retrospective and provisional. Had she accepted the closure of destiny—a destiny imposed upon her, androcentric in every sense, intolerant of her poverty—she would never have achieved what for her is probably a relatively desirable condition. She recognized, seized, and activated the available possibilities and made them, within a narrow and equivocal compass, her own.

NOTES

This article was originally prepared for the conference on lamenting organized by Steven Feld at the University of Texas, Austin, in April 1989 and funded in part by the National Endowment for the Humanities. It has benefited substantially from the discussions that took place at that time, as also from a seminar held in the Department of Anthropology, Harvard University, in December 1991. I would also like to thank the following people for providing careful criticisms of the text: Margaret B. Alexiou, Loring M. Danforth, Kenneth M. George, Kathleen Halme, J. Lorand Matory, Peter Loizos, Mary M. Steedly, Stanley J. Tambiah, Nur O. Yalman, James L. Watson, Rubie S. Watson, and reviewers for the *American Ethnologist*. Neither my colleagues nor the Endowment can be said to hold any responsibility for the opinions expressed here. I would also like to acknowledge the assistance of Vassos Argyrou in the delicate task of transcribing an extremely difficult tape recording.

1. The singers of laments are almost exclusively female in Greece. For a possible if rare exception, see Herzfeld 1981b:130.

2. *O,ti ghrafi dhe kseghrafi.* "Writing" and literacy are key symbols of power in Greece, and the complex idiom of a writing fate carries over into the popular imagery of bureaucratic power.

3. From *mira* (fate) and *loya* (words). A common "folk etymology" gives *mirioloya*, from *miria*, literally, "ten thousand" (cf. English "myriad") (see Alexiou 1974:110–118).

4. A full ethnographic account is given in Herzfeld 1985.

5. I particularly want to acknowledge the contribution that Jane K. Cowan has made to my awareness of the dangers, central to my present argument, of overstating the presence of resistance or subversion and of identifying it with too much certainty. Her perspective, which was extremely helpful in formulating the argument of Herzfeld 1991, is also crucial to several sections of her own recent ethnography (Cowan 1990).

6. The lament text in my earlier article is misrendered in line 1, and should read "*dakhtilidhaki mou khrouso, koumbaki m'asimeno*" (1981a:54). For further discussion of these themes, see Alexiou 1974:202–203 and Danforth 1982:106–108.

7. See Alexiou 1974:83–98. It is not necessary to argue even a sketchy folk memory of actual events. In fact, the laments for the fall of citadels in particular do not seem to reflect the historical perception of those times, when the local population often saw the Turks as deliverers from a harsh Western yoke, while the laments served no less effectively to express the views of Greek-speaking *Muslims* (that is "Turks") when the new Greek state assumed control (see Herzfeld 1973). The importance of these sources, or the models provided by the *Virgin's Lament* (see Alexiou 1974:62–78), is not that of a literal historicism.

8. I use this term in the semiotic (Peircean) sense.

9. Such appeals to an encompassing collective history are a common means of rendering personal experience accessible to an audience. See, for example, Coplan 1987; for additional, well-contextualized Greek examples, see Seremetakis 1991:226, 237. On a Glendiot male equivalent, see Herzfeld 1985:9–10. On conflation with

religious figures, see Kligman 1988:223. Trawick (1988) is more concerned with the merging of contemporaneous and co-present identities.

10. Male silence inverts a normative structure in which control of words stands for control of the body and of social relations (Herzfeld 1985:182; cf. Seremetakis' [1990:490] view of men as a "silent chorus" acting in contrast to the vocal women). Female identity in Greek male ideology conjoins images of the silent Virgin Mary and of the gossipy devil. Since the Virgin Mary image is associated with sexual restraint and that of the devil with unbridled sexual incontinence, it does not seem unreasonable (*pace* Friedrich 1988:188) to assume an implicit parallelism between the contrasts of self-control with license in the two domains, language and sexuality, especially as the alleged female propensity for uncontrolled speech (gossip) is often blamed for the collapse of reputations for chastity.

11. Nationalist folklore scholarship has found in the laments an extraordinary conformity to the principles of ancient tragedy. See, for example, Zambelios 1859; but cf. Herzfeld 1981a.

12. Villagers may have given Kalokiris an idealized view of the past, claiming that the distinction between male and female roles was clearer than it is today. This raises troubling questions about Seremetakis' (1991:222) interesting but perhaps undemonstrable claim that today's sharp gender dichotomization has resulted from penetration by ideologies of modernization, although, if she is right, the villagers' view may also reflect the impact of such a process on modern perceptions of the ideal state of society.

13. I have also heard it said on Nisiros that women would often pass the time in the fields singing laments to themselves. Note the conflation (from an Anglophone perspective) of different kinds of intense emotion in such Greek terms as *kaimos* (grief, enthusiasm) and *lakhtara* (longing, terror).

14. Greeks often describe marriage in general as a woman's "destination" (*proorismos*) and thus as the object of unremitting effort because to remain unmarried would be a severe social failure. No woman knows, however, who her specific marriage partner will be; that is the decision of cosmological forces, particularly "fate," whose ultimate decision one may try to manipulate in advance but cannot alter after the fact.

15. The situation was relatively unusual in that, since women commonly marry in their mid- to late teens, few are fatherless by this stage; of these, some have at least one brother (who may be younger than they) to assume a protective role. On the other hand, the sisters did have two matrilateral uncles and a first cousin in the village, as well as sundry agnates of their late father. The lack of interest on the part of these male kin, many of whom were themselves of precarious social standing, probably reflects their unwillingness to express in public their connection to a family of such dramatically low status.

16. Since at the husband's death neither sister still lived in Glendi, they both might have felt freer to voice discontent had they wished to do so; but the younger sister's silence also almost certainly shows that she understood the older sister to be as unfree an agent of the male-authorized morality as she was herself.

17. This is consistent with a common form of Greek evaluative diction, in which a foreigner may speak "better Greek" than the native and in which an impoverished old woman who offers a guest one olive and a glass of water achieves greater social worth than a big spender who scatters his largess around the community.

18. I do not claim, however, to have understood the lamenter's conscious intentions. Interpretations that even closely related fellow villagers might have made, while contributing to a social poetics in the sense intended here, do not permit us to gauge her own thoughts at the time. The theoretical argument on which my use of "poetics" is based derives from the Jakobsonian concept of the poetic function but extends it

beyond the realm of language alone; see Herzfeld 1985 and 1991. The category of performative utterances includes "perlocutionary acts," and these may have unintended consequences (Austin 1975:107; see also Giddens 1984:9–14). A gender-sensitive poetics must also account for the difficulty of ascribing conscious intent if the idea of an active "making" is not merely to reiterate the hegemonic assumptions that it seeks to counter; see Miller 1986 and Showalter 1986.

REFERENCES

Abu-Lughod, Lila. 1986. *Veiled Sentiments: Honor and Poetry in a Bedouin Society.* Berkeley: University of California Press.
Alexiou, Margaret B. 1974. *The Ritual Lament in Greek Tradition.* Cambridge: Cambridge University Press.
Anonymous. 1977. "Justice for Cyprus Pledge at Makarios Burial." *The Times* (London), 9 August:6.
Austin, John L. 1975. *How to Do Things with Words.* 2nd edition. Cambridge: Harvard University Press.
Baud-Bovy, Samuel. 1935. *Chansons du Dodécanèse.* 2 vols. Athens: G. N. Sidéris.
Beeman, William O. 1981. "Why Do They Laugh? An Interactional Approach to Humor in Traditional Iranian Improvisatory Theater." *Journal of American Folklore* 94:506–526.
Bloch, Maurice, and Jonathan Parry. 1982. "Introduction: Death and the Regeneration of Life." In *Death and the Regeneration of Life,* ed. M. Bloch and J. Parry, 1–44. Cambridge: Cambridge University Press.
Bourdieu, Pierre. 1977. *Outline of a Theory of Practice,* trans. R. Nice, Cambridge: Cambridge University Press.
Campbell, John K. 1964. *Honour, Family, and Patronage: A Study of Institutions and Moral Values in a Greek Mountain Community.* Oxford: Clarendon Press.
Caraveli, Anna. 1986. "The Bitter Wounding: The Lament as Social Protest in Rural Greece." In *Gender and Power in Rural Greece,* ed. J. Dubisch, 169–194. Princeton: Princeton University Press.
Caraveli-Chaves, Anna. 1980. "Bridge between Worlds: The Greek Women's Lament as Communicative Event." *Journal of American Folklore* 93:129–157.
Coplan, David B. 1987. "Eloquent Knowledge: Lesotho Migrants' Songs and the Anthropology of Experience." *American Ethnologist* 14:413–433.
Cowan, Jane K. 1990. *Dance and the Body Politic in Northern Greece.* Princeton: Princeton University Press.
———. 1991. "Going Out for Coffee? Contesting the Grounds of Gendered Pleasures in Everyday Sociability." In *Contested Identities: Gender and Kinship in Modern Greece,* ed. P. Loizos and E. Papataxiarchis, 180–202. Princeton: Princeton University Press.
Danforth, Loring M. 1976. "Humour and Status Reversal in Greek Shadow Theatre." *Byzantine and Modern Greek Studies* 2:99–111.
———. 1982. *The Death Rituals of Rural Greece.* Princeton: Princeton University Press.
de Boulay, Juliet. 1974. *Portrait of a Greek Mountain Village.* Oxford: Clarendon Press.
de Certeau, Michel. 1984. *The Practice of Everyday Life,* trans. S. Rendall. Berkeley: University of California Press.
Fernandez, James W. 1986. *Persuasions and Performances: The Play of Tropes in Culture.* Bloomington: Indiana University Press.

Friedrich, Paul. 1988. "Four Meanings of 'Critical.'" *Anthropological Quarterly* 61:187–198.

Geertz, Clifford. 1988. *Works and Lives: The Anthropologist as Author.* Stanford: Stanford University Press.

Giddens, Anthony. 1984. *The Constitution of Society: Outline of the Theory of Structuration.* Berkeley: University of California Press.

Herzfeld, Michael. 1973. "'The Siege of Rhodes' and the Ethnography of Greek Oral Tradition." *Kritika Khronika* 25:413–440.

——. 1980. "Honour and Shame: Some Problems in the Comparative Analysis of Moral Systems." *Man* (n.s.) 15:339–351.

——. 1981a. "Performative Categories and Symbols of Passage in Rural Greece." *Journal of American Folklore* 94:44–57.

——. 1981b. "An Indigenous Theory of Meaning and Its Elicitation in Performative Context." *Semiotica* 34:113–141.

——. 1985. *The Poetics of Manhood: Contest and Identity in a Cretan Mountain Village.* Princeton: Princeton University Press.

——. 1991. "Silence, Submission, and Subversion: Toward a Poetics of Womanhood." In *Contested Identities: Gender and Kinship in Modern Greece,* ed. P. Loizos and E. Papataxiarchis, 79–97. Princeton: Princeton University Press.

Johnson, Elizabeth L. 1988. "Grieving for the Dead, Grieving for the Living: Funeral Laments of Hakka Women." In *Death Ritual in Late Imperial and Modern China,* ed. J. L. Watson and E. S. Rawski, 135–160. Berkeley: University of California Press.

Kalokiris, S. 1970. *Ta Anoya.* Athens.

Kligman, Gail. 1988. *The Wedding of the Dead.* Berkeley: University of California Press.

Loizos, Peter, and Evthymios Papataxiarchis. 1991. "Introduction: Gender and Kinship in Marriage and Alternative Contexts." In *Contested Identities: Gender and Kinship in Modern Greece,* ed. P. Loizos and E. Papataxiarchis, 3–25. Princeton: Princeton University Press.

Machin, Barrie. 1983. "St. George and the Virgin: Cultural Codes, Religion and Attitudes to the Body in a Cretan Mountain Village." *Social Analysis* 14:107–126.

Mandel, Ruth. 1983. "Sacrifice at the Bridge of Arta: Sex Roles and the Manipulation of Power." *Journal of Modern Greek Studies* 1:173–183.

Menardos, Simos. 1921. *Istoria ton lekseon Traghodhia ke Traghoudho.* [Athens].

Messick, Brinkley. 1987. "Subordinate Discourse: Women, Weaving, and Gender Relations in North Africa." *American Ethnologist* 14:210–225.

Miller, Nancy K. 1986. "Arachnologies." In *The Poetics of Gender,* ed. N. K. Miller, 270–295. New York: Columbia University Press.

Rosaldo, Renato. 1989. *Culture and Truth: The Remaking of Social Analysis.* Boston: Beacon Press.

Seremetakis, C. Nadia. 1990. "The Ethics of Antiphony: The Social Construction of Pain, Gender, and Power in the Southern Peloponnese." *Ethos* 18:481–511.

——. 1991. *The Last Word: Women, Death, and Divination in Inner Mani.* Chicago: University of Chicago Press.

Showalter, Elaine. 1986. "Piecing and Writing." In *The Poetics of Gender,* ed. N. K. Miller, 222–247. New York: Columbia University Press.

Trawick, Margaret. 1988. "Spirits and Voices in Tamil Songs." *American Ethnologist* 15:193–215.

Tsouderos, Yannis E. 1976. *Kritika Miroloya.* Athens.

Tuffin, Paul. 1972–73. "The Whitening Crow: Some *Adynata* in the Greek Tradition." *Epeteris Kendrou Ethnikon Erevnon* (Nicosia) 6:79–92.

Zambelios, Spiridon. 1859. *Pothen i kini leksis traghoudho.* Athens: Soutsas Ktenas.

Suffering and Its Professional Transformation

Toward an Ethnography of Interpersonal Experience

ARTHUR KLEINMAN AND JOAN KLEINMAN

INTERPRETATION AND EXPERIENCE

An effective strategy in medical anthropology is to demonstrate how a patient's illness complaints and convictions reproduce a particular moral domain. Via visible social archetypes and invisible social processes, pain and lay modes of help seeking are shown to replicate a cultural world, one, moreover, that the anthropologist can validly interpret. The theory may come from Durkheim, Weber, Marx, Freud, or Foucault, and the style of ethnographic writing may be no-nonsense naturalism or vexed post-modernism yet the accomplishment is to show that illness is a socially constructed reality to which the ethnographer has privileged access.

This interpretive strategy is often followed by a second analytic feat in which the anthropologist reveals how the clinician reworks the patient's perspective into disease diagnoses and treatments that reproduce the health profession and its political economic sources. The semiotic iteration of the suffering of lay men and women into the taxonomies of healing professionals is then shown to distort the moral world of patient and community.

Thus, when a psychiatrist transforms the misery that results from political calamity—say, the horror of the Cambodian genocide or the numbing routinization of poverty in urban ghettos—into major depressive disorder, post-traumatic stress or sociopathic personality disorder, the anthropologist claims that, notwithstanding technical and ethical intentions to the contrary, psychiatry ends up delegitimating the patient's suffering as moral commentary and political performance. At least by implication, psychiatrists are held to trivialize the experience of their subjects, and even perhaps render them more difficult to work through. The anthropological accounts, then, claim to make a fundamental critique of the psychiatric transformation of that irreducible existential quality of illness. That professional transformation, it is claimed, sometimes with more than a little suggestion of moral superiority, recreates human suffering as inhuman disease (Cassel 1991).

The anthropologists' *interpretive dilemma* is that they participate in the same process of professional transformation. The interpretation of some person's or group's suffering as the reproduction of oppressive relationships of production, the symbolization of dynamic conflicts in the interior of the self, or as resistance to authority, is a transformation of everyday experience of the same order as those pathologizing reconstructions within biomedicine. Nor is it morally superior to anthropologize distress, rather than to medicalize it. What is lost in biomedical renditions—the complexity, uncertainty, and ordinariness of some man or woman's world of experience—is also missing when illness is reinterpreted as social role, social strategy, or social symbol . . . anything but human experience.

Please do not misinterpret our intention. We are not positing an anthropological oxymoron like suffering as experience taken neat, without its cultural meanings and historical changes. There can be no such acultural, ahistorical human phenomenon. But we are suggesting that anthropological analyses (of pain and passion and power), when they are experience-distant, are at risk of delegitimating their subject matter's human conditions. The anthropologist thereby constitutes a false subject; she can engage in a professional discourse every bit as dehumanizing as that of colleagues who unreflectively draw upon the tropes of biomedicine or behaviorism to create their subject matter.

Ethnography does participate in this professional transformation of an experience-rich and -near human subject into a dehumanized object, a caricature of experience. That it occasionally resists such transformation seems to have more to do with the constraints imposed by participant observation as an empirical practice—by its very nature a way of knowing difficult to isolate from the messiness and hurly-burly of daily living—than with anthropological theorizing about experience and its modes.

CATEGORIES FOR THE ETHNOGRAPHY OF EXPERIENCE

What categories might an ethnography of experience, in particular one concerned with the study of illness and other forms of suffering, draw upon to resist the tendency toward dehumanizing professional deconstruction, or simply to become more self-consciously reflective about the human core of human experience? It is our opinion that a contextual focus on experience-near categories for ethnography should begin with the defining characteristic of *overbearing practical relevance* in the processes and forms of experience. That is to say, *something is at stake* for all of us in the daily round of happenings and transactions.[1]

Experience may, on theoretical grounds, be thought of as the intersubjective medium of social transactions in local moral worlds. It is the outcome of cultural categories and social structures interacting with psychophysiological processes such that a mediating world is constituted. Experience is the felt flow of that intersubjective medium. In Bourdieu's (1989) terms it is the social matrix out of which habitus is structured and where shared mental/bodily states in turn structure social interactions. Yet, in practical terms, that mediating world is defined by what is vitally at stake for groups and individuals. While preservation of life, aspiration, prestige, and the like may be shared structures of relevance for *human conditions* across societies, that which is at stake in daily situations differs (often dramatically) owing to cultural elaboration, personal idiosyncracy, historical particularities, and the specifics of the situation.[2] What is at stake in life settings, then, is usually contested and indeterminate (Kleinman 1992).

Ethnographers enter the stream of social experience at a particular time and place, so that their description will be both a cross-sectional slice through the complexity of on-going priorities and a part of the temporal flow of changing structures of relevance. That such structures are contested, indeterminate, novel and changing means that the ethnographer's descriptions are always about a local moral world that can only be known incompletely, and for which the relative validity of observations must be regularly recalibrated. Moreover, what the ethnographer experiences matches how individuals encounter the flow of experience (Dewey 1957:269). They do not dominate it, or invent it, but rather are born or thrown into the stream of lived interactions. (See Jackson [1989:1–15] for a review of phenomenological sources for this existential appreciation of experience.)

A central orienting question in ethnography should be to interpret what is at stake for particular participants in particular situations.[3] That orientation will lead the ethnographer to collective (both local and societal) and individual (both public and intimate) levels of analysis of experience-near interests that, we hold, offer a more valid initial understanding of what are social psychological characteristics of forms of life in local worlds than either professional sociological categories (roles, sets, status) or psychological terminology (affect, cognition, defense, behavior).[4]

The focus on what is at stake encourages the ethnographer to build up an ethnopsychological inventory of key indigenous conceptions, but not to stop the analysis at that point. The level of indigenous categories *qua* categories can quickly become artificial—as the misadventures of ethnoscience clearly disclose—because it leaves out precisely what orients those categories to practical experience. Moreover, a list of ethnopsychological categories in itself can only partially provide the grounds for understanding what is shared in human conditions and what social psychological processes mediate experience. The former, the conditions of being human, refers to the existence of certain defining rhythms and limits to experience—birth, life cycle change, moral development, death, and bereavement. Human conditions—e.g., the subject of this essay, suffering—constrain lived experience. They offer a resistance in the flow of life to the elaboration of life plans.[5] The dialectical dance between these shared resistances and the culturally elaborated yet simultaneously idiosyncratic structures of relevance creates the "bewildering inexpediency" of human experience (Manning 1981). It also shapes the character of danger, the scope and possibilities of transcendence, and the other existential quiddities that taken together represent whatever is meant by the expression human nature. That is to say, the flow of experience is not the product of a human nature (personality, instinct, etc.) but the condition for its emergence as both shared and culturally particular, and therefore far from the determinative agency that has been claimed by psychoanalysts, cognitive behaviorists, or most other psychological theorists.[6]

The upshot of this phenomenological vision is that viewed from close up, the density of personal awareness (the actors' and the observers') of the richness of human experiences is difficult to express and uncertain owing to its repleteness, subtlety, and complexity. Yet when viewed from afar the historical shape of experience is apparent as are cross-culturally shared elements and rhythms. The ethnographer's focus moves back and forth. The task is to interpret patterns of meaning within situations understood in experience-near categories; yet, ethnographers also bring with them a liberating distance that comes from their own experience-near categories and their existential appreciation of shared human conditions. That means that ethnography, like history and biography and psychotherapy, holds the possibility of a way of knowing more valid to the dialectical structure and contingent flow of lived experience than reductionistic forms of knowing which by definition distort the existential conditions of life. This perspective also suggests why understanding ethnopsychological categories, though essential, is insufficient: we know much more than we can say or understand; we are awash in the meanings of experience; the historical flow and cultural elaboration of experience lead us to organize figures out of grounds that are greatly relevant to particular occasions. (Our informants and our audiences are also trained in varying levels of irony, as Geertz 1988 puts it.) Getting at mediating psychological processes requires that eventually we shift to the view from afar—we cannot otherwise abstract universalizing processes from the particularizing content of ethnopsychological meanings—but to understand actual situations we must use both lenses.

In sum, then, what is at stake for particular men and women in their local worlds offers an example of the type of category we regard as crucial for advancing an ethnography of experience.[7] In discussing this category, we have all too quickly touched upon other aspects of experience—e.g., the existential pressure for coherence and unity (see Oakeshott 1985), the immediacy of its felt quality (Cassirer 1962:78; Merleau-Ponty 1962), the confusing multiplicity and indeterminacy of its flow (à la Bergson [1889] and William James [1981:279–379]), the notion that it is emergent, achieved and contested not preformed (as in Dewey 1957:269), the character of brute resistance to life plan that must be transcended and that expresses the finitude of experience (Jackson 1989:1–15), the existential responsibility to come to terms with its teleology (Sartre 1956:553–556; Frankl 1967:84–93), and so on. These recognizable aspects of experience suggest other categories that must inform our ethnographies. For the purposes of this essay, however, a single category will be all that we can handle, though we shall return to certain others later on.

HUMAN SUFFERING

We will examine the suffering that is a concomitant of illness and its social sources as an illustration of the ethnography of experience. Biomedical interpretations of illness have properly been criticized for leaving the experience of suffering out of assessment of the disease. In order to depict suffering, anthropological accounts disclose how the idiosyncracies and divided interests and cross-purposes of personal life lived under the strenuous constraint of disease processes are actually culturally patterned into recognizably shared forms: e.g., the desperate withdrawal and isolation of seriously ill Gnau patients near the Sepik River in New Guinea (Lewis 1976), the neurasthenia of Chinese with major depression in Beijing or Taipei (Kleinman 1986), the nervios of Puerto Rican immigrants to inner city ghettos on the East Coast of the United States (Guarnaccia 1989) and so on. To accomplish this analytic feat the illness experience is frozen at a certain moment as if the illness narrative had reached completion or the illness course had terminated at a final stop. Of course, in the actual flow of illness experience, there is no final stop. Even death is followed by bereavement and the further and influential trajectory of the remembered past (for the family and the practitioners). The anthropologist creates the illusion of finality and continuity and coherent meaning, when in fact even the simplest illness episode has more complex resonances than can be accounted for by the analytic models that are available to us. The abstraction of a definitive cultural form out of the inchoate transitoriness and recalcitrant uncertainties of the everyday experience of illness does violence to the personally idiosyncratic and the situationally particular, to the "blooming buzzing" confusion of the stream of living. As the first author has shown in The Illness Narratives, cultural representation is only one of at least several discrete kinds of illness meanings—the others include the personal and interpersonal meanings in a local setting—yet in numerous medical anthropological accounts it is all that we learn about an illness. We hold that the anthropological tendency to create cultural archetypes out of the always messy and uncertain details of a personal account of illness—an approach to which we too have contributed— is as invalid an interpretation of the human core of suffering as is the biomedical tendency to create a purely biological metaphor for pain. Both render the peculiarly human quality of suffering—that which is most at stake for the participants—fungible. By alienating the illness from what is at stake for particular individuals in particular situations, cultural analysis creates an inhuman reality every bit as artifactual as the pathologist's disease entity. If there is no purely "natural" course of disease, there also can be no purely "cultural" symptomatology.

Suffering can be defined from the historical and cross-cultural record as a universal aspect of human experience in which individuals and groups have to undergo or bear certain burdens, troubles and serious wounds to the body and the spirit that can be grouped into a variety of forms. There are *contingent misfortunes* such as serious acute illness. There are *routinized forms of suffering* that are either shared aspects of human conditions—chronic illness or death— or experiences of deprivation and exploitation and degradation and oppression that certain categories of individuals (the poor, the vulnerable, the defeated) are specially exposed to and others relatively protected from. There also is *suffering resulting from extreme conditions*, such as survivorship of the Holocaust or the Atom Bomb or the Cambodian genocide or China's Cultural Revolution. The cultural meanings of suffering (e.g., as punishment or salvation) may be elaborated in different ways for current day Sri Lankan Buddhists or Medieval Christians, but the intersubjective experience of suffering, we contend, is itself a defining characteristic of human conditions in all societies.

To illustrate this point in order to draw out its significance for understanding human suffering as the focus of an ethnography of experience, we will turn to a case of the bodily mode of experiencing personal and political distress— i.e., somatization—in Chinese culture.[8]

Case Illustration

Huang Zhenyi is a worker from a rural county town in his late twenties suffering from depression. He attributes his chronic headaches and dizziness to a traumatic childhood experience during the Cultural Revolution, about which he can talk only to his wife. During winter vacation from school Huang Zhenyi returned to the schoolyard. Someone had tacked up a piece of paper with "Throw down Chairman Mao!" written in bold characters across it. Not knowing what to do about this anti-Mao slogan, he ran to see his close friend, who told him to quickly inform their commune leaders. This he did, and those cadres responded by calling in the public security (police) agents. Three of them interviewed Huang Zhenyi at his school. They asked him who wrote the poster, and when he could not respond they accused him. The policemen threatened that if he didn't confess they would not let him return home. Frightened after being interrogated for several hours in a small room at the school, from which he was not allowed to go to the toilet in spite of a painful urge to urinate, he told the police that he had found the slogan but was not the one who wrote it. He was angry at his friend for not supporting his story by telling what had actually happened. Eventually, late at night, his interrogators allowed Huang to return home. There he found his mother distraught over his absence. He explained the problem to her and assured her he was not at fault.

The next morning the three agents came to Huang Zhenyi's home and took him to the public security building. Brutally, they assured Huang Zhenyi that this time he would never leave the small interrogation room until he confessed. Terrified that he would not be allowed to eat, relieve himself, or see his mother again, Huang Zhenyi signed the confession, accepting sole responsibility for writing the poster.

When he returned home he told his mother that he had written the poster, fearing that if he told her the truth it would only create greater trouble for her and for him. Huang Zhenyi still recalls with obvious pain his mother crying and cursing him, "If I knew before you'd end up like this, I wouldn't have wanted you." He remembers breaking down in tears, but he found himself unable to tell his mother the truth. "I felt like a coward. I couldn't tell her."

This experience recalled for him an earlier one. At age eight he had gone with several classmates to fish in a nearby pond, instead of walking to school. They were very late getting to class. The teacher punished them by locking the boys in a small mud-walled room. They escaped by knocking a hole in the wall and hid in a nearby cotton field. Their teacher, who was known for being a strict disciplinarian, ran after them and caught Huang Zhenyi's two friends but not him. "I was so frightened I froze in my place. I could not move." Later in the evening he returned home, and the next day went back to school. The teacher, greatly angered by Huang's behavior, ordered him to do menial work around the school rather than study. Huang Zhenyi refused to do the hard labor, and this led his teacher to criticize him severely in front of other teachers. After this experience, Huang Zhenyi reported "my liver became small, and I became frightened, cowardly." From this time onward he felt "paralyzed" whenever he had to "stand up" for himself before adults.

Because of his confession, the twelve-year-old Huang Zhenyi—who again felt "paralyzed," unable to break his silence before his adult accusers—was marched through the local county town wearing a duncecap, carrying a sign around his neck on which he had written a self-criticism for the "terrible act," surrounded by thousands of local peasants and cadres, who cursed him, spat at him, and threw dirt and pebbles at him. The next day he was sent to work as a peasant at a local production team. He was expected to do the work of an adult. No one would talk with him at first. The heavy labor was so exhausting that Huang Zhenyi thought he would not survive. Each day he had to undergo self-criticism, while local groups of children jeered at him. In a mass criticism session he felt himself go numb, as if paralyzed. He wanted to yell out the truth but couldn't get himself to do it, to break his silence. No one would believe him, Huang Zhenyi reasoned. He had been patient so far, he would endure the unendurable, since there was no way out. Finally, after a year of hard labor, a year during which he several times thought he could no longer stand the work and the isolation, his fellow peasants praised him for doing the work of an adult and enduring his punishment in silence. They pleaded on his behalf with the local authorities that he be allowed to return to school, which he did.

Eventually Huang left this commune and moved to a county town in another province, where he finished high school and where his past was unknown. He became a key worker and joined the Communist Party. He was able to do the latter since the local party officials, owing to the chaos of the time, knew nothing about his past and because of his highly regarded poor peasant background. He never told his mother his version of what had happened. When she was dying he thought of confessing to her the full story but decided against it. "I was too frightened to speak out and didn't think it would do any good." Huang's mother died not knowing of her son's innocence, a point he returns to again and again as a palpable reason for his current feelings of desperate shame and self-hatred. Now looking backward, he feels depressed, hopeless, desperate. He retains great anger at the three policemen and at his classmate, who would not admit to the interrogators that Huang Zhenyi had told him he had found, not written, the anti-Maoist poster. He feels a searing sense of injustice, a feeling that he associates with a burning sensation in the head, dizziness and exhaustion. He is fearful that someone in the party will learn of his past and expel him on account of it.

Huang believes he will never recover from this event. "It has affected my character. I am withdrawn; I don't like to be too friendly with others. I am a coward. I cannot trust others." He sees his only hope as writing a novel about his experience that would fictionalize it to protect his anonymity and generalize it so that it comes to represent the "losses and defeat" his generation has experienced. "Like me we are a lost generation that has suffered so much." But Huang Zhenyi doubts he will accomplish this goal. He has no formal training or natural skill to write fiction. He actively fears the consequences of others learning about his past. He feels trapped. Each time he takes up a pen to write the story, he is overcome by a self-defeating lassitude, dizziness, and sense of his inefficacy. Hence Huang's physical complaints are amplified (perhaps created) by the literal embodiment of chronic frustration, inability to act—if we use his word, "paralysis," but of will not muscle—and the unbearable inner hurt of shameful "injustice" that he can neither publicly articulate (save through the personally unavailing neurasthenic pain) nor privately expiate.

Huang Zhenyi's own statement that his losses during the Cultural Revolution represent those of his generation signifies a collective awareness in China that the Cultural Revolution deeply affected the lives of entire cohorts of Chinese, in this case adolescents. Unlike others I have interviewed to understand the relationship of neurasthenia to political oppression, his losses during these terrible times were not the physical loss of close family members (his mother died after the Cultural Revolution). Instead Huang is talking about the loss of self-esteem, self-confidence, the normal developmental period of becoming an adult, the normal relationships with family members, and also of hope in his future and that of his society.

Doubtless there are parallels in pre-Communist China and in other societies, the United States included. We are not trying to suggest that what happened to Chinese in the Cultural Revolution is without precedent or cannot be compared to social sources of misery in other societies. But it is also the case that we mean to implicate an entire generation in Huang's distress. His demoralization and anguish may be (and probably are) greater than that of others, owing to his personal vulnerability and the magnitude of the crisis he experienced. He developed a disorder, most others did not. Yet it is precisely because Huang's disorder exposes the inner hurt the Cultural Revolution caused that we may suspect this type of psychological wound is fairly widespread among the members of his generation. To our minds, it represents the personal effects of a society-wide delegitimation crisis; a loss of engagement with the dominant moral order. For most members of that generation the psychological effects of the Cultural Revolution are unlikely to have led to the despair that Huang experiences. We do not know with what intensity and quality of distress it has afflicted them. We can be sure it has left its mark, however, and that that mark is more like a wound than a blemish. China's leadership seems to have written this "lost generation" off, concentrating instead on the new generation of students, who are expected to be better prepared, educationally and psychologically, to take maximum advantage of the new emphasis on technological and economic growth.

The first author of this paper published the story of Huang Zhenyi, including the interpretive paragraphs, in 1986. Writing in September 1989, it seems eerie reading the closing words. In the Tiananmen Massacre and its repressive aftermath, the Chinese government has gone on, it would seem, to create a second "lost generation." There is a popular cultural delegitimation of the Party and the State every bit as widespread and deeply felt as at the end of the Cultural Revolution. One can only wonder what has happened to the man to whom I gave the pseudonym, Huang Zhenyi; or how many other Huang Zhenyis will arise out of the ashes of the latest democracy movement? In the face of such terrible oppression is it surprising that bodily idioms of distress are commonplace, that neurasthenia again seems on the rise?

A student of Chinese culture will experience little difficulty interpreting even this brief illness narrative in light of core Chinese cultural configurations. One of Huang Zhenyi's chief complaints, dizziness or imbalance, *tou yun*, resonates with a central metaphor in traditional Chinese medicine, balance or harmony between macrocosm and microcosm, between the constituents of the body/self and the social world. Huang Zhenyi's disharmony is in the circulation and amount and forms of his *qi* (vital energy), and in his past experiences; they in turn disharmonize his emotions and create illness. To be dizzy—a common though usually unmarked symptom of neurasthenia in the past and of chronic fatigue syndrome at present in the West—is to be unbalanced, to experience malaise, to be dis-eased. Dizziness was understood by our informants to be the embodiment of alienation. The broken moral order was quite literally dizzying. To experience dizziness was to live and relive the memory of trauma. It was as close as many could come to express political opposition and cultural criticism, at a time when overt expression of such hidden viewpoints could lead to dangerous political outcomes: public violence, humiliation, demotion or job loss, forced self-criticism, exile, imprisonment. Dizziness also expressed for some the felt experience of falling (or fear of falling) from a higher to lower social position. The topsy-turvy cycles of the Cultural Revolution spread this experience across all social positions. One group ascended via struggle, was in turn struggled against, and then was passed by, as another group grasped for higher position, only to fall in turn.

His exhaustion and pain can be analyzed in the same way. Exhaustion from sleeplessness, and the paralyzing fatigability and weakness associated with it, recalled shared traumatic events. Months of working frenetically in political campaigns, often at contradictory purposes, convinced sufferers that they and perhaps the nation had reached the end of revolution. Vital resources were exhausted. Personal and collective efficacy had been drained. Fatigue and weakness in traditional Chinese medical theory express loss or blockage in the flow of qi. Devitalization is understood to affect the body-self and the network of connections, the microcosmic local context and the macrocosmic society.

Pain—headaches, backaches—also recreated the effects of the Cultural Revolution's turmoil on human lives. This lived metaphor, like the others, was easily extended from personal anatomy to the social body, from the anatomical network of muscles, bones, nerves, and blood to the social network of interpersonal experience in conflicted work and family settings. Pain, inner resentment, collective suffering, and social resentment merged. Each complaint, elaborated in the context of a story that integrated social and bodily suffering, extended the metaphoric reach of the pain, exhaustion and dizziness as moral commentary, first, about the self and its local life world, ultimately, about the society. That is to say, somatic complaints expressed what was at stake in the flow of experience. There is not one source of symptoms; different social experiences engage the same culturally prepared bodily processes (Kleinman and Kleinman 1994).

A student of Chinese culture could follow this line of emic analysis to interpret Huang Zhenyi's physical complaints as a somatopsychic idiom of distress that expresses the psychosocial effects of political problems in a politically acceptable and culturally sanctioned collective rhetoric of complaint. Indeed, one could (and one of us has done so) write an entire book on the relationship of neurasthenia to depression in China and its mediation through culturally shaped bodily experience among patients whose complaints are similar to Huang Zhenyi's.

Yet Huang Zhenyi's tale has so very much more in it than the cultural semiotics of symptoms and disease, which we also do not mean to disvalue, that violence would be done to the account—we would suppress its echoing misery—if we stopped at this level of analysis. If we left off at that point, we would turn Huang Zhenyi into a passive object, a caricature unworthy of the tragic tale he had told us and the moral significance it held for him that he wanted us to take away from the encounter to transmit abroad. The same inauthenticity would occur if we interpreted this story solely in psychodynamic terms or even as a political tract. Those implications are also present, but they, like the illness experience, are only facets of a complex narrative of suffering, the human veracity of which is its concentration of multiple divergent meanings. What is most at stake for Huang Zhenyi—the historical injustice, the obdurate sense of shame, the frustrated desire to express his grievance and right a terrible wrong, and the practical need to protect himself from the machinery of oppression—was only in part at stake for the Chinese psychiatrists who listened to his story, and was not at all relevant for us. Yet understanding what was at stake in this encounter, we are now convinced, tells us something more valid about Huang Zhenyi's actual experience of suffering than separate cultural, political or psychodynamic interpretations.

SUFFERING IN CHINESE CULTURE:
THE LIMITATIONS OF CULTURAL ANALYSIS

Take a recent piece in *ETHOS*, the *Journal of The Society for Psychological Anthropology*, by Sularnith Heins Potter (1988), a Berkeley anthropologist who has conducted field research in China. In that anthropological article, Potter contributes to a growing literature that seeks to distinguish non-Western cultures from North American and Western European cultures by emphasizing the point that whereas Western societies are individual-centered, non-Western societies are sociocentric. This dichotomy seems to be one of the basic orientations of contemporary psychological anthropology.

Potter's argument asserts, based on her rural field research, that Chinese regard emotions as irrelevant idiosyncrasies lacking in serious implications for social relationships. The Chinese, she tells us, do not locate significance in the connection between the emotions, the self, and the social order. For them, emotions are "a natural phenomenon" without important symbolic meaning for the maintenance and perpetuation of society. Emotional experience and expression of feeling have no formal social consequences. Suffering, she avers, is not understood by the Chinese as inner personal experience. Nor would the personal experience or expression of suffering, by extension of her argument, hold social significance in Chinese society. Rather a Chinese person's anguish, resentment, ominous feeling of menace, bitter demoralization, hopeless despair, or raging alienation are of no intrinsic importance to the social order.

Feelings are never the legitimating rationale for any socially significant action undertaken by Chinese, insists Dr. Potter. Americans, of course, are described as the absolute obverse of this caricature. For us, emotions are everything. They are the "legitimating basis that establishes a relationship between a person and a social context." Social action for us is spurred by feelings, the form and meaning of our lives derive directly from our emotions.

Thus, we have Edward Said's (1978) *Orientalism* equation, albeit with a reversal in the values, now favoring the formerly colonized. The cultural other is the alien opposite of what we hold ourselves to be. What is flawed in our world is perfected in theirs. But to accomplish this interpretive feat what evidence is adduced must (1) portray homogeneous, unidimensional stereotypes, not real people; (2) it must discount examples of the opposite, which of course abound in Chinese (and also in American) culture; and (3) above all it must leave out any shared human qualities that suggest there is an obdurately panhuman grain to human conditions. The upshot of Potter's transformation comes dangerously close to what Said accused the orientalists of accomplishing: narrowing the humanity of the other and thereby of ourselves.

To make such comparisons, one tends not to, one *must not*, emphasize actual experiences of suffering or narratives of personal misery; they are too powerfully human; their concrete details—always original and affecting and usually plural and ambiguous enough to contest—disintegrate abstract dichotomies; they smudge the cold prose of social analysis with the bitter tears of moral sentiment. It is not that Huang Zhenyi after all is not more sociocentric than his North American counterpart, but that that very sociocentric orientation to the world is the medium in which his individuality is expressed. Or rather, as Nan Lin (1988) has pointed out in a powerful recent essay on the Chinese family, Chinese, like Huang Zhenyi, are both sociocentric members of family groups and rugged individualists. Different patterns of transmission from generation to generation of moral authority and material property, argues Lin, foster a divided orientation of the self. (See also Basu [ms.] on divergent constructions of the self among Chinese.)

Any culturally valid theory of psychosocial dynamics for Chinese society would have to transcend the simplistic sociocentric/egocentric dichotomy and also, to our mind, would find inadequate and distorting a number of standard psychoanalytic presumptions. Rather we should begin with a historical reconstruction of Chinese cultural categories of personal experience and interpersonal engagement. Emotion (*qing* or *chih*) is not presented as an independent phenomenon, separable from the rest of experience. The Su Wen section of the pre-Chin Huangdineijing (*The Yellow Emperor's Classic of Internal Medicine*) sets out an indigenous theory of the emotions as they relate to health and illness. Suicidal grief, immobilizing sadness, manic passion, and other extreme emotional states are held by the dominant Chinese medical tradition of systematic correspondences up to the present to be etiological factors that cause organic pathology; they are also signs of social pathology. They are *pathogens,* internal etiologic factors (*nei yin*) that create organic dysfunction. In Traditional Chinese Medicine (TCM) emotion is not a general phenomenological descriptor. Instead, there are seven specifically named entities, the *qiqing,* seven kinds of situationally embedded emotional reactions, namely joy (*xi*), anger (*nu*), melancholy (*you*) [also translated as anxiety/depression], worry (*si*), grief (*bei*), fear (*kong*), and fright (*jing*). These, if excessive, may become pathologic factors. They include excessive joy, anger, and melancholy, over-worrying or thinking too much, and fear. They are said to influence the normal circulation of *qi* and the blood in the internal organs, thereby causing morbid conditions. In this view, the human body as well as its pathological changes are in a continuous state of adapting to the variations of the "natural environment." This is the concept of *tian ren xiangying*—nature and man adapt to each other—and here "nature" includes the four seasons, the physical and social environment, and the physical structure and physiological processes of the individual himself. Thus, emotional pathology may become both sign and cause of social pathology, and balancing the emotions means harmonizing social relations and vice versa. Dizziness or imbalance is a sign of illness. Suffering simultaneously affects and is affected by the relational balance between body-self and the natural world. (In a vast civilizational culture like China's, plural traditions abound and we could find a few exceptions to support another interpretation of the emotions. But this we take to be the paramount view.)

From at least Zhang Jiebin's (1710) *Qing Yue's Medical Text* right up to the most recent writings of China's leading theorists of psychopathology, the prototypical Chinese view of emotions and emotional disorders has recognized various sources and consequences of depression and anxiety states, while holding a somatopsychic view within which the causal line from environment to person is held to be mediated by the body. The body is also regarded as the main idiom or medium through which psychological, social and psychosomatic problems are expressed.

Francis Hsu (1985) points out that *affect* in Chinese culture is understood as *specific* feelings: love, hate, loyalty, sympathy, betrayal, aspiration, despair, and so on. It is further understood to be inseparable from the performance of particular tasks in specific situations that are part of one's social role, says Hsu.

In Taiwan today there is a major movement by academic psychologists to sinicize psychological theory and methodology. A leading figure in the sinicization movement is K. K. Hwang, professor of psychology at the National Taiwan University, who offers, to our mind, the most conceptually satisfactory interpretation of emotion among Chinese. Hwang (1987) defines *renqing* (the emotional response of an individual who confronts various concrete situations in daily life) as the essential meaning of emotion. *Renqing* is happiness, anger, fear, love, hate, and desire.[9] If a person understands other persons' emotional responses to various circumstances in life, and if he can respond empathetically to their reactions, then he is said to "know *renqing*." Emotions need not be expressed openly. A sensitive person "knows the tone" (*zhih yin*). For example, close friends are "those who know me" (*zhih jizhe*).

Thus, emotion means a contextualized response, a response one feels or senses in experiencing the concrete particularity of lived situations. The person who knows *renqing* reads his and others' responses to the situation through all the senses: sight, smell, sound, and other sensations, including an inner resonance. *Renqing* is also a *resource* that is part of social exchanges. Affection like goods or services is exchanged. But unlike money it is difficult to calculate. Indeed, it is said that "one is never able to pay off debts of *renqing* to others." And that is why social relations involving establishment of networks of influence so central to Chinese daily life transactions turn on whether *renqing* is withheld or given as gift. Thus, "reading," "exchanging," and "repaying" *renqing* (here understood as favor) constitute what is at stake in relationships. Finally, Hwang argues, *renqing* is also a set of social norms by which one has to abide in order to get on well with others in Chinese communities. Hwang relates *renqing* to *mianzi* (face) and to *la guanxi* (creating networks of relationships or connections) and *bao da* (repayment or reciprocity) as the central Chinese models of experience. *Renqing* is both social and deeply personal; it captures the dialectical quality of experience; it is individual and interpersonal. It represents the moral core of experience. Sociocentricity alone is an inadequate category to interpret what the Chinese mean by emotion; this term points to something that is simultaneously sociocentric and individualistic in experience.

The methodological question is how to elicit both sides of the dialectic. And here there is a major problem. For as the leader in the movement to sinicize psychology, Yang Kuo-shu (1987), also a professor at the National Taiwan University, has shown, research must confront the tripartite division of all social relations among Chinese. The nearest compartment is occupied by family and close friends. Here trust is unconditional, and certain private feelings can be revealed. The second compartment contains distant family and friends. Here trust is conditional, and feelings will only occasionally be expressed, and always with great caution. The most distant compartment contains relations with strangers, including researchers (i.e., professional strangers). Here there is an absolute lack of trust, and inner experience is not to be expressed lest it is used against one's family and social network. Such a worldview is likely to lead the researcher toward certain conclusions (i.e., the Chinese are sociocentric) and away from others (i.e., the Chinese are also strongly individualistic).[10]

Other key indigenous sources that create a more valid understanding of experience, and therefore of the experience of suffering, include the third century text *Renwu zhi* (On Human Personality) by Liu Shao, who presents a political and transactional view of the self. The ideal person is to be *bland*; he is to blend with others and situations ". . . like salt, that by itself is not salty. He is clear, but not sharp; substantial, but not overbearing; attractive, but not obvious . . . decisive and cautious, there is no knowing all he is capable of. With this he can regulate and control." Balancing emotion and situation is essential to master social relations with others. Demonstrating strong feelings, including the menaced and aggrieved affects of suffering, is dangerous, because it gives others power over relationships and restricts one's flexibility to respond effectively. Ultimately, uncontrolled emotional displays threaten one's position in a world of power. Balance, blandness, control provide greater access to power and protect one from the feared effects of power: loss of resources or status or life.

As far as Potter's deconstruction of emotion among Chinese, one has only to point to a few classical sources to challenge her conclusion that emotions in Chinese society are irrelevant to the legitimation of the social order.[11] Qu Yuan (332–295 B.C.), hero of the Li Sao (Encountering Sorrow), has traditionally exemplified the delegitimation of an unjust social order.[12] His tale of sorrow is that of the wanderings of an upright official outcast from a corrupt court, a lonely individualist. The poem is a deeply moving meditation on his grief. The poetry's haunting sadness becomes the idiom of moral accusation. Qu Yuan's suicide is the ultimate act of delegitimation of the social order; a paradigmatic moral exemplar for Chinese remembered each year at the time of the Dragon Boat Festival (the fifth day of the fifth moon); and embodied in the eating of zonqzi (glutinous rice wrapped in leaves), both by participants in the festival and, after they are thrown in the water, by Qu Yuan's spirit. (Perhaps, Huang Zhenyi, who came from Qu Yuan's homeland, even had Qu's lament in mind as a model for his own dirge of personal suffering and political injustice?)

From pre-Chin times the songs or odes of the land, defined as shi yan zhi ("verbalized emotion") were gathered together to record, somewhat like an ancient Gallup poll, how well the realm was governed. These songs were not thought of as only the upwelling and outpouring of personal sentiments; instead the songs were held to derive from the social ethos. Joy, sadness, and disgruntlement, as conveyed in the odes, were believed to express the tangible conditions in the political order and to comment on the moral climate of the times. Confucius indicates this quite clearly in the Great Preface to the Book of Odes The She King (Shi Jing).

> . . . in an age of good order [the odes are] quiet, going to be joyful;—the government is then a harmony.
> . . . in an age of disorder [the odes are] resentful, going on to the expression of anger;—the government is then a discord.
> . . . when a State is going to ruin, [the odes are] mournful, with the expression of [retrospective] thought;—the people are then in distress. Legge (1960)

Classically, Chinese poetry explored concentrated life experiences, like the endurance of suffering, for their echoing emotional quality and universal significance. Writing such poetry was itself a way of witnessing and also of protesting one's times. Here is Arthur Waley's (1940:75) translation of Zuo Si's (Tso Ssu) third century classic, *The Scholar in the Narrow Street,* a scholar-official's criticism, through the portrayal of suffering, of himself and his era. (The moral sentiment is as appropriate for intellectuals in present-day China as for those in past periods.)[13]

> Flap, flap, the captive bird in the cage
> Beating its wings against the four corners.
> Depressed, depressed the scholar in the narrow street:
> Clasping a shadow, he dwells in an empty house.
> When he goes out, there is nowhere for him to go:
> Branches and brambles block up his path.
> He composes a memorial, but it is rejected and unread,
> He is left stranded, like a fish in a dry pond.
> Without—he has not a single farthing of salary:
> Within—there is not a peck of grain in his larder.
> His relations upbraid him for his lack of success:
> His friends and callers daily decrease in number.
> Su Ch'in used to go preaching in the North,
> And Li Ssu sent a memorandum to the West.
> I once hoped to pluck the fruits of life:
> But now also, they are all withered and dry.
> Though one drinks a river, one cannot drink more than a bellyful;
> Enough is good, but there is no use in satiety.
> The bird in a forest can perch but on one bough,
> And this should be the wise man's pattern.

The tradition of using the emotional response of readers or an audience to indict the system of political power extends right down to modern times through the writings of Lu Hsun, Lao She, Ba Jin, and many other Chinese authors. Shame, menace, loss, grief, and other emotional expressions of suffering are master symbols of China's revolutionary literature. For Lu Hsun (1963), the most influential of all Chinese writers in this century, the suffering of common people, as depicted in the social roots of their sorrow and desolation, represented the moral delegitimation of cultural as well as political authority. In the revolutionary theater put on for villagers by local representatives of the CCP during the years of civil war, their emotional response to memories of suffering under cruel landlords was used to sanction land reform and the destruction of their class enemy. The campaigns of the Great Leap Forward, Anti-Rightists, and Cultural Revolution reenacted this bitterness of experience as the transformation from "eating bitterness" (i.e., suppressing resentment and grievance) to expressing it publicly, often in the most extreme forms, against those designated at the time as the enemies of the people. The killing of landlords, the ritual degradation of intellectuals, the expulsion of

Party leaders, the erasure of alternate political memories—all were sanctioned through the conjuring of intense emotional reaction to the experience of suffering. The literature of the wounded following the Cultural Revolution, to which Huang Zhenyi's story belongs, is another example of the political uses of public sentiment; here used to delegitimate the Cultural Revolution.

In *Social Origins of Distress and Disease,* the first author describes the case histories of individuals whose distress and disease resulted from the excesses of the Cultural Revolution. The stories of suffering they told to us and to others were meant in large measure to articulate pain and despair as a moral commentary on the sources of their tragedy. Their idea was the classical one we have described; ruinous social policies ultimately ruin personal lives, the felt experience of whose haunting tragedy becomes the most telling political commentary on the times; precisely because that account is lived and power-fully felt, it has moral authority. Those stories were told to us as a moral witnessing of the Cultural Revolution: personal bitterness and defeat passed a sentence of condemnation.

To interpret such problems, because of the bodily idioms that frequently accompany them, solely as illness is to medicalize (and thereby trivialize and distort) their significance. The idea of *post-traumatic stress disorder* in North American psychiatry, which is increasingly being applied to victims of political trauma such as Cambodian and Salvadoran refugees, is the latest example of this invalid transformation of moral into medical meanings of suffering (see Young 1989). For here the intimate physiological consequences of political violence are converted into an anonymous medical euphemism. In so doing, their moral significance is weakened or even denied entirely.

Think of what "stress" means for an elderly Chinese as opposed to a similarly aged North American. The former has lived through the breakdown of social order in the 1920s and 1930s when epidemics and other conse-quences of a disintegrating social order dominated personal experience. What would be the equivalent in North America of the "stress" of the Anti-Japanese War, when 20 million died and 180 million were uprooted? During the first 8 years of the People's Republic, Mao Zedong admitted that 800,000 counter-revolutionaries were killed. The aftermath to the 1989 Democracy Movement has taught us what counter-revolutionary means! From 1959–61, following the disastrous policy of the Great Leap Forward, China experienced perhaps the most deadly man-made famine in history: perhaps as many as 30 million died of starvation. And so on. The very idea of post-traumatic stress as a disorder invalidates the moral and political meaning of suffering. After all in both traditional Chinese and Western cultures, the idea of suffering turned on the idea of having to endure or bear great hardship. The idea of suffering carried the moral significance of endurance, and in its Buddhist and Christian senses, there is the idea of transcendence. Those teleological connotations are lost when suffering is configured as a stress with which we cope (either adaptively or ineffectively) or a disease that can be "cured." Foucault's analysis of the practice of the professions in modern society emphasized that the responses of experts to stress and disease—experts, that is, who define *rationality* as a self-designation of what they think and who regard suffering to have no teleological significance but rather to be an opportunity for technical intervention—becomes a very powerful, perhaps the most powerful source of social control for just this reason.

One need only read Susan Sontag's (1989) recent cultural analysis of *AIDS and Its Metaphors* in our society to see that for the other side of our comparison—suffering in the U.S.—we would need to fashion an equally rich and complex indigenous analytic framework to get at the cultural elaboration of personal experience in North America, a society by the way where to bear or endure hardship for most of its members seems to run counter to the now dominant secular text of a world without pain or suffering.[14] The ideas of personal responsibility for suffering, hidden contagion silently transforming genetic codes into cancer or AIDS and thereby threatening at the very core our society's myth of technological control and our penchant to view as predictable and therefore insurable, risks the quiddity of human tribulations, the banishment of death from our response to AIDS, and even Sontag's utterly American wish to remove the meanings AIDS inflicts on sufferers—all are examples of the significance of suffering among North Americans that we can only mention in passing. They show obvious differences but also a few surprising similarities with our Chinese materials (see Kleinman 1988:100–120,146–157).[15]

And then? Having in hand different analytic frameworks and different accounts of suffering, then what do we do? If we stick to the texts, we might be tempted to throw up our hands over radical untranslatability. But we will not do this, we believe, if we stay close to the ethnographic context of experience.[16] For there is, we hold, something panhuman in the experience of distress of the person, in the bearing of wounds, in the constraints to the human spirit, in the choke and sting of deep loss, in the embodied endurance of great burdens, in the search for coherence and transcendence. There is something definitively human at the core of the experience, which to be sure is elaborated in greatly different ways in different cultural settings, but something that would emerge as universal from cross-cultural translation in the final stage in cultural analysis, if we focused ethnographic descriptions more self-consciously on experience and its modes. Translation, that is, must be, as Stanley Tambiah (1990) has put it, not the first but the last step in cultural analysis. Not the first, as it all too often is in psychiatry and psychology, because then we lose the valid cultural grounding of experience. But at the last it must be carried out—because if we fail to compare, we are not merely left with cultural solipsism, but with inhumanity: something less than the moral grounds of human experience.

CONCLUSION

Thus, just as biomedicine delegitimates the suffering in somatization by entifying it as *disease,* so too do the other professions and institutions of postmodern society (including all too frequently medical and psychological anthropology) transform somatization into something other than human experience.

Taussig's (1987) writings are to our mind among the more troubling examples of doing violence to the authenticity of the flow of lived experience; they undermine the status of suffering as a legitimate moral domain; but he is not alone.[17] We, each of us, injure the humanity of our fellow sufferers each time we fail to privilege their voice, their experience. Nations and Rebhun's (1988) account of the responses of poverty-stricken mothers in the *favelas* of northeastern Brazil to the high rates of death among their children, and Veena Das's (1994) description of the experiences of survivors of inter-ethnic violence and of the Bhopal disaster, are exemplary contributions to the anthropology of suffering precisely because they privilege the experience of sufferers to such an extent that it simply is no longer possible to disregard or disguise their grief, and to deny its implications for our understanding of the experience of the moral orders behind the distancing categories of public health or anthropology.

Earlier we contended that the professionalization of human problems as psychiatric disorders, undeciphered anthropological codes, or class warfare causes sufferers (and their communities) to lose a world, the local context that organizes experience through the moral resounding and reinforcing of popular cultural categories about what life means and what is at stake in living. We are far along in this process of inauthenticating social worlds, of making illegitimate the defeats and victories, the desperation and aspiration of individuals and groups that could perhaps be more humanly rendered not as representation of some other reality (one that we as experts possess special power over), but rather as evocation of close experience that stands for itself.[18]

We live in the flow of daily experience: we are intersubjective forms of memory and action. Our experiences are so completely integrated—narratized moments, transforming narratives—that the self is constituted out of visceral processes as much as expressed through them. Because the order of that flow is historical and cultural, what we feel and see and recall is a symbolizing physiology. Because of the social construction of the flow of experience, psychosomatic processes are transmitters and receivers of cultural codes. Because of the psychophysiological grounding of experience, cultural codes cannot make of each of us precisely what they will. There is also a panhuman constraint on the continuities and transformations that represent our lives and our networks which derives from the limited number of social ways of being human. Because of the political economy of experience, that panhuman constraint is itself twisted and turned by the local contexts of pressure that encourage or oppress our aspirations, that defeat us, that defend us, that are us.

Can there be a society without sadness? Can there be a culture without menace? Can the flow of experience, no matter how fantastically different is its cultural elaboration of loss or how serene, optimistic or trivial its historical configuration of that which must be endured, escape suffering?

We do not wish to be misunderstood. We are not saying that anthropology or psychiatry provide invalid knowledge. Far from it. We believe these two fields have greatly enriched our understanding of the social and psychological origins and consequences of illness, and of the powerful influences of social context and psychological orientation on the forms and processes of care. Even when it comes to the experience of suffering, both fields have opened up important directions for investigation. And yet, the materials required to understand suffering are of such a different order that we believe research approaches to it must deal directly with an experiential domain which heretofore, perhaps with the exception of the work of phenomenologists (which has its own problems), has been the grounds of art.[19] How social and behavioral science is to transform that realm into a suitable subject matter is not entirely clear to us. We feel certain, though, that this must happen if human suffering *qua* experience is to be part of the problem framework of our disciplines. Inasmuch as outstanding works of ethnography, biography, and history aspire to engage the phenomenon of experience, we feel comforted that the challenge, though a great one, can be met. By the way, that challenge is not to create a universal science of human suffering, which we hope this contribution has shown would be archly ironic.[20]

We also most definitely are not insisting that the topic covered in this paper is the most central or important topic for psychological or medical anthropology. The study of experience is simultaneously both another subject and a way of examining several of these fields' concerns. It deserves a place in medical and psychological anthropology.

Finally, we are not saying that suffering defies understanding or that it cannot be defined. We are not implying an irrational or mystical quality to suffering. Human beings find their plans and actions resisted by forms of resistance in the life course, in social relations, in biophysical processes. Out of these forms of resistance emerge what is shared in our human condition: loss, deprivation, oppression, pain. Human conditions are shaped as well by our responses to those forms of resistance: grief, rage, fear, humiliation, but also by what Scheler (1971:46) called transcendent responses: endurance, aspiration, humor, irony. Yet these are so greatly elaborated by systems of meaning and individual idiosyncrasy that human conditions must always contain great divergence too. Suffering is constituted out of these shared forms of resistance and by our greatly different ways of reacting to inevitable misfortune. Suffering and transcendence are among the things most at stake in the practical forms of daily experience. For that reason they deserve to be the self-conscious subject matter of ethnography and cross-cultural comparisons.[21]

NOTES

This chapter is a revised and expanded version of a paper that was originally published in *Culture, Medicine and Psychiatry* 15(3):275–301, 1991. The expansion draws upon materials from Arthur Kleinman and Joan Kleinman: "How Bodies Remember." *New Literary History* 25:707–723, Summer 1994.

1. The idea that experience, whatever else it may be, is of overriding practical relevance to the persons engaged in transacting a lived world can be found in the writings of scholars from a wide range of orientations: John Dewey (1957); William James (1981); Alfred Schutz (1968); Helmut Plessner (1970), the most important if the least well known of Continental phenomenologists; and is echoed in Dan Sperber and Deidre Wilson's (1986) recent criticism of contemporary studies in psychology and anthropology, which they claim lack an appreciation of this central orientation. Calling "relevance" that which is at stake in living—i.e., for survival, for coherence, for transcendence—has a long provenience in literature; it has become revivified for us as a resonant theoretical category in a dialogue with Unni Wikan (1987), with Veena Das (1994), with Vera Schwarcz (ms.), and with the present and past members of the Harvard Seminar in Medical Anthropology: Byron J. Good, Mary-Jo Delvecchio Good, Thomas Csordas, Mitchell Weiss, Peter Guaranccia, Pablo Farias, Norma Ware, Joyce Chung, David Napier, John Sugar, Robert Desjarlais, et al., including our present and former graduate students: Paul Farmer, Paul Brodwin, Anne Becker, Jim Kim, Lawrence Cohen, Maya Dummermuth Todeschini, Richard Castillo, Scott Davis, Ana Ortiz, Tara AvRuskin, Karen Stephenson, Catherine Lager, Kate Hoshour, Eric Jacobson, Terry O'Neill, Linda Hunt, Liz Miller, Don Seeman, Matthew Kohrman, Cheungsatiansup Komatra, among others.

Michael Jackson (1989) develops a sophisticated argument for radical experientialism in ethnography whose focus is the personal experience of native informant and ethnographer. Writing earlier, in the same tradition, Renato Rosaldo (1984) draws upon his own experience of grief, following the death of his wife, to understand the "force" of emotion among the Ilongot. Stoller (1989) is another contributor to this group. His focus on the sensory appreciation of cultural processes in taste, smell, sight, and sound suggests that ethnomusicologically informed ethnographies, such as Feld's (1981), as well as studies that focus on dance (Chernoff 1979), deserve to be included in this grouping. Francis Zimmermann's (1989) ethnomedical reconstruction of Ayurveda though metaphors of the terrain and taste of healing spices orients his work toward the experiential foundations of therapeutics. Roseman's (1990) multichanneled sensory approach to Malaysian aboriginal healing rituals would also deserve to be categorized under the rubric of experience-near ethnography.

What we have attempted to do in this paper is to develop a somewhat different understanding of experience, though we do not mean to deny certain resonances with the works mentioned above. We define experience not as a subjective phenomenon—something that a single person "has"—but as an interpersonal medium shared by, engaged in, and also mediating between persons in a local world. Here we elaborate the Chinese paradigm into a position that claims cross-cultural validity.

Our intention is to dissolve the individual/collective dichotomy. Interpersonal experience is the grounds of sociosomatic mediation (in illness) and transformation (in healing). In the local field of experience, chunks of unified processes of memory, affect, and physiology can be described at a variety of levels—personal, familial, network, community. Yet it is the novel idea of experience as an interpersonal medium of mediation that we wish to emphasize, rather than its more usual categorization as a personal form. For this reason, we describe our approach as the ethnography of interpersonal experience, though perhaps we could equally well describe it as the sociodynamics of cultural experience, because we regard culture to be constituitive through the everyday processes and practices, the interpersonal routines and rhythms of experience.

2. By *human conditions,* we mean to signify that there are only a limited number of ways of being human. We all must experience physical growth, personal transformations, hunger, injury, sickness (both minor and serious), fear, death, bereavement, etc. We use the plural, however, because we wish to indicate that even human conditions may vary within and among groups. Not everyone will experience a grave childhood disorder or bereavement for an infant son or daughter, yet many will, and some groups will have more than their share of such experiences. That which is at stake for men and women is constrained by shared human conditions, and, at the same time, it is elaborated by the particularities of local life worlds and individuals. Thus, human conditions supersede the dichotomy between "universal" and "particular" forms of living.

3. Including, of course, what is at stake for the ethnographer—by which we mean to convey a much wider set of self "interests" than is captured by the post-modernist emphasis on intellectual paradigm and style of writing. Something akin to the ethnographer's countertransference of passions, abiding and momentary, is what we have in mind, but without the psychoanalytic specification of their allegedly universal content.

4. Here we argue that "cognition," "affect," "defense," and "behavior" are not only hegemonic Western psychological categories, but that they are particularly inadequate as categories for the ethnography of experience. The separation of cognition from affect, in spite of all the words spilled to show the distortions produced by the residual dichotomies of the Western cultural tradition, is now taken for granted not just in psychology but in virtually all the human sciences. Yet, even a moment's self-reflection is enough to illustrate amply that this dichotomy rends the unity of experience. Commitments to measurement make most researchers deaf to these objections. Defense, of course, carries the entire weight of the psychoanalytic paradigm, which converts the multiplicity and uncertainty and sheer originality of experience into "truths" whose validity and reliability have almost never been rigorously tested, while their use has infiltrated the everyday language of social scientists and physicians. The ethnography of experience would be better off if it were defenseless. "Behavior" reifies the narrowest possible vision of living, and is underpinned by theories that are the most vulnerable to dehumanizing applications. All of these terms reify an overly individualistic account of experience that obscures the intersubjectivity we wish to emphasize.

5. Max Scheler (1971:14, 52–53) defines the quality of resistance as the very essence of the person's experiencing of reality as real. "Representations and mediated thinking [inferences] can never give us anything but this or that quality in the world. Its reality as such is given only in an experience of resistance accompanied by anxiety" (52–53). Here Scheler's notion of what is the realness of our experience of the world is what we denote by its quality of overriding relevance: namely, that which absorbs our attention. Social absorption, then, is the shared core of human conditions.

6. We are not saying there is no human nature. Rather, we insist that human nature is emergent in local worlds of experience; it is achieved and contains both universal and

culturally specific elements. Melzack (1989) theorizes from considerable research in the neurosciences that the brain-self is a neuromatrix open to experience, yet largely preceding it, that gives rise to a particular neurosignature of the lived body. While we disagree with Melzack's biological reductionism, our vision of human nature encompasses a notion of the body-self that is the continuously achieved result of the interaction of social world and psychobiological processes (including the neuromatrix). In this dialectical model, human nature is emergent: constrained yet elaborated.

7. The concept of local moral worlds is developed further in Kleinman (1992). For our purposes here the idea is a kind of shorthand for the focus of ethnographic studies on micro contexts of experience in village, urban neighborhood, work setting, household-networks, or communities of bounded relationships where everyday life is transacted.

8. This case is republished with a few alterations from Arthur Kleinman: *Social Origins of Distress and Disease: Neurasthenia, Depression and Pain in Modern China* (New Haven: Yale University Press, 1986), pp. 127–131.

9. See the *Li Ji* Book of Ritual: all men are born with the seven emotions.

10. J. C. Scott (1985, 1990) refers to the "hidden transcript" as that set of ideas which subordinates in a contested field of power relations cannot express publicly because of the sanctions of their superordinates. The idea is close to the Chinese understanding save for the emphasis Scott places on class conflict. In the Chinese version, the hidden transcript is expressed only in the first and second compartments. The third compartment, even with members of the same social class or political stratum, still contains the public transcript.

11. Of course, the story of the victims and survivors of the Tiananmen Massacre and the present period of repression of the democracy movement would be another and more powerfully charged way to challenge Potter's argument that emotions in Chinese society are irrelevant to the legitimation of the social order. The grief and anger of overseas Chinese and students from the People's Republic in the West have been emphasized as a sign of moral revulsion with the current government, and with Communism more generally. In the democracy movement, emotion was central to the hunger strikes and to resisting the troops who were sent to Beijing. In both cases, its significance as moral authorization for resistance was widely understood by all.

12. This is one of the reasons why Mao Zedong, who came from the same region of China, the area of the ancient Kingdom of Chu, held Qu Yuan to be one of his cultural heroes.

13. Compare Liu Binyan's (1990) account of the life of an intellectual under Chinese Communism.

14. Compare Phillippe Aries's (1981:614) sardonic summary of the meaning of death in the modern Western world for professional thanatologists: "They [a small elite of anthropologists, psychologists, and sociologists] propose to reconcile death with happiness. Death must simply become the discreet but dignified exit of a peaceful person from a helpful society that is not torn, not even overly upset by the idea of a biological transition without significance, without pain or suffering, and ultimately without fear."

15. Compare Dreuilhe (1988) or other personal accounts of persons with AIDS to see how Sontag's cultural analysis leaves out, purposefully as she indicates in her "Introduction," precisely that lived experience of suffering that we take to be the focus of the ethnography of suffering.

16. Recent examples of such ethnographies include Ellen Basu's (ms.) study of the felt experience of conflicting commercial and familial modes of interaction in the life of a Chinese merchant in India; Michael Jackson's (1989) description of the intersubjective

flow of experiencing everyday life activities in a Sierra Leone tribal society; and Steven Feld's (1981) attempt to render the sensibility of bereavement among the Kaluli of New Guinea across several sensory domains.

17. We have in mind Taussig's tendentious interpretation of shamanism solely as political resistance of colonized Indians in Colombia, and his denigration of both the personal pains and distress that sick persons bring to shamans, which shamans try to cure, and the practical responses of the public health system to control diarrheal disease as a source of the high infant mortality rates afflicting Indian families. For critiques of the interpretations of suffering as resistance see Das (1994) and Kleinman (1992). Taussig's use of the fantasy and illusion of hallucinogen-derived montage makes for some extraordinary literary excursions; yet it obscures what is at stake in local worlds. His radically self-experiential experimentation, though innovative, distorts the authenticity of the worlds of others; it also inverts the legitimacy of their local accounts for the priority of a totalizing analysis of hegemonic ideology that is his own source of authority. That political inversion creates what Scott (1985:346–350), following Barrington Moore (1978:459), rejects as a false sense of inevitability in the discourse on hegemony that "fails(s) completely to capture the texture of local experience." As Scott puts it ". . . to see the causes of distress instead as personal, as evil, as a failure of identifiable people in their own community to behave in a seemly way may well be a partial view, but it is not a wrong view. And not incidentally, it is quite possibly the only view that could, and does, serve as the basis for day-to-day resistance" (348).

A not insignificant contribution, however, is Taussig's experiment with a form of writing aimed at challenging the authority of the author in describing the realities of other worlds. Genre and style of writing are clearly crucial to the ethnography of interpersonal experience, and either can clarify or obscure human conditions. Yet the vexed prose of post-modernism shows itself to be as corrosive for the voice of the subject as it is of the authorial voice, so that Taussig's flawed experiment eventually substitutes one abuse of language for another. Nonetheless by forcing attention to the language of ethnography, Taussig provokes a useful question about the words and style most suited to describe the flow of interpersonal worlds. Perhaps, one of the benefits of the ethnography of experience is that it challenges the ethnographer to search for an authentic voice that can match both the scholarly and ethical requirements of its subject.

18. As for the magnitude of abuse, the professional transmogrification of experience via psychiatric or anthropological rhetoric is serious but certainly not nearly as dangerous as, say, the nineteenth-century idea of degeneracy and its twentieth-century revivification in the murderous eugenics of Nazism (Pick 1989). It would be a terrible scholarly error to exaggerate the former form of abuse. Even today the new eugenics strikes us as the most dangerous of discourses with respect to potential political abuse. Nonetheless the medicalization (or socialization) of suffering—what Latour (1988: 116–129) might call the Pasteurization of suffering by biomedical (or social science) reductionism—is still a significant example of the dehumanizing consequences of contemporary professional discourse.

19. The chief problem with phenomenological theory is that it has over time become a special language whose conventions, accepted by initiates, are opaque to general readers. The neologisms invented by Husserl, Heidegger, Merleau-Ponty, Gehlen, Plessner, and others obscure more than they illuminate about the felt quality of the flow of experience, and ultimately take on an essentialist tenor that is unacceptable for social analysis. Indeed, phenomenological theory often hides behind these abstruse terms. It has not taken on the responsibility of popularizing its conceptual advance through a rapprochment with broader intellectual currents. Nonetheless, as Jackson (1989)

shows, the insights of the phenomenologists can be outstanding and breathtaking when effectively translated into ethnography.

20. The ethnographic and comparative historical analysis of suffering would provide something altogether different than a cross-cultural science of suffering. For example, suppose the Chinese materials canvassed in this essay were compared, say, with the moral meaning and political uses of suffering in the Polish tradition. Longina Jakubowska (1990:12) evokes the imagery of Jesus Christ on the cross as symbol of "despair, sacrifice and death, but also resurrection," and notes the popular association of "Jesus the Sorrowful," *Jesus Fasobliny*, with Poland itself. That historical and ethnographic comparison would contrast these quite distinctive religious and political images, but would also be enriched by taking into account how they contribute to the structuring of experience in local worlds in each society. We would also want to know what such an empirical comparison can tell us about the moral order and its significance for human conditions. The upshot would not be a new science (behavioral or otherwise) but an integrating focus for historical and anthropological and psychological/psychiatric studies.

21. Presented by the first author, at the First Conference of the Society for Psychological Anthropology: "On Current Thinking and Research in Psychological Anthropology," San Diego, 6–8 October 1989; the current paper is a revision of a revision of the original draft.

REFERENCES

Aries, P. 1981. *The Hour of Our Death*. New York: Knopf.
Basu, E. ms. "Individualism, Holism and the Market Mentality: Notes on the Recollections of a Chinese Entrepreneur."
Bergson, H. 1889. *Les Données Immediates de La Conscience*. Paris: Alcan.
Bourdieu, P. 1989. "Social Space and Symbolic Power." *Sociological Theory* 7(1):14–24.
Cassel, J. 1991. *Expected Miracles: Surgeons at Work*. Philadelphia: Temple University Press.
Cassirer, E. 1962. *An Essay on Man*. New Haven: Yale University Press.
Chernoff, J. M. 1979. *African Rhythm and African Sensibility: Aesthetics and Social Action in African Musical Idioms*. Chicago: University of Chicago Press.
Das, V. 1994. "Moral Orientations to Suffering." In *Health and Social Change in International Perspective,* ed. L. C. Chen et al., 139–167. Department of Population and International Health, Harvard School of Public Health. Cambridge: Cambridge University Press.
Dewey, J. 1957 [1922]. *Human Nature and Conduct*. New York: Modern Library.
Dreuilhe, E. 1988. *Mortal Embrace: Living with AIDS*. New York: Hill & Wang.
Feld, S. 1981. *Sound and Sentiment*. Philadelphia: University of Pennsylvania Press.
Frankl, V. 1967 [1946]. *The Doctor and the Soul*. New York: Bantam.
Geertz, C. 1988. *Works and Lives: The Anthropologist as Author*. Stanford: Stanford University Press.
Guarnaccia, P., et al. 1989. "The Multiple Meanings of Ataques de Nervios in the Latino Community." *Medical Anthropology* 11:47–62.
Hsu, F. 1985. "Field Work, Cultural Differences and Interpretations." In *The Chinese Family and Its Ritual Behavior,* ed. J. C. Hsieh and Y. C. Chuang, 19–29. Taipei: Institute of Ethnology, Academic Sinica.
Hwang, K. K. 1987. "Face and Favor: The Chinese Power Game." *American Journal of Sociology* 92(4):944–974.

Jackson, M. 1989. *Paths toward a Clearing.* Bloomington: Indiana University Press.
Jakubowska, L. 1990. "Political Drama in Poland: The Use of National Symbols." *Anthropology Today* 6(4):10–13.
James, W. 1981 [1890]. "The Consciousness of Self." In *The Principles of Psychology,* 279–379. Cambridge: Harvard University Press.
Kleinman, A. 1986. *Social Origins of Distress and Disease: Neurasthenia, Pain and Depression in Modern China.* New Haven: Yale University Press.
———. 1988. *The Illness Narratives: Suffering, Healing and the Human Condition.* New York: Basic Books.
———. 1992. "Pain and Resistance: The Delegitimation and Re-legitimation of Local Worlds." In *Pain as Human Experience: Anthropological Perspectives,* ed. M. J. Good et al., 169–197. Berkeley: University of California Press.
Kleinman, A., and Kleinman, J. 1994. "How Bodies Remember." *New Literary History* 25:707–723, Summer.
Latour, B. 1988. *The Pasteurization of France.* Cambridge: Harvard University Press.
Legge, J., ed. 1960 [1935]. *The Chinese Classics.* Volume 4. Oxford: Oxford University Press.
Lewis, G. 1976. *Knowledge of Illness in a Sepik Society.* London: Athlone Press.
Lin, N. 1988. "Chinese Family Structure and Chinese Society." *Bulletin of Institute of Ethnology.* Academica Sinica (Taiwan) 65:59–129.
Liu, B. Y. 1990. *A Higher Kind of Loyalty.* New York: Pantheon.
Lu, Hsun. 1963. *Selected Stories,* trans. H. Y. and Gladys Yang. Peking: Foreign Languages Press.
Manning, O. 1981 [1960]. *The Balkan Trilogy.* New York: Penguin.
Melzack, R. 1989. "Phantom Limbs, the Self and the Brain." *Canadian Psychology* 30:1–16.
Merleau-Ponty, M. 1962. *The Phenomenology of Perception,* trans. C. Smith. London: Routledge & Keagan Paul.
Moore, B. 1978. *Injustice: The Social Basis of Obedience and Revolt.* London: Macmillan.
Nations, M., and Rebhun, L. A. 1988. "Angels with Wet Wings Won't Fly: Maternal Sentiment in Brazil and the Image of Neglect." *Culture, Medicine and Psychiatry* 12(2):141–200.
Oakeshott, M. 1985 [1933]. *Experience and Its Modes.* Cambridge: Cambridge University Press.
Pick, D. 1989. *Faces of Degeneration: A European Disorder, 1848–1918.* Cambridge: Cambridge University Press.
Plesner, H. 1970. *Laughing and Crying: A Study of the Limits of Human Behavior.* Evanston: Northwestern University Press.
Potter, S. H. 1988. "The Cultural Construction of Emotion in Rural Chinese Social Life." *Ethos* 16(2):181–208.
Rosaldo, R. 1984. "Grief and a Headhunter's Rage: On the Cultural Force of Emotions." In *Text, Play and Story: The Construction and Reconstruction of Self and Society.* S. Plattner and E. Bruner, eds. Washington, D.C.: American Ethnological Society.
Roseman, M. 1990. "Head, Heart, Odor and Shadow: The Structure of the Self, the Emotional World and Ritual Performance Among Senoir Temiar." *Ethos* 18(3):227–250.
Said, E. 1978. *Orientalism.* New York: Pantheon.
Sartre, J. P. 1956. *Being and Nothingness: An Essay on Phenomenological Ontology,* trans. H. E. Barnes. New York: Philosophical Library.
Scheler, M. 1971 [1928]. *Man's Place in Nature,* trans. H. Meyerhoff. New York: Noonday Press.
Schutz, A. 1968. *On Phenomenology and Social Relations.* Chicago: University of Chicago Press.

Schwarcz, V. ms. *Mnemosyne Abroad: Reflections on the Chinese and Jewish Commitment to Remembrance.*

Scott, J. C. 1976. *The Moral Economy of the Peasant.* New Haven: Yale University Press.

———. 1985. *The Weapons of the Weak.* New Haven: Yale University Press.

———. 1990. *Domination and the Arts of Resistance: Hidden Transcripts.* New Haven: Yale University Press.

Sontag, S. 1989. *AIDS and Its Metaphors.* New York: Farrar, Straus & Giroux.

Sperber, D., and Wilson, D. 1986. *Relevance: Communication and Cognition.* Oxford: Basil Blackwell.

Stoller, P. 1989. *The Taste of Ethnographic Things: The Senses in Anthropology.* Philadelphia: University of Pennsylvania Press.

Tambiah, S. 1990. *Magic, Science, Religion and the Scope of Rationality.* Cambridge: Cambridge University Press.

Taussig, M. 1987. *Shamanism, Colonialism and the Wild Man.* Chicago: University of Chicago Press.

Waley, A. 1940 [1919]. *Translations from the Chinese,* 75. New York: Knopf.

Wikan, U. 1987. "Public Grace and Private Fears: Gaiety, Offense and Sorcery in Northern Bali." *Ethos* 15:337–365.

Yang, K. S. 1987. *The Chinese People in Change.* Vol. 3 in series *Collected Works on the Chinese People.* Taipei: Kuei Kuan Book Co. (in Chinese).

Young, A. 1990. "Moral Conflicts in a Psychiatric Hospital Setting: Combat-related Postraumatic Stress Disorder." In *Social Science Perspectives on Medical Ethics,* ed. G. Weisz, 65–82. Dordrecht, Netherlands: Kluwer.

Zhang, J. B. 1710 [1624]. *Qing Yue quan shu* (Qing Yue's Complete Works). Guiji: Guiji Lushi Ranben.

Zimmerman, F. 1989. *Le Discours des Remedes au Pays des Epices.* Paris: Editions Payot.

Hand Drumming

An Essay in Practical Knowledge

SHAWN LINDSAY

Knowledge which is not projected against the black
unknown lives in the muscles, not in consciousness.
—John Dewey (1922:177)

HANDS

Nick and I are sitting in a practice room at the Music School. We each have a djembe held between our legs, tilted forward slightly, uneasily. Our palms are face up, extended. Before we begin drumming, Orlando wants to look at our hands. We had hemmed and hawed about how much we practiced the strokes he taught us on our last meeting. Now he is grabbing us by the wrists and inspecting our palms. "You need to practice more," he tells us, as if at the end of each lesson we could somehow misinterpret the soreness, the rawness of our hands.

The inspection of hands became a weekly ritual for us in the fall of 1992. The story of how our paths crossed is brief. I wanted to make the knowledge of drumming a basic part of my ethnographic tool kit, a way of integrating myself into the song performances I would research in southern Africa. Nick Baham, a fellow graduate student in the Anthropology Department, had just returned from a summer of fieldwork in Ghana. He brought back some large djembe drums which he was selling on behalf of the National Dance Company of Ghana, which needed the money to buy video equipment. I bought a djembe and together Nick and I agreed to find an instructor.

Juan Dies, President of the Indiana University Ethnomusicology Students Association, put me in contact with Orlando Cotto. A *puertoriqueño* via New York, Orlando was in Bloomington finishing a master's degree in percussion. His primary interest was the marimba, but he considered himself an all-around percussionist, and he had earned a reputation as a formidable conga drummer. He had been taking on students since his funding from the School of Music dried up. My acquaintance with Orlando lasted until the summer of 1993, when he was given funding to pursue a doctorate at another institution.

In his approach toward the drum, Orlando displayed a practical attitude not restricted to pedagogy. Inspecting our palms was but one instance in which he revealed an understanding of music as practice, a disposition that comes from the body. Orlando's practical knowledge of drumming enabled him to wow audiences, orchestrate rhythmic backdrops for jazz improvisation, sustain hot rhythms to encourage dancers, lead novices through percussion workshops, and pass down drumming techniques to his private students.

My experiences of learning to drum with Orlando provide a ground for investigating issues in the anthropology of embodiment and practice. One aim of this essay is to describe how complex musical performances are generated through bodily praxis. In bringing together phenomenological and ethnographic modes of description, this essay is also an experiment in style. The experiment is a success if it suggests ways in which ethnographers can incorporate practical knowledge into their disciplinary tool kits, their customary approaches to thinking and writing about culture.

PRAKTOGNOSIS

It seems self-evident that practical engagement in an activity should be a prerequisite to having a knowledge of that activity (Oakeshott 1990:90). Yet in the writings of European philosophers from Aristotle to Kant, practical knowledge has been denigrated by an episteme which places abstract reflection prior to the fact of embodiment. A serious rupture in the dominant episteme can be seen in Edmund Husserl's concept of intentionality, the idea that consciousness is always a consciousness of something. Intentionality implies that *Verstehen* ("understanding") is not a moment encapsulated within a realm of pure ideas. Rather it is constituted by a relation between the subject and its phenomenal world. Given a supposition of intentionality, consciousness can be construed as an activity which refigures the contrast between subjective and objective poles of meaning. The character of the subject's engagement with an object of knowledge cannot be construed as given, or even ascertainable in every circumstance, because the consciousness of the world is in constant motion (Husserl 1970:109). Objectifications attain a measure of validity insofar as they are able to accommodate the indeterminacies that are a condition of their construction and deployment. Hence the experience of the subject as a participant in the continuous and sundry reconstructions of the objective world comes to be seen as co-foundational to a theory of knowledge (Jackson 1989:2–4).

Although Husserl acknowledged that theoretical activity might be subsumed under a principle of "universal practical reason" (1974:32), it was Martin Heidegger who first provided a framework for a phenomenology of practical knowledge. Heidegger's key contribution is the idea of being-in-the-world, an analytical *premise* of the existential subject, *Dasein*. Like the mature

Husserl's "lifeworld," the hyphenated unity of being-in-the-world presents lived experience as a given structure of intentionality. Practical understanding is regarded in this view as an originary expression of intentionality and, therefore, all knowledge (Okrent 1988:24;4–5;130–131). A crucial passage in Heidegger's *Sein und Zeit* indicates the extent to which being-in-the-world undercuts traditional metaphysical foundations of knowledge:

> In ontic discourse we occasionally use the expression "understand something" in the sense of "being able to manage something," "being up to the challenge," "being able to do something." In understanding as an existential, that of which we are competent [*Gekonnte*] is not a what, but rather being as existing. *Dasein's* way of being lies existentially in understanding as being-to-be-able. (1977:190–191,143)

This idea of *praktognosis* is more succinctly and accessibly expressed in Merleau-Ponty's maxim: "Consciousness is in the first place not a matter of I think that but of I can" (1964:137). Whereas Heidegger investigated the environmentality of being, its horizons of possibility, Merleau-Ponty uncovered the body as a primary horizon, taking the phenomenological critique of mind-body dualism to its extreme intimacies. For anthropology, practical understanding is a potentially incisive tool for rethinking its empiricist-intellectualist notions of culture, custom, norm, rule, pattern, and so on. A locus of anthropology's critical self-appraisal has been the concept of habitus, which intimates descriptions of culture sensitive to practice as a mode of bodily understanding.

HABITUS

The first anthropological use of the Latin *"habitus"* can be credited to Marcel Mauss (1973). For Mauss, *"habitus"* signified the habitual "techniques of the body" which are socially patterned. In the habitus one sees the "work of both collective and individual practical reason" (1973:73). Pierre Bourdieu, who has popularized the concept of habitus, makes up for a number of insufficiencies in Mauss's formulation, chiefly by refiguring the dichotomy of collective vs. individual as a conflict between structure and practice. This maneuver permits the habitus to be characterized as a structured disposition, an "acquired system of generative schemes objectively adjusted to the particular conditions in which it is constituted" (1977:95).

Bourdieu's stringent portrayal of the body's objective reality presents several obstacles to the study of music making as an "intelligent habit" (Dewey 1922:77). For starters, Bourdieu's peculiar dialectic of practice and structure downplays the role of human agency in the necessarily *partial* embodiment of surroundings which habit achieves (Dewey 1922:51). Bourdieu draws attention to bodily praxis as a generative locus of social structure. However, the logic of bodily practice which he traces out rubs against the premises of intentional-ity and being-in-the-world. Bourdieu's logic of practice operates through a sort of reversal of the analysis of intentionality. Rather than viewing habit and practice as the body's direct appropriations of its world, Bourdieu sees the acquisition of habits as the "appropriating by the world of a body thus enabled to appropriate the world" (1977:89). This tactic differs from the phenomeno-logical recognition of the givenness of the lifeworld in that it *a priori* separates the active body from its world. The exclusion of the subject from intentionality spells out a concept of habitus which is overly predetermined by "structure." As a consequence, it is unable to encompass "those moments in social life when the customary, given, habitual and normal is disrupted, flouted, suspended and negated" (Jackson 1989:20).

Bourdieu's concept of habitus assumes *a priori* a homology between events, a homothesis of the conditions of original production and the conditions under which the habitus is brought into play (1990:54–55). It is reasonable to generalize about the conditions of existence, to talk about homologies in cultural practices; but to explain similarities in practice as being structurally determined beforehand—it is similarities of habitus and not of practice itself which Bourdieu actually discloses—this strikes me as an overcompensation for the extravagances of subjectively inclined hermeneutics. The pragmatic cri-tique of reification deserves to be reiterated: "anything defined as structure is a character of events, not something intrinsic and *per se*" (Dewey 1926:72). By leaning too hard on structure, Bourdieu's theory of practice violates an under-standing of activity as ongoing and reticulated throughout the totality of experience (cf. Oakeshott 1962).

Of course, Bourdieu recognizes the fallacy of "occasionalism" (1977:81). Bourdieu's attack on occasionalism derives from his more general concern for replacing "rule" with "strategy," and reincorporating into social analysis the concept of time, "with its rhythm, its orientation, its irreversibility" (1977:9). Bourdieu shows a remarkable sensitivity to the rhythms of life, to kairotic, everyday manipulations of time. Nonetheless, in stressing the structural nature of homologies in the habitus, his analysis risks falling back on the categorizations of time against which *kairos* is deployed. This difficulty is evident in the problem of repetition, which is at the core of any argument against occasionalism.

The word "habit" carries a connotation of repetition, but it is possible to hold to a concept of habit which treats repetition as an after-the-fact attribu-tion. Against the idea that habit is defined by repetition, John Dewey argued that the "essence of habit is an acquired disposition to *ways* or modes of response, not to particular acts" (1922:42). Both Dewey and Bourdieu under-mine the reduction of meaning to isolated instances of action. By foregrounding ways as opposed to homologies, Dewey's formulation of habit works with the flow of time, not allowing it to appear chopped up. Bourdieu's account of habit, on the other hand, acknowledges human strivings for likeness, strivings which the connotations of "habit" reveal. The categorical sameness implied in the concept of repetition can be deproblematized by recognizing the intentionality of practical knowledge. Repetition, as a capability of habit, may be actively practiced and acquired, a bona fide strategy in itself. Where repetition is not aimed at, it may more useful to speak of reiteration, readjustment, reworking, and so on. These words stress that it is always an activity which is "repeated," taken up again in an ongoing engagement with the world.

The habitus actualizes the conditions of its production in making a virtue of a necessity (Bourdieu 1977:77; 1990:54). When what is given in the body's experience is set on an equal footing with the structures of the surrounding world, the conceptual pair of contingency and necessity must be reexamined. Before the habitus can "make a virtue of necessity," the body-subject must have already performed a "transformation of contingency into necessity by the act of taking in hand" (Merleau-Ponty 1962:170). To stress the contingency of the productions of the habitus presumes a kind of part/whole relationship, an incompleteness of being (Dewey 1926:64–65). To be coherent with the analysis of being-in-the-world, a secondary normative concept of the social world cannot be used to position the "what" of the contingent-upon or the necessary-for. Necessity is always necessity for something (Dewey 1926:65). The intentionality implied in being necessary-for involves the active incorporation of things into the immediate sphere of the body.

The primary movement of the habitus should not be seen as retreat or withdrawal, because falling back on a habit carries with it the potential for recovering and rearranging patterns of intentionality—being of the world. Necessity-for is the product of a "factic" appropriation of that which is on hand, and this process of taking to hand never occurs except as an intrinsic expression of being-in-the-world. To recognize movement *from* the total world-structure of existence requires that the habitus not be misconstrued as generating its "conditioned and conditional freedom" (Bourdieu 1990:55) as a by-product. Contingent freedom is a precondition for practice in the habitus's constitution and genesis. In the words of Merleau-Ponty: "All that we are, we are on the basis of a *de facto* situation which we appropriate to ourselves and which we ceaselessly transform by a sort of *escape* which is never an unconditional freedom" (1962:170–171).

On the basis of not just the possibility but the actuality of "escape" as a structure of existence, the habitus must be envisaged as possessing the capacity for generating practices which are not in themselves "inherent in the particular conditions of its production" (Bourdieu 1990:55), but are actually transformative of those conditions. Here lies the difficulty for the anthropological gaze, accustomed as it is to disclosing the obvious social contingencies of dispositions and assuetudes: to investigate the conditions of production of the habitus without denying the possibilities of being (the being of another person).

A diplomatic path out of the thicket of being and contingency begins with a recognition of what Merleau-Ponty calls inter-existence in the intentionality of the body-subject. Intentionality is the expression of an existence which stretches out laterally in the world and *toward* the world (Jackson 1989:130). Being-in-the-world as a precondition for intentionality contains in itself the basis for considering social contingency as a part of the existential structure of *Dasein* (see Ostrow 1990:11–14). From such a starting point, it should be possible to work out an understanding of hand drumming which bypasses explanation in terms of structures and norms, and yet recognizes the social conditions which are "em-bodied" in making music (cf. Bourdieu 1977:89).

TRANSPARENCIES

After taking leave of Orlando, Nick and I sought out a practice room. Orlando had just taught us a handful of patterns meant to be fitted together, and we were eager to try them out in a more casual setting, without supervision. Gradually we worked into a groove from which we could stray without getting lost. As I became comfortable with the rhythm I was playing, I looked over at Nick. I was just staring at his drum, the space between us woven with gestures. My strokes were extending into a transparency, as if they could not be contained in the space between my body and my drum. We had learned enough to actualize the identity of gestures and sounds, and the result was uncanny. It was as if we were dancing, wrestling, fencing without visible signs of contact. In reaching out to grasp a rhythm not entirely of its making, my body had become invisible to me, although it maintained a sensual presence. It surpassed itself, becoming for a moment "co-extensive with the world" (Sartre 1956:420).

There is a structure to the body's disappearance implied in the activity of drumming, a predisposition for the body to disappear in a certain way. The initial acquisition of a skill often involves an uncomfortable awareness of one's body. Novel gestures require more concentration to perform than the casual listener might imagine. But the body rendered "perspicuous by difficulty" soon disappears (Leder 1990:31). If you stick with it, practice every day, an activity will become incorporated into the space and everydayness of your body. An identity will be established between self and habitus. The body's awkward parts will soon "disappear."

Following Leder (1990:31), the incorporation of a new skill into the habitus can be interpreted as an extension of bodily absence. Working with Michael Polanyi's analysis of bodily knowledge as composed of "from-at" and "from-to" structures, Leder argues that our normal mode of experience is *from* the body, toward contact with the world. Thus the "absent body" is comparable to a Husserlian null point of the perceptual field (1990:15–16). Learning a movement means taking it into the world of the body, becoming able to "aim at things through it" (Merleau-Ponty 1962:39). This ability, which is none other than habit, defines sensual practical understanding.

The learning of a new skill presents a threat to the habitus in that it entails a reworking and revitalizing of the body's corporeal schema (Merleau-Ponty 1962:142). The disruption of the habitus concomitant with acquiring a skill can lead to a loss of sureness, a temporary loss of verticality that is designated by the status of "student" or, in a sense, "apprentice." For some students, the crisis is met by a retreat into the habitus, by seeking to produce a milieu to which the habitus is as "pre-adapted" as possible (Bourdieu 1990:61). There is always an aspect of this protective behavior in human endeavors. For other temperaments, the critical challenge to the habitus exhilarates. It provides the resistance needed to make contact with the world, to actualize the self in taking the attitudes of an other, in grasping the dispositions of things.

The drummer makes music *from* his body. It is only in learning or attempting to explain how to drum that the at-ness of the body becomes an issue. The disappearance of the body in drumming has a unique structure which can be examined using Leder's (1990:26) distinction between focal and background disappearance. In reference to drumming, "focal disappearance" principally concerns the self-concealment of hands. For the skilled drummer, hand techniques cannot be available for scrutiny. To thematize body movements past the initial stages of acquiring mastery can easily lead to confusion, "dys-appearance" (where the body appears to awareness), or a breakdown in performance (Leder 1990:85). Like all artisans, drummers are forever practicing new techniques, trying out new gestures. But in advanced stages of mastery, these inventions call upon what is given in the habitus as it has been reengineered. There is a logic of practice which allows for artistic complexity, but only as the basis of what can be taken as given from the body.

"Background disappearance" refers to the non-awareness of those parts of the body which are not immediately needed in order to drum. Background disappearance, like focal disappearance, is an actively structured phenomenon, and if it is disrupted, the flow of activity can come to a halt. Any time we extend outside of our usual absences, the body appears as an awkward and dysfunctional obstacle to our performance.

On the evening when the reciprocity of musical gestures and intentions became transparent to me (cf. Merleau-Ponty 1962:185), Orlando had taught us much more than a handful of rhythms. He drilled into us the need to listen to each other, to be responsive to each other's tempos and dynamic levels. He continued his technique of playing complex rhythms on the bata while we practiced new, simple rhythms. Orlando admitted to using the technique of playing bewildering accompaniments in order to confuse us, to force us to *dwell* on our hands. He also did this to get us to listen, to make our hands disappear in the sound of a "resultant" rhythm, a polyrhythm. That evening, Orlando was particularly concerned that we work together. He insisted that we know how to play each other's parts so that we could switch back and forth with ease. He provided us with a number of simple rhythms, rhythms which involved the least amount of attention to our hands. We did not practice our *secos,* the most difficult stroke, at all that night.

The ability to play each other's parts added a vital immediacy to our conversation of attitudes (see Schütz 1957:77–79), but there were other forces at work in my experience of transparency. My body was in the midst of a "habitus shift" which has altered my perception of complex meter (e.g., 6/8). I now immediately hear complex meter as hemiola (two pulses played against three), and adjust my hearing when listening to European concert music. All of the patterns Orlando taught us that night could be counted in complex duple meter.

The way I had been accustomed to playing complex meter created an asymmetrical division of one beat. When tapping out rhythms, I had habitually let my left hand play the thesis (one) while my right hand followed up with the arsis (two, three). This tack gave my right hand more freedom to improvise. Orlando quickly moved to correct this bias, stating that the right and left hands must be "even." Every drill performed on the right hand must also be performed on the left. Both hands must be strong and sure. The drum itself must be incorporated into the bilateral symmetry of the body. It has a left side and a right side which should not be crossed. The bilateral approach to handling complex meter is to alternate strokes between the left and right hands, placing a slight accent on every third stroke. Thus the strokes on each pulse remain evenly divided between right and left hands but the accent shifts from left to right.

At first I was wary about reading too much significance into my experience of becoming transparent. However, the next time we met something happened which convinced me that what I was feeling was not entirely my own fantasy, but was enmeshed in a mode of inter-experience. Nick, Orlando, and I sat facing each other in a sort of triangle. After a quick review of the basic strokes, Orlando announced that he wanted to show us something. First he told Nick to play a simple three-pulse pattern. Then he asked me to play the same pattern starting from Nick's second pulse, so that the parts overlapped. Finally he began to play rhythms which emphasized Nick's third pulse (my second). As I gazed out across my drum head a triangle appeared, hovering above the drums. It spun around from drum to drum, following the main beat of each part. Orlando started playing with the triangle. He shouted at us to concentrate as he tilted and bent the triangle, dropping his beat slightly before or after Nick's three. Orlando's hands were now flying around the two heads of his bata as the triangle wobbled on a moil of rhythms. (For me the triangle symbolized change—but how can I deprive this moment the name of action? Orlando definitely intended to show us something, to give us a glimpse at the power of rhythm.)

I cannot adequately explain my need to visually grasp the encounter. However, the form it took in my imagination, the fluid triangle, is open to hermeneutic inquiry. Orlando was playing with rhythms of interaction typical of drumming within a bata ensemble. Following Dewey (1934:44), the pattern of any experience can be defined in terms of a relationship established between alternating senses of doing and undergoing. In bata ensembles, particularly in the early stages of mastery, this alternating movement can produce a special variety of corporeal disappearance:

> Playing bata is a group undertaking. While any of the rhythms, for any of the drums, may be relatively easy to perform by itself, this is often not the case when performing within the ensemble. Each drum has its own specific rhythmic identity, but when combined in ensemble performance the various parts interlock to create what may be an entirely different rhythmic sensation for each of the musicians. In fact, in the early stages of learning it is not uncommon to lose track of the very sounds that one creates on his own drum amongst the broader sounds of the ensemble. While disconcerting at first, this may also be a positive sign, for it suggests that one's ears are experiencing and assimilating the totality of the ensemble rather than being locked onto a single musical line. (Amira and Cornelius 1992:25)

John Amira and Steven Cornelius's comments on communication in bata performance suggests that inner time and polythesis are not always constitutive of what Alfred Schütz (1957:79) called the "mutual tuning-in relationship" established between musicians in performance. The meaningful, grasped time that is shared by bata drummers appears to be more like the "spatialized outer time" which Schütz sees as necessary to all social interaction. Schütz's study correctly underlines the multidimensionality of time experiences that are shared in making music, but the distinctions he draws are best regarded as provisional. In place of a contrast between inner *durée* and spatialized outer time, it would be more instructive to discuss how making music together accomplishes an integration of different modalities of bodily attention. Leder's notion of disappearance is crucial here. While the hands disappear into drumming, the ears and eyes and voice are available for interaction. The successful drummer must be able to focus all of these activities on the activity at hand, to engage with dancers, fellow musicians, and spectators.

Through the triangle encounter, Orlando demonstrated an interactive quality of rhythm. We worked through our bodies, achieving a fusion of doing and undergoing which helped us to realize the experience of rhythm as an integral connection between our bodies, a social performance in which each individual contribution is both essential and partial. In my encounters with African musicians, I have had several "flow" experiences similar to my experiences with Orlando, moments when I could feel the pull of a rhythm so strongly I would swear it was tangible. If flow effectively merges action and awareness (Csikszentmihalyi 1993: 183), in traditions of African and Afro-Caribbean music, this merger has a social feel, a practical polyrhythmicity (Chernoff 1977). It is not only one's technical fluency, but one's social abilities which are refined and put to the test in making music together. The misunderstanding of this ethical-aesthetic aspect of performance explains the general failure of members of the men's movement to self-actualize at African percussion workshops.

As the symbolic form of our interaction, the triangle articulates well with habital ways of drumming bata. The bata is a double-headed, asymmetrical hourglass drum which originated during the reign of Sango in Old Oyo (Thieme 1969: 183–186). In the New World (but not in West Africa), bata drums are almost always played in groups of three. The bata is placed on the lap, so that the left hand plays the small head while the right hand plays the large head. In teaching me to play a 12/8 rhythm on the bata, Orlando had me tap my foot so as to circulate pulses: small-foot-large, small-foot-large. In my awkwardness, the triangle Orlando traced over my body appeared foreign to my understanding of my appendages and their movements. As I practiced the rhythm, the triangle sank in, lodging itself in what I was doing. I found I could work through it.

Orlando himself seldom taps his foot while playing the bata, but he does sway his trunk as if to point an off-beat away from his body, toward another rhythm. Such habitual nuances reveal the openness of bata drumming to interaction, a disposition toward making music together that is carried in the body and the drum. In essence, the whole activity of drumming, its implements and situations, is carried in the practice of the skilled drummer. What I learn from Orlando is always more than the few simple patterns I can name: the clave, "Afro," el caballo, the seis, the salsa. These are invitations to participate in a complex cultural world, invitations extended through the body.

HAND-EAR COORDINATION

Orlando spent more time teaching me basic strokes than anything else. The three basic strokes are open, closed, and the seco (the "slap"). Other fundamental strokes are "walking," a heel-toe movement of the palms of the hands in the center of the drum; the open palm, in which the flattened palm strikes the center of the drum so as to produce a boom; and the closed seco, in which one hand presses flat on the surface of the drum while the other hand slaps. These movements must be very precise. Orlando corrected me for everything, for holding my fingers too far apart, not applying the right amount of pressure, striking too close to the edge of the drum, not curving or flattening my hand properly, and not using enough wrist.

These precise movements of the hand are not a language of silence. "You have to hear the difference," Orlando insisted. A rhythm does not sound right if the strokes are sloppy. Orlando once spent almost an entire session listening to me play open strokes and slaps. While he listened he said "good," or, when the strokes were sloppy, just shook his head. It would be false to conclude that because these strokes are attuned toward sonic referents, their production is governed by a purely intellectual semiosis. Hearing a *seco* is a path that the ear travels first alone, and then in tandem with the hand. What is achieved in making a proper *seco* is much more than an ability to play that particular stroke (cf. Oakeshott 1962:96–97). It is a reorganization of corporeal schemas which enables a fuller capacity for participation in percussive music. Orlando led me to the ability to hear strokes and sounds as intimately connected, whether I am listening to a mambo, the drumming of Ephat Mujuru, or Hawaiian *hula pahu*.

There is some literature which suggests that the motor perception of a rhythm may be different from the perception of its sonic counterpart, and that the exploitation of this difference might be basic to an understanding of African rhythm (Kubik 1985; Hornbostel 1928; Blacking 1955). This phenomenon is secondary to actually learning the basic strokes. Let me give a simple example. The phrase "dakada kadaka" describes a rhythm in 6/8 time in which the hands simply alternate from right to left. Thus the alternation of strokes can be heard as basically 3/4 time: "daka daka daka." This however, would be an incorrect perception of the rhythm. Potentially, it could be perceived as shifting to 3/4, depending on how it interlocked with other patterns, but the primary sense is 6/8. In learning to produce this result, I often found myself keeping time in my shoulders, swaying in 6/8 time so as not to be misled by the "daka daka daka" of my hands. I often noticed Orlando swaying in this way too, so I do not think of it as bad form. It is an essential part of the "feel" of a rhythm. Had Orlando been teaching me "to follow a baton" in a symphony orchestra, such movements would have been discouraged. They are regarded by classical musicians as a distraction to other players, rather than subtle cues to the possibilities inherent in a rhythm.

No proper rhythm can result from indistinguishable strokes. A movement such as the *seco* is grasped by incorporating it into a repertoire of skills and habits. In the process of this grasping, the hands attain an invisibility to themselves. In cooperation with the ears, the hands are brought out to be played from, to be surpassed toward the activity of drumming. As I come to understand the movements involved in making a *seco*, consciousness of my hand gives way to the sound of the stroke. The pain I feel in slapping the drum recedes as I learn to concentrate on the larger flow of rhythm. Experiences of this process of disappearance surely vary, but when one really begins to learn to hear on the basis of grasped significances, the muscular "how" of a sound becomes an integral element of its perception.

COUNTING

There are some rhythms which are just plain tricky. In my earliest stages of studying with Orlando, I often became frustrated with my inability to play certain rhythms correctly. On several occasions I simply laid down my hands and demanded: "What's the count?" Orlando would then oblige me by playing the rhythm in question while counting the meter of a cross rhythm.

Commenting on the fact that African drummers rarely count, Koetting (1986:60) remarks that, like the paradiddle familiar to snare drummers, a pattern such as vertical hemiola may best be understood as a whole gesture, "a non-counted rhythm—one that is merely felt as a pattern." Felt correspondences may provide the basis for mathematical operations as complex as those that proceed from the concept of number (Sheets-Johnstone 1990:73–76). Ruth Stone (1988:132) makes the important assertion that in African music "qualitative" time is not necessarily imprecise or unsophisticated. Neither is it totalizing. It may be true that during performance somebody will invariably be keeping a rhythm, a "time line." But there is no reason to believe that these patterns are a constant source of focal attention. Drummers set patterns in motion by relating their rhythms to others. Once the body is "set in motion," there is no way of determining where the experience of rhythm will go (1988:134).

Orlando sometimes relies on counting in his teaching, but like many percussionists, he also makes use of syllabic mnemonic formulae. To teach me *el caballo,* Orlando started with the phrase *"café con pan." "Café con pan"* is a mnemonic phrase used for the *seis,* a rhythm which can be heard in a variety of Puerto Rican music genres. Like the clave in Afro-Cuban music, it forms a constant rhythmic background against which one sets one's parts. As with his habit of counting in cross rhythms, Orlando's mnemonic phrases interlock with rather than duplicate the gestural sequences they refer to. Orlando taught me the *seis* as a sequence starting from *"con."* The rhythm of the *seis* employs a borrowed division, which in itself is a minor difficulty. It also requires a silent gesture in preparation for a closed slap which falls between *"con"* and *"pan."* Hearing the phrase *"café con pan"* helps to keep the anticipatory gesture silent.

Phrases such as "dondo kiki takaTi katika kiki takaTi ka-" (the salsa rhythm over two measures) represent extremely sophisticated encodings of gestural sequences, as well as the relationship of parts to the larger context of rhythm. In this example, rhythms other than the one "in my hands" are suggested. The clave always starts with my first walk (taka-). In the verbal form, the progress of the clave is marked by the "ti" of katika, which, if it merely represented the flatness of my gestures, could well be simply "kataka." The strongest drum beat is the *seco* (-ti-), but in the rhythm of the mnemonic formula, its force is minimized by a division of the measure into a sequence of two-, three- and four-pulse beats. The common practice of starting formulas at the end of my gestural phrases also contributes to taking the rhythm away from my body, orienting my performance toward a larger idiom of musical activity.

The mnemonic formulas represent just one technique for teaching me the appropriate uses of my body in drumming. Learning a rhythm such as a salsa requires an abeyance of the body, a restructuring of the way rhythm feels and

sounds. Orlando sometimes had me listen to recordings and try to imitate what
was being played. He told me I needed to "feel" the rhythm. The feel of a rhythm
is not ambiguous in the way of poetry. Feeling a rhythm is way of approaching
a gestural sequence, of knowing its sonic consequences. Orlando used the
word "feel" in a technical sense, forcing me to examine my body's awareness in
order to correct a problem of execution, to orient my playing toward an
ensemble of parts.

Musical counting is primarily an educational device, although in performance, experienced musicians may resort to it in moments of unclarity (Schütz
1957:95). For some musicians, counting is a habit indispensable to their
experience of music. Steadfast counting is a strategy for the attunement of the
body. When a violin student is taught to count the smallest divisions of pulse
which appear in a score, she often uses a formula such as "one-ee-and-a, two-
ee-and-a. . . ." She learns to read a triplet as "tri-pa-let," and she is able to
produce triplets with stunning precision. The mathematical operations are not
performed on paper or "in the head," but through an alternative, non-focal
modality of the body. The logic is one of substitution and displacement.
Counting need not represent a prioritization of quantitative time. First and
foremost it is a practical means for getting a handle on difficult passages.

In counting or using formulas, the difference between the movements of
the hands and the whole of a rhythm are brought out in order to correct the
body's clumsiness. Classical musicians' counting directs attention toward a
pre-established score with a tempo marking that can be set by a metronome.
Orlando's counting in cross rhythms and his use of mnemonic phrases orient
the body toward other performers. They teach an awareness of how one's part
fits into the whole, and they implicitly prepare the body to interact in fluid
performance situations.

"YOU HAVE TO RELAX"

An essential aspect of feeling a rhythm is being able to relax your entire body.
Orlando once impressed upon me the importance of relaxing by mimicking an
uptight, mechanistic player. With a puppet-like grin, he smacked the drum in
a gesture that resembled dog-paddling. It came from the shoulders and elbows
instead of the wrist. Orlando's clowning worked. I became aware of the tension
in my shoulders and back, and began to work on achieving more fluidity in my
strokes.

Relaxation is not a lack of energy. Orlando can move from a relaxed
disposition to a vigorous attack in a blink. Nor is relaxing a matter of simply
letting your wrists do all the work of drumming, although refraining from
using your whole arm when executing a stroke is a part of learning to relax.
Swaying or rocking the shoulders can become an integral part of keeping the

feel of a rhythm. The best way to feel any rhythm is to come to it relaxed. In this sense, relaxation defines an approach to the drum, an attitude starting from the body.

At times, I mistook Orlando's postures of extreme relaxation for a lack of interest. His arms were kept draped over his drums or on his legs. This is how he showed me to comport myself. He said, "It's important to look like you know how to drum." This meant keeping your hands in a warm relation to the drum, not flailing about like a geek. When he wanted me to focus on developing strong strokes with both hands, he alternated hands on the drum, letting the hand not in use slump on his leg. To emphasize how easy it is to build up strength, Orlando rested his chin in his hand and walked with the other: "You have to practice every day. You can do this while you watch TV." When I began to learn to play patterns on two drums, the importance of relaxing the arm not immediately on the drum really hit home. You cannot move smoothly between drums if you are too tense.

One evening when Nick was present I glanced over at him and discovered that he was a different person. I had never seen him so relaxed. After Orlando left, I asked Nick about feeling the music. He recited the graduate student's mantra: he said he was tired. We had talked about the "high" that comes from a good drumming session, but it had not occurred to me to link that high to relaxation. Drumming can be good therapy, a kind of release. A skilled drummer, however, avoids the dionysian catharsis of the amateur. Relaxing is practiced in a mundane sense. As a possibility of the drummer's habitus, the ability to release oneself in drumming is always renewable and present at hand.

A subsidiary awareness of being relaxed should be incorporated as one of a drummer's basic skills. The "background disappearance" required for this skill involves letting music come from not just any body, but a body that is actively, habitually relaxed. Achieving a state of habitual relaxation constitutes a rearrangement of the habitus. The reticulations of being relaxed can work themselves into other activities, such as typing. I take my experience of becoming more relaxed as an indication of the plasticity of what is given to our bodies in the cultural world.

Relaxation in drumming is a generative capability. Friedman (1982:127) offers the only discussion of relaxation in hand-drumming of which I am aware. Relaxation is definitely an aim of *bata* performance traditions, but Orlando's use of relaxation extended into a much wider array of drumming practices. If you don't relax, he said, you will get tired. Drummers, unlike concert pianists, must be prepared for situations in which people want to dance, and there are always people who want to dance all night. The habit of relaxing is generative in that it can be taken into typical performance situations and used to effect. A relaxed disposition can also be used to better aim the body at similar tasks (that is, tasks in which the body can assume similar sitting postures).

THE DRUM AS TOOL

For an understanding of drumming praxis, one of the more useful consequences of Heidegger's investigation into the conditions of intentionality lies in
his discovery of the ontological character of things. Things (*pragmata*) are not
something accessory to intentional being. Rather, they reveal their character of
being things in praxis, which must be understood not as mere doing, but as a
caring or concerned engagement in the world (Heidegger 1977:92/68). It is our
concern with the world which defines things as tools, extensions of our being
invested with the disposition of habitus.

As manifestations of our engagement in the world, tools have an existence
utterly unlike the fetish of the commodity. "The way of being of a tool (*Zeug*) in
which it manifests itself as itself, we call its 'at-handedness' (*Zuhandenheit*)"
(1977:95/69). The drum is a mute thing until it is incorporated into the at-
handedness of my bodily space. This implies that the disappearance of the
from-structure of my body necessary for drumming carries with it a temporal
aspect which pervades the idiom of the activity. The drum can have no meaning
for me unless I bring to it the possibility of drumming and everything entailed
in the activity of drumming.

By defining "things" in terms of practice, instead of the other way around,
we arrive at what Okrent (1988:33–37) identifies as the holistic character of
practical understanding. Knowing what a drum is means knowing in what
context drumming is appropriate, knowing intimately the details of its
situatedness. This knowledge is demonstrated in conducting oneself properly
in playing the drum, by simply being able to get along with other drummers,
musicians, dancers, singers, spectators, roadies, recording engineers, stage
crews, or what-have-you.

Orlando taught that a good drummer must know how to play all sorts of
percussion instruments. What Orlando usually meant by playing the drum
involved knowing "where" the clave is, hearing it as a part of what the hands are
doing. Popularly referred to as "the heart of salsa," the clave is the constant
referent which sets the tempo and feeling of a performance. Its analogue in
African music is the handclap (Jones 1954) or the bell pattern (Nketia
1979:132). Not only must you always listen for the clave, you must hear it
when you are practicing alone.

Hearing the clave when it is not being played is not an example of subjective
fancy. It is a knowledge implied in the drum, its being as something to be
brought out. When I drum without hearing a clave or bell pattern, the drum I
am playing is qualitatively different from the drum which Orlando played and
taught me to play.

The existence of the clave in the drum cannot be meaningful to me until I
have in some measure incorporated the drum and its rhythms into my body
space. Like the relaxed body, the drum must become settled into my subsidiary

awareness. I accept it existentially by dwelling in it (Polanyi 1958:59). The drum must be held between my legs with a slight forward tilt so as not to muffle its sound. After I have incorporated the drum into an habitual background disappearance, I then learn the strokes. When these have been understood, the surface of the drum no longer seems distant and strange. Contact is anticipated, heard. Finally, having passed through these initial stages of mastery and becoming invisible to myself, I am ready to hear the clave, to feel my rhythms correctly.

The drum is but a manifestation of the body's projecting around itself a cultural world of habit which it can incorporate and so find new meanings for itself (Merleau-Ponty 1962:146). The imaginative act of projecting a conceptual linkage between the drum and the clave does not depend on a faculty of disembodied intellect. It is enabled in practice and the reliance upon tools, which never exist except in the capacity of being handy. The reliance on tools expresses a commitment to the world (Polanyi 1958:61). Therefore it carries with it the possibility of uncovering being-in-the-world. The habitus can thus be conceptualized as the cultural expression of the possibility of the self revealing itself to itself through a reciprocity of gestures consistent with the structure of being-in-the-world. The notion of ipseity brought to an understanding of disclosure in practice is anything but solipstic. It is in the capacity of being committed to the world that the disclosure of being as open to the world is possible.

DETACHABLES

A practical understanding of hand drumming accents the way musical ideas are embodied in the habitus, a disposition toward making music together. When being-in-the-world is taken as a foundation for practice, the potential for contingent freedom that exists in the habitus must be acknowledged as one of its essential constituents. The principle of plasticity in the habitus is not a matter of allowing for a subjectivist concept of will. It is a characterization of the relationship of habitual dispositions to the ongoing nature of human activity.

In approaching activities which are as close to our bodies as music, the faculty of "*empathic* understanding" (Jackson 1989:134) defines a crucial strategy for using experience as a basis for interpretation. Praxiological and theoretical knowledge need not be kept at arm's length, but may be used to complement each other, as I have tried to show in this essay. As ethnographers assemble and reassemble their theoretical tool kits, they would be well advised to consider learning the basics required to engage in new patterns of living. The hoe, the drum, the hatchet, the water jar: knowing how to properly use these things is a first step toward understanding the rhythms of social life.

REFERENCES

Amira, John, and Cornelius, Steven. 1992. *The Music of Santeria: Traditional Rhythms of the Bata Drums*. Crown Point, IN: White Cliffs Media.

Blacking, John. 1955. "Some Notes on a Theory of African Rhythm Advanced by Erich von Hornbostel." *African Music* 1(2):12–20.

Bourdieu, Pierre. 1977. *Outline of a Theory of Practice*, trans. Richard Nice. Cambridge: Cambridge University Press.

———. 1990. *The Logic of Practice*, trans. Richard Nice. Stanford: Stanford University Press.

Chernoff, John Miller. 1979. *African Rhythm and African Sensibility: Aesthetics and Social Action in African Musical Idioms*. Chicago: University of Chicago Press.

Csikszentmihalyi, Mihaly. 1993. *The Evolving Self*. New York: Harper.

Dewey, John. 1922. *Human Nature and Conduct*. New York: Modern Library.

———. 1926. *Experience and Nature*. Chicago: Open Court.

———. 1934. *Art as Experience*. New York: Putnam.

Friedman, Robert A. 1982. "Making an Abstract World Concrete: Knowledge and Structural Dimensions of Performance among Bata Drummers in Santeria." Ph.D. diss. Indiana University.

Hornbostel, Erich von. 1928. "African Negro Music." *Africa* 1(1):30–62.

Husserl, Edmund. 1970. *The Crisis of European Sciences and Transcendental Phenomenology*, trans. David Carr. Evanston: Northwestern University Press.

———. 1974. *Husserliana. Gesammelte Werke*. Vol. XVII. The Hague: Martinus Nijhoff.

Jackson, Michael. 1989. *Paths toward a Clearing: Radical Empiricism and Ethnographic Inquiry*. Bloomington: Indiana University Press.

Jones, A. M. 1954. "African Rhythm." *Africa* 24:26–47.

Koetting, James. 1986. "What Do We Know about African Rhythm?" *Ethnomusicology* 24(3):393–415.

Kübik, Gerhard. 1985. "The Emics of African Rhythm," in Daniel Avorgbedor and Kwesi Yankah, eds., *Cross Rhythms* 2:26–66. Bloomington: African Folklore Publications, Trickster Press.

Leder, Drew. 1990. *The Absent Body*. Chicago: University of Chicago Press.

Mauss, Marcel. 1973. "Techniques of the Body," trans. B. Brewster. *Economy and Society* 2:70–88.

Merleau-Ponty, Maurice. 1962. *Phenomenology of Perception*, trans. Colin Smith. London: Routledge & Kegan Paul.

Nketia, T. H. Kwabena. 1979. *The Music of Africa*. New York: Norton.

Oakeshott, Michael. 1962. *Rationalism in Politics and Other Essays*. London: Methuen.

Okrent, Mark. 1988. *Heidegger's Pragmatism: Understanding, Being and the Critique of Metaphysics*. Ithaca: Cornell University Press.

Ostrow, James M. 1990. *Social Sensitivity: A Study of Habit and Experience*. Albany: State University of New York Press.

Polanyi, Michael. 1969. *Personal Knowledge*, ed. Marjorie Green. Chicago: University of Chicago Press.

Sartre, Jean-Paul. 1955. *Being and Nothingness*, trans. Hazel Barnes. New York: Philosophical Library.

Schütz, Alfred. 1957. "Making Music Together: A Study in Social Relationship." *Social Research* 18: 76–97.

Sheets-Johnstone, Maxine. 1990. *The Roots of Thinking*. Philadelphia: Temple University Press.

Stone, Ruth. 1988. *Dried Millet Breaking: Time, Words and Song in the Woi Epic of the Kpelle*. Bloomington: Indiana University Press.

Thieme, Darius L. 1969. "A Descriptive Catalog of Yoruba Musical Instruments." Ph.D. diss. Catholic University of America.

On Dying and Suffering in Iqwaye Existence

JADRAN MIMICA

> Here (among the Iqwaye), man just dies, mother
> gives birth. You-me walk (i.e., we live)—you feel
> you will die, you die. . . . It is not like white man.
> —Omalycaqulyi (in Yalqwaalye, 1985)

This statement was made by an Iqwaye man, sometimes called in Tok Pisin *kasman* (cards-man, i.e., gambler) because of his frequent involvement in the endless gambling games to which Iqwaye and other Yagwoia men have become addicted in the last three decades. Our conversation was about the general character of Iqwaye life, and Omalycaqulyi's comment was spurred, I think, by my remark that westerners keep statistical records of births as well as deaths, and that virtually all other aspects of westerners' lives have a different kind of orderliness, a number attached to everything. Omalycaqulyi made his comment with a broad, mischievous smile and he provoked laughter in all of us. For it is true that, by comparison with whites, Iqwaye were, and many still are, born without dates, and live and die without dates, in the sumptuous stench of their decomposing bodies. So we all laughed.

Every so often, usually an older, sick man or woman will declare in a mode of immediate intention—"I'll die!" (*napoqwomne*). For instance, an old woman greeted me exactly in this manner upon one of my returns to the Iqwayaana (Iqwaye homeland). Her body was drained and pained by sickness and she was waiting to die. Dying was her immediate self-expectation in living. Although people are afraid of death there is a sense of acceptance of its imminence, especially among older Iqwaye. I recognized fully the reality of this attitude whenever news arrived that somebody in the village had died, and then it turned out that the person had only "half-died," i.e., had not really died yet, but would. In 1985 this was the case with a man who had been very sick for a long time. I saw him at the funeral of his neighbor. He looked sick, and because of his sickness he was closer to the dying mode of his life, thus sharing an inner moribund affinity with the condition of his decomposing neighbor who was being mourned in a hut. The sick man was already thought of as being dead, but as it turned out he was only half dead, and he managed to recuperate. At the burial, I observed him for a while as he sharpened arrows and watched others making the coffin in which his neighbor would be buried. But he did not die because of his sickness. Several months later, contrary to all expectations, he committed suicide by hanging himself at the grave of his wife who had died the year before. For this alone, he would be remembered by many Iqwaye.

Another case will illustrate more acutely this oscillation between life-as-dying and death-as-living. By mid-August 1979, Amcaqulyi-ule-Taqalyce had been sick for more than two weeks. A curing seance was performed for him and for some of his affinal relations, but his condition did not improve. Every time I went to Kaloqwalnaquli hamlet I could see him either lying or sitting in his wife's earth-oven shelter, wrapped in a bark cape and a worn-out blanket. One evening, I was walking back to my hut accompanied by several boys and an older man, Omalyca-Malycaqulyi. We watched men and boys playing dice. The sick man's patrilateral half-sister Palycipu passed by with a worried expression on her face. She stopped to tell Omalyca-Malycaqulyi, who was walking behind me, that her brother had died. A few steps later he told me the news. I was taken by it. Then, since none of the young men were keen to return to the place where the men gambled in order to deliver the news, I decided to go and do it myself. I was curious to see the reaction.

I told people that old Taqalyce died. Several men went quiet. Younger boys asked: "Who died?" My chief informant and friend Palyc-Caqapana-ule-Omalyca-Taqalyce[1] and others pondered the news for a moment, their faces sullen. Wiy-Caqaponya asked: "Who was extracting the sickness (napalye) from him?" He was referring to the curing seance. No answer. Than Taqalyce commented that old Taqalyce was the last of Amcaqulyi's older children. With him, all of Amcaqulyi's older descendants were gone. Then he told me: "That was it! That dream I was telling you about. It meant that someone would die. The dream wasn't in vain. You see now."

Although we had been working on his dreams for the past three days, Taqalyce had not mentioned any dream which allegedly portended a death. This invocation of a past dream experience as a way of rendering a novel situation as something precognized, and a confirmation of one's clairvoyant potential, is also a way of shaping events which have an extraordinary quality. The appeal to a dream affirms the egocentric sense of a person's relevance in relation both to the event and the newly emerging situation, which otherwise is wholly independent of those who are now surprised to learn about it. The claim that one has dreamt it at once amplifies the extraordinariness of the event and attenuates its unanticipated otherness for one who has already had a precognition of its inevitability.

Inside the "dead" man's wife's kitchen-shelter were gathered a number of the dead man's relatives. He was covered with a bark cape, and his young son was lying next to him. I asked if it was true that Taqalyce had died. His affine

(WB) and a classificatory patrilateral brother told me that whoever told me so was lying. There, they pointed out, old Taqalyce was still alive; his leg was moving. I saw no movement. The relatives, however, were waiting for him to die. Later, in my hut, when I told several initiated youths and Malycaqulyi that Taqalyce was dying, rather than that he had already died as was initially thought, an initiate remarked that, nevertheless, he would die during the night. It became clear that the prevailing opinion was casting Taqalyce as already dead.

But in the morning old Taqalyce emerged from his comatose state and was, it seemed, quite cheerful. He explained to his younger classificatory matrilateral brother Taqalyce that he had once before been in a similar state. Now he decided that it would be best for him to go to the "haus sik" (hospital) in Kwaplalim. Accordingly, his two classificatory (male) mothers (kanei),[2] Taqalo-Malyconya and Taqaly-Amce, made a stretcher and carried him away. A third man followed them to assist the bearers. Palyc-Caqapana-ule-Taqalyce and I watched them as they walked uphill and downhill through the Yalqwaayle hamlets. He commented that there would be a substantial payment due to the two bearers For when mothers (especially male) provide some such service, or render any care for the well-being of your body, they have to be repaid amply. Shortly after, Taqalyce half-jokingly reprimanded old Taqalyce's wife, Unguyipu, for not going with her husband to the hospital as soon as he was carried away. He told her that being a woman (i.e., a wife rather than a sister or mother) she did not think much about the well-being of her man (husband). She only thought about who would be her next husband if this one died. In this comment, Taqalyce underlined the Iqwaye reality of gender relations, in particular the practice of leviratic widow remarriage and the men's view of women as being perennially oriented toward men other than the ones they happened to be married to.

Two weeks later old Taqalyce returned home. His health improved but he was not cured. He died some years later, though I do not know if he went through any more comatose episodes.

DEATH AS A HORIZON OF EXISTENCE

For the Iqwaye, death is an imminent horizon of existence. For some, this imminence can sink into the consciousness as a definite expectation, so that one's daily life is lived essentially as an expectation of one's own death. But unlike the situation in Western urban cultures, death in the Iqwaye life-world is neither experienced nor ideologized as a radically alien event, wholly external to, or as an inadmissible intrusion into, the realm of human life, which would be opposed to it. Like disease, pain and suffering in general, and death too, are lived factualities of human existence. That does not mean that they are not resisted. The Iqwaye resist them as much as any other human beings, but in the Iqwaye life-world death is lived as a modality of life, and it is wholly assimilated into everyday sociality. In this sense, Iqwaye dying is just as much an everyday social activity as life itself, though life is less anxious. Regardless of how and where it occurs, death is not excised from the realm of daily affairs but, on the contrary, becomes properly fulfilled as a fact of someone's social existence by being attended to by those who live on and who, thereby, come to co-constitute the factuality of that person's death. Death is thus neither an abstract event nor a substantial entity. It is not a menacing otherness, such as one sees depicted in Medieval iconography as a skeleton with a scythe. Death is not an entity that preys upon people and snatches them from life. Rather, it is humans who live themselves into their deaths through their own or some- body else's actions, or by suffering life in its more burdensome manifestations, such as disease, which is often inflicted by the virulent spirits of dead relatives. In this sense there is no death as such, but only a myriad of often contingent ways of dying, of becoming dead and of being after death.

Like sickness, the ubiquity of dying is attested to by Iqwaye of all ages. Nobody is immune to it, though a particularly high incidence occurs among infants and older people. And it is this ubiquity, i.e., the fact that sometime and somewhere everybody dies without exception, that seems to confer a categori- cal typicality upon the factuality of dying, producing thus the illusion of death as a being unto itself. Furthermore, most deaths appear in their *post facto* factuality in the memory of living Iqwaye as average events. In a census I conducted, the most frequent replies to my routine question—"How did this person die?"—were "Just died," "Died from sickness," or "Died for no reason" (simply expired). Such answers indicate the bare fact of average, typical human death in Iqwaye experience, though in actuality each ordinary death is the result of specific circumstances and bodily conditions. Still, there was nothing outstanding about them apart from the fact that these persons died. But there are also memorable deaths, and these are remembered precisely because they are extraordinary, and this transforms the factuality of dying as a universal occurrence into an outstanding event. Every death in warfare, or by the killing of one human being by another, has this aura of extraordinariness, as does suicide. Equally striking are those spectacularly accidental deaths whose individual factuality supremely exemplifies the contingency of Iqwaye dying and becoming dead amidst the most unassuming everyday life engagements. Here are several such cases.

1. During my census in the Iwola'a-Malycaane, I recorded the name of a woman who was killed in her new garden. While burning the undergrowth, she happened to burn the base of a tree. When she went to plant taro and yams, the tree, weakened by fire, collapsed and killed her.

2. In the rainy period of 1985, Malycaqulyi brought the news to Yalqwaalye that a young Hyaqwang-Ilyce woman and her child had been drowned. She had been crossing a bridge which, like so many others, was a rickety structure made

of a few trunks strung together and placed across the river. All such crossings, especially in the rainy season, are extremely hazardous, for it is easy to momentarily lose one's balance on the shaky bridge and fall into the torrent. The chances of surviving such a fall are minimal, since the body gets smashed against the numerous boulders in the river. This is what happened to the young woman. However, it was not she who fell outright into the flooded river but her child, whom she carried in a string bag suspended from her forehead. As she jerked to regain her balance, the string bag snapped. The woman screamed as she realized what had happened, and instantly jumped after her baby into the torrent. I do not know whether their bodies were ever retrieved.

While telling me about this incident, Malycaqulyi was grinning, and so was I—not because the report was funny, but because it was awesome. Disastrous incidents occur quite regularly in the rainy period, so much so that humans-falling-off-bridges-and-drowning is characterized in Iqwaye experience as an entailment of the rainy season itself. Rainy season and falling-off-bridges and drowning-in-the-river are virtually as intimately linked as fire and smoke (in the period 1984–85 there were two other cases of such drownings).

3. The death of Hilyce-Taqalyce from Iwola'a-Malycaane was also a memorable one. He was killed by a wild pig which, in a savage attack, ripped off his genitals.

4. In Yalqwaalye, particularly astounding was a man's death some twenty years ago. It happened in the forest while he was splitting a tree with an axe. A branch accidentally split off and forcefully transfixed his leg to the ground. He was found dead. Local opinion was that his bone marrow (nenena)—his vital seminal substance—completely ran out of his body, which is why he died.

5. An Ung-Waace man died on his way home from Iwola'a-Malycaane in the Vailala headwaters. He saw a marsupial entering a hole under a large rock. No Yagwoia man would ignore such an opportunity, so the Ung-Waace man began to burrow after the marsupial despite his wife's protests. As he burrowed, he paused from time to time to look inside the hole. But in doing so, he loosened the rock under which he had tunneled, and next time he stuck his head into the hole the rock collapsed and decapitated him. Then and there his wife began lamenting that he should have heeded her.

Accidents resulting in death during marsupial hunts are quite common, because they regularly involve a hunter climbing a tree to inspect a lair or chase an animal from a tree crown. Such undertakings may end with a hunter falling from a tree, in which case the outcome is often fatal. In a few instances, men who survive such falls suffer severe injuries, which leave them with permanent deformities. It is also true that some men survive such falls without injury.

There are also instances of accidental deaths caused by a pandanus nut landing on a person's head after the nut is cut or shaken from the crown of a palm. An accident related to this rather commonplace activity occurred some years ago, and was self inflicted. During his work at a coastal plantation, an Iqwaye man procured a special cutter for coconuts, which he thought he could just as easily use to cut pandanus nuts. However, the razor-sharp cutter was so weakly attached to its handle that, on one occasion, when he tried to cut a pandanus nut, the blade detached and, as it fell, slashed his throat. He survived, thanks to a British nurse posted at Kwaplalim station, who stitched the ghastly wound. He now bears a thick, glossy scar which looks like a rope tightly tied underneath his chin, stretching between his ears.

The Yagwoia life-world has a very high "coefficient of adversity." One does not have to cross a stream, go into a garden, enter a forest, or wage war for this to become manifest. The domestic abode itself, with its central open fireplace, has its own ever-present danger potential. Some Iqwaye children suffer severe burns, sometimes death, because they accidentally fall into the home fire. Adults are more vulnerable while asleep. Occasionally a sleeper stretches his or her leg beyond the edge of a fireplace, only to wake in pain with a burning foot, bark cape, or blanket. One man, who went to sleep wearing his recently acquired canvas "patrol" boots, woke screaming in panic with his boots on fire.

Some remembered deaths are characterized by an extraordinarily whimsical self-affirmation by individuals who thereby assert their irreducible and unshakable egoic self-regard in the very act or context of dying. For instance:

6. Amco-Qwoqwapana from Yalqwaalye died after eating a species of poisonous bean. He probably ingested the beans by mistake. As he was vomiting from the effects of the poison, he became sexually aroused and told his wife he wanted to have sex with her. And so they did. He expired in coitus. Unable to extricate herself from her husband's mortal grip, Palycipu began to yell for help. Eventually her sister's husband (ZH) Ung-Yaquye heard her and freed her. I first heard of this death from Taqalyce, who had heard it from Ung-Yaquye. Taqalyce said that she subsequently became pregnant and gave birth to her last son. I checked this detail with other men, including Ung-Yaquye himself, who claimed that this was not so. This mortal sex produced no offspring. What is impressive for the Iqwaye (men and women alike) and for me is that this was a death in sex in which Qwoqwapana affirmed himself over and against his deadly accidental poisoning.

7. Amce-Kamacaqulyi of Iwolye died in his late thirties, leaving two widows and six children. It was not his death as such that was impressive, but the way he faced it. Before he died, he killed all five of his pigs and ate them with his family. I was told that he died from a sore in his throat. He ate one pig as soon as he became sick. When he returned from hospital in Lae, where he was surgically treated, he and the family ate another pig. Three more were finished off while he languished from his illness. His wife and another relative told me that he had reasoned: "It's not good that I die and the pigs stay alive." His body was hot (with fever) so he wanted to give himself some *aalye* (water, fluid) to cool off his body. But because he had no maternal uncles to give him "water" (pork), he gave it to himself.

Eating one's own pigs is, for Iqwaye and other Yagwoia, an incestuous mode of behavior (see Mimica 1991). The self turned in upon itself in a total ouroboric self-closure is the ultimate desire of Iqwaye social being. Although socially proscribed, individuals live this desire in various degrees and modalities of realization. In the face of his imminent death, Kamacaqulyi chose to negate the fundamental presuppositions of Iqwaye sociality. By eating his own pigs he was effectively eating himself, motivated by the exigencies of triple self-deprivation: (a) he was dying; (b) after his death his pigs would be eaten by somebody else and the money and valuables obtained from them would be "eaten" by his children, specifically his sons, not himself; (c) no maternal uncle (male mother) was forthcoming with the socially appropriate pork to fill his stomach, make his body cold, and reduce his imminent bodily self-deprivation. The metaphor of pork as water means semen. The male mother's (MB) gift of pork has this generative-nourishing identity which simultaneously relates it to the mother's milk that primordially nourished a person's body and flesh.

In this socially depriving context of dying, Kamacaqulyi decided to affirm himself for himself, regardless of how socially depraved it was. He was dying, i.e., running out of himself as his body was languishing. He saw clearly that no matter how much his closest relations embodied his sociocentric identity and his bodily being, his own children, maternal relatives, and pigs would remain other. They would live on, making use of his pigs for their own purposes, while he as his particular self would be irreversibly dead. Accordingly, he decided to reverse the social flow of life-giving goods, and alone, with his family, eat his own pigs. He, *qua* his pigs, would be the source of the "water" for his languishing body, rather than his mothers, who offered no life-substance. This is why Kamacaqulyi's self-consumption in the face of his own death was impressive. He became an egoic singularity in which the life-flow (*qua* social exchange), contrary to its normal social regulation, short-circuited and closed in upon itself. Indeed, in hindsight, his wife and relatives acknowledged that they were now pigless, and his little sons left without any viable wealth to provide them a future accumulation of bride-price. In this reprehensible sense, Kamacaqulyi is a man who did not think about the well-being of his own children, who embody and perpetuate his "bone" (patri-)identity. But, by the same token, this further amplified the radicality of his deed, and his singularization in the face of death. He was the kind of man who could undercut his own social otherness and turn in upon himself—eat his own pigs. He was indeed impressive. Everybody tacitly acknowledged this, for everyone is captivated by the desire to possess oneself for oneself in totality.

All of the above examples show the omnipresence of the possibility of dying in the flow of everyday existence—of dying as a result of the unintended consequences of more or less unexpected and circumstantial connections of events and actions. This very contingency is one of the contributing factors to why such deaths are extraordinary, and why a person is more likely to recall them in their specificity rather than to subsume them under the notion of the typical, i.e., as merely factual deaths, devoid of any singularity. Only on account of this categorical factuality could one say that death is always the same everywhere, or one death is like any other. Similarly, one could assert the same about all human life. But in the immediacy of its impact, many a death, particularly if it is unexpected, provokes a sense of outrageous and irreplaceable loss which cries out for equivalent requital. Formerly this was facilitated by warfare. There were always human beings available who could be readily put to death, viz. one's enemies. They could be killed with impunity, not just because they were already responsible for killings, but because they were alien enough to suit the purpose of atoning for the rage provoked by the loss of life which, as such, may have had nothing to do with the enemy group. I became aware of this aspect of Iqwaye intersubjectivity when I documented the intricacies of an intra-village conflict which happened in the late forties. But the same sense of outrage over the loss provoked by death is still alive. The following incident, which happened in 1992, illustrates this rather poignantly.

8. Palyca-Unguyeulaqwa's life was miserably wasted. He was about nineteen when he fell from a pandanus palm in November 1991 and broke his spine. His brothers has tried to dissuade him from climbing, because it was quite late in the afternoon, but he had ignored their warnings. After unsuccessful treatment in Lae, he was sent home. He was now a paraplegic, and depended on a urinary rubber tube protraction which facilitated infection of the urinary tract. Not long after his return to Yalqwaalye, numerous sores erupted all over his back, groin, and genitals. I was living in the Iwola'a-Malycaane area, and saw him only a few times. Subsequently, all reports emphasized that the lower part of his body literally disintegrated, and that he expired fully conscious. From the abdomen down he was an amorphous lump of pus-oozing, rotten pulp, and I was told by several people that urine was seeping from everywhere in his groin except his penis. He watched himself rotting away, though pronounced himself a strong man, which is why he was still alive. Another man would not have hung on for so long. Two local curers, specialists in bone adjustment, were called upon, but they gave up as soon as they saw him. They said that they should have been called when the injury was new. Unguyeulaqwa said he was going to die when his penis fell off. And so he did. His father, Hitana, did not order the prolonged mourning accompanied by dirges, known as *aa'ma kaace*, because he thought the corpse was stinking so badly that prolonged social contact with his son would be unbearable.[3]

Following the burial there was an uneasy reconciliation between Hitana and his surviving sons, whom he had threatened two months before. In his grief and despair over his favorite youngest son's demise, he declared that they, and particularly his first wife's first-born son, were responsible for his outrageous loss. The young Unguyeulaqwa's life had been cut short. After the burial, Hiwoye and Unguyaqulyi, the deceased son's elder brother, tried to smooth out the situation by explaining that Hitana's rage had been misrepresented. Hitana never meant to kill his own sons because his youngest favorite died so wastefully. However, in time of war the situation would have been different. They could go looking for one or more persons in enemy territory and kill them. In this way the grief for and the loss of the relative would be atoned. And this would be something that they, as Unguyeulaqwa's brothers, would carry out; that was all right. But it was never Hitana's intention to kill his own sons because one of them died. This was bullshit and *"tok win"* (wind talk) disseminated by other people.

I will not dwell here on Hitana's deep attachment to and identification with his deceased son. Of 19 children by three wives (he had four wives in all), Unguyeulaqwa was undoubtedly the embodiment of his "bone." When I saw him two years later, in January 1994, he told me that he was waiting to die, and soon would be buried where he was living, in the garden his father had made, next to his son Unguyeulaqwa. The history of Hitana's violent conflict with his sons exemplifies the tensions and ambivalence which constitute the Iqwaye father-son relationship. What is important in this context is the reality of self projection into the social world, where a sense of loss, experienced as a profound deprivation of oneself, is structured as a desire for a reciprocal destruction of another life which thus makes good the loss. Hitana blamed and threatened the lives of his other sons. The deceased's elder brother and a patrilateral classificatory uncle rationalized the father's actions, but in reference to the past availability of enemies for the restitution of grief and loss.

This experience of loss has its basis in the dynamics of narcissism and envy. In this predicament, any other has the value of one's own negation and deprivation, and is projectively seen as such. Someone is responsible for the loss of my child (sibling/relative), regardless of the specifics of circumstance. But the attribution of responsibility is here determined by the prior totalizing structure of primordial narcissistic-parasitic self-projection which can be formulated as follows: You are other than myself by your very separateness— i.e., by not being myself—and, as such, you are depriving me of myself. Here, the other as an object of envy is determined by the desire for total self-affirmation, i.e., a self-possession whose anxious aim is to annihilate all potential for the loss of the self. In this sense, every other becomes the mirror of oneself. The object of envy is me-in-any-other. Here, self's identification with the envied other equals his/her total incorporative destruction. Therefore, any other is a potentially good enough restitutory victim, precisely because he or she signified, latently, my envy, my own loss of myself in every other human being. Because I have lost myself in my child, any other is accountable for the loss of myself, on the grounds of this *a priori* deprivation of myself by being other than myself. This is not an "eye for eye, tooth for tooth" reciprocity, though the Iqwaye also recognize this principle in practice. The loss and rage over death, the sense of "injustice" that this implies, are due to a more primordial and totalizing narcissistic self-projection, whereby all other human beings owe myself to myself by the sheer fact that they are *alive* and thus deprive me of myself. The newly incurred loss only aggravates that primordial loss and envy of myself in others. It can be said that in this totalizing narcissistic modality, life and death become not just the maximal limits of each other but, simultaneously, are maximally self-consummated.[4]

II

Iqwaye death and dying are eminently intersubjective experiences. A person's subjective awareness of death incorporates the imminent possibility of his or her own demise *and* a life-destiny shared with all other human beings. The articulation of death in self-awareness is due to one's experience of the death of other living beings, human and non-human: a close and loving relative or friend, or a total stranger, such as a victim of an accident that one happens to witness. Or, prior to any such direct experience of human death, one might learn of it in abstract from one's parents, or in the context of handling a dead animal, perhaps a pet, or even a squashed insect. Still more primordially, there are the reverberations of the intra-psychic matrix of pre-oedipal intersubject-ivity in which the dialectic of symbiotic dependencies, separation, and indi-viduation effects the first ambivalent differentiation between life and death within an ambiguous horizon of archaic narcissism marked by a blend of cosmic omnipotence, equally cosmic helplessness, and immortality.

To the extent that death as a subjective experience is truly my own (because I myself can only die my own death, without any real substitute) it is also intersubjective. That is, until my death truly becomes my own as the outcome of my own dying, rather than being merely my phantasy, I mostly experience and live actual death and dying as the factuality of somebody else's being with whom I share my life. In relation to these dying and dead others I may live their predicament as *my* sorrow, grief, bereavement, loss, anger, outrage, awe, shock, or as total relief, pleasure, and lack of interest. I can express these lived experiences through crying, lamentation, rolling in mud, eating earth, self-laceration, homicide, leering, silence. But no matter how I experience, express, and comport to other people's death (ordinary or extraordinary), such experi-ence is a primordial source of awareness of death as a radically terminal and indeterminable horizon of my existence. In short, through the death of another human, friend or foe, I am confronted by both death and dying in general and my own mortality. Death and dying are just as much constituted through the experience, actions, and practices of living individuals as they are by those who die. In fact the social reality of every death is always a reality-in-relation-to-and-for-the-living, which in Iqwaye culture is co-extensive with the reality of the dead, for in their existence as spirits they inhabit the same human world, and as such continue to interact with the living, much to the latter's annoyance.

III

I shall now outline several moods, attitudes, and situations of Iqwaye life that illuminate the reality of hardship and suffering and their relation to dying. Each of these aspects of existence exemplifies different degrees of experiential proximity between living and dying which accrue into a single flow of existence.

The Self-pitying Mood of Hardship and the Pain of Everyday Living

I shall partly follow Heidegger's (1962) formulation of moods as human attunement with the world. They emerge from that level of our being where self-conscious volition does not effect lasting self-alteration. For instance, a depressive mood will not subside as we will it. Moods articulate the primary bodily condition of our existence and as such are structured into an evaluative self-schema. This is not a conceptual schema but a dynamic pattern of affectivity and narcissistic equilibrium whose core is formed by the early experiences and introjections which calibrate our spontaneity. Our life situations, and our experiences of them, are always shaped and co-constituted by ongoing self-projections through our moods. Thus our experiential attendance to and existence in the world takes place through familiar, fluctuating opacities, viscosity, luminous exhilarations, and abatements of moods.

   The specific mood that I describe here relates to the sustained experience of the hardship of everyday life. For instance, a person returns home tired and drenched by rain. He/she goes straight to the fireplace, squats, and begins to grin and groan—"yooiy"—while, within minutes, due to the heat from the fire, steam starts to emanate from his/her body and attire. The grin and groans are expressions of relief from as well as acquiescence in the experienced hardship. Or, one can get caught in the rain in the forest and, if there is no shelter, spend an entire night huddled inside a hollow tree. Taqalyce spent one such night in the forest with his wife and daughter during a pandanus nut–gathering session. He said that for a while he was disgruntled at not having gone home earlier. Eventually he comported to the situation, and made it as comfortable as possible by contriving a shield of pandanus leaves which protected him from rain. Taqalyce recounted this with the characteristic expression of self-pity which I often saw in him and other Iqwaye in situations where discomfort and small but pervasive suffering are appreciated as the sweet pain of existence. Essentially, such a mood attests to a basic Iqwaye attitude toward suffering in life, namely that in spite of all hardship it nevertheless can be pleasurably assimilated into the bodily condition of existence. As a concrete embodiment one lives, endures, and suffers life. A few leaves of pandanus, and one's predicament is changed. Although this man and his family were frustrated and discomforted by the rain, they still managed to make it into a somewhat lesser hardship, in consequence of which they could feel pleasurably sorry for themselves and expect from others corroboration of their mood.

This is why such a mood is employed as an excuse. For instance, during the second initiation ceremony, held in 1979, I arranged with Taqalyce to meet at a bachelors' house late at night (about 4 A.M.). From there we were supposed to go to the forest to take part in the ceremony. When I arrived, Taqalyce and some other men were already gone. Fortunately I spotted another man, Yaqu-Ca'paqulyi, who was just leaving, and went with him. But we got lost in the thicket which grows in the forest fringe area. Anxious not to miss the ceremony, I became annoyed with Ca'paqulyi's failures to find a passage through the thicket which separated us from the footpath. Accordingly, I told him to follow me as I forced my way through it, regardless of the scratches and cuts that I copiously received in the process. Startled by what he saw as my severe disregard for the well-being of my own skin and flesh, he came through the passage I had made. Upon our arrival at the forest site, we found Taqalyce and some men sitting around the fire, while others pounded with heavy sticks at the bases of pandanus palms and trees. The forest was resounding with thuds. Somewhat angry, I asked Taqalyce why he had left without me. He simply replied pitifully, with a mild smile: "Oh, I am pained," soliciting my pity, for no matter what our agreement had been he was now pleasurably pained by the situation—in the forest, sleepless, trying to keep himself warm by a weak fire, amid the thuds that resounded around us. And so was I, evidently roughed up and scratched, which was one more reason for me to acquiesce in his sorrow for himself, since I could feel just as sorry for myself. In that sense we commiserated, and therefore I could not, as it were, reproach him with my annoyance with the way things had turned out.

Rather than pitching this kind of hardship and frustration at the level of an angry regard for self and/or others, the mood of self-pity makes the pain and frustration sweet and turns hardship into an ameliorative pleasure with oneself, though this does not cancel out the fact that in life, on the whole, one endures suffering and is vexed by it to varying degrees of gravity and intensity. This self-pitying mood can be said to articulate a basic appreciation of existence, in which suffering is not an outrageous negativity but an assimilable, even a pleasurable factuality of life.[5] The hardship of everyday life is lived in sufferance and suffering, in the same way that death and dying are irreducible aspects of existence. They do not impose themselves on Iqwaye experience as radically problematic, which is how they are construed in many world cultures where humans, on account of such a problematic appreciation of suffering (for instance as cosmically enunciated by the Buddha's first noble truth, "Existence is suffering") practice a variety of projects of salvation from existence. In the Iqwaye life-world, life, which includes death, is no more and no less than the incessant flow of existence. That, in its factuality, is all there is. Here, human existence does not apprehend itself as problematic in its very factuality, and therefore seeks no salvation. Salvation from what? From existence itself!? Given the character of the Iqwaye life-world, the idea of salvation is absurd.

I do not wish to give an impression that the Iqwaye's sufferance toward suffering is some self-consciously heroic endurance of hardship. This is why I emphasize that self-pitying sufferance is a mood of Iqwaye existence, not an ideologically elaborated attitude toward living. In this sense, it is not something they live for themselves as a thematized moral virtue. The self-pitying mood expresses an affective attunement to existence which neither excludes nor holds sway over the other moods and attitudes which articulate the Iqwaye sense of existence.[6] Bodily injury cogently brings to the fore these other aspects, and in particular, the intersubjective character of the endurance of suffering.

Bodily Injury and the Intersubjectivity of Pain

A notable characteristic of the Iqwaye attitude toward sickness and pain (I make no distinction between psychic and bodily pain) is an ambivalent willingness to assimilate them into the general condition of existence and to live with them. Although they do not want to be ill, and seek assistance with differential apprehension and expectations from local and Western medical experts, Iqwaye are just as much disposed to submit themselves to disease and suffer it in their daily living. For many Iqwaye, therefore, living also becomes an interminable assimilation of sickness, which can hold sway over them with a greater or lesser intensity. Their self-professed desire to be free of disease is, in terms of concrete action, a passive endurance of suffering since, often, it is not only easier to live with sickness but nothing else can be done.

When sickness and pain beset Iqwaye, such afflictions have to be understood in terms of Iqwaye intersubjectivity: as predicaments which occur in the context of coexistence with other people. Every self is *a priori* a relational being whose existence for itself is vitally determined by others who share a common life-horizon, including death. Neither sickness nor pain are modes of personal being; nor are they experiences which, in their manifestations, are exclusively restricted to the person subjected to them. However, no matter how much one can empathize with another person's condition and experiences, this remains a vicarious participation. My response to a person whose body is riddled with scabies, disfigured by leprosy, or infected with a tropical boil with four sealed orifices, or whose face has been cut with the blunt side of an axe, is not his/her predicament but my response to it. But it is also true that a person does not attend to the totality of his own experience as being exclusively his own, despite the fact that factually it is so. One is stuck in one's own embodied self whether one likes it or not. Experientially, then, one's own pain, like any predicament, is lived in a mode of fluctuating self-possession and self-decentering. It is lived in relation to, and as ongoing attunement to and detachment from, the experiences, responses, and expressions of others to oneself. Sickness and pain, like any other human situation, have to be understood in terms of this fluctuating field of intersubjective experience and lived communication, constellated by specific cultural pre-understandings of what constitutes and what is proper sociality. I shall illustrate this with a few observations.

1. An uninitiated boy had a boil of the size of a ping pong ball on the top of his head. His mother and sister's husband (ZH) took him to the river, though he violently resisted, so much so that the latter struck him firmly several times with a hand across the face. At the river, the ZH ruptured the boil and a thick jet of oily blood sprayed for almost a meter. The boy was screaming, his whole body jerking, while the mother wept and chanted about her child's blood being spilled.

This example of a mother's emotional participation in the painful experience of her child can be taken as an archetypal case of intersubjective empathetic participation in the predicament of another person. The child was born out of her body, and nourished by her. The child's body, its very flesh and blood, was derived from her own bodily substantiality, and bore a maternal substantial identity (see Mimica 1991). The basis of the empathetic identification was this primordial bodily identity—the source of all Iqwaye constructions of human identity, and of the articulation of intersubjective emotionality as a whole.

2. The following example (1979) comes from a village court hearing over which Taqalyce presided. All of those present were directly embroiled in a quarrel over ownership of some cowrie shells. Among them were Taqalyce's father, the most notorious Iqwaye warrior, and his much younger wife Hyaqalycipu. Their deceased son had been buried the day before. As Taqalyce was pontificating about the issue of the shells, a man in his early fifties, Omalyca-Hyaqalyce, walked into the hearing, since it also concerned him. He was Hyaqalycipu's FZS, i.e., her classificatory son. Reciprocally, she was his MBD, a classificatory mother. He was also slightly older than she. Recently incapacitated by sickness, he walked slowly with the help of a stick. Ordinarily a very strong man with a stocky, muscular body, he was now like an old man, truly pitiful in appearance. At the sight of her noye[7] Hyaqalycipu broke into tears and began lamenting the decrepit condition of his body. Immediately, her husband, the old warrior Palyc-Caqapana, began to weep rather painfully, since his mouth was half closed. His whole face became contorted. It looked as if his grief was forcing itself through every available orifice—ears, nostrils, skin pores—none of which would let it freely flow out. The sick noye was at once deeply affected. Overwhelmed by their grief for him, he knelt between Hyaqalycipu and Palyc-Caqapana. Still leaning on the stick, he began to weep bitterly. He choked through his tears: "I am badly pained, my body is wrecked. . . ."

While all this spontaneously unfolded and orchestrated itself into well-tuned grieving, Taqalyce continued to expatiate more or less unperturbed. He only paused for a moment as the trio withdrew from their common sphere of communication in order to emotionally close in on themselves, then he resumed talking. Similarly, the others chose to remain unperturbed. Slightly annoyed, Taqalyce asked me to pay attention to him. He said: "The man is wrecked so they cry for him," i.e., their momentary self-absorption is inconsequential for the hearing. After a few minutes, the weeping ceased and the trio gradually turned their attention to the issue of shells.

Adult Iqwaye of both sexes do not hesitate to weep in the presence of others in any context, both as an expression of self-concern and/or concern for others. The two modes are strictly interdependent. In the Iqwaye experience of themselves there is no possibility that a person be concerned with or feel sorry for another person without this being grounded in self-concern. In the present example, this is implied by the very nature of the relationship between the three persons: the classificatory mother, father and sick child, Omalyca-Hyaqalyce. The classificatory mother laments *over her* own bodily identity, which her incapacitated son incarnates in his own decrepit body. This mutual self-concern was also conditioned by the fact that the incident occurred only a day after Hyaqalycipu's and Palyc-Caqapana's little son was buried, so that their already mournful mood was readily exacerbated when they saw their classificatory son in his misery. It also fed their own sense of loss.

The proclivity to break into tears varies from person to person, relative to a given situation. But some people are well known for this, and may be characterized as "those who readily weep." In this regard a problem such as the "genuineness of emotion," often encountered in anthropological literature, stems from a deeply entrenched misconception as to the nature of human emotionality. This apparent problem is based on a tacit presumption about the nature of affectivity. To the extent that it is articulated by a volitional person, affectivity, it is assumed, must also be spontaneous, and uncontaminated by wilful guidance. What is misconceived here is the connection between spontaneity of affectivity and its genuineness. For affectivity, like the rest of being, does not exist as a closed-off interiority of somatic spontaneity. The of emotions lies not merely in themselves, but in relation to a concrete egoity in the concrete situations in which a person is living his/her own emotionality. And this living of oneself unfolds on the basis of spontaneous choices of one's own being in a given situation. As such, every person—be he or she deliberately phony and hypocritical, or sincerely genuine or naive—lives his/her emotionality as an already socialized and structured flow or scheme of spontaneity. This constitutes a person's affectivity as a style of being-oneself, a style more or less flexible, more or less open to situational modifications and choices. Trance behavior or delirium, too, is manifested as a specific style of the self within the parameters of an already personalized and therefore socialized scheme of spontaneity which instantiates a distinctive spectacle of possession, soul-loss, or self-disintegration. In this view, when one's emotionality is feigned, what matters is not that it is feigned but rather *why* the person has chosen to be himself or herself in a given situation through such feigned emotionality.

Although the realm of human affectivity goes beyond the volitional sphere of egoity, nevertheless those involuntary regions of seemingly uncontaminated spontaneity themselves constitute a primordial egoic sphere characterized by self-concerns, through which a person gives direction to and chooses him/ herself in the innermost spontaneity. There is no doubt that implicit in the problem of the "genuineness of emotion" are moral-aesthetic presuppositions of modern Western sensibility concerning the proper way of being-an-emotional-subjectivity. The very notion of the "genuineness" implies a moral-aesthetic view of the virtues of sincerity and self-suspension, i.e., an absence of volitional irradiation and pre-meditated self-interests in emotional self-expression. Only on the basis of this specific cultural moral-aesthetic view of affectivity can there arise the problem of the "genuineness" of emotions. Otherwise there is no reason why emotions should not have a volitional gradient, including the fact that they can be volitionally feigned to the same extent that they can be volitionally genuine. In every outflow of emotion there is a gradient of volitional modulation and control, practiced in good and bad faith. Among the Iqwaye, to have a vested self-interest in concern for others is the very substance of intersubjectivity, and accordingly emotionality is managed. Indeed much of their emotional involvement with each other entails payments.

Here is a minor example of the sociality of the concern for the pain of another person. Many years before I came to know him, Taqalyce decided to have a stripe tattooed on his face. Tattooing was a new fashion, which the Iqwaye and many other Angans in Menyamya Sub-Province began to practice following the example of men who worked on coastal plantations. When subjected to this operation, Taqalyce's cheek was cut and bloodied. Observing this was his father's patrilateral half-brother's daughter's husband, i.e., his classificatory ZH, Ung-Auqucoqwa, who burst into tears at the sight of this mild mutilation. He was sorry and concerned for his WB, which prompted the latter to give him a small amount of money as payment for his tears, sorrow, and concern. Ung-Auqucoqwa duly took it. Apart from being affines, the two men were also co-initiates (i.e., they were nose-pierced in the same ceremony)— something the Iqwaye regard as defining a very close and emotionally intense male relationship. I will not explore here the meanings of concern for others in relation to payments. The significance of the present example is merely to underscore one of many presuppositions of Iqwaye intersubjectivity, namely that one's concern for the suffering of another person often places the sufferer in a position of indebtedness vis-à-vis the concerned person, so much so that this has to be discharged through a payment. In short, concerned empathy, fellow-feelings, and commiseration do not necessarily imply symmetry between persons. More often than not, concerned empathy binds people into asymmetrical power relations; it can restrict, assault, oppress, as well as console, placate, encourage, and liberate. To that effect, Iqwaye affectivity is a fluctuating intersubjective field, a socialty of very diverse passions and self-interests, at once constituted by and constituting social relations.

Moreover, in the Iqwaye life-world it is not the person as a "spiritual" entity who suffers and who is attended to with fellow-feeling, but the person as a concrete bodily being whose body bears the indelible identity of the mother and father, and as such is *owned* by many other relations. The body is the irreducible dimension of Iqwaye selfhood and the matrix of kinship relations (see Mimica 1991). Empathy and emotional attunements, therefore, have to be understood as participation in an embodiment which is egoically sociocentric. The egocentricity of embodiment is the condition of its sociocentricity, both within the framework of kinship and of (patrilineal descent) group relations.

Empathetic participation also extends to animals, such as pigs and dogs, all of which bear the patrilineal descent group names of their owners. As pets, pigs and dogs are fondled, deloused, fed, and occasionally slept with in close embrace, under the same cover (in the case of pigs, only while they are still very small). A man or woman will wholeheartedly weep over the decrepit condition of his/her dog. Likewise, a man may show concern for a pig when it is about to be killed, by trying not to upset it unduly.

In addition to the relationship between parent and child, the relationship between mother's brother (MB) and sister's child (ZCh), especially sister's son (ZS), cogently exemplifies this primordial significance of empathy. In this relationship, concern and grieving also unequivocally presume a compensatory payment from ZCh to MB. The former is insuperably indebted to the latter for the very fact of his/her bodily existence. One of many instances that might be cited is the case of two brothers, Omalyce and Omalycaqulyi, related to Taqalyce as his father's patrilateral half brother's daughter's sons (i.e., classificatory ZS) but who always felt very close to him. In 1976, they had a quarrel which led to a fight. Omalyce, the elder brother, had used his younger brother's bow, which accidentally broke. He showed no intention of making reparation to his younger brother. Accordingly, the latter in retaliation broke several of his brother's arrows. A fight broke out and Omalycaqulyi ended up badly beaten by his much stronger elder brother. Bruised, he went to Taqalyce's house where Taqalyce immediately broke into tears. Two brothers who were his children had fought each other, not two strangers. But though it is undesirable, fraternal discord (including fratricide) is an intrinsic, structural aspect of Yagwoia social existence, just as discord is between fathers and sons, expressing the immanent patricidal and filicidal dynamics of this relationship.

Omalyce followed his younger brother, and when Taqalyce saw his bruised face he intensified his lamentation. Tearfully he admonished both for their behavior, pointing out that he himself was "one piece," i.e., a single child, without a true brother or sister (born out of the same net-bag, i.e., womb, the same mother). When two brothers fight, it is indeed bad. In the course of this tearful admonishment, their father arrived. Immediately he learned what had happened, he went for his elder son with a bush knife, but the latter was resolved to defend himself. The maternal uncle prevented further escalation by intensifying his crying with another admonishment to the effect that it was now a son turning against his father. The situation was contained, and some time later Taqalyce made a new bow for Omalycaqulyi.[8] In turn, the elder brother, Omalyce, made a payment to his maternal uncle of 3 Kina and two sets of 5 cowrie shells. This was a very high payment, not only because the maternal uncle's grief had to be expiated as a matter of course (lest one jeopardize one's own well-being), but also because Taqalyce gave a gift to the ZS, so showing tangibly that, apart from grieving, he truly cared for him.

This case is instructive, both in regard to the emotional structure of the MB/ZCh relationship and the inner significance of the empathetic concern of a maternal uncle for his sister's sons in a specific situation. In his admonishment, this maternal uncle stressed that he himself was brotherless, thereby underscoring how precious one's own brother is and, therefore, why brothers should not fight. So Taqalyce, in fact, thematized the sorrowful concern for himself through which he lived his concern for his sister's children. The fact that he is a single child lends pathos to Taqalyce's self-experience. He is a precarious person, caught in his own kinship singularity. Without a true brother or sister, he lacks a true relational double who is literally the extension and replication of himself (his own identity). But at the same time, this pathetic condition, which is his insuperable lack of egoic being, is also the source of his foremost self-fulfillment. In this irreducible lack of his kinship-determined narcissistic equilibrium, he is also morally superiorized for being himself over and against everybody else who, not lacking a sibling, father, or mother, can take themselves for granted, and therefore do not have to worry about themselves. They exist with self-substitutes, other siblings, doubles of themselves. Hence the force of Taqalyce's injunction to his sister's sons, who plainly do not know what it is to be brotherless. They fought each other, whereas they should appreciate that each is a substitute for each other. Brothers should really look after each other, because being against one's brother is like being against oneself. Taqalyce's response, then, was at once an empathetic and a moral concern for the well-being of his sister's sons, but its inner vehicle was his genuine pity for himself as a solitary kinship singularity, "one piece." Moral admonishments to others are thus also a self-gratifying exultation of one's own moral worth, borne out of irremediable lack, the lack of oneself in the others who are born out of the same womb and are therefore identical to oneself.

For Iqwaye, this pathos of irreplaceably singular selfhood, which as such is at once the lack and the fulfillment of one's own egoic being, is also an intersubjective cultural value. In many situations, individuals will declare that they are singular—"one piece"—despite the fact that they have true siblings. This gives salience to the immanent dialectics of narcissistic dynamics which is at the foundation of Iqwaye selfhood and its social matrix—kinship relationships. Those for whom the lack of siblings (or parents or children) is a real fact willy-nilly live this pathos in its more acute mode of realization.

All this shows that, among the Iqwaye, emotions in general are integrated with sociality, whose structure derives from interpersonal dependencies, symbioses, and bodily identifications, which in turn articulate multiple autocentric and allocentric concerns.[9] And these can range from merciless exploitation to compassionate immersion in the predicament of another person. The latter possibility is often evidenced by grandparents, especially maternal, vis-à-vis their grandchildren. Here is an example.

In December 1985, Omalyca-Hyaqalce-ule-Omalyca was making a set of shelves for me. Just as he was adding a few final touches to the boards, he lopped off the small finger of his left hand with a knife, just below the fingernail. I was translating a tape with a close friend, Palyc-Caqapana, when in the back room we heard Omalyca muttering in Tok Pisin: "It went where?! It went where?! Fuck!!" Then he said in vernacular that he had completely severed his finger, and Caqapana, quite startled, related this to me. Omalyca did not scream or moan. He just asked angrily where it was. The *it* was his finger-tip, which he could not find. At first, I felt slightly annoyed because I thought he was joking, and I was engrossed in the translation work. Then Yaquye-Omalyce, his younger classificatory matrilateral brother went into the room, and in horror confirmed that Omalyce's finger was gone. He dashed out as I went in to see Omalyce copiously sweating, still searching for his finger tip, while the stump slowly exuded a thick stream of blood. At the sight of his stump, currents of anxiety and repulsion infused my body. I quickly cut a piece of gauze and proceeded to dress his finger. He began to succumb to the impact of the experience. He blew-whistled several times; his head was sweating.

At that moment, the children who ordinarily hung around my house flocked inside. With them came Omalyce's true maternal grandfather, Palyca-Nguye, the oldest and most important Iqwaye leader. When he saw several thick drops of blood on the bamboo floor, and his grandson's bleeding finger-stump, the old man broke into tears and soon began to sing-weep about his grandson's mishap and the spilling of blood. He did not remain on his feet but sat on the floor and intensified his lamentation. Omalyce, who until now had been leaning against the wall, slowly slid onto the floor. Although overwhelmed (his pain by now was becoming more prominent), he began explaining how it had happened that he had lopped off his finger tip. Everybody present was arrested by the incident, which truly made Omalyce the powerful center of attraction in this situation. For a while everybody was transfixed by him-and-his-finger. They were stunned. For a moment, Omalyce looked as if he would faint, but he only gasped several times, closed his eyes, and turned his face away with an expression of pain and frustration. Yaquye-Omalyce spat some water onto his face, then Omalyce slaked his thirst. I found the severed finger tip on the floor and put it in a cellophane biscuit bag. I was later told that it would be smoked, and attached as a pendant to a necklace or bandolier for Omalyce's young son. Omalyce gave his wrapped finger tip to a boy to put in his net bag.

Palyca-Nguye sent a boy to get a few cordiline leaves for the *yakale* (spell) which he was going to make in order to stop the bleeding. Omalyce told me that he would wait for his grandfather to sing the spell, then he would go to Kwaplalim station, some 5 km down from Yalqwaalye, to receive medical treatment. The boy returned with a bunch of cordilines; the old man swallowed his tears, and performed the spell.

In this example, the dramatic reaction to Omalyce's accident demonstrates the striking character that such an event always has: the subject of the accident is momentarily obliterated, in the sense that he is lost in a vortex of inter-subjective perceptions focused on the point of the accident—in this case the severed finger. There is hardly anything more fascinating and repellent than the sudden upsurge of a mutilated human body or its part into one's unprepared consciousness. But while Omalyce's immediate reaction was to look for the severed piece of himself (this is why the finger tip was eventually smoked), others were mostly startled by his mishap. They were quickly drawn into his situation, and the emerging empathy became the intersubjective condition in terms of which they all, included the sufferer, further lived the situation in a variety of feelings—as growing anxiety, fascination, repulsion, indefinite shock, distantiation, resistance, unbidden commiseration.

But the sufferer's grandfather, Palyca-Nguye, lived his fellow-feeling as a unilaterally compassionate and painful sorrow for his grandson. I could not help but reflect on the inverse symmetry between them: the grandson's agonizing pain did not result in an unbidden screaming and weeping. Instead he was literally sweating his pain out. The grandfather, however, wept it out and was groping around in tears. Seldom did I witness such intense participa-tion in another's person's suffering during my fieldwork among the Iqwaye. This intensity was so pronounced, precisely because it lacked all the common dramatic repertoire of self-representation of grief, such as wallowing in mud, cutting the forehead with knife or a stone, etc. This intense commiseration was borne out of their concrete, life-long relationship as grand-kin. The situation accentuated the whole configuration of affectivity which is at the foundation of the MF-DCh relation. For instance, one of the preferred genealogical specifica-tions of every person's identity is a reference to the name of his maternal grandfather. Accordingly Omalyce is "Palyca-Nguye kayeqwa" (Palyca-Nguye his-grand-kin-male, i.e., grandson). This particular relationship between per-sons in alternate generations entails a sense of symmetrical power which may neutralize the asymmetry of relationship between the person and his matri-kin, especially between MB and ZCh, which presupposes the perpetual indebtedness of the latter to the former. For instance, if the MF decides to bury his deceased DCh, this may be intended as an act which waives the mortuary payment to the maternal relatives. However, this is primarily a possibility, not a regular practice, and if it does occur (it happened once during my first fieldwork) it will most likely result in a violent quarrel or fight between the grandfather and his son—the maternal uncle, the main recipient of the payment.

The substantial identity embodied by the GCh, and which belongs to his/ her mother's patri-group (and which, therefore, is also the inner identity of the maternal grandfather, mediated by his daughter), is thus not an ossified structure of categorical affectivity which shapes Iqwaye social experience, but something lived in the contingencies of ongoing social life. The case of Omalyce's severed finger exemplifies this anew. A week after the incident, as I was walking back to Yalqwaalye from Menyamya station, where I settled the compensation payment with Omalyce, I met Palyca-Nguye some 10 kilometers away from his abode, pulling his curved body up the hill. He was worried about his grandson, so he had come to meet him on the road.

The fate of Omalyce's finger tip is also significant. As already described, it was smoked with the intention of preserving it for his son. Similarly, Omalyce was advised to save the compensation money for his children and wife. Instead, I soon learned, he decided that he would spend most of it on beer to be drunk by him and his ZH and young classificatory male mothers, i.e., maternal uncles' sons. I was told that he said that his wish was to "eat his own finger." That is to say, qua beer, he ate back his own finger. Although Iqwaye social organization is founded upon primary proscriptions on auto-sexuality and auto-cannibalism, the logic of their kinship system, social classification, and exchange systems is such that the obviation of autocentric prohibitions, which regulate endo and exo relations, ultimately results in their substitutive affirmation (Mimica 1991).[10] Although Omalyce's compensation could have been used as the body payment to his maternal relations, who are entitled to eat it, Omalyce acted auto-cannibalistically. But then, for the Iqwaye, the wisdom of social existence consists in minimizing the draining and disincorporation of one's own body, qua payments, by those who have vested interest in it.

IV

In the ethnographic examples above, one can see the intersubjective character of Iqwaye suffering, where people adhere to each other in the immediacy of any given situation. For some Iqwaye, however, being sick is a dominant way of living, so that one's daily life completely acquires moribund determination. Such insidiously long and creeping sicknesses are assimilated into a habituated endurance. Such a person lives the sickness as he or she lives with, say, all manner of festering sores. It is there, gnawing from within the body, and one may attend to it only to abandon oneself to the endurance of suffering which propels one irreversibly into death. In such instances, living is a long, draining process of dying, and the sufferer as well as everyone else becomes numb, almost completely oblivious, to the condition. Such intersubjectivity is characteristically saturated with the inertia of the predicament; the sufferer is more or less left to himself (herself) and is minimally attended to, because nothing can be done to change the moribund condition.

During my first fieldwork I learned of a man who had died some years before from an "enormous sore," which eventually disintegrated one entire half of his face. It was probably cancer of the jaw. People said that when he drank, water would drain out through the open pulp where his jaw had been. The sore stank so badly that, in the end, no one wanted to visit him in his hut. They were afraid, for he was a ghastly sight to look at, and the stench permeated the entire dwelling.[11]

In another case, a woman aged about 40 was dying for three months. I first saw her at her homestead while conducting a census in the lower Yalqwoyi valley. She was seated under a bush, completely wasted by disease, dumbstruck and devoid of any vitality. It appeared that for some time she had defecated and urinated in the same area where she lived. I arranged for a "haus sik" (hospital) car from Menyamya to drive her to the hospital next day. Just as the car was about to drive off, I saw her at the back of the car, being embraced by her husband, and I caught her gaze. It was the last evanescence of human embodied vitality, a vitality which surfaced through the stupefied cast of her face and clung desperately to its own existence. Never before have I experienced such an irradiation of human life, which in its very vitality was its own death. Perhaps what I saw in her gaze was the same vision of death-in-life which Iqwaye render in their mortuary dirges as the image of "*hiye mapiye*" (literally, "marsupial sun"). It is the shimmer of the cold light which remains after the sun has already disappeared behind the ranges.

That same night, her corpse was driven back for burial.

NOTES

This paper is a shortened version of a chapter from a projected monograph on the experience of death and mortuary practices among the Iqwaye people of Papua New Guinea. They are one of the five politico-territorial groups or tribes which occupy the border region of the Morobe, Eastern Highlands, and Gulf Provinces. Collectively they are known as the Yagwoia people. This is the heartland of the Angan (formerly Kukukuku) cultural and language area (Lloyd 1973). Three other Angan groups, the Sambia, Baruya, and Yeghuye, are well known in the anthropological literature through the works of Herdt (1981; 1987), Godelier (1986), and Fischer (1968).

All Yagwoia words are given in an impressionistic transcription. However, the character c designates an affricate phoneme [ts] (as in church) with both voiced and voiceless variants. The voiced variant appears after nasals. The voiceless variant appears word-initially where it also alternates as [ts] and [s]. The same affricate phoneme fluctuates as [ts] and [s] between vowels. The character t designates a sound which oscillates between a tap [r] and, sometimes in slow speech, a voiceless dental t. Glottal stop is marked as '. In the Yagwoia language all stops are voiceless but most of the time fluctuate between voiced following the nasals, to voiceless aspirated in word-initial positions (Lloyd 1973:53). When it features in word-initial positions the sound h is frequently not realized, e.g., hilyce/ilyce. In combination with y, they both fluctuate, e.g, hyeqwa: yeqwa/heqwa. The morpheme -qa in the name of the territorial group Iwolaqa-Malycaane alternates as 'a, thus also Iwola'a-Malycaane.

I wrote the first version of this chapter in March 1987 while on a post-doctoral fellowship in the Department of Anthropology, Research School of Pacific Studies, Australian National University. I presented it in several departmental seminars in Australia and England in 1987 and 1988. I am grateful to the seminar participants at the ANU, University of Sydney, University College London, University of Manchester, and Oxford University. I also wish to thank Michael Jackson for including this piece of my ethnography in his book. My thanks are also due to the Australian Research Council for financial support in 1984, 1992, 1994 and 1995; to the Papua New Guinea government and the provincial governments of Morobe and Eastern Highlands for allowing me to pursue ethnographic research among the Yagwoia. Finally, my wholehearted thanks to the Iqwaye and Iwolaqa-Malyce for their friendship and everything that, through them, I came to learn about living and dying.

1. He has the same patri and matri names as the man who was supposedly dead. Hence my patrifilial specifications which indicate that they are different individuals. However, the two Taqalyces are related both patrilineally (as FFBS/FBS) and matrilaterally as the classificatory matrilateral brothers (MBDS/MFZS).

2. In the Iqwaye (Yagwoia) kinship classification (Omaha type) all maternal relatives (*males and females*, related to one's mother and mother's brother) both patrilineally (i.e., belonging to the same patrilineal descent group) and as classificatory matrilateral siblings, are categorically classified as *mothers* (1st person singular *naqa*; 3rd person singular *kanei*).

3. Regardless of its repulsiveness, stench is extremely important in Iqwaye sociality of dying and decomposition. In this regard few societies can match the intensity of Iqwaye mortuary practices. Stench is a substantial medium of incorporative identification of the living with the decomposing relative. Decomposition is the manifest activity of the process of death, i.e., the dissolution of the deceased's body, his/her identity, and its reabsorption into the cosmic body, the Yagwoia territory. Dirges and the long mourning period which, albeit all changes, still includes the monitoring of the decomposition of the interred corpse (previously corpse smoking was also practiced; see Mimica 1991) are vital aspects of the process of death. It can be said that death is fully realized after the body (flesh) has completely disintegrated and only the bones are left.

4. This is only a sketch of the primordial narcissistic dynamics and envy constitutive of the Iqwaye intersubjectivity. In another work I explore in detail its narcissistic structures and the modalities of the self-other totalizations especially through the practice of suicide and homicide.

5. Jimmy Weiner observed among the Foi of the Lake Kutubu in the Southern Highlands a similar moody appreciation of life. On various occasions when he and his companions, after a conversation, would lapse into silence and simply attune to the tranquility that permeated the entire landscape, sometimes marvelling at the sunset,

somebody would, all of a sudden, make a perplexing statement: "I think we'll get fucked up now!" According to him it is the Foi mood of human existence as ultimately sustained by immanent hardship, or more strongly, the inescapability from hardship. My sexual gloss renders the Tok Pisin word *bagarap*. Both are quite adequate for the purpose of a summary translation but they focalize the sexual metaphorization of the grip and roughness that the world exerts on human beings. In the vernacular usage of both the Iqwaye and the Foi, the verbalization of the described mood is in reference to bodily pain which assails the person. The tacit metaphoric horizon in the Yagwoia lingual articulation of pain and suffering, however, implies both eating activity (one is being eaten, devoured) and bodily incision, cutting and intrusion. The verb for sexual activity is the same as arrow shooting.

6. This basic Iqwaye attitude toward and the moodiness of existence can be amplified by comparing them with a profoundly different appreciation of the human existence as a predicament but which also, so it seems, does not imply a soteriological problematization of existence. Rather, the humans relate to the world, appreciated as the source of suffering, in a mode of symmetrical retribution. The life-world in question is that of the Bororo Indians of the Central Brazil (Crocker 1986). "This society regards the physical world as ripe with menaces to the well-being and comfort of human persons. Constantly in songs, myths, and verbal formulas, there are endless lists of natural agencies which hurt mankind: thorns that pierce the flesh, stinging insects, venomous snakes, beasts that tear with teeth and claws, even rocks that bruise and wound the feet. The Bororo seem to consider all such injuries as fundamentally wrong, as damages wantonly and capriciously inflicted upon an innocent humanity. Consequently, one of their most important social institutions is dedicated to redressing these crimes of nature against society. Called *mori-xe*, it involves the rule that, whenever a Bororo is injured by a natural element, another Bororo is obliged to kill or destroy the culprit (or a member of the same species). The avenger gives the dead creature to the victim, who must reciprocate with an ornament belonging to his social group" (ibid.:57). Crocker comments: "I do not think the Bororo are especially sissy, although they certainly spend a great deal of informal time as well as ritual moments complaining how badly nature hurts them" (ibid.:343).

7. *Noye* is any person, male or female, related to an ego as the ZCh, true or classificatory child. In this instance FZS=ZS=S.

8. I learned of this incident when a year later Omalycaqulyi sold this bow to me. Taqalyce then made the point that the bow was not just any bow but had a deeper significance attached to itself, namely that it was a bow specifically made by the maternal uncle for his sister's son in response to the specific circumstances related above.

9. For a discussion of the basic aspects of the Iqwaye social organization, see Mimica 1991.

10. For a comparative account on the problematics of the self and its self-relatedness, see Gell 1979.

11. I have already mentioned the intersubjective significance of stench in the Iqwaye experience of death. But regardless of how positively socialized stench is among them, the above example attests to a common human sense of aversion which among the Westerners is not due just to "a higher level of civilizing restraint," as Elias (1985) seems to be suggesting. An example from his little monograph can be read in relation to the Iqwaye example:

Dying, however it is viewed, is an act of violence. Whether people are the perpetrators or whether it is the blind course of nature that brings about the sudden or gradual decay of a human being is ultimately of no great importance to the person concerned. Thus, a higher level of internal pacification also contributes to the aversion toward death, or more precisely toward the dying. So does a higher level of civilizing restraint. There is no shortage of examples. Freud's protracted death from cancer of the larynx is one of the most telling. The growth became more and more ill-smelling. Even Freud's trusted dog refused to go near him. Only Anna Freud, strong and unwavering in her love for the dying father, helped him in these last weeks and saved him from feeling deserted. Simone de Beauvoir described with frightening exactness the last months of her friend Sartre, who was no longer able to control his urinary flow and was forced to go about with plastic bags tied to him, which overflowed. The decay of the human organism, the process that we call dying, is often anything but odourless. But developed societies inculcate in their members a rather high sensitivity to strong smells. (ibid.:88–89)

REFERENCES

Crocker, C. 1985. *Vital Souls: Bororo Cosmology, Natural Symbolism, and Shamanism.* Tucson: University of Arizona Press.
Elias, N. 1985. *The Loneliness of Dying.* Oxford: Blackwell.
Fischer, H. 1968. *Negwa: Eine Papua-Gruppe Im Wandel.* Munich: Klaus Renner Verlag.
Gell, A. 1979. "Reflections on a Cut Finger: Taboo in the Umeda Conception of the Self." In *Fantasy and Symbol,* ed. R. H. Hook. London, New York: Academic Press.
Godelier, M. 1986. *The Making of Great Men.* Cambridge: Cambridge University Press.
Heidegger, M. 1962. *Being and Time.* Oxford: Blackwell.
Herdt, G. 1981. *Guardians of the Flutes.* New York: McGraw-Hill.
———. 1987. *The Sambia: Ritual and Gender in New Guinea.* New York: Holt.
Lloyd, R. G. 1973. "The Angan Language Family." In *The Linguistic Situation in the Gulf District and Adjacent Areas, Papua New Guinea,* ed. K. Franklin. Canberra: Australian National University.
Mimica, J. 1981. "Omalyce: An Ethnography of the Iqwaye View of the Cosmos." Canberra: Ph.D. diss., Australian National University.
———. 1988. *Intimations of Infinity: The Mythopoeia of the Iqwaye Counting System and Number.* Oxford: Berg Publishers.
———. 1991. "The Incest Passions: An Outline of the Logic of the Iqwaye Social Organization, pts. 1, 2." *Oceania* 62(1,2):34–58; 81–113.
———. 1993. "The Foi and Heidegger: Western Philosophical Poetics and a New Guinea Life-World." Review of James Weiner's *The Empty Place. Australian Journal of Anthropology* 4(2):79–95.

If Not the Words

Shared Practical Activity and Friendship in Fieldwork

KEITH RIDLER

The world is not what I think,
but what I live through.
—Merleau-Ponty 1962:xvii

We attain the valuable relationship of friendship
only when we cease to think about it
and concentrate on the friend.
—Telfer 1991:267

About to return again to Italy, I find myself constantly traveling in thought and memory between the antipodes, one part of myself engaged with the New Zealand valley in which I live most of the time, another anticipating the "Green Valley" eight thousand miles away, at the foot of the Brenta massif, where I have also lived from time to time while doing fieldwork. Central to this is the memory of friendships, some of which are about to be renewed. In this essay, I explore the nature of fieldworkers' friendships and provide a partial account of some personal friendships formed in the field. I suggest that there are systematic discursive and existential reasons why fieldworkers are ambivalent about the notion of friendship. These reflections provide a point of entry into a consideration of the anthropologically vexed area of the phenomenological description of friendship, congruent with the practice of a "mimetic" style of anthropological fieldwork.

TWO FIRST ENCOUNTERS

I first arrived in the village I will here call Verzone in early winter, a few weeks before Christmas 1980. I had spent a memorable month traveling and walking in the Italian Alps searching for a fieldwork site, until at dinner one night in Milano, friends of my host invited me to use their holiday house there for a week or so while I assessed whether this village might prove suitable. They themselves would be there for the weekend and would introduce me to people in the village and show me how things worked at their place. On that first trip, discovering that Verzone offered exactly what I had been searching for, I stayed on for almost two years.

The first person I met in the village was Pier Paolo. Carlo, my Milanese contact, who had met the bus, took me into the *salumeria* (delicatessen) and introduced us. It was a quiet time of day, and Pier Paolo led us out the back to admire a batch of salami he was hanging to season in the cool cellar behind the shop. The smell there was marvelous and completely unfamiliar: a pungent mixture of odors of salted meat, garlic, spilled wine, and the damp pine sawdust on the stone floors, so powerfully intoxicating as to distract me while he talked of the tradition of salami making in the village. My first memories of Verzone were thus connected to food: perhaps a good omen, for the main idiom of congeniality there is food and drink.

On the wall of the dark corridor leading to the cellar hung a photograph of Pier Paolo's great-uncle, who had been a delegate to the parliament at Innsbruck in the nineteenth century, when the Trentino was part of the Austro-Hungarian empire.[1] Like Pier Paolo, his brother, his father, and many generations of men from this village who came after him, he too had been a *salumiere* (salami-maker), traveling during the winters as far afield as Mantova, Trieste, and Vienna to make salami during the *stagione morta,* the dead agricultural season.[2] Pier Paolo's family, I learned in those few minutes, had once been substantial peasants, gradually moving into business and playing a central part in local politics.

When I explained my reasons for coming to Verzone, to study the social impact of tourism development on alpine communities, Pier Paolo responded enthusiastically by telling me about his activities in ecological politics and the current plans to turn the mountains surrounding the valley into a national park. There was considerable local discussion, he assured me, about the issues which interested me, and he invited me to have dinner at his home the next day to meet his family and talk further. He also offered to introduce me to one or two people he thought could be helpful with my research on the social history of the village, and others who were involved in various local organizations concerned with tourism. His manner was very animated and positive, and as Carlo and I left carrying paper bags of delicatessen goods, I remember wondering with some astonishment if my fieldwork had already begun, literally within moments of arriving.

A few days after this, I met Augusto, or rather, he made a point of meeting me. I was working in the beech woods above the house, concentrating on preserving my hands and feet while I cut wood with a chainsaw, a tool that was new to me. I was working slowly, methodically, and with a reasonable degree of success, when I had the vague but undeniable feeling that someone was watching me. I turned and saw an old man dressed in checked shirt and jacket, rough trousers, and mountain boots, leaning on a stick observing me silently from a few feet away.

"*Siete pratico?*" he asked, which after a moment I realized meant "Are you experienced [at this work]?"

I bent the truth a little and said I was, explaining that where I came from, in New Zealand, we heated our houses with wood mainly, and, unlike Italy, only rarely had central heating. Augusto made no comment, then introduced himself as the *proprietario* (landowner) who had sold this piece of hillside to Carlo and Monica, telling me that he still made hay on the terraced pastures around the house. I asked about the boundaries, and he pointed them out precisely, indicating a rock here, there a line of old chestnut trees, and finally, with the delicate gesture of a magician completing a trick, a small gully to our left where, in late afternoon, roe-deer descended to drink. As he did this, there was in his manner a great gentleness; in his talk, a kind of open, non-judgmental curiosity which I liked immediately.

We fell into conversation. Augusto asked about my work and what New Zealand was like. In return, he told me about himself, his family, the names in Italian and dialect of the various trees and plants we could see, and a little about the history of the village. He was surprised and amused, it appeared, to have found a *professore* working with a chainsaw.

Both these relationships, begun in the first few weeks of my fieldwork, became friendships which lasted through various successes and troubles in our separate lives. Over the intervening years, Pier Paolo lost his first wife in tragic circumstances, remarried, and then separated. His children grew, became teenagers; the *salumeria* was sold to the village supermarket and then closed down; he struggled, retrained, and developed another career. During this period, he transformed himself, professionally at first, but also personally. The enthusiastic *salumiere* became a rather more reserved and urbane businessman, who, in his increased leisure time, began to explore the *vie ferrate* (fixed-rope routes) on the Dolomites. He traveled more, developed his long-standing love of choral music, and, since I last saw him, has become active in organizing various music groups locally.

Augusto too lost his wife, Francesca, a couple of years before his own death, and his last years were a time of sadly endured domestic solitude, cared for by his sons and daughters-in-law. Eventually, he stopped going out to the countryside, began attending Mass in the mornings, and spent his late afternoons playing cards, local games like Tre-sette or Briscola, in the cafes with his contemporaries. His remained an active life for a man of his age, though, in letters to me in New Zealand, he wrote that he was melancholy, and feared he was losing his memory.

Over the same period, I found my first academic job, married, had children, and fought, for a couple of years, a prolonged illness which kept me away from Verzone for some time. I became involved in establishing the teaching of visual anthropology in New Zealand, initially a distraction from my research on alpine tourism, later a major part of it. I found I spent less time mountaineering, a life-long passion, becoming absorbed by the world of home and children in a way that I would not have understood, I now think to my detriment, at the time that I began fieldwork.

In the decade or so since I had met Augusto and Pier Paolo I visited the village another four times, alone or with my wife, Judith, sometimes for six or seven months, at others for only a few days while in Europe for other reasons. Each time returning, whether the visit was long or short, I experienced that confusing mixture of feelings characteristic, I suspect, of all ethnographers going back to a previous fieldwork site: anxiety about how one will be received, anticipatory pleasure at seeing again old and new friends, and hope for whatever projects one has in mind. The first page of my notes from the last short visit reflects this:

6 November 1990

Arriving, again, in Verzone, laden with New Zealand gifts, Carver's poems and short stories, tapes of Barber's and Rodrigo's music. In the dark, glimpses of snow: at the Bar al Mulino, a familiar back curved over a glass of wine . . . a square of light on the piazzetta, construction barriers and cars streaming through the center of the village.

To Giorgia and Claudio's . . . Giorgia so warm and welcoming with presents for the [future] baby ("al la futura mammina, che da noi portano fortuna"). Their flat, as ever, spotless—the craft of public housewifery showing—a glass of white and news. Claudio a councillor, Matteo "Sindaco" (mayor) (finally), Sergio to marry, after so many false starts . . . so many threads picked up instantly from the last visit, less than two years ago.

Though almost ten since I started—December 9th, 1980 the day I arrived on the same bus, perhaps even the same driver, to be met by Carlo and accompanied to meet Pier Paolo at the salumeria (now long gone) and for a drink at the Bar al Mulino, changed but somehow still the same.

How to measure ten years—the jumble of continuities and ruptures, Verzone's and my own? All the notebooks, searching for some sense of it, of a story, theme, uniting thread: when all there is are the fragments of people's lives, changing, reforming, moving through and toward other shapes, themselves moving toward yet other shapes and projects, never fixed or defined for even a moment.

What does remain, and is renewed each time after the initial anxiety, is the sense of the familiar, even if only half-caught, like someone's voice echoing down a hall—the wave of sound, if not the words.

Now, after more than ten years of visiting, thinking about, and describing Verzone, this half-caught wave of sound or sense has become a part of my life which I cannot simply reduce to the activity of carrying out ethnographic research. As with most anthropologists who carry out long-term fieldwork, the memory of place and people is so deeply inscribed in my own experience that it has come to form part of my own transposable history.

Soon, I am returning for the first time with my family, and as I write, something other than words is already flooding back; I find myself rereading old notes trying to decipher its form, hungering for polenta and salami in the evening, browsing old photographs and looking, implausibly, for the faces of Verzonesi in street crowds on the other side of the world. I am caught by a deep curiosity about the ways in which familiarity and of enigma are so indissolubly mixed, and am revisiting relationships in memory, wondering about their future.

THE "NATURAL STANDPOINT" AND ITS IRONIC SUSPENSION

I am certain that many ethnographers recall this potent yet qualified feeling of familiarity about returning to a known place, and rely on the pre-analytic and associative sense of being-in-place that this affords to reorient themselves in the field. We often teach, after all, that a contextual, broadly lateral style of inquiry is a crucial element of the ethnographer's stock-in-trade, and that it is the creative force that runs between this "background" mode of knowing and the verbalizations foregrounded in notes, lectures, and publications which distinguishes the ethnographer, ultimately, from the tourist and other travelers. It is part of what we mean when we speak of the "anthropological perspective": yet, in producing ethnographies, most of us relegate this sense to the sphere of the intangible and hence inexplicable, useless for our attempts to generate anthropological knowledge.

Husserl describes this domain of the unquestioned familiar as an immediately intuited "world of facts and affairs, but, with the same immediacy, as a world of values, a world of goods, a practical world" (Husserl 1967:73–74). It is, he says, an amalgam of both immediate perception and "a dimly apprehended depth or fringe of indeterminate reality" (ibid.:69). It is the pre-reflexive topos of what we accept, assume, preconceive, without knowing that we do so. He calls it "the natural standpoint" and describes it as "prior to all 'theory'" (ibid.:73).

Experientially, as Victor Turner has pointed out, it is also prior to that form of delineated, storyable experience which, as he puts it, "like a rock in a Zen sand garden, stands out from the evenness of passing hours and years and forms what Dilthey called a 'structure of experience'" (Turner 1986:35). In attempting to fix "the natural standpoint" we are dealing with everything that we know, without *consciously* knowing it, in order to foreground any perception or conception of discrete experience. It is the intangible, phenomenal knowledge from which experiences, meanings, and ultimately narratives are born. The "natural standpoint" is thus constitutive of the *flow* of experience, forming the bedrock from which, by virtue of verbalization, accounts are hewn.

Despite this, it remains shadowy from the point of view of representing ethnographic realities. Writing about the smell of Pier Paolo's cellar, the careful way he might slice a fresh salami, complaining of the bluntness of the knife, or about Augusto's presence, his strong hands holding a rake or scythe, endeavoring to make these things stand in *themselves,* I am breaking with that unstated convention whereby raw, immediate, intuited social experience is discounted in favor of theorization. Yet it is the smell of the cellar, Augusto's presence as a person, which—in the first instance and in memory—engage me with Verzone, and are the ground, in a literal sense, on which I am able to stand when I return there.

I want to suggest that for anthropologists in the field, this backgrounded, umbral aspect of experience is both foundational to understanding and yet neglected for systematic experiential and discursive reasons. These reasons are intrinsic to the existential character of the fieldwork situation and to the process of moving from experience to account.[3] They have to do with the nature of anthropological encounters as lived *toward* the writing of ethnography, and, as I argue below, deeply affect the social role of the ethnographer, his/her relationships in the field, and the accounts s/he produces.

The textual reductions practiced by anthropologists have by now, of course, been almost overly discussed in the literature (Clifford 1986; Geertz 1988; Marcus and Fischer 1986; Rosaldo 1989). What has been less remarked is that this representational reduction is effected in two directions, and is not only discursive but also existential. The anthropologist lives partial realities in the field for many reasons: one of them is the necessity of shaping experience toward representation. In this sense, the discursive objectives of anthropological research lead fieldworkers to (re-)shape experience both *retrospectively* (s/he shapes the account of that experience narratively) but also, and prior to this, *projectively* (the ethnographer lives experience toward a text).

To live a moment through the optic of research, with the ulterior motive of representation, is already, *at the outset,* to be committed to the construction of a deeply interpreted, hence selective, experience. The social reality of the ethnographer, in this sense as much as all the others, is existentially different from that of the people with whom we work. Representation constitutes our "project," our means of making totalizing sense of experience.[4] The politics of fieldwork are framed by this ultimate objective.

While such an existential project may (rarely) coincide with the intentions and experiences of those we work with, the more typical case is one of experiential disjuncture, rendering interpretation more complex, multiplying significances and meanings. In itself, the sheer fact of experiencing projectively sets up ambiguous correspondences and contradictions between the anthropologist's and informant's lifeworlds.

This disjuncture struck me very forcibly after Augusto's death, one evening as I sat writing up some notes a few days after his sad, rainy funeral. His intellectual generosity, his willingness to impart knowledge of the transhumance system and of life at the *malghe* (high Alps), his sharing of the details of village history glimpsed at our first meeting had extended over the years, and crucially helped foster my first clear picture of what life in Verzone had been like, before tourism transformed it. His sense of continuity was powerful, rooted in his own daily work as a *contadino* (peasant), a word he used with pride. He had told me once, as we were haymaking together, that he had used the same scythe for more than sixty summers: "The blades have changed," he said, "but it's always been the same handle."

By contrast, the early evening had been spent visiting Pier Paolo and his second wife, Carla. Pier Paolo, elegantly dressed and sporting an expensive new watch, was talking about the difficulties he had faced in retraining as an investment broker, how stressful he had found the examinations, and how satisfied he felt that he had been able to achieve a new direction. His conversation on this theme was occasionally studded with stories about his and my experiences together in the past, largely for the benefit of Carla and Jude. As he spoke he absentmindedly adjusted his tie, glanced at his watch, attended to our drinks from an elegantly designed and well-stocked bar beside the sofa.

Entertaining us in his own home in this way, Pier Paolo might have stepped from the pages of one of the glossy Italian lifestyle magazines, a portrait of the successful, urbane businessman. The memory of him sitting in his three-wheeler delivery van a few years earlier, smiling happily as I took his photograph, surged into my mind, then quickly disappeared.

Pier Paolo was, indeed, a "changed man," and saw himself as one: happy that he had remarried, and that his professional horizons had expanded. His story was a tale of hard-won transformation. As he spoke, I was struck by Don Federico's words about Augusto at the memorial Mass—*"era un uomo umile"* ("he was a humble man")—requiem for a villager of the old school. The conversation with Pier Paolo made it clear that he thought of himself as a new type of villager. Even as he spoke, Pier Paolo's telling of his recent experience suggested itself as a way of making an anthropological point. Later, remembering Augusto, thinking of Pier Paolo, I wrote:

8 Feb 1987
Pier Paolo is, in his own eyes, the exemplar, perhaps, of the peasant made good: from peasant to artisan to manager or professional. The story he is telling, at another level, is also . . . the sociological narrative of this valley, one which is given poignant contrast by Augusto's funeral, its sense of a continuity lost. For where Augusto was the man unmade by these times (his life and style having moved from center-stage), Pier Paolo is the man who is made by them, or is given the space to make himself in them. . . .

. . . All of this, of course, amounts to another kind of performance—my own performance (increasingly suspect) of an act of anthropological interpretation whereby I reduce this lived experience to a kind of sociological narrative in which Augusto and Pier Paolo play the role of dramatic tokens in another kind of play. . . .

Pier Paolo's story was, of course, like many one is told in the field, *already* a sociological narrative, if cast as a moral tale about progress, which became embedded in my own. Like me writing my notes, he was also narrating several histories; related through a series of equivalences between his view of change in the valley and the changes in his own life. At this level, there was a certain coincidence between his narrative and my own.

But how close was it? The stories we (locals/anthropologists) might tell, the metaphors we establish, even biographical/historical equivalences, might be similar, but the *punctum* (to borrow Roland Barthes' evocative term) is radically different. The emotional point of Pier Paolo's account of his own transformation was precisely that of explaining/performing to a friend the nature of his own intentions; my story, at this moment, became one in which Pier Paolo typified structural changes in the valley. While the outer surfaces might seem similar, the core of meaning, in my telling, involved a reduction away from experience: in Pier Paolo's a revelation of it.

Reflecting later on this evening it struck me again, though here experientially rather than discursively, the extent to which my project collided with that of my friends, creating a degree of what one might call epistemological violence which distorted my understanding of this situation and perhaps of many others. Although disturbed by this realization, as time has passed, I have come to appreciate that many fieldworkers' relationships or moments within them are typified by similar existential ambiguities and narrative expectations. Handelman, for example, has recently written movingly about his relationship with the Washo shaman Henry Rupert, describing their engagement, initially at least and on Handelman's part, as a form of "projective typification" (Handelman 1993:136; 143–44). Likewise Crick, in recounting his relationship with "Ali," a street-trader in Sri Lanka, finds the instrumentalization of anthropologist's relationships in the field so problematic that he is led to question whether it is ever appropriate to use the term "friend" in this context (Crick 1989b). It appears that many anthropologists find or construct friendships in the field which are framed in terms of this kind of projective typification, or of emotional dependency, instrumentalization and forms of psychological boundarying which they contrast with the search for mutuality, compatibility, recreation, and openness conceived of as more typical of their relationships at home.

Some years ago, Geertz, on a somewhat broader canvas, found the same note when he wrote:

Usually the sense of being members, however temporarily, insecurely, and incompletely, of a single moral community, can be maintained even in the face of wider social realities which press in at almost every moment to deny it. It is fiction—fiction, not falsehood—that lies at the very heart of successful anthropological field research; and because it is never completely convincing for any of the participants, it renders such research, considered as a form of conduct, continuously ironic. (1968:154)

The moral irony operating here is not only contextual or political. More immediately at issue is what might be termed the "poetics" of fieldwork, the construction and performance of relationship. At stake is the fieldworkers ability to grasp, in its own terms, the "natural standpoint" of those s/he lives with and encompass it, as far as possible, within his or her own.

"RESONANCE" AND MUTUALITY

This recognition of the ironic existential context for the research practice of the most humanistic of social scientific disciplines has been, in recent years, the strongest driving force behind the deep impulse toward reflexivity not just in anthropology but in many cognate disciplines. However, the problem of thinking through the epistemological question of appropriate method, strategy, or stance has remained problematic. Strongly articulated recent reactions to the "interpretive turn," wrongly construed as a form of idealism, from genetic structuralists (Bourdieu 1990), neo-Marxists (Roseberry 1989), or neomodernists (Comaroff and Comaroff 1992), sidestep the issue by encouraging us to return to principally structural or textual analyses. Yet the pivotal epistemological question posed by an existentially and phenomenologically informed anthropology simply will not go away. Is there, we continue to ask, a way of moving beyond this situation of colliding projects and "continuous irony" toward forms of inquiry which ground themselves more easily in the unquestioned field of meanings of others?

A useful entry-point to a consideration of the issue is provided by Merleau-Ponty's discussion of the *Phenomenology of Perception*. Arguing against sensationalism, on the one hand, and transcendental idealism on the other, he early in this work establishes one of its central themes, that it is meaningless to see perception as divorceable from the world which it grasps. On this understanding, the phenomenological method, unlike the textual and experiential reductions I have discussed above, is less an act of translation than one of rediscovery:

> The eidetic reduction is, on the other hand, the determination to bring the world to light as it is before any falling back on ourselves has occurred, it is the ambition to make reflection emulate the unreflective life of consciousness. . . . The self-evidence of perception is not adequate thought or apodeictic self-evidence. The world is not what I think, but what I live through. (Merleau-Ponty 1962:xvi–xvii)

With the later Husserl, Merleau-Ponty holds that our perception of the material world is intrinsically engaged, practical, and embodied. In the social field, knowledge is founded in the inter-subjective fabric of the lived experience of relationship or, as in R. D. Laing's phrase, in "inter-experience" (ibid.:364; Laing 1967:17).

Similarly, in some non-Western cultures, this idea is rendered explicit, encompassing both a social epistemology and a moral schema. As Uni Wikan has elegantly described, in Balinese thought, for example, the notion of *ngelah keneh* ("creating resonance") describes both a dimension of relationship and a complex epistemology in which feeling and thinking are not radically distinguished (Wikan 1990:268–276). Resonant feeling/thinking allows balanced and ethical understanding to emerge. In this way, Balinese epistemology bases itself in a deep sense of shared space, variously defined, in which mutuality forms the ground of social understanding. Flowing from this, Wikan observes, the Balinese notion of resonance extends to an explicit rejection of forms of social knowledge which are based on ontologically and emotionally disengaged intellection alone. As her discussions with friends and colleagues demonstrate, this provides the Balinese with a trenchant critique of forms of anthropological knowledge about their culture in which such mutuality of experience is neglected (ibid.:282–83).[5]

This Balinese construction and critique "resonate" strongly, in another sense, with Merleau-Ponty's discussion of "Other People and the Human World" (1962:346–365). Like the Balinese, Merleau-Ponty insists that our engagement with, and our relationship to others in the social world is never objectified because we can never existentially remove ourselves from it:

> We must therefore rediscover, after the natural world, the social world, not as an object or sum of objects, but as a permanent field or dimension of existence: I may well turn away from it, but not cease to be situated relatively to it. Our relationship to the social is, like our relationship to the world, deeper than any express perception or any judgement. (1962:362)

The social thus possesses an "existential modality" founded in inter-experience for Merleau-Ponty which is not reducible to object relations between social players. Similarly, though expressed in a different idiom, for Wikan's Balinese friends, resonant engagement is an inseparable mode of both being-in and knowing-of the world (*mekeneh*). *Negelah keneh* is thus both conceptually foundational, and, at the same moment, profoundly *practical* in that it allows *mekeneh* to exist (Wikan 1990:275–277). From the Balinese perspective, as from that of phenomenological philosophy, the dominant Western episteme which effects an objectifying theoretical reduction on experience and lived relationship is itself irrational. Both these standpoints insist that knowledge of the social, to echo Wilhelm Dilthey's beautiful phrase, consists in the "rediscovery of the I in the Thou."

This rediscovery is the same one which every anthropologist performs in the construction of friendships in and out of the field. What is remarkable, although generally unremarked in the anthropological literature, is the extent to which relationships founded in recognition of *mutuality* (as opposed to *difference*) provide both the conditions under which fieldworkers are able to exist as real social beings at their fieldwork sites, and the source of much of what we consider data. What Balinese epistemology asserts, as does the phenomenological argument, is that the discovery of mutuality is both intrinsic to our definitions of self and other and existentially prior to and foundational of other knowledge of the social.

THE PRACTICAL SPACE OF FRIENDSHIP

In the conduct of fieldwork, the existential marginality and ulterior motives of the fieldworker mitigate against this realization. The reasons are complex and often personal; more generally, the nature of fieldwork as a culturally dislocated experience encourages forms of engagement and disengagement, styles and rhythms of sociability, which contrast with those the anthropologist experiences in his or her own culture. One of the most transformative and unsettling aspects, and one of the most often remarked, is the mutation of one's sense of oneself as a result of this contrast (Crick 1989a).

A chief aspect of this is how we participate, or fail to, in the flow of practical, daily activities of the people around us. Informally, fieldworking anthropologists have often contrasted accounts of intensive, methodologically systematic, primarily verbal research activity with descriptions of the lived-experience of fieldwork as characterized by long periods of waiting, "down-times," failures to connect with activities or people seen as necessary to furthering their projects. Frequently, such periods are described as filled with displacement activities which relieve the stress of existence in an unfamiliar culture by disengaging one from one's cultural surroundings.

Such accounts may be symptomatic of many ethnographers' need to effect a psychological and sometimes physical distancing from the repetitive and mundane actions of local people to better observe and document them. Indeed, when similarly mundane tasks are performed by anthropologists, they are often considered irrelevant to the main purposes of fieldwork itself, or merely unilluminating, precisely because of their immediately pragmatic character (Jackson 1989:134). At another level, however, this detachment, and the displacements which accompany it, echoes the dualistic detachment effected in Western culture between the activities of the mind and those of the body. It also reflects a traditional Western devaluation of physical work: one in which manual labor comes to stand for membership of the subaltern classes, contrasted with the values of intellectual production.

Insofar as it is shaped by this intellectually privileged and privileging framework, at an immediate level, fieldworkers impoverish their experience of the sensual dimension of the lifeworld by removing themselves from the sensate patterns and rhythms which furnish its texture and fabric.[6] Jackson has made this point incisively with regard to the specific question of the phenomenological understanding of bodily practices:

If we construe anthropological understanding as principally a language game in which semiotic values are assigned to bodily practices, then we can be sure that in the measure that the people we study make nothing of their practices outside of a living, we will make anything of them within reason. But if we take anthropological understanding to be first and foremost a way of acquiring social and practical skills without any a priori assumptions about their significance or function, then a different kind of knowledge follows. By avoiding the solipsism and ethnocentrism that pervade much symbolic analysis, an *empathic* understanding may be bodied forth. (ibid.)

In searching for such empathic understanding of embodied practices, Jackson encourages us to think toward an analogical and "mimetic" mode of anthropological inquiry in which the practice of physical tasks informs an embodied understanding of other's experience. The "methodological strategy" of allowing participation to be an end in itself, he argues, "of literally putting oneself in the place of the other person," is necessary in order to grasp the embodied sense of an activity (ibid.:135–136).

In a comparable way, I maintain that empathic relationships, characterized by the emotions and practices of affection, loyalty, trust, and finally revelation, are fostered primarily by and through the sharing of embodied practical experience. The point can be made even more strongly, as does the philosopher Elizabeth Telfer, who suggests that such "shared activity" is a *necessary* if not sufficient condition for friendship (Telfer 1991:251). It is in this embodied and social domain that the commonalities (and divergences) of experience are tested; here, in practical experience, that the "natural standpoint" as an encultured, habitual form of knowledge reveals itself as the crucial "unsaid" of congenial interaction; here, finally, that we reveal and recognize our own character and selfhood in dialogical encounter with others.[7]

Both the practical and the shared character of carrying out mundane activities in company are germane to the process of forming and maintaining friendships. Indeed, it is significant that this pattern emerges very early in life. In the same way that children who have made the transition from parallel to cooperative forms of play (a transition which occurs specifically when a child is first able to differentiate and project into the experience of an other), adults sharing practical activity experience an intensification and extension of their engagement both with the activity itself and with others who participate. And, like children's cooperative play, which markedly involves the sharing of objects and fantasies, shared activity is often a medium for exchange and revelation not only of knowledge and practical skills but of intention.

In the case of adults' friendships too, the ongoing and repetitive nature of many practical activities establishes a chronology which forms a framework for reciprocity, mutual obligation, and deep awareness of a shared history of experience itself. These dimensions are universally buttressed by narrative accounts born from such histories. Much of their experiential force is, as an outsider is always aware, derived precisely from the supposition that teller and listener have in common enough background understanding to celebrate together their unspoken meanings and associations.

In the most tangible way these aspects of "friendly" relationship, which lie beneath yet are seamlessly connected to the various cultural idioms in which friendship is cast, express concretely the "existential modality" of the social. The dense fabric of friendship, its close-woven texture, multiple—sometimes conflicting—role expectations, its emotional weight in carrying us beyond the conceptual boundaries of self, all remarked repeatedly as *general* characteristics of the social in ethnographic writing yet seldom attended to *per se or in detail*, express a lived reality which, as Merleau-Ponty asserts, is prior to analysis or theory. Yet, such relationships are the heart of the ethnographic encounter as it is experienced in fieldwork. To the extent that fieldworkers are unable or unwilling to take "things as they are" in this sphere, we remove ourselves in a structural and positional way from the ongoing process of relationship. Our sometimes sporadic and partial participation in shared activity, inability or reluctance to assume the ongoing mundane obligations of daily life in another culture, and discursive neglect of emotional connection mitigate against our recognizing the importance of the simple fact of "being together" with others. Yet attended to in their own right and for their own sake, friendships provide the ground for entering and exploring another epistemology of the social, one which seeks to encompass the "natural standpoint" and to create "resonance" in a way which has, by and large, been problematic for anthropologists.

EMPATHY AND MEMORY: TWO DESCRIPTIONS

The hills and peaks around Verzone are the setting for a great deal of local socializing. In spring and summer, many local families spend weekends at *monti*, mid-mountain settlements nowadays modernized for leisure, cooking traditional foods such as *salamini*, polenta, and *funghi*, playing cards, singing in groups, gathering winter wood supplies. Men in particular also use these settlements in winter, climbing on skis to hunt or just for the pleasure of "*la compagnia.*"

On still higher terrain, alpine activities are not confined to tourists, but include locals who visit the high *rifugi* (climbing huts), several of which are operated by Verzonesi, and climb local peaks in the Adamello-Presanella and Brenta massifs. The high peaks and the glaciers surrounding them figure prominently in local history, songs, poetry, and in the local economy, with many villagers working in the industries connected with mountaineering and skiing. To ski and climb well are skills which younger local men admire in each other: many friendships are built around these activities, either organized informally or through organizations such as the local section of the Club Alpino Italiano.

In the early years, I climbed extensively in the Adamello-Presanella Massif to the west of the valley, but never in the Brenta Massif to the east. Geologically, from a mountaineering perspective, these have a curious and convenient feature: occasional bands of softer rock between horizontal strata have eroded out, leaving open-sided ledges and paths along which a climber can traverse for long distances. The ledges vary in width and degree of exposure, in places broad and secure above relatively wide basins, in others as narrow as a foot-width, suspended above air. Where a fall would be dangerous, many have been equipped with steel fixed-ropes and sometimes ladders, to which climbers clip themselves with karabiners connected by slings to their harnesses. For an experienced mountaineer, these *vie ferrate* provide a relatively easy form of travel, particularly in good weather, with ample protection from falls and no route-finding difficulties. Nonetheless, they remain an exciting challenge for climbers of every level, and day trips along them are popular in July, August, and September with both tourists and locals: distances are not great and in the basins between peaks the *rifugi* offer comfortable accommodation, good food and drink, relaxed surroundings in which to rest.

Over the years that I had known Pier Paolo, we had talked often of these peaks, and of the establishment of the park which now includes them. In many ways, Pier Paolo's and my common interest in the environment and eco-politics, revealed at our first meeting, had been the moving thread that sustained our friendship. I had learned a great deal from Pier Paolo: his love of his landscape, his extensive botanical knowledge, both abstract and related to his former profession as a *salumiere*, his interest in the politics of the alpine environment had fueled many conversations. But while we had walked the lower hills together we'd never reached the higher peaks which were are for me one of the great beauties of this part of the world.

In August of 1988, Pier Paolo invited me to join him and his friends on a section of the Sentiero SOSAT, a *via ferrata* which passes under the highest peaks of the Brenta, directly above and visible from the village. We climbed on a perfect day from a *malgha* (high alp) in a lateral valley toward the Cima Brenta itself. Our route led through a surreal landscape of jumbled blocks of rock: below us lay gentle scree basins covered in alpine anemones and ranunculus; above, rock walls broken with crusted avalanche runnels and shattered, discolored ice. To the west, we enjoyed limpid, sweeping views of the terrain on the Adamello-Presanella I had climbed on in previous seasons, and of the hills above the village. From this height, the landscape seemed to me to fit together in a new way: spread before us were not only the peaks, but the entire topography of settlements, a fine network of roads and paths linking villages to each other and to the mid-mountain settlements and high alps. By contrast with the New Zealand alpine landscape, this was literally inscribed by its history in the forms of terraces, rock walls, and now-disused irrigation channels. On this day, cast against this backdrop, Pier Paolo was the energetic guide: herding us along with solicitous concern, identifying plants and places, pausing and waiting constantly to help others across more difficult parts of the route. Yet there was something strained in his manner, uncomfortable with himself.

The crux of the route is a point, about an hour after the ledges begin, where a deep vertical gully, almost a huge chimney, cuts the track: here two long steel ladders face each other across the chasm. When we arrived a family of tourists were negotiating these, belaying their children with a rope down one side and up the other. We waited, Pier Paolo in silence, his eyes on the gentler peaks across from us; his hands, I remember, were trembling slightly and, uncharacteristically, he smoked one of my cigarettes. Eventually, when the path was clear, he led down the first ladder before carefully crossing the steep floor of the gully and climbing the long ladder on the other side. Everything seemed to be happening very slowly, and he was visibly relieved when we were all gathered on the other side. Shortly, when the path again widened, he suggested we take a break. We sat together for a few minutes without speaking before Pier Paolo turned to me and confessed that for most of his life he had suffered severely from vertigo.[8] Since childhood, he said, he had wanted to climb, but not until recently had he been able to control the symptoms. Now, it was as if another world had opened up: one that all his life he had heard described, sung about, and had seen from a distance, but never experienced.

That evening, at dinner at Pier Paolo and Carla's, as he presided at the table, Pier Paolo was exuberant about the day on the Brenta. He wanted immediately to plan future trips, and spoke at length about his involvement in the continuing campaign to turn this area into a national park, and about the ambivalence of local people regarding the management of their environment. The central issue, he said, was who would control the administration, whether it would be the bureaucrats at Trento, or the local *communi* (local administrative bodies), who, for two thousand years, have nurtured this environment to ensure their own survival.

I remembered our first conversation, some eight years before, when I had first arrived, and reminded him of it. He laughed, and said that for him, being able to travel the *vie ferrate* had become a conscious expression of connection with his place, the history and natural environment of the valley, his positive sense of himself and of his friends.

That day, for the first time in our friendship, though others have followed, I found myself sharing with him a way of being in the mountains which I love. And now, years later, I find in thinking about why it was so important to him to physically inhabit those spaces, I discover I have come to understand something more about what it is to be a *montanaro* (mountain-dweller) at a time when traveling the mountains, especially for the men of Verzone, is not just for work, but for pleasure, and to remind themselves of where they have come from.

On the wall of my study at home hangs a photograph of Augusto and Francesca, taken a few months before her death shortly after the end of my first period of fieldwork. Augusto stands rock-solid as he was almost until the end: confident, centered, an old man enviably at ease in his world. He is wearing the same checked shirt he had on when I met him, his sleeves rolled to the elbows the only concession to the heat of the day. Beside him Francesca, wearing a floral print dress and mountain boots, stands in much the same way, relaxed and in no hurry. Neither of them is smiling, though they were both happy that afternoon; they gaze directly at me behind the camera, as interested in the moment of the photograph as in its result. The image, for me, captures a unique quality of their way of being together: they seem wordlessly linked to each other in the work they are about to do.

Resting in their hands are wooden rakes which also lie across a pile of hay we have gathered together into a mound, to be tied into a *couvert* (a large sacking-cloth), and carried down the field to the horse and cart waiting on the track below. In the background there is one already tied, solid and heavy against the hazelnuts, waiting to be lifted onto my back and stacked with the others Augusto and I had already carried down. The wooden rakes are ones Augusto himself had made, carving each wooden tooth-peg and forcing it into a hole drilled in the rake head. The handles are industrial, dowelled on a modern machine. In Augusto and Francesca's hands, these tools seem to me to tell part of the material story of their lives. Perhaps this struck Augusto too, for after Francesca's death, he kept this photograph, chosen from a number I had given him, on the sideboard in his austere kitchen, studying it as he ate the bread boiled in broth that was his usual evening meal.

The afternoon it was taken we were making hay below the house where I had lived the first time I went to Verzone. They had found my efforts hilarious, laughing as they watched me stagger under the sixty kilos of the bundles, their unfamiliar shape and weight throwing me off-balance, the hessian and hay prickling, sweat stinging my eyes. Augusto, already in his eighties, could still carry one with relative ease, swinging its bulk onto his back with Francesca's help. The motion when they did this was fluid—not effortless, but superbly economical. They worked together without speaking, tying with four hands the awkward knots that secured the *couvert*.

We had been working together most of the day, raking the long, dry hay from the first cut of the season. As we worked, they talked about other times they had done this work, describing the various cuts of the summer season, and the movements of cows, sheep, and goats up and down the mountainside connected with the rhythm of haymaking. Later, as we paused to drink a glass of cool wine and listen to the crickets whirring in the heat beneath the larch trees, they told me the story of their marriage, after the death of Augusto's first wife, Silvia.

Francesca and Silvia had been close friends in childhood, traveling with their families up to their adjacent *monti* (mid-mountain settlements) in the summers before the Guerra Bianca, the war fought between Italy and Austria on the glaciers of the Adamello-Presanella massif and ending with the treaty of St. Germain en Laye in 1919. The two young women passed their time working in the *frate*, the small alpine gardens where rye and vegetables were grown. They also kept their families' pigs, collected nuts and berries, and went mushrooming together in the woods. Their most important job was to milk their families' milch-goats, and to make cheese with the surplus milk.

Augusto's family were nearby, and in the evenings, he would visit Silvia to drink a bowl of fresh milk. Francesca would often be there, keeping company with her friend. She herself, she said, was never courted. Later, Augusto and Silvia married and had two sons.

During the war, the Austrians requisitioned war materials and food supplies from the villagers, imposing great hardship. As happened elsewhere, even the church bells were taken away and melted down. The women of the village were made to carry these supplies on foot many miles up to the military posts scraped into the rock above the glaciers at almost three thousand meters. Francesca remembered this cruel work with bitterness, recalling that she and Silvia often supported each other in this forced labor. Food was so scarce, she added, that families were reduced to eating grass and weeds with their polenta ration, which was a mere three hundred grams of meal a day.

When Silvia died, in her thirties, Augusto—left with two young boys to raise—was devastated. His situation was exacerbated by his poverty: he had little land and few cows, and he could not imagine how he would cope with two boys too young to work. He "took" Francesca, as he put it, to be their mother. She spent their wedding night knitting clothes for the children.

Francesca sat on the bench in front of the *baita*, her feet swinging just above the ground, smiling as Augusto finished speaking.

"I always fancied him, you know, even when we were young and he would visit Silvia, who was so beautiful. But I never thought, all those years, that he would have me."

Just after this, as we went back out into the afternoon sun, thinking of how at ease with themselves and with each other they looked, I asked if I might take their photograph. It was, I later learned, the last photograph of them together.

ABOUT REVELATION: AN INDETERMINATE CONCLUSION

Friendships are of all relationships those which play most freely in the interspace between individual intention and cultural constraint, between agency and structure, in the lifeworld as it is concretely experienced. In this sense, they are by nature indeterminate, open to future possibility in unpredictable ways, and finally, enigmatic. In writing about specific friendships, there is an indefinable yet nonetheless real point at which they defy motivational analysis or reflection, while simultaneously providing a richly suggestive field for thinking outward toward an understanding of our own experience and beyond that, of cultural practice.

Thus the partial and fragmentary accounts of my friendships with Pier Paolo and with Augusto I have offered here cannot be said to provide a key to the "essential" culture of Verzone or to irreducibly typify the "existential modality" of life there. In recalling them, the nebulous movement between ambiguity and revelation, enigma and familiarity, reveals as much about my shifting sense of my own engagement with a time and place as it does about these friends.

Such an approach may in itself may be a first step toward reasserting a balance in studies of friendship. Anthropologists, when they have addressed the topic of friendship, have concerned themselves largely with institutionalized forms, stressing functional dimensions to the relative neglect of the experiential.[9] I have suggested that there are reasons for this emphasis which find their roots in, among other sources, the existential characteristics of the fieldwork situation. To the degree that these lead us to objectify, experientially and discursively, our relationships in the field, we are left formulating accounts of the social which render it opaque both to ourselves and our readers.

Independently of idiom what is central is that friendship is engendered by the sharing of practical and mundane activity. This experience of shared embodied recreation or work, as I learned again from Pier Paolo and Augusto, permits a form of revelation of self which is precluded by the ulterior pursuit of instrumentalized relationship. Without revelation, ambiguous and nuanced as it may be, resonance and an empathic understanding are impossible. Such understanding is the ground of social knowledge, and the principal means we have available to understand the "natural standpoint" of others.

Beyond instrumentalization, then, lies the practical sharing of activity for its own sake. There are dangers for the anthropologist in pursing this methodological strategy, not the least—at the extreme—the attractions of abandoning ethnography. In the present state of anthropology, this seems to me to be a slighter risk to understanding than a countervailing tendency to reduce our own indeterminate experience of relationship to invisible and silent memory.

NOTES

This paper is dedicated to the memory of the couple who appear here as Augusto and Francesca, and to Pier Paolo. I should also like to thank the people of Verzone who have, for so long, and in so many tangible ways, offered their friendship and support of my project. I am also grateful to Guido Bemporad and Constanza Vincenti for their support in the past, and to Michael Jackson, Judith Loveridge, Gregor McLennan, and Peggy Trawick for their discussions and encouragement in the course of writing this paper.

1. The modern Trentino became part of Italy with the signing of the Treaty of St. Germain en Laye on 10 September 1919. For a general discussion of the convoluted political history of the region by the leading contemporary Italian historian, see Zeiger (1981). On the history of various autonomist movements see Faustini (1985) and Rusinow (1969). A brief but useful treatment of the political history of the area appears in Cole and Wolf (1974), who also provide an extensive argument regarding the impact of its political borderland status on the culture of the area.

2. An extensive discussion of the various forms of occupational migration of the people of this area and documentation of migrant's argot, known as "Tarón," are provided by Franchini (1980, 1984). A full ethnohistorical treatment of the experience of the migrant *salumieri* has yet to be written.

3. A recent collection which brings together papers from a session on this topic held at the Second Conference of the European Association of Social Anthropologists (Prague, August 1992) is Hastrup and Hervick (1994). This came to hand as I was writing this paper and with the exception of Handelman (1994) I have not been able to incorporate material from this work as comprehensively as I would have liked.

4. I have followed Sartre in using these terms. By project Sartre broadly intends intentionality directed toward the transformation or resolution of Being; by totalization, the understanding of past action and future possibility on which such projects are founded. Like many of Sartre's neologisms, however, both terms receive a number of related glosses in his later work. Useful introductions are provided by Sartre himself (1976:45–47; 79–94; 97–100), while for a lucid overview of Sartre's later philosophy, see Poster 1982:49–112.

5. Space precludes doing justice to Wikan's original and fascinating exploration of Balinese social epistemology, or to her compelling arguments for a reconceptualization, in the light of Balinese views, of the relationship between emotion and knowledge in anthropological thought and practice. My intention here is simply to highlight in comparative perspective a phenomenological starting point for a discussion of the nature of fieldworkers' friendships.

6. A parallel if somewhat more specific argument which is relevant here is that put recently by Stoller (1989) and Classen (1993) for a revaluation in fieldwork of attention to sensory experience beyond the visual (Stoller), and for an exploration of the cultural and historical formation of the culturally specific hierarchies of the senses (Classen).

7. The psychologist Nathaniel Branden has referred to this as the Principle of Psychological Visibility: "Human beings desire and need the experience of self-awareness that results from perceiving the self as an objective existent, and they are able to achieve this experience through interaction with the consciousness of other living beings" (Branden 1993:72).

8. At its extreme, this is a condition which can terrify and physically paralyze the sufferer, resulting in an uncontrollable loss of balance and a dramatic sense of panic. It can be triggered by looking down into depths and results in a kind of dizziness in which the world appears to be revolving, whirling rapidly even, around one.

9. For a major comparative discussion of friendship in cross-cultural perspective see Brain (1977). At the core of Brain's argument is the view that regardless of institution-alized form, and *contra* a prevailing popular Western view, friendship is universally at once "prosaic and romantic," simultaneously a medium for numerous modes of experience and for the furthering of variously compatible pragmatic projects. In discussing such forms as bond friendship in Tikopia, "blood-brotherhood" in West

Africa, *camradia* for Mayan Chinautleco, and *compadrazgo* in a variety of Mediterranean and South American contexts, Brain finds that well defined and/or ceremonially elaborate functional and structural frameworks of friendship do not preclude, as has often been supposed, the development of an emotional recognition of mutuality but often provide an enduring framework for it. Brain's work remains a pioneering study in this area.

REFERENCES

Bourdieu, P. 1990. *In Other Words: Essays towards a Reflexive Sociology.* Cambridge: Polity Press.

Brain, R. 1977. *Friends and Lovers.* Frogmore: Paladin.

Branden, N. 1993. "Love and Psychological Visibility." In *Friendship: A Philosophical Reader,* ed. N. K. Badhwar. Ithaca: Cornell University Press.

Classen, C. 1993. *Worlds of Sense: Exploring the Senses in History and Across Cultures.* London: Routledge.

Clifford, J. 1986. *The Predicament of Culture: Twentieth-Century Ethnography, Literature and Art.* Cambridge: Harvard University Press.

Cole, J. W., and Wolf, E. R. 1974. *The Hidden Frontier: Ecology and Ethnicity in an Alpine Valley.* New York: Academic Press.

Comaroff, J., and Comaroff, J. 1992. *Ethnography and the Historical Imagination.* Boulder: Westview Press.

Crick, M. 1989a. "Shifting Identities in the Research Process: An Essay in Personal Anthropology." In *Doing Fieldwork: Eight Personal Accounts of Social Research,* ed. J. Perry. Geelong: Deakin University Press.

———. 1989b. "Ali and Me: An Essay in Street Corner Anthropology." Paper presented to Annual Conference, Association of Social Anthropologists of the Commonwealth, University of York, April 2–6.

Faustini, G. 1985. *Trentino e Tirolo dal 1000 al 1900: Brevario Storico dell' Autonomia.* Trento: Casa Editrice Publilux.

Franchini, A. 1980. *Odissea Giudicariese.* Trento: Libreria Paideia.

———. 1984. *Tarón: Gergo di Emigranti di Val Rendena.* San Michele all'Adige: Museo degli Usi e Constumi della Gente Trentina.

Geertz, C. 1968. "Thinking as a Moral Act: Ethical Dimensions of Anthropological Fieldwork in the New States." *Antioch Review* 28:139–158.

———. 1988. *Works and Lives: The Anthropologist as Author.* Stanford: Stanford University Press.

Handelman, D. 1993. "The Absence of Others, the Presence of Texts." In *Creativity/Anthropology,* ed. S. Lavie, K. Narayan, and R. Rosaldo. Ithaca: Cornell University Press.

Hastrup, K., and Hervik, P., eds. 1994. *Social Experience and Anthropological Knowledge.* London: Routledge.

Husserl, E. 1967. "The Thesis of the Natural Standpoint and Its Suspension." In *Phenomenology: The Philosophy of Edmund Husserl and Its Interpretation,* ed. J. J. Kockelmans. Garden City: Doubleday.

Jackson, M. 1989. *Paths toward a Clearing: Radical Empiricism and Ethnographic Inquiry.* Bloomington: Indiana University Press.

Laing, R. D. 1967. *The Politics of Experience and The Bird of Paradise.* Harmondsworth: Penguin Books.

Marcus, G. E., and Fischer, M. M. J. 1986. *Anthropology as Cultural Critique: An Experimental Moment in the Human Sciences.* Chicago: University of Chicago Press.

Merleau-Ponty, M. 1962. *Phenomenology of Perception*. London: Routledge & Kegan Paul.

Poster, M. 1982. *Sartre's Marxism*. Cambridge: Cambridge University Press.

Rosaldo, R. 1989. *Culture and Truth: The Remaking of Social Analysis*. Boston: Beacon Press.

Roseberry, W. 1989. *Anthropologies and Histories: Essays in Culture, History and Political Economy*. New Brunswick: Rutgers University Press.

Rusinow, D. I. 1969. *Italy's Austrian Heritage 1919–1946*. Oxford: Clarendon Press.

Sartre, J.-P. 1976. *Critique of Dialectical Reason I: Theory of Practical Ensembles*. London: New Left Books.

Stoller, P. 1989. *The Taste of Ethnographic Things: The Senses in Anthropology*. Philadelphia: University of Philadelphia Press.

Telfer, E. 1991. "Friendship." In *Other Selves: Philosophers on Friendship*, ed. M. Pakaluk. Indianapolis: Hackett.

Turner, V. W. 1986. "Dewey, Dilthey, and Drama: An Essay in the Anthropology of Experience." In *The Anthropology of Experience*, ed. V. W. Turner and E. M. Bruner. Urbana: University of Illinois Press.

Wikan, U. 1990. *Managing Turbulent Hearts: A Balinese Formula for Living*. Chicago: University of Chicago Press.

Zeiger, A. 1981. *Storia della Regione Tridentina*. 2d ed. Trento: Dolomia.

After the Field

JIM WAFER

I left Bahia in August of 1988 and went away, to Bloomington, Indiana, to write about it. This resulted in a book and a separation. The book was called *The Taste of Blood*, and the separation was from the person who had been both my lover and "principal informant" in Brazil. In the book he is called "Archipiado." He and I did not see each other again until December of 1989, when we went to live together in Turkey Thicket, Washington, D.C. It was snowing as I rode the metro to pick him up from Washington National Airport. He arrived in a light cotton shirt with short sleeves. I gave him a layer of my clothing for the metro journey back. We were too poor to afford a taxi.

From Washington we went to live in the Darwin suburb of Nightcliff, in Australia's tropical north. This was in mid-1991. We were looking for a climate that was more like Bahia's. One day we drove south about sixty kilometers to the Territory Wildlife Park, "one of the most exciting tourism ventures developed in Australia's north," according to the brochure. The park is carefully designed to create the illusion that the animals are living in their natural habitat rather than in captivity. The exception is the aquarium, which would be hard put to disguise the artificial nature of the environment it provides for its denizens. It is an enormous tank, with a Plexiglas tunnel for the tourists. As you walk through the tunnel the marine life swims around you and above you. At one point the waterscape changes, and, instead of being under the sea, you are in a riverbed.

Archipiado and I took our time strolling through the tunnel, letting ourselves be dazzled by the play of refracted light on scales, fins, gills. When we reached the riverbed a large crocodile was lying at head-height, half-submerged, on the bank, only about a foot away from the Plexiglas. I caught his eye, which was above water level. Or perhaps he caught mine. We stared into each other's eyes for so long that several groups of Japanese tourists had time to pass us by. Then I glimpsed a thin, opalescent piece of reptile flesh, like a crooked finger, emerging from his lower underbelly, beneath the surface. It began to jerk back and forth, and, shortly, puffed a few little squirts of viscous white fluid into the water. The stuff congealed and floated down gently onto the Plexiglas. The crocodile's facial expression did not change.

Most definitions of "ethnography" are premised on the notion of "the field," conceived of as a clearly delimited area of the anthropologist's experience, with neat geographical and temporal boundaries. Writing ethnography then becomes an exercise in containing the social world of the field, in subjecting it to the kind of logic that renders it controllable. For modernist ethnography this was the logic of the zoological garden. For most postmodernist ethnography it is the logic of the wildlife park.

"The field" has various resonances; it evokes, simultaneously, peripherality and nature (since fields are in the country), and "the real world" (as distinct from the library or the laboratory). It is thus a romantic notion, because it suggests the possibility of an alternative to the centralization, artifice, and "unreality" of contemporary intellectual life. There is something almost mythological about the opposition between the world the ethnographer leaves behind to go to the field and the field itself. It is like the opposition between profane and sacred spaces that underlies rites of passage.[1]

In van Gennep's classic study, rites of passage are divided into three types, which often also constitute three phases of the same rite: preliminal rites (rites of separation), liminal rites (rites of transition), and postliminal rites (rites of incorporation) (1960:11). The first two phases have been dealt with extensively in the anthropological literature; but the phase of incorporation, reintegration, or return is, by and large, undertheorized. It is often treated as a more or less unproblematic reversal of the original separation, such that the person undergoing the rite leaves behind all traces of the sacred space in his or her return to the profane world. Barbara Myerhoff provides a lovely example: "Elaborate precautions must be taken so that not the tiniest part of Wirikuta [the Huichol mythical homeland] is left on the body or clothes of the pilgrim. Each one is ritually cleansed of every bit of dirt or cactus spine. . . . Thus boundaries are scrupulously observed; the things of the sacred and the everyday are kept apart rigidly . . . [and] all remnants and traces of the experience [of Wirikuta] are left behind" (1975:42–43).

The initiate, in fact, always brings something back, even if it is only the memory of the experience of the sacred. In the case of ethnographers, they return, like the Prophet Muhammad after his time in "the cave of research," where he was visited by the angel Gabriel, pregnant with a book (or at least a few articles). Gabriel was like most informants in that he could not be brought back to the profane world, except as text. The bringing back of more concrete entities, such as fire, or living beings, is a more complex matter, and usually seen as more dangerous, because it poses a serious threat to the boundaries between sacred and profane, and also suggests the theft of a generative power that properly belongs only to the sacred.

The post-field experience is worth examining not just for its own sake, but also because it may suggest new lines of approach to the postliminal or "return" phase of rites of passage. It is obvious that the "return" cannot be as simple as it is often treated as being, because the person coming back from the sacred space is necessarily transformed, and returns to a "profane" reality that has also changed, not just as a result of the passage of time, but also because the one returning can no longer experience it in the same way.

Roy Turner has pointed out that the constitution of the field as an area of scientific inquiry, which entails a distinction between "field" (as reality) and "lifeworld" (as appearance), reminiscent of the separation between sacred and profane, has a tainted political history (1989:13–16). If I focus here less on the politics of this distinction than on its metaphoric associations, it is because I am concerned to understand the cultural ramifications of the separation between the field experience and the post-field experience, and the ways they manifest themselves in the imagination.

I remembered the crocodile several years later, when we were living in Newcastle, on Australia's east coast. We had moved there from Darwin, in mid-1992, and found ourselves a flat in a block called "Olympus," near Bar Beach. One hot day we came home from the beach sweaty, salty, and smeared with suntan oil. Archipiado filled the bath and we wallowed in it for a while, slopping waves out onto the floor. Then I turned onto my stomach and Archipiado fucked me from behind, under the water.

It was around this time that a Brazilian anthropologist friend was in the United States on a lecture tour and sent us a postcard from the Art Institute of Chicago. On the front was a reproduction of D. G. Rossetti's "Beata Beatrix," and on the back he had written a note to Archipiado, in Portuguese: "Aren't you Jimmy's Beatrice? Beata Beatrix! Kisses" and his signature.

I had applied for a job in Newcastle because the city and its surrounding areas of Lake Macquarie and the Hunter Valley are where I was conceived, born, raised, and educated, and where my family had lived for several generations. I had a nostalgia for "home"; but I think I was only dimly aware that home is the place where you cannot escape the consequences of your own actions and those of your forbears.

Newcastle has what Erving Goffman (1963) calls a "spoiled identity." During my school days it was called, by students from rival cities, "Newcastle, the arsehole of Australia" (chanted so that "Newcastle" rhymed with "arsehole"). When I came back to the city in middle age I saw, on a wall of one of the steep streets leading up to the Hill, a graffito which read, "NEWCASTLE—COLOS-TOMY BAG OF THE UNIVERSE" (such is progress).

In contemporary Australian folklore this spoiled identity is associated with heavy industry, pollution, and working class culture. But it has a long history. Newcastle, at the time of its occupation of the Aboriginal site of Muloobinba in the early nineteenth century, was what Governor Macquarie called "a recep-

tacle for our worst characters" (Elkin 1955:13). It was established as a settlement for transported convicts guilty of secondary offenses, who were brought
here principally to mine coal. According to anthropologist and Newcastle
diocesan chronicler A. P. Elkin, "many of them [were] of a violent type," and
this "gave the district an undesirable name" (1955:13).

The convicts were followed by free immigrants, mostly from Britain and
Ireland, who continued to work the coal mines, and, later, labored in the heavy
industries. As the settlers expanded into the surrounding areas they destroyed
most of the local Aboriginal peoples. The violence of the region's history is
symbolized for me by the fate of my great great-grandfather. He died, according
to his death certificate, by "poison self-administered"—a discreet way of saying
that he committed suicide by drinking sulfuric acid.

Most of the male members of my immediate family worked, during their
early adulthood, in the heavy industries, which are still the biggest employers
in Newcastle. It scarcely needs to be said that, by avoiding this fate, I missed out
on an important part of the local version of masculine socialization. Of the
various facets of the dominant male ethos of Newcastle, the most relevant to the
present discussion is a deep suspicion of intellectuals, wogs, and poofters. Or,
at least, that is how I experienced it during my brutalized adolescence.

It was to this environment that I returned, after an absence of almost two
decades, to take up a position at the university. I came with a Black Brazilian
boyfriend sixteen years my junior. I came to stand my ground.

If the return has meant standing my ground on my native turf, it has also meant
recognizing the need to stand my ground on the symbolic turf of academic
discourse. So far I have evaded this. In my publications for a "general" (that is,
implicitly heterosexual) academic audience, I have positioned myself as a
"neutral" (that is, not explicitly gay) author; and the publications I have written
from the vantage point of an openly gay man were destined for a readership of
other queer academics.

This essay provides me with the opportunity not only to address a general
audience as a gay man, but also to explain why doing so is not just an act of
confessional self-indulgence. Feminist anthropologists have already developed
a sophisticated body of theory, neatly synthesized by Helen Callaway, to argue
that gender makes a difference "in how anthropological knowledge is created"
(Callaway 1992:36). "What," she asks, "are the implications of the anthropologist as a gendered knower? Of field research as a process of personal interaction
and flawed understandings, involving what may be vastly different—and not
always easily recognized—patterns of gender relations between that of the
anthropologist and the society being studied? In what ways does rational
inquiry have gendered dimensions? Since there are no ungendered lives, can
there be ungendered texts? How does gender relate to the production of
knowledge and its power structures (publishers' decisions, professional legiti

mation and so on)?" (Callaway 1992:30). She believes that the gendered nature of subjectivity needs to be made explicit in ethnographic writing because "a deepening understanding of our own gendered identities and the coded complexities of our being offer the best resources for gaining insights into the lives of others" (Callaway 1992:30).

Everything she says of gender applies, *mutatis mutandis*, to sexual identity. The traditional genre conventions of ethnography, in which "the transcendent authorial voice [is] separated from the embodied person and from historical time and place" (Callaway 1992:30), force ethnographers (and their readers) into a subject position that is not only implicitly male but also implicitly heterosexual. Challenging the heterosexist bias of ethnography requires, then, attempting to transform the *practice* as well as the underlying assumptions of anthropological writing.

If feminist theory is well developed in anthropology, queer theory has been late coming to the discipline. It has flourished in less tradition-bound fields such as media studies (see, for example, Gever et al. 1993, Ringer 1994). Queer theory's particular contributions to the debates we are concerned with here are the challenge it poses to essentialist understandings of gender and sexual identity, and its recognition of the "regulatory aspects of identity categories" (Kotz 1993:87). Instead of theorizing lesbian and gay experiences as "somehow 'outside of' or apart from the structures of the wider, 'patriarchal' culture, these contemporary analyses insist on the importance of understanding how lesbian and gay identities and cultural practices are articulated within and in relation to their cultural and historical contexts" (Kotz 1993:86–87). For queer theory, gender and sexual identity are not given, but are created and transformed through the process of their own performance.

There is also much anthropology could learn from the dynamic cultural production that has come out of the queer world's confrontation with AIDS. The proximity of death in the lives of people affected by AIDS has given their work an urgency that requires radically new modes of expression. The result has been the emergence of hybrid cultural forms that break down the distinction between theory and art, politics and religious vision, the commonplace and the sublime. (A good example would be Bill T. Jones's dance performance, "Last Supper at Uncle Tom's Cabin.") The ugly concreteness of AIDS seems to have acted as a catalyst for social and cultural change in a way that more abstract threats to survival, such as the possibility of the extinction of the human species in a global war or ecological catastrophe, have not.

Bahia, like Newcastle, is also a city with a spoiled identity. Ruth Landes provides an illustration in her account of reactions to her decision to do fieldwork there in 1938: "'Must you go there?' my Brazilian teacher wailed. She screwed up her cheerful young face and shivered in mock horror. Then she laughed. "'Let Bahia stay there!'" she quoted a song, "'and we'll stay here!'"" (Landes 1947:8).

The reasons for its spoiled identity are not entirely dissimilar to those I have discussed in relation to Newcastle. In both cases the image of the city has developed out of its early association with a group of humans stigmatized by their own oppression. Bahia was Brazil's main port for the traffic in African slaves, whose descendants, after emancipation, came to constitute the bulk of the city's unemployed or underemployed poor. Newcastle's convicts lived in conditions of "near slavery" (Elkin 1955:53), and the cheap labor that replaced them after the convict era formed the basis of the city's industrial work pool.

There are particular spots in Newcastle, especially around the Hill and especially in summer, where Archipiado, the Soteropolitan, and I, the Novocastrian, have been struck by certain visual similarities to Bahia. Both cities are ports adjacent to the ocean; both have harbor-side city centers that have developed around a steep hill; both have silhouettes punctuated with church towers and spires; and the January full moon hangs above both like an irresistibly succulent but unattainable fruit.

But most of the time, when we compare the two cities, which we do endlessly, we focus on the differences.

Ruth Landes put her finger on one of the most salient characteristics of Bahia when she called it "theatrical" (1947:10). Everyday life in Bahia is routinely treated as a performance. This is one of the things that made it most difficult for Landes, and also for me. In Newcastle, I think, there is quite a strong inhibition on self-expression. I have no simple explanation for this inhibition, but it probably results from a number of factors: the heritage of Victorian religion and morality; the destruction of expressive folk arts such as dance, music, and story-telling by the rise of industrial capitalism; the bodily disciplines entailed by the surveillance procedures of the modern bureaucratic state; and something like the local version of the folk wisdom of not drawing attention to yourself, enunciated in its classic form by Chuang Tzu: "They say it is the beautiful markings of the tiger and the leopard that call out the hunters" (1964:91).

These factors have operated, no doubt, in most areas of the Anglo-Saxon world; but I think in Newcastle they have been relatively undiluted by outside influences, such as the African American tradition that has been so important in the development of American expressive culture. Because Newcastle's period of industrial growth took place before the major influx of non–Anglo-Saxon immigrants to Australia, it remains one of the least ethnically diverse big cities in the country.

Whatever the reasons for this inhibition, Archipiado has no patience with it. One of his favorite forms of self-expression has been the progressive decoration of our flat, with paintings of naked men by our friends Eli Braga, Fernando Azevedo, and Gary Lee; safe sex posters depicting anal intercourse by David McDiarmid; photographs of ourselves naked or dressed as Sisters of Perpetual Indulgence; a cartoon by Eli Braga depicting the two of us in drag;

and a variety of sculptured erect penises—a small ceramic one belonging to a miniature Greek warrior's tomb, by our friend Ron Hunter; a large one, with a red tip, attached to a pottery mug from Belém; and four metal ones attached to figures engaged in an Igorot masturbatory ritual. He has also set up a number of parodic shrines around the house, strongly influenced by the assemblage aesthetic of the Afro-Brazilian religions. There is a skull with red eyes and an electric light bulb emerging from the top, surrounded with offerings of cigarettes and five-cent pieces; a small metal Exu behind the front door, with offerings of foreign coins; images of the Sacred Heart of Jesus and the Sacred Heart of Mary in the bathroom; and a series of shelves in the living room with religious paraphernalia from various parts of the globe, surrounded with beads, shells, stones, feathers, flags, candles, dried flowers, vases, goblets, and musical instruments.

It is probably unreasonable of me to attribute the responsibility for our interior decoration entirely to Archipiado. I have at least acquiesced, and at times even colluded, in the process. I have allowed him to teach me. But it is certain that I would never have taken the initiative to decorate the flat this way. I would have been too nervous about the reactions of the members of my family who occasionally visit.

My nervousness was acute when my turn came to host the annual family gathering, on Christmas Day of 1994. My parents were bringing my sister, my grandmother, who is in her late eighties, and my grandmother's sister; and my brother and his wife were bringing my nephew and one of my nieces, who are both in their early teens. I assume my grandmother knows I am gay, since she has met Archipiado at most of the family gatherings since we have been living in Newcastle, and has visited us at home before. But the matter is never discussed; and my great-aunt, whom I remembered from my youth as being a bit conservative, had never met Archipiado. As for my brother and his family: when they had been to our place before, it was always on flying visits, which I interpreted, no doubt unfairly, as my brother's way of protecting the children from our eccentric influence.

When my grandmother and great aunt arrived we left them in the living room, where most of Archipiado's interior decorating efforts have been focused, while we went to get them drinks. In the couple of minutes we were in the kitchen with my sister and my parents, we heard hoots of laughter coming from the other room. I would love to know what comments my grandmother and her sister exchanged; but at least, I thought, if the comments were about our taste in *objets d'art*, they were good humored. The good humor continued when my brother and his family arrived and we started to exchange presents (Archipiado and I received identical kinds of gifts), then got down to the business of eating and drinking.

Archipiado's present to my family was a video he had made about them called "The Wafers' Story." Archipiado was studying ethnographic video for his honors degree in anthropology at the university, and this had been a little five-finger exercise for him. He had shot most of the Australian footage at a previous family gathering at my brother's place, and at a soccer tournament that had happened earlier on the same day, when my twelve year-old nephew's team was playing in the grand final match of the season.

As the evening wore on there was a lull in the festivities, and Archipiado decided the moment was right to premiere his video.

The opening credits, which are superimposed on slow-motion shots of the members of my family in characteristic poses, give the impression that the video is focused on the oldest member, my grandmother, and the youngest, my nephew. The video is subtitled "As told by Nanna R.," and the first family member to be introduced is my nephew, who is called "Soccerman." The other family members are presented in terms of their relationship to Soccerman. For example, my brother is "Soccerman's body guard. Just in case." I am "Soccerman's prodigal uncle"; and the goldfish in my brother's house is "Silver the Fish (Soccerman's best mate in a defeat. It says nothing and listens too)." The accompanying music is a child's wavering voice singing a sentimental song to piano accompaniment.

My niece became excited because she recognized the music. Slowly she remembered that Archipiado had, by chance, brought his video camera to Young People's Theatre when she was rehearsing a dance sequence for a tribute to the theatre's ailing founder. The song was one the latter had written, and was sung by one of the other dancers.

The other family members were clearly amused to see themselves as "stars."

In the opening scene my grandmother is talking to my mother about a house where her own grandmother had lived. (My grandmother complained about how old the camera made her look.) We see the house (which is in West Wallsend, near the soccer field where my nephew's match took place); then, as my grandmother begins to reminisce about her early years and now deceased relatives on the soundtrack, the visual images show the setting and the other people in it: the deck at the back of my brother's house, set in bushland in Charlestown. My brother is cooking at an elaborate barbecue, and the other family members are helping themselves to food, except for my older niece, who is strolling with her boyfriend by the pool. The scene is obviously one of considerable affluence—and spaciousness; but suddenly it fades and is replaced by a title saying "Somewhere on the planet a few months earlier. . . ."

The next sequence begins with a Black priest ascending the sanctuary steps of a church and starting to pray in a foreign language. The prayer continues as the perspective moves to show the densely packed congregation, then a highly embellished crucifix. Next, the camera pans down the façade of a baroque church to show, at its base, a crowd of tens of thousands of people dressed in white, waving their arms from side to side in the air, or carrying vases of flowers on their heads. The camera focuses on an elderly white-haired man who is struggling through the crowd, having his hand shaken and his head patted. The sequence ends with a group of religious officials dressed in maroon robes in procession outside the church. The music is a hymn, played out of tune by a brass band.

I could not restrain myself from pointing out to my family the brief shots of Archipiado and me in the crowd inside the church. We had been there for the baptism of a group of young members of his family. He was the godfather of one of his nieces, and I was the godfather of his little female cousin, whose mother, Archipiado's youngest aunt, is like a sister to him. The baptism took place in the Church of Our Lord of Bomfim, the symbolic heart of Bahia, and had been arranged by Archipiado's mother to coincide with our return visit to the city (with video camera) in the (southern hemisphere) summer of 1993–1994.

Archipiado's editing gives the impression that the crowd outside the church was there at the same time we were inside. But in fact these shots were filmed some weeks earlier, during the annual procession called "the washing of Bomfim." The man with the white hair is Archipiado's least favorite politician, Antônio Carlos Magalhães, several times governor of Bahia. The music is the hymn of our Lord of Bomfim.

Meanwhile in Charlestown, Archipiado talks to my nephew about his team's loss in the grand final. My nephew says, "I didn't like losing though," followed by shots of his soccer trophies. "We got it last year. Some people never make it, some people do. Just the luck." This is followed by a slow motion sequence of my younger niece dancing in long flowing robes, during her rehearsal at Young People's Theatre.

And on the other side of the planet, I am sitting, eating, in a crowd of people (Archipiado's family and their neighbors and friends) in a long room (a bar run by Archipiado's brother's ex-wife). A young man (another brother) is holding a baby as he eats. He jokingly opens his shirt and puts the baby to his breast. A well-dressed woman (Archipiado's mother) is evidently supervising the proceedings (the celebration after the baptism). A man (Archipiado's aunt's boyfriend) gives me something across the table, which I pop into my mouth.

Meanwhile in Charlestown soccer is being played. The music is a song that came out after the success of Sydney's bid to host the 2000 Olympics. It opens with the voice of a reporter at the scene of the announcement: "Well there's pandemonium here." The perspective moves back and forth between the stage of the soccer field's pavilion, where my nephew and his teammates are receiving their trophies; the match itself, including a slow motion sequence of my nephew running to head the ball and being beaten to it by a member of the other team; the audience, including family members; and my nephew in candid moments off-field, looking very glum (as the president of the International Olympic Committee says, "There is only one winner"), and, later, being hugged by his mother, and striding along with his father.

At some point in all of this my mother had started to laugh. I think she had got it.

Back to the other side of the globe, where dancing is happening: a circle of little girls dressed in white, like a round-dance of angels from a Botticelli painting, followed by less angelic scenes of solos, couples, and groups, with body contact front to front, front to back, men with women, men with men, women with women, children with adults. And in the midst of it all a strange, stick-insect-like figure, a White man, Ichabod Crane perhaps, or Don Quixote: belly dancing with a ravishingly beautiful young woman, both of them with handkerchiefs veiling the lower half of their faces; being surprised to find Archipiado's mother close behind him; dancing, in his angular way, with a well built young man, their chins on each other's shoulder; dancing in the street, at the entrance to the bar, with Archipiado (shirtless) and his aunt. . . .

Back in Charlestown the story goes on according to Nanna R. But because the story has to reach The End: Archipiado and I are sitting in our living room in front of a ficus tree decorated with colored lights, baubles, and little golden angels playing musical instruments. Behind the tree is Eli Braga's painting of two naked men whirling around each other in the pattern of the yin-yang symbol. We are discussing, in Portuguese, what sequence we will do our performance in. I take up a wooden flute and he takes up an *agogô* (a metal percussion instrument) and we play, very badly, "We wish you a merry Christmas." Then we sing it.

Our Newcastle family joins in: "and a happy New Year!"

The screen goes blank, but for a few seconds the discussion in Portuguese continues. It is drowned out by a surge of talk as those present come to terms with what they have seen.

What they saw was the creation of a "virtual family,"[2] a utopian kin group that transcends boundaries of race, nationality, and language, made possible by jumbo jets, hi-tech electronics, and the sterile union of two gay men. What they saw also was themselves made strange but more real, perhaps hyper-real, by the refraction of their bodily images in a medium where time is not necessarily linear, space does not necessarily imply distance, and social relations are not necessarily ordered according to taxonomic hierarchies.

Archipiado also sent the Brazilian branch of our family a handcrafted video as a Christmas present. The genre he is developing, which he is teaching me by example, I call "virtual ethnography." This term is meant to suggest a kind of ethnography for which "the field" is no longer constituted geographically but rather aesthetically, and which is not underpinned by the logic of containment and control, but rather by the fractured dialectic of social performances made interactive through the artifice of juxtaposition. The distinction between field and post-field (and thus, implicitly, between sacred and profane) is no longer a disjuncture in time and space, but rather a contrast between alternative perspectives.

The nature of these perspectives is nicely expressed by Arjun Appadurai when he says that inhabitants of the contemporary transnational world make an "ironic compromise between what they could imagine and what social life will permit" (1991:198). Virtual ethnography sharpens the contrast between these two perspectives in order to expose and question the compromise.

According to Appadurai, "the historical role of anthropology was to fill the 'savage slot' in internal western dialogues about utopia. A recuperated anthropology must recognize that the genie is now out of the bottle, and that speculations about utopia are everyone's prerogative" (1991:209). This means, also, understanding who the savage is. We have met the savage, and it is us.

It is all very well to recognize that one is a savage in the abstract, but what does this mean in terms of the pragmatic constraints of the "academic family" that ethnographers come back to "after the field"? The only work I know of that attempts to deal with the "return" to the university as an ethnographic problem is Sarah Williams's unpublished doctoral dissertation entitled "Professing Culture: Anthropology among Anthropologists" (1991). Williams carried out fieldwork with Turkana women, then returned to "the abyss of the university" (a notion she borrows from Derrida; 1991:vii) to study anthropologists. She makes clear why such an exercise is so rarely undertaken: because "academic privilege is what is at stake" (1991:129).

Williams has written her text in such a way that "the act of reading situates the reader as a participant-observer within the field of anthropology" (1991:1). She achieves this by developing a research strategy that makes her an actor in her own text, a performer rather than a producer of human science (1991:39). This "performative" strategy is based on the recognition that "because of our historical situatedness in relation to the categorical powers—the characterizations—of human science . . . it is not possible to think beyond or think outside of the constraints—the cultural histories—of the human sciences, or the human identities and sexual subjectivities reflected and performed in language. However, it is possible to parody these constraints and our knowledges of them" (1991:37).

For Williams, the feminist performer of "(hu)Man science" (1991:17), the paradigmatic form of parody is (inevitably?) drag (1991:37). But her experiment with transvestism is explicitly restricted to her text (1991:3). In my own experience of the return to the academy I have, over time, found it necessary to go beyond textual parodies in order to develop an embodied performative approach to the existential quandary of the university. Like Williams, I have been inspired by the richness of the metaphor of transvestism. Ethnographers routinely engage in practices that make them what Christian Feest has called "cultural transvestites" (quoted in Green 1988:42), by attempting to live like the people they study in the field. But when they come back to the academy they often treat their role there as somehow natural or grounded, rather than as a cultural product.

In 1994 Archipiado and I, along with four students, founded the Convent of Original Sins at the University of Newcastle, affiliated with the cosmic order of gay male nuns called the Sisters of Perpetual Indulgence. Archipiado's religious name is Sister Immaculate Consumption, and mine is Sister Wanda Bonk of the Mission to Se(a)men.

We first joined the order in Darwin, when it was being formed with the specific political objective of pressuring the Northern Territory Government to include sexual orientation in its proposed anti-discrimination legislation. (The campaign was successful.) We formed a missionary chapter of the order at the University of Newcastle in 1993, during Queer Awareness Week. That year we hired our habits and passed in procession through the Shortland Union's ambulatory and refectory, censing the lunchtime crowd with a borrowed thurible and sprinkling them with holy water, as we exorcised homophobia using a chant I had written to the tune of the Dies irae.

In 1994 we received a visitation from our beloved Mother Abyss, of the Sydney House, accompanied by her sewing machine. We had organized a sewing bee to make our own habits. The habits of the Convent of Original Sins have a special Newcastle component in the form of a yellow gamp. (The gamp sits around the neck and covers the upper chest like a bib. Yellow articles of clothing, in particular socks, are traditionally associated with gay men in Newcastle.) Our manifestation at the university was more ambitious than in 1993. After opening the convent in the courtyard of the Shortland Union, we proceeded across campus to the Hunter Union. The lunchtime crowd was less dumbfounded than they had been the previous year. I began to wonder whether we were already becoming institutionalized.

Shortly afterwards the Sisters manifested at the Newcastle premiere of "The Adventures of Priscilla, Queen of the Desert," which I was asked to open. After my speech, a university colleague of mine who was in the audience divulged to a third party that I moonlighted as a lecturer in anthropology.

Early in 1995 we were visited by our Brazilian friends Selmo and Air, who live in Sydney. They came with Selmo's mother, Dona Marta, who lives in Belo Horizonte but was in Australia to spend three months with her son and his partner. Dona Marta told me I spoke Portuguese like her local priest in Belo Horizonte. She stayed in our spare room—the one decorated with David McDiarmid's safe sex posters. She did not comment on the posters, but told Archipiado she loved the holy pictures of the Sacred Heart of Mary and the

Sacred Heart of Jesus. She wondered, however, why we had them in the bathroom. On the second day of her visit we all went to One Mile Beach. Dona Marta did not want to go beyond the rocks, because Selmo had warned her that there were naked sunbathers there. But Air encouraged her to go and see for herself, which she did. The next day, Sunday, Selmo took her to mass at the Sacred Heart Church in Hamilton; but, to demonstrate her independence, she insisted on walking back by herself.

At the end of her visit Archipiado had to go into her room to get his habit, which he was packing for the trip to Sydney. Dona Marta asked him what the habit was for. He explained that he was a Sister of Perpetual Indulgence, and that he was driving back to Sydney with them in order to take part in the demonstrations against the Pope's visit. (John Paul II was about to arrive in Australia to beatify the country's first potential saint, Mary MacKillop.) He went on to tell her how the Vatican encourages discrimination against gays, and to point out how its policies also disadvantage women. Dona Marta became quite animated in her concurrence, and, for the first time, I heard her use the word "gay" (which is the same in Portuguese).

Dona Marta went to see the Pope in Sydney. I watched the coverage of his visit on television. During the service of lauds at Saint Mary's Cathedral he blamed the desire of women to become priests on "a mistaken anthropology."

Which anthropology, I wondered, was he talking about? Surely the anthropology I am familiar with cannot be so influential. Who takes any notice of us scavengers in the semiotic rubbish dumps of the late twentieth century?

At the end of *Tristes Tropiques*, Lévi-Strauss exchanges a wink, "heavy with patience, serenity, and mutual forgiveness," with a cat (1964:398). At the beginning of this essay I stared into the unmoving eye of a crocodile. For Lévi-Strauss the experience was part of his "farewell to savages," and represented a kind of spiritual homecoming. Anthropology is no longer so innocent. But does this mean that the practice of ethnography is unavoidably alienated? This is a question the reader will have to answer for herself.

Meanwhile, I am planning to learn to roller-blade, so that, during her next manifestation, Sister Wanda Bonk will be able to fly.

NOTES

1. It was apparently Margaret Mead who first compared fieldwork to a puberty ritual. See Scheper-Hughes 1983:113.

2. The inspiration for this term comes from a new discussion group on the Internet devoted to "virtual cultures." (Archipiado, who is a dedicated net-surfer, tells me there is also a Brazilian Spiritist discussion group on the Internet, where spirits communicate with each other via psychography. . . .)

REFERENCES

Appadurai, Arjun. 1991. "Global Ethnoscapes: Notes and Queries for a Transnational Anthropology." In *Recapturing Anthropology: Working in the Present,* ed. Richard G. Fox, 191–210. Santa Fe: School of American Research Press.

Callaway, Helen. 1992. "Ethnography and Experience: Gender Implications in Fieldwork and Texts." In *Anthropology and Autobiography,* ed. Judith Okely and Helen Callaway, 29–49. London: Routledge.

Chuang Tzu. 1964. *Chuang Tzu: Basic Writings,* trans. Burton Watson. New York: Columbia University Press.

Elkin, A. P. 1955. *The Diocese of Newcastle: A History of the Diocese of Newcastle, N.S.W., Australia.* Sydney: Australasian Medical Publishing Company.

Gays and Lesbians Aboriginal Alliance. 1994. "Peopling the Empty Mirror: The Prospects for Lesbian and Gay Aboriginal History." In *Gay Perspectives II: More Essays in Australian Gay Culture,* ed. Robert Aldrich, 1–62. Sydney: University of Sydney (Department of Economic History and The Australian Centre for Gay and Lesbian Research).

Gever, Martha, Parmar, Pratibha, and Greyson, John, eds. 1993. *Queer Looks: Perspectives on Lesbian and Gay Film and Video.* New York: Routledge.

Goffman, Erving. 1963. *Stigma: Notes on the Management of Spoiled Identity.* Englewood Cliffs, N.J.: Prentice-Hall.

Green, Rayna. 1988. "The Tribe Called Wannabee: Playing Indian in America and Europe." *Folklore* 99(1):30–55.

Kotz, Liz. 1993. "An Unrequited Desire for the Sublime: Looking at Lesbian Representation across the Works of Abigail Child, Cecilia Dougherty, and Su Friedrich." In Gever et al., 86–102.

Landes, Ruth. 1947. *The City of Women.* New York: Macmillan.

Lévi-Strauss, Claude. 1964. *Tristes Tropiques.* New York: Atheneum.

Myerhoff, Barbara G. 1975. "Organization and Ecstasy: Deliberate and Accidental Communitas among Huichol Indians and American Youth." In *Symbol and Politics in Communal Ideology: Cases and Questions,* ed. Sally Falk Moore and B. G. Myerhoff, 33–67. Ithaca: Cornell University Press.

Ringer, R. J. (ed.). 1994. *Queer Words, Queer Images: Communication and the Construction of Homosexuality.* New York: University Press.

Scheper-Hughes, Nancy. 1983. "Introduction: The Problem of Bias in Androcentric and Feminist Anthropology." *Women's Studies* 10(2):109–116.

Turner, Roy. 1989. "Deconstructing the Field." In *The Politics of Field Research: Sociology beyond Enlightenment,* ed. Jaber F. Gubrium and David Silverman, 13–29. London: Sage.

van Gennep, Arnold. 1960 [1908]. *The Rites of Passage,* trans. M. B. Vizedom and G. L. Caffee. Chicago: University of Chicago Press.

Wafer, Jim. 1991. *The Taste of Blood: Spirit Possession in Brazilian Candomblé.* Philadelphia: University of Pennsylvania Press.

Williams, Sarah. 1991. Professing Culture: Anthropology among Anthropologists. Ph.D. diss., University of California, Santa Cruz (History of Consciousness Program).

CONTRIBUTORS

MICHAEL JACKSON is College Professor in the Department of Anthropology at Indiana University, Bloomington. He has done fieldwork among the Kuranko of Sierra Leone (1969–1970, 1972, 1979, 1985), among the Warlpiri of Central Australia (1989, 1990, 1991), and among the Kuku-Yalangi of Cape York Peninsula, Australia (1993–1994). He has published four volumes of poetry and two works of fiction, as well as several ethnographic monographs, the most recent of which is *At Home in the World* (Durham, 1995), a study of the experience of home and belonging, based on his fieldwork in Central Australia. He writes: "Perhaps the most central question in my work has always been how human beings everywhere seek, alone or in concert with others, to strike a balance between a sense of closure and openness, between being acting upon and acting, between acquiescing in the given and shaping their own destiny. Most of my books explore the ways in which inherited customs, habits, and dispositions both constrain activity and consciousness *and* are reconstructed, resisted, and replenished in quotidian practices, rites, narratives, and unspoken experience. As I see it, one of the most urgent tasks of anthropology is to close the gap between theoretical and practical knowledge, exploring the immediate, intersubjective underpinnings of abstract forms of understanding, disclosing the subject behind the act, and the vital activity that lies behind the fixed and seemingly final form of things. At the same time as one explores and discloses connections between ideas and the lifeworld, one endeavors to test out ideas—personal, theoretical, ethical and political—in this lifeworld, and in so doing critique and revise them. One's goal is never absolute knowledge, but rather a deepened pragmatic understanding of the possibilities of human coexistence in a pluralistic world."

LILA ABU-LUGHOD is Associate Professor of Anthropology at New York University. Her fieldwork in an Awlad 'Ali Bedouin community in Egypt's Western Desert began in 1978 and continued intermittently until 1989. It resulted in two ethnographies, as well as numerous articles. *Veiled Sentiments: Honor and Poetry in a Bedouin Society* (Berkeley: University of California Press, 1986) was concerned with the way women and young men use a form of oral poetry to express sentiments such as vulnerability and attachment that would violate the moral code and compromise their images if expressed in ordinary language in public. *Writing Women's Worlds: Bedouin Stories* (Berkeley: University of California Press, 1993)—a book of stories about and by a small group of related women in this settled Arab Muslim Bedouin community—was meant as a critique of ethnographic typification. Arguing for a "writing against culture,"

I deliberately chose chapter titles such as "Patrilineality," "Polygyny," "Reproduction," "Patrilateral Parallel-Cousin Marriage," and "Honor and Shame" that
represented the standard anthropological concepts by which society and
culture in the Arab world were grasped. The complex contents of the chapters,
with their stories of distinct individuals arguing, joking, posturing, and suffering, were meant to undo the titles and suggest how inadequate generalizing
language and cultural generalization are for rendering the lives of others.
Writing Women's Worlds was awarded the 1994 Victor Turner Prize for Ethnographic Writing.

ROBERT DESJARLAIS is Assistant Professor of Anthropology at Sarah
Lawrence College in Bronxville, New York. After completing his Ph.D. in
cultural and psychological anthropology at the University of California, Los
Angeles, in 1990, he undertook a two-year post-doctoral fellowship in psychi-
atric anthropology, funded by the National Institute of Mental Health, in the
Department of Social Medicine, Harvard Medical School. He is the author of
Body and Emotion: The Aesthetics of Illness and Healing in the Nepal Himalayas
(Philadelphia: University of Pennsylvania Press, 1992), an ethnography which
includes a study of the aesthetic sensibilities and cultural dynamics that form
and inform sensate experience of loss, illness, and shamanic healing among the
Yolmo Sherpa, a Buddhist people of Tibetan descent who live in the foothills of
North Central Nepal. He is also co-author of World Mental Health: Problems and
Priorities in Low-Income Countries (New York: Oxford University Press, 1995).

He writes: "My current work involves an attempt to advance our understanding of the social, cultural, and political makings of phenomenal realities.
It is focused on the everyday concerns of a handful of men and women who
reside in a shelter, in downtown Boston, for people considered homeless and
mentally ill. While my work in Nepal led me to focus on the profound role that
sensate experience plays in the lives, pains, and healings of the Yolmo, it was
only through my ethnography of shelter life, conducted from March 1991 to
August 1992, that I began to question many of my previous assumptions about
the nature, primacy, and ubiquity of human "experience," "agency," and
"subjectivity." As part of this inquiry I am trying to develop a critical phenomenology that will help us not only describe the nature of subjective experience
for a given person or people, but to understand how this and other ways of
being come about through a complex play of political, cultural, social, and
linguistic forces."

RENE DEVISCH is Professor of Social Anthropology at the Catholic Universities of Leuven and Louvain in Belgium, and member of the Belgian School of
Psychoanalysis. Since 1972 he has carried out fieldwork among the Yaka of the
Bunduundu region, SW Zaire, and from 1986 he has spent about six weeks a
year doing research in Kinshasa. He has written extensively on the relation

between culture, body and psychic symbolism, and symptom formation, as well as on cosmology, healing and the management of misfortune. A trained psychoanalyst, with experience in family therapy in Belgium and Tunisia, and anthropological work in Ethiopia and South-Saharan Africa, René Devisch has developed a "semantic-praxiological methodology" which "reaches beyond mere participant observation, beyond the neutral stance of the scientist," by placing his own fieldwork and field experience squarely *within* the practical, quotidian lifeworld of the other. Devisch relates this stance to the need to decolonize ethnographic consciousness, as well as to a methodological aim to make interpretation grow out of field experience, accepting indigenous symbols and practices on their own multilayered terms, and reaching for an understanding of how meaning is intersubjectively produced and life actively regenerated in critical, transitional moments of communal life. His monograph study of the *khita* healing cult among the Yaka, *Se Recréer Femme: Manipulation Semantique d'une Situation d'Infécondité chez les Yaka du Zaïre* (Berlin, 1984) was recently revised, expanded and translated as *Weaving the Threads of Life: the Khita Gyn-Eco-Logical Healing Cult among the Yaka* (Chicago, 1993). René Devisch is presently collaborating with Claude Brodeur on a two-volume work, *Forces et Signes*, which explores oneiric, imaginary, and bodily aspects of human experience—especially the "forces" at play in the collective and individual unconscious, and in body symbolism—through ethnographic and psychoanalytic analyses of violence and dysphoria in postcolonial Kinshasa.

CHRISTINE HELLIWELL is Senior Lecturer in Anthropology and Comparative Sociology at Macquarie University in Sydney, Australia. She has carried out fieldwork in Auckland among middle-class New Zealanders (1977–80), and in Kalimantan Barat (Indonesian West Borneo) among Dayak people (1985–87). She has published on a range of issues, from gender to ethnicity, and is currently completing a book on the idea of "development" as it operates in the Western imaginary as well as in the consciousness and discourse of people in "Third World" states. The central concern of all her work—reiterated in her essay in this volume—is to explore the ways in which taken-for-granted Western conceptions lead anthropologists and others to misrepresent social relations, in the West as well as elsewhere.

MICHAEL HERZFELD is Professor of Anthropology at Harvard University. He views his work as an exploration of the ways in which personal, local, and national histories are brought into conjunction through social experience. He was trained in archaeology as an undergraduate at Cambridge University (B.A. 1969), and in Greek folklore at the Universities of Athens (1969–70) and Birmingham (M.A. 1972). While these interests later led him to probe the role of Greek intellectuals in the construction of national identity (*Ours Once More: Folklore, Ideology, and the Making of Modern Greece*, Austin: University of Texas

Press, 1982), his doctoral research at Oxford, conducted under the supervision of J. K. Campbell, focused on categories of exclusion and inclusion in a Rhodian village, and paved the way for the concerns with meaning explored in his study of a Cretan community (*The Poetics of Manhood: Contest and Identity in a Cretan Mountain Village*, Princeton: Princeton University Press, 1985) and in his article in this volume. His analysis of intellectuals' roles in the construction of national and other forms of identity suggested the possibility of an empirically grounded reflexivity that would bring the comparativist project of anthropology to bear on the discipline itself, generating *Anthropology through the Looking-Glass: Critical Ethnography in the Margins of Europe* (Cambridge: Cambridge University Press, 1987). His interest in how the nationalistic project affects everyday relations between state and citizen led to a study of historic conservation on Crete (*A Place in History: Social and Monumental Time in a Cretan Town*, Princeton: Princeton University Press, 1991) as well as to a more general examination of the social and cultural significance of bureaucratic stereotypes and practices (*The Social Production of Indifference: Exploring the Symbolic Roots of Western Bureaucracy*, Oxford: Berg, 1992). Michael Herzfeld is now examining artisan-apprentice relationships on Crete for what they can reveal about the ways in which class as well as other power imbalances come to be experienced and translated into social attitudes as forms of "cultural intimacy" and its violation, and he is also working on the "ethnographic biography" of a Cretan writer in order to compare ethnographic with novelistic representations of shared places. He has also recently initiated research on the social production of taste in Italy. Co-winner of the 1981 Chicago Folklore Prize and winner of the 1989 J. B. Donne Prize in the Anthropology of Art (Royal Anthropological Institute, London) and the 1994 J. I. Staley Prize of the American School of Research, he is currently Editor of *American Ethnologist*. Before moving to Harvard in 1991, he taught at Vassar College and Indiana University, and has held visiting research and teaching appointments at the Universities of Paris-X (Nanterre), Manchester (as Simon Professor), Padua, and the Ecole des Hautes Etudes en Sciences Sociales, Paris.

ALFRED GELL is Reader in Social Anthropology at the London School of Economics and Political Science. He has done fieldwork among the Umeda, New Guinea (1969–70) and in Bastar district, Madhya Pradesh, India (1976–77, 1981–82). His publications include *Metamorphoses of the Cassowaries* (1975), *The Anthropology of Time* (1992), *Wrapping in Images* (1993), and numerous articles. His current interests are in the anthropology of art, Indian and Melanesian ethnography, cultural interpretation, and the history and theory of art and music.

ARTHUR KLEINMAN, the Maud and Lillian Presley Professor of Medical Anthropology at Harvard University, is a physician and anthropologist who has conducted field research in China and Taiwan since 1968. His earlier studies included research on cultural patterning of health and health care in Taiwan, rural health care in China in the 1970s, neurasthenia and depression among Chinese, and the experiences of the survivors of China's Cultural Revolution. In recent years his orientation has broadened to a wider concern with social experience, suffering and the interpersonal processes that mediate how the moral becomes embodied. His collected essays, *Writing at the Margin: Discourses between Anthropology and Medicine,* will be published in 1996 (Berkeley: University of California Press). The project he co-edited on *World Mental Health* (New York: Oxford University Press) was published in 1995.

JOAN KLEINMAN is a sinologist who studies pre-Song Chinese literature. She is currently translating *Qian Zi Wen, "Thousand Character Classic"*—a 6th century A.D. text classically used in the Confucian social education of Chinese. She has also collaborated on field research in medical anthropology in China and Taiwan with Arthur Kleinman, her husband of 30 years.

SHAWN LINDSAY is a graduate student in the Department of Anthropology at Indiana University, Bloomington. He is currently finishing his requirements for a Ph.D., and making plans for a phenomenological study of language in Malawi, where he has conducted preliminary research. His other interests include writing poetry and playing jazz guitar.

JADRAN MIMICA is a Lecturer in Anthropology at the University of Sydney, Australia. He has done extensive fieldwork among the Iqwaye of Papua New Guinea: 1977–79 (23 months), 1983 (1 month), 1984–86 (14 months), 1992 (6 months), 1994 (1 month), and 1994–95 (2 months). He writes: "Over the years, I have visited all four central Yagwoia groups, but my intensive research has been focused on the Iqwaye (Menyamya Sub-province) and the Iwolaqa-Malyce (Merewaka District, Eastern Highlands Province). In my paper on dying and suffering in Iqwaye existence, occasional shifts of reference from the Iqwaye to the Yagwoia are intended as generalizations valid for all four central politico-territorial groups. I also frequently refer to an Iqwaye man, Palyc-Caqapana-ule-Omalyca-Taqalyce or just Taqalyce. He is one of my closest Iqwaye friends and informants. Our collaboration still continues.

"My approach to ethnography and anthropology, as to life in general, is grounded in Husserlian and existential phenomenology, and psychoanalysis. Apart from death and mortuary practices, I have researched virtually every aspect of Iqwaye and Iwolaqa-Malyce life. My current work is focused on Iqwaye curing practices and the realities of illness."

KEITH RIDLER is a Lecturer in Social Anthropology at Massey University, New Zealand. He has also lectured at Victoria University, New Zealand, and

l'Universita degli Studii di Padova. Since 1980, he has carried out fieldwork in
the Trentino, Italy, focusing on the social impact of tourism on alpine communities. Much of his work has been in visual anthropology, involving documentation of Maori and Italian rituals and social practices. His interests span
anthropology and cultural studies; he is former General Editor of *SITES: A
Journal for South Pacific Cultural Studies.*

JIM WAFER is a Lecturer in Anthropology at the University of Newcastle,
Australia. He was born in Australia, in the city of Newcastle, and has lived in
Auckland, Canberra, Stuttgart, Willowra, Alice Springs, Rabat, Bloomington,
Bahia, Washington, and Darwin. He writes: "I began my working life as a
teacher in an Aboriginal school in central Australia. Since 1980 I have carried
out research for land claim proceedings in various Warlpiri and Arrernte
communities in that region. I studied anthropology in the United States, at
Indiana University, and conducted field work in Brazil, in the city of Salvador
(more commonly known as Bahia) for a brief period in 1986, for a longer period
in 1987–1988, and for another brief period in 1994. In Bahia I met my present
partner, Hédimo Santana. My main publications are *The Taste of Blood: Spirit
Possession in Brazilian Candomblé* (1991), and a long essay written in collaboration with a group of Aboriginal gays and lesbians called 'Peopling the Empty
Mirror: The Prospects for Lesbian and Gay Aboriginal History' (Gays and
Lesbians Aboriginal Alliance, 1994). I am currently carrying out research into
Islamic perspectives on homosexuality, the social history of lesbians and gay
men in Newcastle, and lesbian and gay alternative religious movements. The
central concern of my anthropological work is to problematize two boundaries:
the one that separates 'anthropological experiences' from the rest of the
anthropologist's life; and the one that separates 'anthropological knowledge'
from other forms of knowledge. I touched on these issues in *The Taste of Blood*
and 'Peopling the Empty Mirror.' The essay included in this volume is an
attempt to work through these questions in more detail."